THE FOURTH GOSPEL
AND ITS
PREDECESSOR

From Narrative Source to Present Gospel

THE FOURTH GOSPEL AND ITS PREDECESSOR

ROBERT TOMSON FORTNA

Fortress Press   **Philadelphia**

Library of Congress Cataloging-in-Publication Data

Fortna, Robert Tomson.
   The Fourth Gospel and its predecessor. From narrative source to present Gospel.

   Bibliography: p.
   Includes index.
   1. Bible. N.T. John—Criticism, Redaction.
   I. Title.
   BS2615.2.F648   1988   226'.5066   87-45889
   ISBN 0-8006-0860-7

3219K87   Printed in the United States of America   1-860

For
Gertrude Tomson Fortna
Jean Fortna
Virginia Page Fortna

Contents

Preface

This book is the sequel to my earlier monograph, *The Gospel of Signs,* in which I sought to reconstruct the text of the Fourth Gospel's "predecessor." Here I make use of that text, altered slightly in the light of subsequent discussion, so as to apply redaction criticism by comparing it to the text of the present Gospel. The purpose is to return to 4G from the source and to understand both documents in ways that only a redaction-critical approach can afford.

I intended at first to entitle this work "The Evangelist John and His Predecessor," in deliberate allusion to the pioneering redaction-critical work by W. Marxsen: *Der Evangelist Markus.* But the proposed title would not do, and for two reasons.

In the first place, the new literary criticism of the Bible has taught us to give attention to the text itself and not simply to the author, real or implied, behind the text. We have the book, but the one who produced it, together with that writer's mind and purpose, can only be extrapolated from the text. First of all, then, we had better seek to understand what that text on its own intends. But against the excessive claims of the newer criticism I maintain that to read only the text, without asking also how it came to be and what its original context was, even what its author intended, renders it oddly timeless. So we study both Evangelist and Gospel. Why then avoid speaking of the former in the title?

Because, in the second place, the provisional title was sexist, most obviously in the possessive pronoun "his" but also in using the traditional name "John." The feminist movement in biblical studies has convinced me that these conventions, supposedly innocent in intent and justified by the canon, must be given up. Just as we have no idea of the Evangelist's identity and name, so also of his or her gender. And like all of the Gospels, that according to "John" is in fact anonymous, its apostolic attribution added roughly a century after it was written and on spurious grounds. We cannot know even the degree of likelihood that the writer was a male. So the custom of calling "him" by the traditional name "John" ought to be abandoned.

In the case of this Gospel we have no problem. Except in chapter-and-verse citations we can avoid the name John (which in the Gospel itself refers mainly to the Baptist) by speaking of the Fourth Gospel (4G) and the Fourth Evangelist (4E), and often simply of the (present) Gospel and the Evangelist, respectively.

I continue to refer to the Gospel's wording or thought as "Johannine," trusting the adjective to be understood as gender-free. It can then be contrasted with "pre-Johannine," which designates the text, and also the tradition, prior to its present state. For it is precisely the relation between the present Gospel and the document from which it hypothetically developed—namely, between the Fourth Gospel and its predecessor—that engages us.

I have tried to write this book in a way that will include the non-specialist: by transliterating Greek words, citing the text always in English, and giving explanations of technical terms. Translations from the Greek text of the Fourth Gospel or the source are my own, but often are reminiscent of the Revised Standard Version.

The Introduction is for all readers, whether or not they are approaching redaction criticism of the Fourth Gospel for the first time. The notes are primarily for the scholar. Similarly, the analyses, the third subsection of each numbered section of part 1, are for reference only, tracing the detailed reconstruction of the source's text (see The Plan of the Book, in the Introduction).

Finally, a disclaimer. Some of my students, caught up in my belief in a pre-Johannine Signs Gospel, have imagined that some day an ancient copy of it might be discovered. As no doubt with those who attempt to reconstruct the text of Q (the Synoptic saying source), I have to confess that such a fantasy is not without its appeal. But it quickly turns to dread. If a manuscript of something like the Signs Gospel were to come to light, I should be most uncomfortable to find in how many respects, large and small, my attempt at what may be called creative sleuthing would appear to be inept. One critic (Carson, "Source Criticism," 419) has estimated my confidence in the reconstruction—overconfidence, he would say—to be about nine on a scale of one to ten. My own sense is more nearly a seven. And, like Brown (*The Community of the Beloved Disciple,* 7), in the end I should be happy if more than half of what I propose is found convincing to others. But what is presented here is a hypothesis whose vindication is not finally based on probabilities or argument about criteria but on its usefulness in coming to terms with this elusive and insistent Gospel.

I am grateful to several institutions for their combined support along the protracted way this book has taken: to Vassar College for research leave and sabbatical; to the American Council of Learned Societies for a fellowship; to the American Philosophical Society for a grant-in-aid; to the

Albright Archaeological Institute in Jerusalem for an annual professorship; and to the Ecumenical Institute for Advanced Theological Studies ("Tantur") for accommodation and scholarly collegiality. Without the almost limitless resources of the library at the Ecole Biblique study in Jerusalem would be impoverished indeed. I especially thank the staff and students of St. Bede's Theological College, Umtata, Transkei, for their warm welcome and friendship offered to my family and me at almost the very end of this volume's odyssey.

To the Vassar College Academic Computing Center I am indebted for much special help with the technical problems of producing this work.

I owe a debt of thanks to a number of people who gave assistance and perspective on various parts of the manuscript: Albert J. van Ackere, Betsy Halpern Amaru, Michael H. Barnes, Thomas E. Boomershine, Pieter D. Davidse, Alice G. Howson, Benjamin G. Kohl, Jerome Murphy-O'Connor, O.P., Bruce E. Schein, Richard C. Schneider, Robert H. Smith, Giulia Battisti Sorlini.

Several students at Vassar College served as research assistants, and many more as members of my seminars endured exposure even to some of the most rarefied arguments of this study and in turn gave both their reactions and new ideas. I regret that I cannot name them all; these in particular I must thank: Anne Gable, Sarah B. Gordon, John Lo Breglio, Paulette Muller-Girard.

Dr. John A. Hollar and Margret McGinnis of the editorial staff of Fortress Press have greatly added to the book's clarity and usefulness, and Stephanie Egnotovich, the Managing Editor of Fortress Press, guided the manuscript through the process of publication. I thank them all.

Chiefly I am grateful to my friend Walter Wink who tirelessly read virtually every line of this book and some earlier versions of much of it and gave needed encouragement and tough-minded criticism. Another friend and colleague, R. Alan Culpepper, also made many especially helpful suggestions for its final shaping.

My dissertation in 1965 was dedicated to my two young sons: Ben, who always wanted a book written for him, and Ned, who had no idea how much his arrival had interfered with it. *The Gospel of Signs* was presented with gratitude to my wife, Evelyn. It is overdue now to dedicate this study—the consummation of many years of work on the Fourth Gospel—to my mother, my sister, and my daughter.

R. T. F.

Abbreviations

4E	The Fourth Evangelist (principal author of 4G)
4G	The Fourth Gospel, the "Gospel according to John"
AB	Anchor Bible
ABD	*Anchor Bible Dictionary* (forthcoming)
BAGD	W. Bauer, W. F. Arndt, F. W. Gingrich, and F. W. Danker, *A Greek-English Lexicon of the New Testament and Other Early Christian Literature*
B & L	M.-E. Boismard and A. Lamouille, *L'Evangile de Jean*
BETL	Bibliotheca Ephemeridum Theologicarum Lovaniensium
BTB	*Biblical Theology Bulletin*
Brown	R. E. Brown, *The Gospel According to John*
CBQ	*Catholic Biblical Quarterly*
ETL	*Ephemerides Theologicae Lovanienses*
IDB	G. A. Buttrick et al., eds., *Interpreter's Dictionary of the Bible*
JAAR	*Journal of the American Academy of Religion*
JBL	*Journal of Biblical Literature*
lit.	literally
LXX	"The Septuagint," the ancient Greek translation of the Hebrew Scriptures
MS(S)	manuscript(s)
NovT	*Novum Testamentum*
NovTSup	Supplements to *Novum Testamentum*
NT	New Testament
NTS	*New Testament Studies*
OT	Old Testament (= the Hebrew Scriptures, the Bible of Judaism)
par(s).	and parallel(s) (among the Synoptic Gospels)
PQ	Passion Source (the narrative source underlying the passion account of 4G)
SANT	Studien zum Alten und Neuen Testament
SBLDS	Society of Biblical Literature Dissertation Series

SBLMS	Society of Biblical Literature Monograph Series
Schnackenburg	R. Schnackenburg, *The Gospel According to St. John*
SG	Signs Gospel (= SQ + PQ)
SNTSMS	Society for New Testament Studies Monograph Series
SQ	Signs Source [*Sēmeia-Quelle*] (the hypothetical narrative source underlying chapter 1 and the miracle stories of 4G)
TDNT	G. Kittel, ed., *Theological Dictionary of the New Testament*
TGOS	R. T. Fortna, *The Gospel of Signs*
TR	*Theologische Rundschau*
ZNW	*Zeitschrift für die Neutestamentliche Wissenschaft*

Introduction

A. THE JOHANNINE RIDDLE[1]

The Fourth Gospel, at once so perplexing and so sublime, has always shown an enigmatic face to its readers. The church very early began to call it the "spiritual" Gospel, but this was a phrase more memorable than precise. (Did it mean least factual or most true? the purest or the most derived? the crown of the Gospel canon or only the unassimilable Fourth?)[2]

What chiefly makes the Gospel problematic is its literary riddle, the all-but-intolerable tension between *narrative* and *discourse:* on the one hand, third-person stories—familiar from the other three Gospels—vivid, brief, and earthy, about Jesus (his miracles and his passion); on the other hand, Jesus' timeless speeches—extended, repetitive, sonorous—in first and second person. And only in the Fourth Gospel (hereafter 4G) do we find the kind of narrative known from the other Gospels alternating with the discrete art form of the discourse, having its own substance and flow.[3]

1. In the *discourses*, Jesus gives voice to a theology of eternal truth, conveying metaphysical revelation about salvation: "God loved the world so much that he gave his only begotten son that everyone who believes in him would not be destroyed but have eternal life" (3:16). In particular, he speaks explicitly of himself, in the normative vocabulary of later classical

---

1. The adjective "Johannine" is used as a convention for anything distinctive of the Fourth Gospel, and particularly of its final, principal author. It implies nothing about the identity of that writer.

2. Kysar's title, *John, the Maverick Gospel,* vividly expresses the Gospel's distinctiveness.

3. There is nothing of this Johannine dichotomy of genres in the other three (the so-called Synoptic) Gospels. They contain, it is true, both narrative—stories about Jesus closely similar to those in 4G—and a form of the teaching of Jesus, but the two are not in tension. A few passages in the Synoptics are sometimes called discourses: the Little Apocalypse in Mark 13 and pars.; the Sermon on the Plain in Luke 6; the five sermons, esp. the Sermon on the Mount, in Matthew; and the brief Farewell Discourse in Luke 22. But all of these are simply gatherings of Jesus' brief sayings into composite constructs, montages of small units of tradition; and they have no distinctive style or common theological tenor. If a very few of the Johannine discourses' elements stem distantly from an older tradition of Jesus' words, their sharp difference from the Synoptic presentation of those traditions is clear.

1

Christianity, as the unique Son of God: I am Life, Truth, the Way; apart from me no one can come to the Father.

In the Synoptic Gospels, Jesus' teaching, by contrast, is concrete, timebound, usually secular. He speaks in the comparatively foreign tones of a first-century Palestinian rabbi, piling up his message in a rush of startling parables and apocalyptic images; he uses phrases that barely come into 4G[4] and never made their way to the orthodox creeds—phrases not about himself but about the kingdom of God, the future Son of Man. It is in the Johannine discourses that we find the more familiar portrait of the Jesus of universal Christianity, uncluttered—it is often held—with ancient and dispensable Jewish elements.[5]

The discourses, in themselves revelatory, stand as the Gospel's greatest characteristic. They define the Johannine Jesus, lending the religious tone we associate with that portrayal. Their poetry seems to float from heaven, giving an unearthly quality to the entire Gospel. Even when Jesus is ostensibly engaged in dialogue, he speaks with that same sonority, drowning out his interlocutors, confounding them with double meanings.

2. But alongside the discourses in 4G, with their predominant tone of a timeless and ethereal Christ, there also stand—and this is the heart of the riddle—traditional stories, the *narratives*. (These are not at all the stories the Synoptic Jesus himself tells about the kingdom; there are none of Jesus' parables in 4G, only narratives told about him.)

These narratives of his deeds, far from sharing the otherworldly quality of the discourses, give a wholly different effect. Even though they recount his miraculous and therefore highly theological feats, they are told in altogether concrete, unspiritual, earthly terms. Here we have the type of narrative about Jesus familiar from the Synoptic Gospels: healings, a raising from the dead, the providing of food (both bread and fish) and drink as well. They are lavish and astounding, often more impressive than in the Synoptics; but far from having been spiritualized, as we might expect in view of the discourses, their matter-of-fact physicality is more pronounced. We read of water—six Jewish stone jars of it, each holding twenty or thirty gallons—changed into wine; an official's son saved from death at one o'clock in the afternoon; a congenitally blind man healed with a mixture of dust and spit; Lazarus, his body decomposing four days in the tomb, brought back to life. The prodigiousness of these deeds belies their

---

4. When the Johannine Jesus speaks of the figure of Son of Man, it does not serve to deflect attention from himself, as most distinctively in the Synoptics, but on the contrary refers self-evidently and unambiguously to himself as Son of Man in the present.

5. The reader will notice the hint of a not-so-subtle anti-Semitism in this common evaluation. In fact, the so-called spirituality of 4G's discourses is thoroughly Jewish, as the discovery of the Dead Sea Scrolls has shown.

fundamental nonspirituality, expressed in concrete and even mundane detail.

Furthermore, Jesus is shown working these astonishing deeds deliberately and as signs, that is, as overt demonstrations and indeed proofs of his messiahship. Here the narrative of 4G goes beyond the Synoptics, whose Jesus refuses so material a manifestation of his authority (Mark 8:12; Matt. 16:4). And, what is more, the signs are contradicted within 4G itself by the Johannine discourses with their sharp critique against signs.

So 4G confronts us with this strange juxtaposition: earthly signs alongside otherworldly teaching against them, the heavenly revealer of pure Christian theology doing deeds that are frankly temporal and even coarse. A Jesus—wholly timeless and non-Synoptic in the discourses—appears in the narratives of 4G as the worker of Synoptic-like miracles,[6] and one even closer to a first-century magician, the so-called thaumaturge, than in the Synoptics. In short, 4G is a document that in the narratives is more synoptic (so to speak) than the Synoptics, yet it is literarily independent of them, and at the same time totally un-Synoptic in Jesus' speeches.

The riddle, then, the finished Gospel's enigma, centers in this disarming combination of two very nearly contradictory modes of Jesus' activity—his narrated deeds and the words of his discourses. The two genres, moreover, are in no way integrated. Highly specific miracle stories simply alternate with blocks of monologue in which all relation to historical setting or developing plot is forgotten. At one place four chapters of monologue stand virtually alone: the Farewell Discourse in chapters 14—17 has only the slimmest of connections to the Last Supper narrative of chapter 13 that ostensibly occasions it. More often discourse (sometimes preceded by dialogue in the same style) appears as an appendage to a miracle story, mechanically joined to it (as, e.g., 5:19–47) and followed just as abruptly by more narrative. Occasionally the dialogue has been interwoven with story (as in chap. 11); but even then a close look shows how the two styles stand out from each other.

In this book we are concerned only with the narratives in 4G, for obviously the narratives and discourses stem from radically different origins (and so far a precise way to explain the discourses' provenance and development has not been found), and they reflect distinct periods in the development of 4G. The narratives almost certainly represent the older, more traditional—the clearly "pre-Johannine"—layer in the Gospel (excluding, of course, Johannine redactional transitions and introductory or concluding comments within it).

6. The exorcism of demons alone is wanting; see further, part 2, n. 50.

3

And so, confining ourselves to the narrative material, we might expect that the tension that exists between the two kinds of material in the Gospel as a whole would be no issue. But that is not the case; within the narrative itself there is a stylistic confusion. The narrative has been invaded, as the form critics would say, by another (obviously redactional) hand at a number of points, in fact by a style very close to that of the discourses. These intrusions appear but fleetingly within the narratives, in a word or phrase or verse or two. Yet they have considerable effect; they produce the difficulties technically known as the Gospel's aporias. These are the roughnesses and tensions—the interruptions and sudden turns, non sequiturs and even contradictions, passages with dense or overloaded wording, the doublets—that so patently characterize 4G and distinguish it from the narrative of the other Gospels.[7] These aporias incongruously dot an otherwise smooth narrative. They are found in the accounts of Jesus' signs that run through the Gospel's first half; they appear also in the other principal body of narrative in 4G, the account of Jesus' death and resurrection of chapters 18—20. So the aporias are a further aspect of the Johannine literary enigma. On a small scale they replicate the juxtaposition of narrative and discourse in the Gospel as a whole.

Let us examine a particular aporia as an example of this textual tension that so distinguishes 4G. The illustration comes from the account of Jesus' healing the official's son (4:46–54). This is a simple, straightforward miracle story like so many in the Gospels (see the roughly parallel story of the centurion's servant in Matthew 8 = Luke 7). Yet just for a moment in its midst we hear that other, lofty Johannine voice, such as sounds in the discourses—and then without explanation the story resumes.[8]

4 [47b]When he [the official in Capernaum] heard that Jesus had come . . . [9]he went out to him and asked that he come down and heal his son, for he was

7. The Synoptics contain a few aporias. There are occasional careless inaccuracies, such as in Mark 1:2 where the author cites Isaiah but first unknowingly quotes Malachi. In other cases the inconsistency may suggest a textual lacuna; thus, in Mark 10:46 we are puzzled to read: "And they came to Jericho. And as he was leaving Jericho . . ." (not unlike John 2:13). In Mark 14:1–2 we learn that the officials intend not to arrest Jesus during the Passover, yet they proceed to do so. (In all of these cases, Matthew and Luke show awareness of the problem in Mark and a corrected, smoother text.) But these Synoptic instances, mostly Markan, are rare, and none of them so blatant as those typical of 4G.

8. In 4G's prologue (1:1–18) we discover just the reverse phenomenon. The hymn to the Word, while not presented as the words of Jesus, is nevertheless similar in tone to his discourses. It is interrupted by the blunt, prose announcement of vv. 6–7; then suddenly the poetry takes over again. Similarly, within the Farewell Discourse (chap. 14), it appears that Jesus brings his words to a close and the passion story is about to begin (v. 31b: "Arise, let us be going"), but then the discourse continues for three chapters. These instances of aporias within the poetry/discourses are rare, and seldom so clear-cut as within the narratives, but they appear to derive from the same kind of compositional process as we shall find lying behind the narrative.

9. For clarity I omit a phrase here.

about to die. [48]Therefore Jesus said to him, "Unless you people see signs and wonders, you refuse to believe!" [49]The official said to him, "Sir, come down before my child dies!" [50a]Jesus said to him, "Go, your son lives."

It is the aporia of v. 48 that causes the problems. The official had not asked for a sign, still less demanded to believe; clearly he believed in some fashion already. So why Jesus' outburst, and what is the logic of the narrator's "Therefore"?[10] Whom is Jesus addressing? Why does he use the second-person plural in speaking, as we are explicitly told, to an individual? And most puzzling of all, why after his reluctance to be a miracle-worker does Jesus proceed to grant the official's request, and specifically to work a "sign" (v. 54), a term treated so polemically in v. 48? Unless we go to extraordinary lengths to vindicate the passage as smooth and consistent, such questions force us to doubt the passage's integrity.[11]

The most natural explanation for these phenomena, then, is that the narrative stems from more than one author: it consists of an older and a younger layer. In short, "redaction" has taken place. Bultmann, in his commentary on 4G, was the first to work out the hypothesis accounting for this literary complexity.[12] Specifically, Bultmann held that the present Gospel derives its narrative from one or more earlier documents, or "sources." Just as Matthew and Luke are thought to stem from Mark,[13] so 4G is a reworking, a redaction of older material: principally a Signs Source (SQ) and, whether still separate or already joined to it, a Passion Source (PQ) as well.[14] The Fourth Gospel as we have it can be understood as chiefly the product of two literary stages, a pre-Johannine narrative source

10. The conjunction used here (oun) can be translated as merely an indefinite "Then," but the paradox seems to demand a stronger sense.

11. Attempts to understand Jesus' word in v. 48 as something other than an objection are wholly unconvincing to me. Another example, similar to this verse, is the word of Jesus to his mother (2:4), interrupting the story of the wedding feast at Cana and seemingly refusing a miracle story before performing it, also later termed a sign. Notice also Jesus' word to his brothers and his subsequent behavior, in 7:6–10. Here we are concerned only to point out the problems in 4:47–50. For answers to them, see part 1, sec. 4.

12. In developing his theory, Bultmann followed a lead suggested by Faure in 1922.

13. On the most widely held view of Synoptic interrelationships. But in any case it is clear there is some form of literary dependence among the Synoptic Gospels, to which 4G's derivation is parallel—and parallel only. Despite recent attempts to show that 4G is dependent directly on one or more of the Synoptics themselves, there is no convincing evidence of that so far as I can find. (See further part 1, excursus B.)

14. Bultmann named the former Sēmeia-Quelle (SQ). Besides recounting the signs of Jesus, it was introduced by an account of the first disciples' conversion and concluded with what is now 20:30–31a. It was, therefore, no mere string of stories but an articulated document, more rudimentary than Mark but nevertheless a self-sufficient source, providing basis for expansion. Bultmann seems to have given no name to the "written source [that] the Evangelist followed [in] the passion story" (quoted by D. M. Smith, Composition, 45; Smith himself simply calls it the Passion Source). To balance SQ my siglum for it imagines a German original: Passions-Quelle.

(or two) and an extensive Johannine redaction, including the composition of the discourses. Its composition, then, is analogous to that of the Synoptics.

But there are two notable differences from the Synoptic source theory, one posing for us a serious problem and the other offering hope of a solution. In the first place, whereas Mark (as probably the principal source of Matthew and Luke) is available to us, the sources underlying 4G are not; they have not survived. Therefore, such pre-Johannine sources are hypothetical. To be studied and understood they must be discovered, embedded in the present text of 4G, and reconstructed, moving backward from it.[15]

Yet—and this is the second difference from the Synoptic situation—the Johannine author who has made use of these sources or an already merged form of them has evidently treated them with far greater respect, so as to retain their original wording, than did the Matthean and Lukan authors in reusing Mark (see n. 21). The aporias are just those points at which a more thorough recasting of the source(s) would have produced a smoother present text without aporias. Consequently, those very points of tension, so problematic in themselves, pinpoint for us the literary seams between pre-Johannine source and Johannine insertion, and the two layers in the text often come apart more or less in our hands.[16]

The aporia, which provides (1) *contextual* evidence for separating source from later additions, is not the only such criterion, though the chief one. (2) *Stylistic* criteria also aid in the process, so far—after some experience in reconstructing the source—as we can recognize aspects of Johannine, and occasionally pre-Johannine, usage (e.g., explanatory parenthesis [1:41–42; 2:9] typical of the Evangelist's style; characteristic of the source: singular verb with double subject [1:35] and gratuitous factual detail such as hour [1:39; 4:52], amount [2:6], or distance [21:8]). (3) Further, *theological* themes (and language, a special form of style) provide a criterion, in a cumulative way. (Thus, "the Jews" in 2:6 or "glory" in 2:11b are Johannine; literal compliance with Jesus' command in 1:39 is pre-Johannine.) (4) Both *form-* and *text-critical* considerations are also of use (e.g., see below on 2:10 [part 1, sec. 3, Analysis] and on 2:3b–4 [part 1, n. 126], respectively). (5) Finally, *Synoptic analogy* can be a criterion—"sideways," so to speak—since the pre-Johannine tradition and the Synoptic appear to have had close affinities; for example, on 21:1–14 and Luke 5:4–10a, see part 1, sec. 5; on 6:1–21, see part 1, n. 204. For a fuller discussion of criteria in source reconstruction, see *TGOS*, 15–22, and my forthcoming article in *ABD*, tentatively entitled "Signs/Sēmeion Source."

15. Like the other hypothetical source "Q" lying behind the sayings of Matthew and Luke. Similarly, we do not possess the sources of Mark, and (though, as we are about to see, it is far more difficult than for 4G) they also must be discerned solely on grounds internal to Mark.

16. Thus, in the illustration, v. 48 is patently Johannine insertion into an otherwise smooth pre-Johannine miracle story. See further part 1, sec. 4, Analysis, on v. 48.

So the problems within the text, the aporias, become a means to their own solution. Furthermore, the discourses by analogy can be attributed to the later author, amplifying the earlier document(s). This author, known traditionally as "John," we refer to as the (Fourth) Evangelist (hereafter 4E). Her or his recasting of the source material was by no means mere editing but, rather, creative transformation, the kind of authorship known technically as redaction. Yet this redaction has been carried out so carefully that *the text of the source survives on the whole intact within the present Gospel* and can therefore be reconstructed with some facility and confidence, often simply by lifting off the patently redactional material.

This may seem quite improbable: that though the putative source has been massively redacted by the Evangelist, yet it stands still recoverable within the present text of the Gospel. The latter would not be true in the Synoptics' case: if we had no surviving text of Mark we could scarcely reconstruct it from either Matthew or Luke or even both together. That is so because of the quite different way that Mark has been treated by the later Synoptics, compared to 4E's handling of the Signs Gospel (hereafter SG). The aporias such as we find in 4G, and only there, are the result of the thorough yet respectful redaction that 4E has done on the source; a more radical rewriting (e.g., as Matthew and Luke rewrite Mark) would have evened out roughnesses of this sort, leaving a far smoother text—without aporias. It is just those stumbling blocks in the reader's path that suggest the survival of SG within 4G, and thus its reconstruction.

The aporias, then, are the points of contact (collision, more often) between source and redaction, points at which the Evangelist as redactor comments on a source, supplements it, corrects it—but does not obliterate it.

This two-layer view of the Gospel's composition, then, accounts for the rise of the aporias.[17] But it does more. The aporias not only resolve themselves and provide us with the clues to their origin and the means to the source's separation from redaction (that is, to its reconstruction); they

17. Bultmann *(Gospel of John)* also held that a third hand had a part in the production of the finished Gospel, a still-later editor of the Johannine redacted source(s). He called this writer the (Ecclesiastical) Redactor—not applying the term redactor, as we do, to the role of the Johannine author. Such a "post-Johannine" writer (or more than one) probably had a smaller role than Bultmann thought. Only the following passages appear to be subject to later alteration: the addition of 4:1a ("when the Lord knew that") and the correcting parenthesis of 4:2 about Jesus' own baptizing; 5:3c–4; the phrase "after the Lord had given thanks" in 6:23; 11:2ab; the addition of chap. 21 as appendix or, if it is an epilogue attached by 4E, then at least 21:24b ("and has written these things") and 25; the story of the adulterous woman (7:53—8:11, but found only in some manuscripts and sometimes in Luke instead). If the prologue (1:1–18) was not originally part of the Gospel, it seems to me nevertheless to be the addition of 4E and not a later redactor. Bultmann further believed that underlying the discourses was an extensive source (the Revelation-Sayings), but this hypothesis has not won scholarly acceptance, so complex and uncontrolled is it in Bultmann's formulation.

also give us the key to clearer understanding of the present Gospel, to interpreting the text that otherwise is so liable to subjectivity. So, the Johannine riddle that we have examined becomes the interpreter's opportunity, as we shall now see.

B. THE RIDDLE BECOMES THE INTERPRETER'S OPPORTUNITY

The means of understanding 4G that the aporias afford is known as "redaction criticism." This method attempts to retrace the literary process—the redaction of source material—that produced the present Gospel.[18] If we can reconstruct the source with some confidence, we can then both understand, far more clearly than by a single-level reading of the text, the circumstances in which the present Gospel arose and also, thereby, perceive the intent of the Evangelist. It is as if we look over that author's shoulder as he or she adapts, corrects, and improves the earlier document.

The redaction-critical method has recently been discounted as antiquarian, seeking to impose on the Gospel an academic and anachronistic concern. For what in the end does it matter—it is argued—how the aporias arose? Are we not simply to come to terms with the text before us, its relevance to us here and now?

Certainly redaction criticism must not distract us from understanding the text we possess as a coherent unity and even an authoritative document.[19] But in fact the redaction-critical method closely *parallels the way the original readers would have perceived and understood the text.* For them the source was undoubtedly familiar, indeed greatly beloved. Therefore 4E as redactor dared not recast its text, but was obliged to let it stand virtually whole, amid the many additions and changes demanding to be made in it. The aporias are just the flags remaining at those points where the source

18. Redaction criticism is fundamentally historical, seeking to recover both the situation within which and the process by which the Gospel material took form; it works "diachronically." The German term for this method *(Redaktionsgeschichte)* might better be translated "redaction history," so long as "history" is understood both as a literary process and as a method of examining it. The more common English term "[redaction] criticism" more explicitly conveys the methodological dimension but not the historical.

19. This obvious priority has been strenuously asserted recently, indeed overasserted, as if the redaction critic would otherwise never get beyond the pre-Johannine process to consideration of the present text. It is true that the source criticism of 4G has by definition focused on the pre-Johannine stage, but redaction criticism, which has so far barely been attempted for 4G, attends to the earlier process precisely so as to move beyond it and comprehend the Johannine stage. Nicholson (*Death*, 13–18, citing M. de Jonge and N. Petersen) is simply incorrect to suggest that the redaction critic understands 4E "on the model of editor rather than author" (ibid., 16). O'Day, *Revelation*, misunderstands source analysis as if an end in itself, and holds that redaction by the Evangelist must then be seen as "secondary" (p. 49) and a "disruption of the source material" (p. 134). In fact the separation of the source is made chiefly so as to treat the redaction as primary, and not as disruptive but as a creative reworking of the entirely secondary source material.

was no longer acceptable or intelligible and was thus in need of alteration. If the present text of the Gospel is meant to be coherent and intelligible as we have it, it also intends to call attention to the two literary levels it contains. So the original historical reader (the "implied reader") would in fact have appropriated it in a way closely analogous to the modern method of the redaction critic, comparing the old with the new.[20]

In this way 4G is quite different from the Synoptic Gospels. It clearly intended to supplant the pre-Johannine source, and it succeeded in doing so—but not by considerably rewording it (as in the case of Mark at the hands of Matthew and Luke). As we have seen, SG remains intact and recognizable at most points within the present Gospel. The aporias show us just where the source is laid aside and taken up again.[21] Not to perceive the contours below the surface of the text is to miss the Gospel's richness and even a good deal of its sense.[22]

The aporias, those enigmatic irritants in the text, then, are not road-blocks in the way of the careful interpreter; rather they are keys to reading the full text as it stands. Although at first they seem to be distracting idiosyncrasies or worse, the aporias provide us the means to a fuller understanding of the document containing them.

There is also a byproduct. We become acquainted with an otherwise unknown early Christian document, one that proves to be altogether unique in the literature and survives within the text of 4G—from those shadowy years before or just after the middle of the first century C.E. The pre-Johannine Gospel[23] is probably the purest example we have of a

20. In technical terms, although the more recent synchronic way of reading 4G is valid and essential, the diachronic method has hardly been exhausted.

21. Matthew and Luke were evidently written for audiences that did not hold the very wording of Mark to be so precious and familiar as the Johannine community regarded the source(s) underlying 4G. Consequently, the authors of Matthew and Luke did not preserve Mark in its original form (and so, no doubt partly for that reason, Mark survived and SG did not). But the "mere fact that a source is no longer extant should not be taken as an argument against its existence," as Robinson observes (*Trajectories*, 239).

Perhaps the Matthean and Lukan authors used Mark chiefly from memory and, even when they thoroughly reworked it, had little thought of violating it but believed that they were correctly interpreting, at most paraphrasing and clarifying. (Here I am indebted to Thomas Boomershine.) The Johannine author, on the other hand, evidently worked from a written text. If it was not necessarily lying on that Evangelist's desk it nevertheless was reproduced in a more precise and faithful way than was Mark. The literal text survives in recognizable (and so for us reconstructible) form. A closer example than the Synoptics is provided by the Pentateuchal sources.

22. On the other hand I have no reservations about the brilliant work by Culpepper, *Anatomy*. He acknowledges the value of redaction criticism while showing that it must now be supplemented by the newer literary criticism that he applies.

23. I call it a Gospel even if SQ had not yet been joined to PQ, for it contains the essential good news of the Christian kerygma, that the Messiah has come (see part 1, excursus A.1). Since eventually (excursus A.2) we shall see that SQ was joined to PQ, without assuming the fact we nevertheless can speak loosely in part 1 of either SQ or PQ as (an element of the combined) "SG."

document written within the context of Christians in the synagogue, by and for Christians who were still part of Judaism. For by the time this pre-Johannine source was redacted by our Evangelist, the rift between Jews and Christians had taken place. This circumstance made the older work obsolete and greatly in need of the correction and reinterpretation 4E gave it.

Our starting point, then, will be to examine the source in its own right, as a unique early Christian document—no longer surviving but identifiable below the surface of 4G. Thus, we presuppose a reconstructed pre-Johannine text; hypothetical and at points questionable as it is, its existence and even wording are the subject of some scholarly consensus.[24]

C. THE PLAN OF THE BOOK

In part 1 we apply redaction criticism story by story, following the Gospel's narrative blocks as nearly as possible in their pre-Johannine order. There are twenty such sections in part 1, and each has three subsections:

First, at the beginning of each section, is set out the hypothetical text of the *Pre-Johannine Source* in English translation (boldface type).[25] This is followed by a close commentary on the meaning of the passage at the pre-Johannine level. The purpose is to give as full an exposition as possible of the early Christian-Jewish document, story by story. The latter constitutes a new thrust, for until now redaction critics[26] have concerned themselves largely with the meaning of the present Gospels, and even then almost entirely with the Synoptics. In this way we learn not only of the pre-Johannine author's intent but also of the early situation that evoked this pre-Johannine work.

Second, we identify the *Johannine Redaction*. (The boldface type in this subsection identifies the wording of the Johannine redaction.)[27] We examine the alterations 4E has made so as to understand for each story the reuse of the narrative source. In this way we are able to trace the movement—the theological shift—from the pre-Johannine to the Johannine stage, to understand the latter more precisely, and also to perceive the context in which the present Gospel was written.

24. See my *ABD* article, "Signs/Sēmeion Source."

25. In all the reconstructions of the source's text, material not certainly to be assigned to the source appears in parentheses ( ), and emendations and hypothetical readings in square brackets [ ]; passages whose position in the source is hypothetical or uncertain are enclosed in double brackets [[ ]].

26. Following the models given by Marxsen for Mark, Bornkamm and others for Matthew, and Conzelmann for Luke.

27. Material in parentheses ( ) is possibly from the source. Words in italics are unchanged in Greek from the source but now have a different translation.

Thus, for each narrative of the source I offer commentary both on the reconstructed source and on 4E's redaction of it; these are found respectively in the first two subsections of each numbered section in part 1. Such comment is not exhaustive; nor do the two together constitute a full-scale commentary on the narratives of 4G so much as a prolegomenon to such commentary, but one that has seldom even been considered, let alone carried out. The intent is to learn what a thoroughgoing redaction-critical investigation can reveal of this enigmatic work: to emphasize the difference between source and present Gospel, the distinctiveness of each, and at the same time to note their continuity. We are concerned with the background of the Johannine Gospel and have the expectation that uncovering its genesis—its origins and subsequent development—will inform our encounter with the meaning of the finished Gospel.

Finally, in the third, more technical subsection (*Analysis*), the detailed reconstruction of the source's text, as found in the first subsection, is justified. This amounts to a revision and up-dating of my earlier source analysis in *TGOS*,[28] and the sum total of these subsections in part 1 comprises a source-critical analysis of the narratives of 4G as a whole. In each case this involves, first of all, identifying the aporias in the present text, thus distinguishing pre-Johannine source from Johannine redaction. The latter is then lifted off from the underlying source, allowing the separate examination given in the two major subsections we have just described. The reader may want to turn to this Analysis in each case before reading the first subsection, which presupposes it.

Thus, part 1 is essentially analytical, distinguishing source from redaction, commenting on each, and—in the appended third subsection—showing how the separation was achieved.

The *Excursuses* to part 1 examine the character of the source, including its genre and its relation to the Synoptic Gospels.

In part 2 we gather synthetically the many theological threads that run through the commentaries of part 1, seeking to view the overall movement from source to present Gospel. We examine these threads according to both the major categories of biblical theology (christology, soteriology, eschatology) and to themes peculiar to Johannine thought (e.g., miracles and faith, Jesus' itinerary). Thereby, we hope to comprehend both the hypothetical Signs Gospel and the Fourth Gospel as we know it. We shall discover not only the meaning of the narratives but a better perspective on the entire Gospel as well.

---

28. Both further reflection and the many suggestions of critics demand this fresh analysis. What is undertaken in these analyses represents yet another stage in the attempt to identify the pre-Johannine source. But because debate of the source hypothesis has been extensive we can hope that a number of major issues have been settled. Fuller discussion of the method of Johannine source analysis is to be found in *TGOS*, 1–25.

Part One

THE NARRATIVE SOURCE AND ITS JOHANNINE REDACTION

The Opening

The Signs Source is more than a gathering of Jesus' miracle stories or a cluster of parallel traditions such as appear to underlie Mark. Rather, the stories' arrangement has structure and articulation, and they begin with a double preparation: the testimony of John the Baptist and the assembling of the first disciples. The latter provides the body of followers who will always be somehow present in the ministry of signs. The Baptist makes known who it is that is about to display himself in the signs. Thus the appearance of John marks the appropriate literary opening of SQ—the narrative Signs Source.[1]

SECTION 1 (1:6–7, 19–34)[2]
JOHN'S TESTIMONY

So dense is this material in its present, canonical form that its source reconstruction is more difficult than for almost any other narrative in the Gospel. This difficulty is to be seen in the Analysis at the end of this section, where the source underlying this passage is reconstructed. (Thus, the reader exploring this method of treating 4G for the first time may want to jump ahead to sec. 2—or better, sec. 3—coming back to this problematic passage at a later time.) Nevertheless, a probable form of the pre-Johannine text can be wrested from it, one that proves coherent in itself and, what is more, occasions the complexity of the Johannine redaction:

Pre-Johannine Source[3]

1 ⁶There appeared a man, sent from God, whose name was John. ⁷He came for testimony, that all might believe through him.

¹⁹And this is John's testimony: When priests and Levites were sent [or

---

1. That SQ did not consist solely of a cycle of miracles, lacking introduction such as we now turn to, is clear from what the first miracle story presupposes by way of background; see further, p. 49. Bultmann did not include this episode in SQ; but Becker, "Wunder," agrees that it belongs.

2. The verse numbers here, as in each section, reflect the outer limits of the pre-Johannine passage, and do not indicate the extent of Johannine redaction within it.

3. For the basis of the reconstructed text of the pre-Johannine source, see each section's Analysis. For the format, see The Plan of the Book and its n. 25.

came] to ask him, "Who are you?" [20]he bore witness, "I am not the Christ." [21]And they asked him, "What then; are you Elijah?" And he said, "I am not." "Are you the Prophet?" And he answered, "No."

[22]So they said to him, "Who are you? What do you say of yourself?" [23]He said, "I am the voice of one crying in the wilderness, 'Make straight the way of the Lord,' as Isaiah the prophet said. [26b]I baptize with water. (There stands among you) [27]the one who comes [or was to come] after me, of whom I am not worthy to loosen his sandal thong. [[[33d]This is he who baptizes with holy Spirit."]]

[29]He saw Jesus coming to him and said, "Behold the Lamb of God! [31bc]I came (baptizing with water) for this: so that he might be revealed to Israel. [32b]I saw the Spirit descend like a dove from heaven upon him. [34]I myself have seen and I testify that this is the Son of God."

This highly compact pre-Johannine account can be seen at a glance to be an amalgam of independent elements in the Baptist tradition. The Synoptic Gospels still only place these elements alongside one another. Here, though densely combined, they have a unity which a single theme provides, that of **testimony** (or "witness"—in Greek the two words are the same: *martyria*). And this thematic unity is evidently the creation of the source's author. The **man ... whose name was John** has solely the function of witness to Jesus—**he came for testimony**; and everything he does is an expression of this one role.

But the role is not simply a human one; though called human being (*anthrōpos*, here translated "man"), John is **sent by God,** he has a divine mission. From the start, the source's story is theological.

And the goal of this theological mission is faith: **that all might come to believe[4] through him.** The question, Who are included in this **all?** must wait, just as the object of the faith to be engendered by John is kept in suspense. (The name "John" refers not to the Evangelist [4E] but rather to the Baptist—in accordance with the Gospel's consistent usage.) What is to be understood now is that he is God's agent; **through** him the belief will arise.

Having thus introduced the Baptist (vv. 6–7ac), the narrative proceeds at once to portray him carrying out this single-minded task: **And this is the testimony of John . . .** (v. 19a). But that testimony is so condensed that we need to unravel, one by one, the various ways in which John fulfills his divine mission as the bearer of witness:

1. The instigating event is the arrival of a delegation—whether on their own initiative or sent by others matters not—of **priests and Levites.** Why do these particular functionaries come? To this there is no hint of an answer; we can only surmise. For SG's readers, perhaps they stand simply

---

4. The Greek aorist subjunctive is used here and very possibly has the inceptive force this translation contains.

for dignitaries sufficiently authoritative[5] to elicit John's formal and forthright answer.

They came only to ask him, Who are you? (v. 19bd). But what occasions their question? Why is it John they seek out, and what makes his identity a matter of formal inquiry? The questions they put to him give us the clue (and it is indirectly supported by Baptist traditions in the Synoptics). There had evidently been sufficient reason to wonder if John were the one sent by God to bring the turn of the ages and establish the kingdom of God. If so there would have been various titles to describe him in such a role: Messiah, the forerunner Elijah, the Prophet promised by Moses (Deut. 18:15). There was, in other words, speculation about John's identity, and the pre-Johannine author has pictured for us a delegation, coming to John and putting the question to him officially: **Who are you?** But he intends to bear witness only to Jesus, and so initially he answers the question of his own identity only negatively, and in a way that will be seen to bear witness tacitly to Jesus.

First he denies that he is in any sense the predominant figure of Jewish expectation, and he does so voluntarily and emphatically: **I am not the Christ** (v. 20). He then still more quickly rejects two other titles proposed by his questioners: he is neither **Elijah**[6] nor **the Prophet**-like-Moses (v. 21).

If in the portrayal of these denials there is any anti-Baptist thrust, as sometimes suggested, any wish to portray John rejecting from the beginning the later view of the Baptist sect that he was the Messiah, the pre-Johannine author has now subordinated that older meaning entirely to the christological affirmation of Jesus that is implied. The concern voiced by the questioners—Who are you?—when applied to Jesus is the only focus of the passage. John's role is accordingly reduced to the single task of providing this focus.

The delegation evidently thought of the three titles as distinct—**What then?** they say, after John's first denial. But the reader is to understand them as more or less synonymous,[7] for all of them will be seen to apply equally to *Jesus* (vv. 41–45, in this part, sec. 2). Thus, in making clear that he is in no sense a messianic figure, even by this repeated and purely negative testimony John already bears threefold witness to Jesus' messiahship.[8]

5. The double phrase is unique here in the NT, but common enough in the OT, the Dead Sea Scrolls, and later Jewish literature. See Haenchen, *John* 1:143.

6. Even the Synoptic view (and perhaps Jesus' own) that John is to be understood as Elijah-returned is therefore rejected.

7. See D. M. Smith, "Milieu," 175.

8. It is not likely that a discrete Baptist tradition underlies this material. Luke knows of a denying on John's part but in a general form and without verbal contact to SG's text here (see Acts 13:25—"I am not 'He' "). Rather, it seems to have been read backward onto John at the pre-Johannine level, from the threefold affirmation of Jesus soon to be made by the first disciples (1:41, 43b [as reconstructed in this part, sec. 2] and 45).

2. But John has not answered the question of his own identity, so it is repeated and restated: **Who are you? What do you say of yourself?** Having cleared up by the denials any potential misunderstanding, he can now declare that he is nothing more than the **voice** prophesied by Isaiah (v. 23); and, following their lead, he says this of [him]self. In all other Gospels it is the evangelists who make the connection between John and this prophecy of Isaiah's, and they focus not on the **voice** itself but on the preparation for the Lord which the voice commands. But simply to be the "voice of one crying in the wilderness," that is, to be the witness, is an apt definition of the role John plays in SG. A witness is one who sees and then speaks; John has seen, as he will tell us (vv. 32, 34), and so now begins to speak, being the vehicle of God's revelation.

In the Synoptics, it is Isaiah who bears the witness; here as throughout this passage John himself does so (**I am the voice . . .**), acknowledging only as afterthought the source of the language he uses: . . . **as the prophet Isaiah said.**[9] But in declaring himself to be this voice he points not so much to himself as to the one of whom the voice cries: **Make straight the way of the Lord.** And we note how SG has rewritten Isa. 40:3 (which reads, "Prepare the way of the Lord/make his paths straight"). John does not "prepare" for the Lord's coming, nor does he call others to do so. Rather, he himself simply fulfills the prophecy of "the voice," the witness.

Strictly, of course, the command to "make straight" is addressed to others; in the Synoptics it is the crowds, and the means of their doing this is to come to baptism. Here nothing of the sort is countenanced. (Certainly it is not the "priests and Levites" who had come to him that are addressed.) If anyone, then, heeds Isaiah's call to smooth the Lord's coming it must be John himself, by his multiple act of bearing witness.

In further contrast to the Synoptic portrayal of John's role, here in SG, despite the citation from Isaiah, he is not strictly the forerunner, the prophet who beforehand announces the Lord's coming—we noticed the omission of the phrase "Prepare . . ."—but only the witness who in retrospect declares what he has seen. This limitation in John's role can be built upon by the Evangelist, in connection with the preexistence of Jesus (see below on v. 30).

The wilderness mentioned here is only a vestige of that tradition in the Synoptics; nothing whatever is made of the venue of John's activity, and description of his style of life is missing altogether, presumably because he is no longer to be understood as Elijah. The source's portrait of John, then, is highly focused—solely on his role as witness.

3. Next John tells us (strictly speaking, he tells his questioners), in line

---

9. This clause is surely to be taken as part of John's words, maintaining the flow of the sentence, not the author's parenthetical comment.

with Synoptic tradition: **I baptize with water** (v. 26b). At first reading, this seems to suggest a new role for John, distinct from that of witness, namely, the role of baptizer, of prophet, and somehow priest. But nowhere in 4G, and so presumably neither in SG, is he called either "the Baptist" or "the one who baptizes." Rather, he only alludes to his baptism and solely to contrast it with that of Jesus, who "baptizes with holy Spirit" (the conclusion of this sentence). And whereas in the other Gospels there are many whom John baptizes (the "you" to whom the saying in its Synoptic form is spoken [Mark 1:5–8 pars.]), here the "you" is missing and the saying will apply only to Jesus (v. 31b).[10] Even his baptizing of Jesus will itself never be shown to us; instead he only bears later witness to what he had earlier seen (vv. 32, 34).

4. In v. 27 a new—and yet a familiar—element surfaces: the contrast between John and the one who "comes after" him. Until now that contrast has only been implied, in John's denials of titles that belong to Jesus. Here he forthrightly declares it. He is wholly inferior to the coming one, inadequate even to provide the service of a slave: **I am not worthy to loosen his sandal thong** (v. 27b, taken over from the tradition).[11] Once again the thrust is christological and not deliberately anti-Baptist. Compared to Jesus even the witness God sends is as nothing.

What of the phrase **one who comes [or was coming] after me** (v. 27a)? Is John after all the forerunner in SG (see item 2, above)? No, the language here is entirely traditional, expressing the long expectation, now fulfilled. Temporally, of course, John came before Jesus (perhaps even for a time Jesus was his follower), but now—if our tentative reconstruction is valid—he declares the presence, **standing in your midst,** of this coming one.

5. John will baptize only Jesus, and alone will describe for us that event. Of the Synoptic account[12] all that appears here is the narrator's statement that John **saw Jesus coming to him**[13] and so even this we perceive through John's witnessing eyes.

It is striking how incidentally Jesus appears on stage for the first time; only 4G will tell us where this takes place (v. 28). In contrast to John the Baptist ("There appeared a man sent from God . . ."), Jesus is nowhere introduced to the reader. Rather we have been prepared for his appearance

10. This limitation, like a number of other points in the present passage, will be contradicted by the independent traditions used by the Evangelist in 3:22–24 (cf. 1:28), where John's ministry of baptism to the general public is acknowledged.

11. Along with Luke, SG lacks the phrase "mightier than I," which overloads the Markan sentence. But nothing is lost thereby, since the sandal saying expresses the same contrast.

12. Namely, that Jesus comes from Galilee to the Jordan where (or in which) he is baptized by John; that as he comes out of the water the heavens open, the [Holy] Spirit descends like a dove, and a voice comes from heaven: "Thou art/This is my beloved Son."

13. Verse 29a; only later in vv. 32, 34 do we hear from John of the Spirit's descent and his own acclamation of Jesus' messiahship; see item 7.

only by John's cryptic allusion to one who is coming after him, is now standing among us, and of whom he is unworthy (v. 27). So it will be John's further task to make clear who this Jesus is (vv. 29–34).

In the source this is the first mention of Jesus' name (1:17 belongs to a later level). Perhaps it is this that evokes John's first explicit declaration of Jesus' identity: **Behold the Lamb of God!** (v. 29b). His very syntax is confessional, almost ceremonial; not "He is . . .," but "Behold. . . ." The observer is summoned to see as John does, expected to recognize and admire.

And what of that title, unique here in Gospel tradition? The text gives us no hint of its origin or reference. And speculation, a common temptation here, is of no value. Rather we must attend to the story, in which before long Andrew, one of the two who heard John make this confession (v. 37), reports simply, **We have found the Messiah!** (v. 41). The title Lamb of God—it must have been evident to the original reader—is but another expression of Jesus' messianic role, so repeatedly and variously asserted in the source.[14]

6. It is of course for baptism that Jesus comes to John. Here is the now-secondary accomplishment of John's mission: **For this I came baptizing with water . . .,** he reiterates (v. 31b). He has spoken before of his baptizing (v. 26), but it has not yet occurred; and unlike the Synoptic John he does not baptize the crowds. He implied that his water baptism will finally prove inferior to Another's baptism; yet even his has its unique and all-important role, which is now to be carried out. We also heard, at the very beginning, that when John appeared he "came for testimony" (v. 7a); here, then, is his ultimate testimony, to baptize Jesus (he continues) **in order that he might be revealed to Israel** (v. 31c). The follower who is the greater is at last to be shown to Israel (the **all** of v. 7c).

7. So the high point of John's work is now about to be accomplished (vv. 32–34). There is here the greatest possible narrative concentration; all is reduced to John's spare report. There has been no preaching by John, no interest in his style of life, and now we find no setting in the wilderness, no crowds, no ascent of Jesus from the water (in fact, there is no mention of the River Jordan or even water!), no opening of the heavens or divine voice, no vision on Jesus' part (the Baptist alone tells us what he saw). Jesus' baptism is reduced to this account: **I saw the Spirit descend like a dove from heaven upon him** (v. 32b). Only this christological moment of the traditional scene is recounted.

The second half of the baptism's report (v. 34), unique in form, brings all to a close. In the tradition the voice from heaven declared Jesus' status, a voice heard either by everyone (Q) or Jesus alone (Mark). But now John

14. So Dodd convincingly argues (*Tradition*, 269).

is our only voice (he takes the place of the *bath qol*) because he was evidently the only witness: **I have seen . . .**, he declares (v. 34a); now at last he completes his role: **and I testify. . . .**[15] And he makes the messianic acclamation himself: **This is the Son of God** (v. 34b).

Here then is the greatest title of all, the climactic christological affirmation. So, at the very end of the source (20:31a), it sums up all the others: **that you may believe that Jesus is the Christ** and Lamb of God, Elijah, the Prophet[16]—that is, **the Son of God.**

John's witness is now complete. The climate in which his testimony is given is without tension—people come to him and ask who he is; he volunteers that he is **not the Christ**. Although terms from juridical procedure can be read in—"testimony" (for "witness"), "confess" (for "testify")—the context is not especially official and certainly not threatening. John announces, proclaims, professes; he does not admit or defend. From the opening verses (6–7ac) it is clear that the setting is a public one. As the one **sent from God** his witness is divinely authorized with universal belief as its goal.[17] Everything, then, is gathered into a single event: the testimony of John.

Our reconstruction is patently hypothetical at various points, yet it turns out to have coherence and a single-minded purpose. Given this thoroughgoing concentration, the lack of so many elements from the Synoptic Baptist tradition in no way suggests a diminution of John's importance.[18]

Johannine Redaction[19]

1 [Vv. 1–5] [6]There appeared a man, sent from God, whose name was John. [7]He came for testimony, **to testify to the light,** that all might believe through him. [8]**He was not the light, but came to testify to the light.**

[Vv. 9–14] [15]**John bore witness to him and cried out saying, "This is he of whom I said, 'He who comes after me is ahead of me, for he was before me.' "** [Vv. 16–18]

[19]And this is John's testimony: When **the Jews from Jerusalem sent** priests

15. On this translation of the perfect tense here (*memartyrēka*), see this part, n. 60.

16. There will be still others: Rabbi, King of Israel, Savior of the world.

17. Though the **all** of v. 7 is surely to be understood only in a Jewish way, it is encompassing, not exclusive.

18. It is only 4E who makes major corrections of John's status, as will presently appear. See further Wink, *John the Baptist*.

19. To save space here we reprint only the redaction within the pre-Johannine narrative material, indicating the hymn to the Logos (and, except for v. 15, any Johannine additions to it) simply by bracketed verse numbers. On the format of the reconstructions of the Johannine redaction, see The Plan of the Book and its n. 27.

and Levites to ask him, "Who are you?" [20]he confessed—**he did not deny but confessed**—"I am not the Christ." [21]And they asked him, "What then; are you Elijah?" And he said, "I am not." "Are you the Prophet?" And he answered, "No." [22]Then they said to him, "Who are you? **So that we can give an answer to those who sent us:** What do you say of yourself?" [23]He said, "I am the voice of one crying in the wilderness, 'Make straight the way of the Lord,' as Isaiah the prophet said."

[24]**Now they had been sent from the Pharisees.** [25]**And they asked and said to him, "Then why do you baptize if you are neither the Christ nor Elijah nor the Prophet?"** [26]**John answered them and said, "I baptize with water; in your midst stands one you do not know,** [27](the) **one who comes after me, of whom I am not worthy to loosen his sandal thong."** [28]**These things took place in Bethany-beyond-Jordan, where John was baptizing.**

[29]**The next day** John saw Jesus coming to him and said, "Behold the Lamb of God, who takes away the sin of the world. [30]This is the one of whom I said, 'After me comes a man who is ahead of me, for he was before me.' [31]And I did not know him, but for this I came **(baptizing with water):** so that he might be revealed to Israel." [32]**And John testified saying,** "I saw the Spirit descend like a dove from heaven **and it remained** upon him. [33]**And I did not know him, but he who sent me to baptize with water, he himself said to me, 'The one on whom you see the Spirit descend and remain on him,** this is he who baptizes with holy Spirit.' [34]I myself have seen and I testify that this is the Son of God."

1. It has been suggested (see this part, n. 33) that the prologue, John 1:1–18, is not the work of 4E, or at least not within that author's original conception of the Gospel, but either an afterthought or a later addition altogether. If the former, we need not distinguish here between original and subsequent Johannine editions. But if the prologue is post- and therefore non-Johannine, it tells us nothing directly about the Evangelist and her or his understanding of this passage. (Nevertheless, the tendency of that redaction is consistent with what we find in the subsequent, certainly Johannine, passages.)

Perhaps the issue cannot be resolved. But it tells against the post-Johannine view of the prologue's origin that it has not simply been added at the beginning of the Gospel but rather interwoven with the opening lines (and not the Evangelist's, but the source's), and further that it has made its impact at one point further on, namely, in v. 30. On the face of it, then, it seems more likely that the prologue is of Johannine provenance.

The Evangelist (or just possibly a later editor) has enclosed and framed SG's opening within the hymn to the Logos—and done this so massively that those few lines now appear an intrusion within the hymn, just the reverse of the case. What observations can we make on the present text of the prologue on the basis of this separation of source and redaction?

a. By giving vv. 6–7ac a place in the midst of the prologue and allowing those two sentences, from the source's opening, to interrupt the hymn so jarringly, 4E obviously intends to affirm the source's portrait of the Baptist as witness. Indeed, it is carefully integrated with what precedes and follows in the hymn (**the light** in vv. 4–5, 9) by the insertion of v. 7b: "John came for testimony, that is, **to testify to the light,** so that all might believe through him." The pre-Johannine role of the Baptist is thus extended by the deeper Johannine christological language; he becomes a witness not only to Jesus in history but also to the cosmological fact of Jesus' preexistence. Perhaps the abrupt notice at v. 15 (see on this verse in the Analysis, below) intends, in part, to show John as witness to the incarnation itself (v. 14). Later, in 5:33–37, John's witness is to be qualified as not in itself sufficient, but even there it is not repudiated.

b. Conversely, and still more important, the involvement of the preexistent Logos in the historical world is anchored by the fact of John's witness.[20] The Baptist provides the vehicle by which timelessness and time come together.

c. It is important to the Evangelist to add immediately after the insertion in v. 7 that John is only a witness and is not to be confused with the one to whom he bears witness: **He was not the light, but came to testify to the light** (v. 8). This comment is best understood as reflecting a corrective of the point of view of followers of the Baptist who were contemporaries of the Johannine community. If such an intent was faintly implied in the source, from its traditions, it now becomes emphatic and stands alongside SG's positive view of John: he bears witness—and does only that.

Verse 15 functions as a further anti-Baptist corrective. If John bears witness not simply to the public appearance of Jesus (as in SG) but to the very incarnation of the Logos, nevertheless we are forcefully made to understand here that he testifies as well to his own inferiority to Jesus: **John testified to him and cried out, ". . . he was before me."**[21] The anti-Baptist corrective is found also in v. 30, which both extends and explains v. 15, and further in vv. 31a and 33a, John's two declarations that even he did not know Jesus, just like his audience (v. 26c).

2. After the prologue, which uses up only the two introductory sentences of the source, the report of John's activity begins and loosely follows the pre-Johannine account. In both SG and 4G this begins at v. 19,[22] and

20. However abrupt the shift in tone and meaning at v. 6, it is clearly acceptable to the Johannine redactor.

21. We find John making himself inferior to Jesus already in the Synoptic tradition and in SG (v. 27), but there it was not so prominent. Here the preeminence of the one who comes last, an important Johannine theme, is asserted from the beginning. So Foster, "John Come Lately."

22. Verse 19a, however, functions slightly differently in source and present Gospel. Originally it served as bridge, leading directly from v. 7a ("He came for testimony . . .") to the content of that witness beginning in v. 19b. Now, after the conclusion of the hymn, it has the function of resuming and reminding us of John's basic task.

4E takes up the source's central and all-encompassing theme of John as witness.

The climate in which his testimony is given, however, is from the start greatly changed. What had been a public declaration, a profession, in response to eager questioning (there was nothing to suggest suspicion on the part of the priests and Levites) now becomes a courageous confession in the context of an official accusation. **The Jews** (or Judeans) send a delegation **from Jerusalem** to investigate John (v. 19) and we soon learn that **the Pharisees,** Jesus' great antagonists in this Gospel, are behind it (v. 24). In other words, the religious establishment of Judaism already ranges itself against John just as it will do later against Jesus. The inquisitors demand that he explain himself, **so that we may give an answer to those who sent us** (v. 22b). And they are quick to press him further when they are not satisfied with his reply: **Then why do you baptize, if you are neither the Christ nor Elijah nor the Prophet?** (v. 25). Only here in any of the Gospels is John challenged to justify not only himself but also the very activity that in all the traditions is synonymous with the man himself.

Yet John, surrounded by this unsympathetic delegation, is neither intimidated nor in any way deflected from his forthright witness. He freely **confessed** (*hōmologēsen*, translated only as "bore witness" in SG) that he was not the Christ. He admits the fact (to the Baptists of 4E's day?) and courageously offers what is in effect a profession of faith in Jesus under official duress. The Evangelist underscores both this fearlessness and this eagerness to confess Jesus by reiterating: **He did not deny but confessed** (v. 20b). At the start, then, we see John in a wholly positive light, courageous and undeviating, so long as it is understood that he is wholly subordinate to the one to whom he gives his testimony.

3. In SG the questioners were only the initial occasion of John's testimony, but now they act as the antagonists throughout the first half into which the evangelist subdivides the source (vv. 19–28).[23] After that they will disappear, but while they are present John accepts their challenge. Verse 26, spoken at large in the source, is now addressed expressly to them: **John answered them and said** (v. 26a) ". . . in your midst stands one you do not know" (v. 26c). He becomes *their* accuser. Already "the Jews," then, are shown as deaf to the message to be proclaimed throughout the Gospel and first announced by John, unable to know the one now about to appear.[24]

---

23. In SG they are finished at v. 22ac. But here their impatient insistence is reiterated (v. 22b), and with the redactional addition of v. 24 ("Now they had been sent from the Pharisees"), they continue on stage and can ask the challenging question of v. 25: "Then why do you baptize . . .?"

24. John's charge that the authorities "do not know" Jesus is of course a basic Johannine theme.

4. Whatever the origin of the datum in v. 28—**These things took place in Bethany beyond the Jordan, where John was baptizing**[25]—it is inserted by 4E to bring to a close this section of John's testimony.

5. With v. 29 (**Next day**) a new scene is created—somewhat artificially, since from the reader's standpoint (and that of SG) the witness of John simply continues. But Jesus, who as in the source now appears, takes the place of the departed and temporarily silenced Jewish delegation. (Such a shift in interlocutors is a common feature of the Johannine scened dramas in chaps. 5, 9, and 18—19.) That this arrival on stage is merely schematic is clear from the fact that Jesus will say and do nothing till v. 38 (in the third scene, vv. 35–42). In that sense his appearance here is premature. Because of the intervening insertions of the Evangelist, he can hardly be seen any longer as coming to John even for baptism. Rather, he appears as the center of christological attention.

John's confessing function now intensifies. Jesus is **the Lamb of God** (v. 29b, as already in SG), to which evidently 4E adds **who takes away the sin of the world** (v. 29c). If this somehow points forward to the view of Jesus' death later expressed by Caiaphas (11:50–52), here its effect is evidently only to heighten the traditional christological title.

6. Verse 30 is the first of three reiterations of the Johannine intention to make John inferior to Jesus. He solemnly and formally declares of the one just now named Lamb of God: **This is he of whom I said, "A man follows me who ranks before me. . . ."** By reminding that he has spoken in this way before (evidently in v. 27), the Johannine Baptist declares that the one predicted has now come. But it is his superiority to John that here defines him. That was implicit in the Baptist tradition. To make it still clearer, the Evangelist adds as both explanation and underscore: **for he was before me** (v. 30c). Jesus' superiority makes his preexistence almost tautological. The Johannine as well as the pre-Johannine christological intent has been overshadowed for the moment by the anti-Baptist corrective.

As if there were doubt about this, the second insertion drives it home: **And I myself [or even I] did not know him** (v. 31a). The very one whose function is to reveal (as the source is about to say—v. 31bc) is ignorant of the one he reveals! John for the moment is little better than the Jews' representatives in v. 26c.

And then, for the third time and following the account of the baptism, we hear again, **I myself did not know him** (v. 33a).

7. What this Johannine doublet frames is the first part of John's all-important revelation to Israel, namely, his report of the baptism of Jesus (vv. 31bc–32). So when now John is made both to reiterate that he **did not**

---

25. The locale here is unlikely to be pure invention on 4E's part. On its function, see on this verse in part 2.F, Present Gospel. Note how the verse's last clause dispels, perhaps unintentionally, the source's total concentration of John's baptizing on Jesus alone.

know him (v. 33a) and then at last to supply the datum of Jesus' Spirit baptism (v. 33bc), postponed by 4E from v. 27, we recognize that a deliberate and important redactional activity is being carried out; it is the Johannine intent here both to emphasize and to qualify:

If the source read only, "I [John] came for this, that he might be revealed . . ." (v. 31bc), the Evangelist has added and thus made explicit the limited extent of John's role, namely, that he came only **baptizing with water.**[26]

Then follows the account of the baptism itself. 4E adds the solemn declaration, "And John testified saying" (v. 32a), simply to ease the density of text. The primary Johannine alteration here is to add that the Spirit not only descended upon Jesus but also **remained on him** (on "remained," see this part, n. 58). What John saw was not just a momentary christological vision, but the permanent condition of Jesus' spiritual nature, visible and effective from that point onward.

Then, the Evangelist repeats the Baptist's disclaimer of all prior knowledge of Jesus (v. 33a). It was only because he had been prepared by a previous disclosure from God that he could recognize and report what is now a greater event than seeing the baptism, even with its christological disclosure.

John recounts that private revelation: (I did not know him [v. 33a]) **but he who sent me to baptize with water said to me** (v. 33b), **"He on whom you see the Spirit descend**[27] **and remain on him** . . . (v. 33c; note the pleonastic "on him" after "on whom") [then, from the source and almost anticlimactically] **this is he who baptizes with holy Spirit"** (v. 33d).

Note that it is now not John but God, speaking through him, who declares Jesus the Spirit-baptizer. He is not so much the one who testifies as only a mouthpiece. John, in the Evangelist's portrayal, has been subtly demoted from the evangel of the good news in his own right.[28]

---

26. Yet because of the phrase "that he might be revealed . . ." this declaration must be joined to the Johannine John's preceding declaration of ignorance (v. 31a) with an adversative conjunction "but" (in the unambiguous form *alla*).

27. In this retelling the traditional likeness to a dove from heaven has dropped out, as perhaps superfluous or too crude.

28. The importance of putting John's role in proper perspective is evident further in two Johannine passages. (1) In 3:22–31 Jesus himself baptizes (v. 22) and "all" go to him (v. 26c). John baptizes too, and "people" come (v. 23), but his pre-Johannine role, as both the only baptist and baptist of Jesus alone, has been undercut. And the brief mention (v. 24) of John's impending imprisonment here suggests not so much his sharing in the passion of Jesus (as it does in Mark) but rather his ministry soon to be curtailed. (Evidently 4E here is in touch with Synoptic tradition, but I can no longer be confident it comes to him in this case via the source.) This gradual diminution of John is epitomized in the (evidently Johannine) saying, "He must increase, but I must decrease" (v. 30), and the contrast of the one "from above" with the one "from earth" (v. 31). (2) Equally, in the summary at 10:40–42, 4E carefully defines the limits of John's role: "John did no sign," we hear, just before Jesus' last and greatest miracle, "but everything John said about this man is true." This recalls 4E's comment in 1:8 ("He was not the light, but came to bear witness to the light").

The Evangelist has chosen to combine the two traditions involving the Spirit, the one in the saying of John about Jesus' superior baptizing, the other in the account of Jesus' own reception of baptism. It is just because Jesus uniquely receives the Spirit that he baptizes with it, or will do so.[29] The contrast between John, the water baptizer, and Jesus is at last fully drawn. The suspension set up earlier by John's isolated assertion, "I baptize with water" (v. 26a)—isolated, that is, in the Johannine redaction—has finally been resolved.

The second half of John's messianic disclosure, the voice of God declaring Jesus his son (v. 34), has until now been ignored. It follows quickly and without change from the source. But due to his demotion by the Evangelist, John's voice now has the quality of a postscript to the more important fact of Jesus as bearer of Spirit.

Yet if John's pre-Johannine role has been systematically downplayed, in the end he remains God's spokesman, and he is now as well the defender of the faith against the hostile delegation. It was only when he had successfully silenced and dismissed the representatives of "the Jews" that Jesus appeared. By the insertion at v. 28 4E has made two scenes from one. In the first "the Jews" are on stage with John, and ranged against him; in the second Jesus replaces them. Thus, almost from the start, the Jews and Jesus stand over against each other, and John's own testimony receives the Jewish opposition that Jesus will later find.[30] Consequently, John is a part of the Christian good news, the indispensable witness to Jesus, and in particular against "the Jews."

This section, then, is no longer only an account of John's witness (which is considerably curtailed), nor finally a christological affirmation (though 4E retains v. 34's messianic pronouncement at the culmination of the double scene). Now it particularly underscores the Conflict between God's Emissaries and Their Opponents.[31]

In section 2 we move on to narrative that is more flowing, less condensed and piled up than in the present case. Thus our interpretation of both

29. If this was implied in the tradition or even in the Synoptics themselves, it is only implied. It is well known that in the Synoptic Gospels this promise is never realized. But if the pre-Johannine source included the passion, it is fulfilled there: The risen Jesus' last word to his disciples is "Receive holy Spirit" (20:22). See this part, sec. 19.

30. We need to distinguish between 4E's anti-Baptist critique here and the more general anti-Jewish polemic. As we shall see (part 2.F), "the Jews" are most characteristically portrayed as the enemies of Jesus, since they evidently were the enemies of 4E's late-first-century Christian community. At most, the latter-day followers of John the Baptist were not enemies but only competitors, whose mistaken view of their mentor needed simple correction. (Polemic, the term generally used of this tendency in 4G, is too strong.)

31. My capitalized summary labels, like those at the end of every Johannine Redaction subsection, are not exhaustive of the redactional focus of the passage in question but call attention to an important Johannine theme that emerges from our redactional investigation.

27

source and redaction can be smoother, briefer, and more confident. But in the meantime, for those who would follow it, here is a detailed explanation of the text of the source used above. (This analysis justifies the reconstructed text presented in Pre-Johannine Source in this section.)

Analysis

Chapter 1 of this Gospel, so unusually dense, and especially the prologue (1:1–18), is not the most auspicious place to begin a source-critical analysis of 4G.[32] But because the source seems clearly to begin in chapter 1, we must consider that material first, to follow the source as nearly as possible in its original sequence ("original" here refers simply to the work of the pre-Johannine author and implies nothing about the historical factuality of the narrative). For convenience we divide the passage in three, at vv. 19 and 24.

1:1–18

Some see the source beginning only at the end of the prologue, with 1:19; but that declaration ("Now this is the witness of John . . .") obviously demands prior introduction of the figure named John and a statement of his role as witness—just what is provided in vv. 6–7ac.

The prologue is unique in the Gospel; its metaphysical and poetic thought is especially puzzling. But while it contains notorious aporias, those points of difficulty are just the clues to a source analysis of the passage, for they lead us to the seams between source and redaction.

There is consensus that the prologue is based on a poetic source, a pre-Johannine hymn to the Logos (the divine Word). Thus, the intrusion of narrative prose at v. 6 might seem to be material invented by 4E. But the situation is not so simple here, for vv. 6–7 in their own right seem to constitute the opening of an independent prose account.[33] Rather, the Evangelist (or a later editor) has added the prologue and so framed the original opening of the pre-Johannine source. It is not so much an intrusion as a vestige.

Prior to their combining, the narrative source would have had no connection with the poetry of the hymn. Thus, we need not try here to solve the many questions raised by the latter. Rather, its poetry's very uniqueness sets off the narrative in bold relief. In the midst of the sonorous measures of a hymn of praise to the divine Logos another style and tonality altogether now breaks in at v. 6, the down-to-earth (though still theological) voice of a narrator announcing a concrete

---

32. Our analysis here will depend at points on the experience gained from a separation of source from redaction in the miracle stories (see Analysis in this part, secs. 3–9), which by widespread agreement comprised the heart of any pre-Johannine source. See also *TGOS*, 22–25 ("A Starting Point: The Miracle Stories").

33. Some have held that the Johannine Gospel itself once began with these words, patent testimony to their introductory character; so Lindars (*Gospel of John*, 76) preceded by Brown and others. But if so we shall see from their pre-Johannine point of view that 4E simply used the first words of the source for 4G's sometime opening, just as the Gospel's original ending— prior to the addition of chap. 21 as epilogue or appendix—reproduces the conclusion of the source (20:30–31a).

event in prose: **There appeared a man, sent from God, whose name was John. . . .**[34] These words fittingly and forthrightly open the narrative source. This historical affirmation now seems to interrupt the timeless verities of the hymn, and almost as suddenly as it begins it disappears. But the impression that v. 6 (together with v. 7ac) has been inserted into the hymn is just the reverse of the case. For, in fact, a narrative that once opened with v. 6 has been enclosed by the poetry of the hymn; it is the latter that has been added to the basis provided by the older narrative. We can, then, easily separate the narrative from the hymn:

• There is clear stylistic and substantive contrast between the abstract poetry of vv. 1–5 (terms such as: the beginning, Logos, life, light, darkness, was) and the circumstantial and declarative prose of vv. 6–7 (appeared, man, sent, John, came, testimony, believe).[35] The latter verses would then derive from SQ. But v. 7 is overloaded,[36] evidently a combination of pre-Johannine and Johannine. The middle clause (**to bear witness to the light**) amplifies v. 7a (**he came for testimony**) by relating it to the Johannine concept "light" from vv. 4–5. Similarly v. 8 editorially qualifies the narrative in view of the hymn and so prepares for the latter's resumption in v. 9. Thus vv. 7b and 8–9 are Johannine, leaving vv. 6–7ac as source.

• Verse 15 is still more intrusive, an obviously editorial parenthesis, inserted as a comment on the hymn.[37] While it picks up John's role of witness from v. 7a, it anticipates incongruously what will not be said till v. 30 and is puzzling even there. So far in the source there has been no allusion to Jesus or question of his relation to John. The verse is Johannine.[38]

1:19–23

• SG resumes at v. 19: **This is John's testimony.** The original occasion of this testimony, in other words, the phrasing of v. 19b, is uncertain. **The Jews** who send a delegation **from Jerusalem**[39] have an obviously Johannine ring, and this generalizing subject of the verb is out of keeping with its very specific object (**priests and Levites,** a phrase found only here in the NT and probably stemming from the tradition underlying this story). Thus we can only conjecture how the sentence originally read. Possibly it had an indefinite "they" as subject, with the force of a passive; alternatively, "priests and Levites" was the subject of a verb such as

---

34. The word translated "man" here is the inclusive term *anthrōpos*, that is, human being.

35. The Jerusalem Bible rightly sets out the prologue in poetic lines, but fails to indicate the prose style of vv. 6–8.

36. There are two uses of the root *martyr-* (testimony/testify) and two purpose clauses with *hina*.

37. In form it is complex and awkward, with quotation within quotation and an odd mixture of tenses (lit., John bears witness to him and cried out saying, "This was the one of whom I said, 'He who comes after me has become before me, for he was first of me'").

38. Boismard and Lamouille (*Jean* [hereafter B & L]) see it as helping to provide chiastic structure to the hymn as 4E shapes it, balancing vv. 6–8.

39. In the Greek the two nouns come together (*hoi Ioudaioi ex Hierosolymōn*). Thus the sentence can also be translated "the Jews of Jerusalem sent [to him]. . . ." The use of the city name here without definite article in Greek is apparently Johannine (see 5:1, in contrast to the pre-Johannine in 5:2).

"came." In either case, what is chiefly specified is the delegation's purpose: **to ask him, "Who are you?"**

• Verse 20a is so emphatically repetitive ("And he confessed and did not deny and confessed") that it probably contains redaction, perhaps reading originally only **he testified. . . .**[40]

• The titles denied by John in vv. 20b–21 as inappropriate to him **(the Christ, Elijah, the Prophet)** anticipate and paraphrase what will appear to be clearly pre-Johannine in vv. 41–45 (the three titles there rightly applying to Jesus—Messiah, [Elijah],[41] the one of whom Moses and the prophets wrote). This suggests that here the questions put to John and his answers were also pre-Johannine.[42]

• The original question **(Who are you?)** has so far had only negative answers, so it is repeated in v. 22a and then paraphrased in v. 22c **(What do you say of yourself?)**; both derive from the source, the latter preparing for the manner of John's reply. The intervening clause (v. 22b: **that we may give an answer to those who sent us**) must be Johannine, consistent with the official interrogation set up by the insertions in vv. 19–20a.

• John's answer to the question follows immediately (v. 23), with the traditional citing of Isa. 40:3, here by John himself: **I am the voice of one crying in the wilderness, "Make straight the way of the Lord," as Isaiah the prophet said.**

1:24–34

The material in chapter 1, as we recognized at the beginning, does not easily lend itself to the separation of clearly defined redaction from a just as clearly pre-Johannine narrative. But so far we have been able to feel our way. From this point, however, the text becomes especially tangled and the going more tenuous, as evidenced by the variety of attempts to distinguish tradition and redaction here.[43]

But in looking for what may be the pre-Johannine elements here we are helped first of all by our knowledge of the more or less parallel Synoptic tradition about John:

the use of the Isaiah prophecy (here in v. 23);

the contrast between water and Spirit baptism (vv. 26b, 33e—see also vv. 31c and 33b);

the announcement of the one coming after John and John's relative unworthiness (v. 27; see also v. 30b); and

the tradition of Jesus' baptism (vv. 32b, 34—see also v. 33c).

A glance at the verse numbers just cited shows how intricately all this has been

---

40. "Testified" (or "professed") is a better translation of *hōmologēsen* in the pre-Johannine context than "confessed" in its usual sense of admission under pressure. But for 4E the latter is more appropriate.

41. As reconstructed in this part, sec. 2.

42. It is further supported by indirect evidence from the Synoptics: the people's and Herod's threefold (and similarly mistaken) identification of *Jesus* as John the Baptist, Elijah, or one of the prophets (Mark 6:14–16 pars.). The difference here is that these titles are mistaken when (with appropriate changes) applied to John, but will be seen to be valid when explaining Jesus' identity. (Here and at other points I am indebted to the analysis of this passage by Paulette Muller-Girard.) With the question whether John is the Messiah, compare very loosely Luke 3:15b.

43. Contrast, e.g., the analyses of Richter, in "Joh 1, 19–34," and of B & L, 80–86.

rewoven in the present Gospel. We can assume that most of these traditions were to be found in some form in the source and that the Evangelist has occasioned the complexity, most often by repetition and paraphrase.

Second, we can identify the most obvious redactional material from evidence to come in analyses below:

not knowing, even on John's part (vv. 26d, 33a);

a high Christology together with John's quoting himself (v. 30—see v. 15);

"remaining" (vv. 32c, 33c);

editorial asides (vv. 24, 28, 29a); and

the creation of doublets by repetition (v. 30 after v. 27, v. 36 after v. 29, v. 33ab after v. 31, and v. 33c after v. 32b).[44]

With these clues from the Synoptic Gospels and other parts of 4G, we can make this analysis:

• The explanatory afterthought of v. 24 (**And they had been sent from the Pharisees**) is related to the Johannine interrogation, and thus redactional.[45]

• John has not yet mentioned his baptizing, so if we can assume a minimum of logical consistency, the question in v. 25—with its challenging tone (**Then why are you baptizing . . . ?**) and the summary of John's threefold admission—belongs to the same interrogation. Along with it stems also the editorial introduction in v. 26a (**John answered them saying . . .**). What follows (v. 26b) does not answer the question why he baptizes (not till v. 31b is that explained) but rather simply states that he does and derives from tradition. It furthers without interruption his testimony (begun in v. 23) in answer to the simple question of his identity (v. 22).

Following on the Isaiah prophecy, then, and here again in his own words, John narrates his activity as the baptizer; in the Synoptics this is first told us by the Evangelists (Mark 1:4 pars.). He begins the traditional logion, **I baptize with water** (v. 26b). The completion of this saying (**he who baptizes with holy Spirit**) now does not come till v. 33d.

• The rest of v. 26, with v. 27, is so dense that redaction has clearly taken place, and the problem is to know how much of that editorial activity is Johannine and how much already the work of 4E's predecessor. These verses, 26b–27, one hopelessly overloaded sentence, contain three relative clauses: (1) "whom you do not know," (2) "who comes after me," and (3) "of whom I am not worthy. . . ." The second[46] and third obviously derive from the tradition. The first clause is most certainly part of the Johannine theme of "not knowing."[47] The principal clause

---

44. In one or more cases, 4E doubles not only the source but something already inserted, so the division of doublets does not simply yield source on the one hand and redaction on the other.

45. Still more clearly so if "from" (*ek*) means that the priests and Levites were chosen from among the Pharisees, which is historically unlikely.

46. It also expresses a Johannine preoccupation anticipated already in 1:15 (cf. v. 30).

47. See 1:10 ("the world did not know him"), 3:10 ("a teacher of Israel and you do not know these things!"), 4:32 ("I have food to eat of which you do not know"), and others. It will be applied even to John himself in vv. 31a and 33c.

("there stands among you") is also unique.[48] But an obstacle in assigning it to 4E is that without it the pre-Johannine sentence has no finite verb. It is possibly, then, pre-Johannine, perhaps the redactional addition of the predecessor, preparing for the otherwise too casual appearance of Jesus in v. 36.

In this Gospel, the traditional mightier-than-I phrase is missing. But in v. 27 the clause "of whom I am not worthy . . ." conveys the same idea and may be the source's simpler version of the Matthean form of the phrase, for the latter saying is slightly redundant, "mightier than I" and "of whom I am not worthy" being roughly synonymous. It is the Johannine author who has inserted whom-you-do-not-know before he-who-comes-after-me, overburdening the sentence, and so is able to postpone the baptizing-with-holy-spirit.[49]

The pre-Johannine text, then clearly enough, would have read: **I baptize with water. (There stands among you) the one who comes [or was to come] after me, of whom I am not worthy to loosen his sandal thong.**[50] **This is he who baptizes with holy Spirit.**[51]

• The whole of v. 28 artificially interrupts John's testimony, which smoothly continues in v. 29 and the following verses. The datum of locale (**Bethany beyond Jordan**) is perhaps taken from an independent, possibly oral, tradition, distantly related to the Synoptic references to the Jordan,[52] but now forms part of a Johannine geographical schema running through the first half of the Gospel (see part 2.F).

• Similarly the scheme of days that punctuates chapter 1, beginning with **on the next day** in v. 29a, is almost certainly the Evangelist's insertion (see also 1:35, 43; 2:1).

• The rest of v. 29 is hard to assign since it is almost identical to v. 36: John sees Jesus coming/walking and says, "Behold the Lamb of God." We may suppose that v. 29 is pre-Johannine and v. 36 the Evangelist's redactional repetition. This

---

48. Except that it is akin to the probably pre-Johannine assertion in 20:19 ("Jesus came and stood in their midst"); but since we do not establish any certain connection between SQ and PQ till later (excursus A.2) we do not use this datum as a clue to the provenance of the clause. The reading *estēken* is now preferred; it is a pluperfect, from the perfect form *stēkein*, and thus has both past and present temporal reference, meaning roughly "has come and now stands."

49. If so, what is suggested here is that the Evangelist has removed this clause, saving it for a later point (and perhaps prefixing "this"). This kind of displacement is not common in the Johannine redaction, but not unique either. We resort to such a solution when no other way of unraveling the text presents itself. In this passage, where the highly compact source has patently been greatly expanded by 4E, it is clearly more likely that this has occurred than elsewhere; see also the similarly intricate story in this part, sec. 7, the raising of Lazarus.

50. The latter clause shows both close parallels to and typically minor divergence from the Synoptics (different word for "worthy"; subjunctive clause rather than infinitive; and "sandal" in the singular).

51. In the Synoptic Baptist's pronouncement the last phrase is, as here, without articles, but is usually overtranslated as "the Holy Spirit," under the influence of later Christian doctrine. That the simpler rendering we use is probably more faithful is evident from the fact that in Q (Matt. 3:11 = Luke 3:16) the phrase is "holy spirit and fire," hardly the hypostatized third person of the Trinity.

52. Mark 1:5 = Matt. 3:6 ("the river Jordan"), Matt. 3:5 = Luke 3:3 ("the region of the Jordan").

likelihood is reinforced by the fact that the format of v. 29 ("saw . . . coming to him and said, 'Behold . . .' ") is found again in v. 47, where it is pre-Johannine (see just below). But the amplification of the Lamb of God title with the explanation **who takes away the sin of the world** (v. 29c) is more in keeping with the Johannine presentation of Jesus' death than the pre-Johannine.[53] Probably, then, it is the Evangelist's insertion here, and so when v. 29 is reiterated by 4E in v. 36 only the shorter, pre-Johannine form need be copied.

• In v. 30, John quotes a former saying of his (**This is he of whom I said . . .**), something not heard elsewhere. The best explanation for this anomaly—all the more striking since it has been prematurely anticipated in v. 15—is simply that the Evangelist here paraphrases v. 27 rather than strictly quotes it. Thus the earlier clause ("he who follows me, . . . of whom I am not worthy . . .") becomes **A man follows me who ranks** [lit., "has become"] **before me.**[54]

• To this paraphrase 4E adds, as an explanatory comment, **for he was before me** (lit., "for he was first of me"—v. 30c). This both resonates with the Evangelist's concept of Jesus' preexistence (see 1:1 and 8:58 ["Before Abraham was, I am"]) and underscores John's inferiority, by way of Johannine anti-Baptist corrective.[55]

• Similarly, v. 31a (**I myself** [or **Even I**] **did not know him**) is 4E's redaction, as also again in v. 33a.[56] John was almost as ignorant as the delegation he addressed (v. 26d).

• Verse 31bc (**For this I came baptizing with water: that he might be revealed to Israel**) is formally akin to the Johannine 18:37 ("For this I was born, and for this I have come into the world, to bear witness to the truth"). But there the Evangelist is perhaps following the model of the present verse, which is informed not by Johannine themes but by the tradition found in 1:6–7. And **Israel** will be found at several points in the source (1:47, 49; 12:13; evidently it is Johannine only at 3:10), presumably synonymous with the **all** of 1:7c.[57] So we can take v. 31bc (less "but")

53. Dodd suggests (*Tradition,* 270–71) that the amplifying clause is not Johannine but perhaps original to the title Lamb of God, only underscoring its general messianic reference. That is possible, yet it never again functions in the source, whereas at the Johannine level it seems to connect with Caiaphas's "prophecy" in 11:51–52 and may also reflect 4E's particular interest in the Passover theme (2:13; 6:4; 11:55).

54. The Evangelist's change in grammatical form (from participle to finite verb) is the reverse of Matthew's adaptation (3:11) of Mark 1:7 or Q (Luke 3:16). Earlier in the source, John is called simply a human being (*anthrōpos*—v. 6); here Jesus is called "man" (i.e., male—*anēr*), a kind of variation common to the Evangelist and consistent with our separation of source and redaction.

55. Thus also the Johannine "I did not know him" (vv. 31, 33), "He must increase, but I must decrease" (3:30), and "John did no sign" (10:41). See further, n. 56.

56. D. M. Smith ("Milieu") believes that the purpose of the source was to convince followers of John that not he but Jesus was the Messiah. In that case, much or all of the so-called anti-Baptist corrective in the Gospel and especially in this section would be pre-Johannine. I find, instead, that most of this anti-Baptist tendency has been added by the Johannine redactor. Yet, if the source's purpose was not primarily to counter the first-century Baptist movement but to convince Jews in general within the synagogue to accept Jesus as their Messiah (see this part, excursus C, on the *intent* of the source)—still there was secondarily a clear motive to restrict John's role to the single and subordinate task of witness.

57. To "manifest" (*phaneroun*) is frequently Johannine (3:1; 7:4; 9:3; 17:6) but also possibly sometimes pre-Johannine (2:11b; 21:1, 14).

to be a resumption of the source after v. 29, following the Evangelist's insertion of vv. 30–31a. The fact of "baptizing with water" is SG's only repetition (from v. 26), but unless it is a Johannine insertion for anti-Baptist effect it is appropriate here as Jesus comes for that rite, which is now about to be solemnly testified to.

• This report (v. 32) of Jesus' baptism is conveyed here, as throughout in our source, not by an offstage narrator but in John's own words, perceived solely through his eyes: **I saw (the) Spirit descend like a dove from heaven . . . upon him.** (The phrase **and remained** is omitted here—probably 4E's insertion; the source's reading is closer to the Synoptics.)[58] The formal reminder (**And John testified, saying**) is probably Johannine, providing a needed pause in the account which is now so turgid because of the Johannine doublets.

• Verse 33a–c (**And I myself [or Even I] did not know him, but he who sent me to baptize with water said to me, "He on whom you see . . ."**) is emphatic Johannine repetition (of 1:6b, 26b, and 32b, all pre-Johannine, as well as of the Johannine v. 31a).[59] It leads to the source's declaration in v. 33d, postponed to this position by 4E. Note that the declaration (**This is he who baptizes with holy Spirit**) is no longer the word of John, but now in the Johannine repetition a direct disclosure from God.

• Verse 34, the last of the traditional material, brings to a climax the source's account of John's testimony—**I myself [kagō] have seen and I testify.**[60] And the burden of the testimony, the goal of John's mission, is none other than the christological fact of Jesus' identity: **This is the Son of God.** These words, of course, are a translation onto the lips of John (like everything in the source) of the voice from heaven in the Synoptic portrayal of the baptism of Jesus.

The foregoing analysis is unusually intricate and contains a number of uncertainties, but a far clearer text emerges when the apparently Johannine themes are removed: a version closely parallel at many points to the Synoptic tradition and at others showing either the variation that such tradition inevitably involves or the redactional intent of the source's author.

SECTION 2 (1:35–49)
THE FIRST DISCIPLES FIND
THE MESSIAH

We saw that the change of scene marked by v. 29 was artificial; the testimony ostensibly begun to the delegation from Jerusalem is only complete on what the Evangelist now describes as the following day, when they have disappeared. But in the underlying content of the narrative there is a scene change at v. 35: there the first disciples' discovery of the Messiah,

---

58. Compare the repeated use of "remain" (*menein*) in the discourses, esp. chap. 15, and the study of this term by Heise, *Bleiben*. On 1:39 see below, in sec. 2, Pre-Johannine Source. Matthew has only "descending and alighting."

59. The use of a form of *pempō* for "sent" is Johannine; SG uses only *apostellō:* 1:6, 19; 11:3; 18:24.

60. This second verb (*memartyrēka*) is also in the perfect tense, but perhaps it means "I now complete my testimony."

as the consequence of John's testimony, begins. Thus, though it flows smoothly out of the first one, we treat the passage as a distinct section.

Pre-Johannine Source[61]

1 [35]Now John was standing with two of his disciples, [37]and they heard him speak, and they followed Jesus. [38](And Jesus turned and saw them following and said to them, "What are you searching for?") And they said to him, "Rabbi, where are you staying?" [39]He said to them, "Come and you will see." So they went and saw where he was staying, and they stayed with him that day; it was about four o'clock.

[40]Andrew (the brother of Simon Peter) was one of the two who heard John and followed Jesus. [41]He first found his brother Simon and said to him, "We have found the Messiah!" [42]He led him to Jesus. When Jesus saw him he said, "You are Simon son of John; you shall be called Cephas."

[43b]And he found Philip [and said to him, "We have found Elijah!" And he led him to Jesus],[62] and Jesus said to him, "Follow me." [44]Now Philip was from Bethsaida, the village of Andrew and Peter.

[45]Philip found Nathanael and said to him, "We have found the One of whom Moses (and also the prophets) wrote in the Law, Jesus son of Joseph, of Nazareth!" [46]And Nathanael said to him, "Can anything good come out of Nazareth?" Philip said to him, "Come and see." [47]Jesus saw Nathanael coming to him and said of him, "Behold a true Israelite." [49]Nathanael answered him, "Rabbi, you are the Son of God; you are King of Israel!"[63]

John's task is almost fulfilled; before he fades from our sight one act of his witnessing remains, and far from the least: to occasion that others find Jesus and become his followers. They will represent Israel (1:31), the "all" to whom John was sent so that they "might come to believe through him" (vv. 6–7).

We hear for the first time of John's followers (v. 35). But he is not so

61. I no longer hold (as in *TGOS*, 179–80) that the tradition underlying 3:23–24 (John baptizing at Aenon) came at this point in the source, between vv. 34 and 35, and then was removed by 4E to its present place in chap. 3. The datum that John baptized the crowds collides with SG's focus on his role solely as witness. The verses are evidently an independent unit in 4E's tradition.

62. See Analysis, below, for this reconstruction.

63. Freed and Hunt ("Signs-Source," 567–70) suggest a refinement of my analysis in *TGOS*, on the basis of stylistic variation, which they take to occur in the Johannine stratum alone. This section, with two or three others, would then be excluded from the source since it shows evidence of such variation. But some of the instances advanced seem to me insignificant, since minor variation within the source is not unlikely; and those places that contain an unusual degree of variation are found within the material I attribute to the Evangelist. The parallel to this passage in 12:21–22 appears to be an instance of Johannine imitation of the source.

much their leader as simply a witness, for when they heard him they immediately went after Jesus (v. 37; see on "follow" below). That John has followers is significant only as it occasions the first conversions[64] to Jesus' discipleship (and is not intended as anti-Baptist propaganda).

The account is paradigmatic, providing a model for Christian conversion. While there is no mention yet of actual belief in Jesus—that will serve as the climax of the first miracle (2:11)—the new disciples' confession of him, their joining themselves to him, stands as a norm. Three verbs, each of them appearing several times within vv. 37–43, and with varying denotation, give this passage its rich meaning:

a. The first is **follow** (*akoluthein*). Like the others, sometimes it is used merely literally. The disciples of John have heard his manifold witness to Jesus; in the midst of it Jesus himself has appeared, and so they now "follow" him (v. 37). That the word is used in a physical way (to "go after") is evident from the next verse where Jesus turns and sees them thus **following** him (v. 38a). The same ordinary meaning, by which no relationship between Jesus and these "followers" is yet implied, on first glance is intended also in v. 40, which simply reminds us of what was said in v. 37: **Andrew . . . was one of the two who heard John and followed Jesus.** Yet the situation is not now the same, for in the meantime they have **stayed** with Jesus (v. 39) and subsequently can announce that they have **found the Messiah** (v. 41). So, perhaps, in v. 40 we should read "followed" to mean more than simply "went after," and to include the sense "joined themselves to." Certainly this fuller meaning obtains by the time of Jesus' command to Philip in v. 43: **Follow me.** Philip had already sought and come to Jesus; now he is challenged to continue as a disciple. The literal meaning has fallen away. But the two other terms have by now come into play.

b. The second term, **stay** (*menein*), at first means simply "pass time." The two who left John and went after Jesus express their interest by asking him, **Where are you staying?** (v. 38b). Evidently they want to know something more about him, perhaps where he can be found, and at his invitation (**Come and see**—v. 39a) they find the answer to their own question (**so they went and saw where he was staying**—v. 39b).[65] By now their initial curiosity has become a commitment to his presence: **they stayed with him that day** (v. 39c).[66] Through the play on the word (as with

---

64. I use this word despite its anachronism: at the time of the source (as of the original disciples) following Jesus, believing in him, did not involve the leaving of one religion for another; that was becoming true only in 4E's time.

65. Note their exact compliance with Jesus' words, typical of SQ (2:7–8, etc.).

66. The odd datum of time ("and it was about four o'clock" [lit., "the tenth hour"]— v. 39d) lends a note of factuality, also characteristic of the source. It may suggest that they began their stay with Jesus shortly before sundown and so, by Jewish reckoning, were with him "that day"—overnight and the next morning.

"follow"), their remaining has gradually become a function of discipleship, a decision to adhere to Jesus.[67]

c. But the components of conversion are not yet exhausted. There is finally the term **find** (*heuriskein*). Andrew[68] did not simply follow Jesus and stay with him; a sequence of conversions ensues. After (i) he had been converted by John, (ii) Andrew himself went out, **found his brother Simon,** and led him to Jesus (vv. 41–42). (iii) Then Simon[69] **found Philip,** his fellow townsman, and led him to Jesus (v. 43b, as reconstructed). Finally, (iv) **Philip found Nathanael** (v. 45), who at his bidding came to Jesus (vv. 46b–47a). Each actively accomplishes the conversion of another first by finding and then by leading[70] him to Jesus.

But between these two physical acts, the term "find" is used again, in a deeper, nonliteral way. For the conversion is brought about in each case by the announcement: **We have found. . . .** John had given testimony to Jesus, elaborately. But prior to that he had implied a question, if he himself was not the Messiah, Elijah, the Prophet, then who was? He had never answered the question. So his disciples set out on a quest; his indirect testimony to Jesus' status had to be confirmed.

Andrew's testimony to Simon is just this: that the search is over, his search and all Israel's. Jewish expectation at last has come to fruition. **We have found the Messiah!**[71] Jesus is no other than the fulfillment of all Jewish hopes. John's testimony had come to a different christological climax (**Son of God**); only by the lips of the first disciples is the consummation of the age-old expectation voiced. This simple declaration forms the essential message of the source, the good news that makes it a Gospel (see further, this part, excursus A).

The succeeding titles do not so much add to this first as explicate it. It

---

67. This wordplay seems to be the germ of the later and more highly theological Johannine use of remain (or "abide") to describe both the intimate relationship between the Son and the Father and that between the believer and God.

68. The other of the two disciples of John in vv. 35 and 37 is anonymous and evidently to be ignored at the pre-Johannine level (see also the "other disciple" in 18:15). At the Johannine level, his mention perhaps is meant as a hint ahead of time of "the disciple whom Jesus loved," in the Gospel's second half.

69. Or possibly Andrew. The subject is indefinite, and the detail that Andrew had "first" found Simon (v. 41) may imply that he next found Philip.

70. Twice this verb (*agagein*) is used. The plot in Nathanael's case is thus more complex.

71. The use of the verb "find" here is far from a literal coming upon something lost or misplaced, or an accidental stumbling upon. Instead it means "discover," "come upon [almost] by divine initiative." The first-person plural may suggest that both Andrew and the other disciple had made the discovery. But thereafter it is retained even for individuals: There emerges a growing community of converts, who one after another testify, "We have found. . . ." Apart from 4:25, which probably imitates it, this is the only NT instance of the Semitic word *Messias* behind the Greek term "Christ." The fact that in 1:20 *Christos* was used, but here *Messias,* may indicate that the term in 1:20 is derivative, the Semitic form being more basic.

was not yet clear what kind of Messiah Andrew had found, but the subsequent declarations begin to tell us, especially that he is not the political, Davidic liberator expected by so many. He is not military victor but healer, a worker of miracles; that is, he is **Elijah,** who had done many such deeds, had not died but rather had been taken up to heaven so that his return was expected. To make it still clearer, Jesus is the Prophet-like-himself that Moses promised.[72] And Moses had had one role in common with Elijah—the working of miracles; indeed, Moses had worked signs. (The connection, simply presupposed by the pre-Johannine author, between Jesus' messiahship and his working of signs, now about to begin, is apparently self-evident within the messianic thinking of that author's audience. John's denial of the titles is therefore understandable, for—as 4E will later observe, presumably on the basis of the lack of tradition to the contrary—John "did no sign" [10:41].)

So this account of the disciples' conversion, with its definitive three titles, is prefatory to the ministry of signs that will follow. Jesus is that awaited agent of God from heaven who would both display himself in signs and accomplish his mission by means of them. Thus the passage prepares for the acts of self-disclosure about to begin; it spells out the language of the source's christology, its understanding of the role and status of Jesus.

A kind of progression takes place as the disciples discover Jesus. At the beginning he is called simply **Rabbi,**[73] a title conveying respect and attributing authority but still without christological intent. Then the three titles of discovery are applied to Jesus—but not addressed to him. So Nathanael brings the drama of conversion to an end by declaring to Jesus, **Rabbi** [again, gathering up the progression], **You are the Son of God. You are King of Israel.** He makes the full messianic confession.

Thus John's climactic testimony ("Son of God" in v. 34) is finally amplified by the oldest form of national hope, "King of Israel" (no political sense is implied by this title; Jesus' revealing himself as Messiah will not be by any nationalistic act but by the working of signs). Just as the two-part preface to the source (the pre-Johannine narrative in chap. 1) begins with the testimony of John, so it ends with Nathanael's. His is more than a testimony, it is also an act of praise (not John's "This is" but "You are") and a confession of faith.

The initiative in this drama is always the disciples'. Jesus is not one who actively calls disciples but rather a quiet presence around whom the story revolves. It is in response to the first followers' question that he invites them: **Come and see** (v. 39a). (And if he previously spoke—that is, if

---

72. This clearly is the referent of "the one of whom Moses wrote in the Law" (see Deut. 18:15). That the title Prophet is thus paraphrased here (but not earlier with respect to John, in v. 21, or again in 6:14) is possibly to remind us initially of its OT basis for Jesus.

73. V. 38b; also translatable as "Master" or "Teacher."

v. 38a is pre-Johannine—it was only with the ambiguous question, "What are you looking for?") When—one by one—Peter, Philip, and Nathanael are brought to him, he responds to each with a declaration; he renames Simon, exhorts Philip, compliments Nathanael. But he only responds, he does not summon them or in any way provoke their faith. We can thus entitle this section "The First Disciples Find the Messiah."[74]

The passage thus contrasts with Jesus' "calling" the disciples by the seaside in the Synoptic Gospels.[75] Here Jesus is the self-evident goal of the old Jewish quest, the one who appears and need only be recognized. This is the source's very purpose, then—to portray Jesus showing himself obviously as Messiah. His activity is not to seek out followers; rather, they initially and quite naturally seek him, and only when they have found him does he perform the deeds of the Messiah, the signs that are to follow. Then they, and after their example all who read of those deeds, will see him for what he is and believe in him.

In contrast to the rather imprecise impression we have so far of Jesus, the portrait of the new disciples is drawn in concrete detail—the name of each of the converts is given, and biographical data about them are supplied. Attention rests on them one by one as they come to Jesus.

Andrew and his unnamed companion[76] had initiated the process of discovery by their immediate response to John's testimony. Jesus did not have to attract them; merely the word about him was necessary.

But it is to his more illustrious brother that Andrew makes the explicit messianic announcement. It is this Simon who, when brought to Jesus, is given the first Christian name, **Cephas.**[77]

Jesus' word to Philip is a simple command: "Follow me." This might be better translated, **Be my follower,** since from the Greek form[78] we should

74. Similarly Martyn, "Elijah," 44–45.

75. The only overlap with the tradition underlying Mark 1:16–20 par. is the word to Philip, "Follow me" (v. 43b). But here in SQ the phrase expresses not a call to Philip but simply Jesus' response to the fact that Philip has already come to him (in the reconstructed text) and thus in some way shown his readiness to be a follower. The technical Synoptic term for Jesus' converting his first disciples, "call" (*kalein*—Mark 1:20 par.), does not appear with this meaning in 4G.

76. Why this superfluous figure? It is not possible, I would hold, that Johannine redaction has created him as, for example, an early preparation for the beloved disciple who appears first in chap. 13. The fact of more than one follower of John's seeking Jesus is thoroughly embedded in vv. 35–39. Apparently this is one of those gratuitous details that the source is so fond of supplying.

77. In the NT, only here and in two of the letters of Paul (1 Corinthians, Galatians) do we find the original Semitic form of the name; elsewhere only the Greek *Petros* is used. Nothing is made of the meaning of this designation ("rock"), such as in the parallel passage in Matt. 16:18; it is enough that Jesus acknowledges him, calls him by his full name ("Simon son of John"), and then gives him the appellation that almost totally supplants his given name in Christian tradition.

78. Present (not aorist) imperative, indicating that the action is ongoing.

understand that it both invites Philip into discipleship and exhorts him to continue in it.

When Philip speaks to Nathanael the threefold confession is complete. Perhaps for that reason the Messiah is at last fully named: **Jesus son of Joseph, of Nazareth.** Nathanael's response is given, uniquely in this section, and at first it is cynical **(Can anything good come out of Nazareth?**—v. 46a). He expresses either mere village rivalry (if he came from nearby Cana, as 21:2 tells us) or astonishment that one of so apparently ordinary a provenance should be the fulfillment of generations of Jewish anticipation. Philip's reply is pragmatic, the by-now expectable **Come and see.** Not theological (or sociological) argument but the self-evident messiahship of Jesus will convert him. Apparently he complies,[79] for Jesus, seeing him coming and despite his skepticism, declares him a worthy convert. He can represent all to whom the source's good news is addressed: **a true Israelite.** Initial disbelief does not disqualify one from discipleship, it simply gives way to belief. The drama comes to completion with Nathanael's extravagant acclamation. (For further discussion on this scene and a comparison of its pre-Johannine treatment with the Johannine, see just below.)

The entire passage is a paradigm. It shows both a process repeated and a progression, exemplifying in each case the way converts are to be won. Underlying the variation of titles and of the individuals involved there is a common pattern, expressed in three elements: the fresh convert goes out and finds someone known to him; he announces the good news to him as a discovery; he brings him to Jesus. A procedure for the missionary enterprise is evidently intended. The initiative rests with the disciples, not with Jesus. (The situation of the church rather than of the historical Jesus is clearly the basis for this. The purpose of this document—a missionary tract, addressed to both potential converts and the Christians who are to approach them—informs this passage.) The process appears to be automatic, the method foolproof.

Johannine Redaction

1 [35]**The next day again** John was standing with two of his disciples, [36]**and seeing Jesus passing he said, "Behold the Lamb of God."** [37]**And his two disciples** heard him speak, and they followed Jesus. [38]**(And Jesus turned and saw them following and said to them, "What are you searching for?")** And they said to him, "Rabbi," **which translated means 'Teacher,'** "where are you staying?" [39]He said to them, "Come and you will see." *Then* they went and saw where he was staying, and they stayed with him that day; it was about four o'clock.

---

79. It was not Jesus' command, so we are not shown explicitly (contrast v. 39).

[40]Andrew (**the brother of Simon Peter**) was one of the two who heard John and followed Jesus. [41]He first found his brother Simon and said to him, "We have found the Messiah," **which is translated 'Christ.'** [42]He led him to Jesus. When Jesus saw him he said, "You are Simon son of John; you shall be called Cephas."

[43]**The next day Jesus decided to go away to Galilee.** And he found Philip [*Here the Evangelist has omitted the announcement to Philip with the messianic title Elijah.*] and said to him, "Follow me." [44]Now Philip was from Bethsaida, the village of Andrew and Peter.

[45]Philip found Nathanael and said to him, "We have found the One of whom Moses (**and also the prophets**) wrote in the Law, Jesus son of Joseph of Nazareth?" [46]And Nathanael said to him, "Can anything good come out of Nazareth?" Philip said to him, "Come and see."

[47]Jesus saw Nathanael coming to him and said of him, "Behold a true Israelite **in whom is no guile.**" [48]**Nathanael said to him, "How do you know me?" Jesus answered and said to him, "I saw you before Philip called you, while you were under the fig tree."** [49]Nathanael answered him, "Rabbi, you are the Son of God; you are King of Israel!" [50]**Jesus answered and said to him, "Do you believe because I said to you that I saw you under the fig tree? You will see greater things than these."** [51]**And he said to him, "Amen Amen I say to you, you will see heaven opened and the angels of God ascending and descending on the Son of Man."**

In comparison to the preceding section (1:19–34), this passage from SG stands relatively intact in 4G; the analysis into source and redaction was consequently far simpler. Whereas the Evangelist greatly transformed the portrayal of the Baptist's testimony, the conversion of the disciples receives only retouching.[80]

If a new scene at v. 35 was implied in the source, it is now made unmistakable: **On the next day again. . . .**[81] What had been a natural continuation of John's testimony (the first mention of his disciples is the only new element) becomes a fresh start altogether. This then demands the addition of v. 36, doubling and paraphrasing the pre-Johannine v. 29: **And he looked at Jesus as he walked and said, "Behold the Lamb of God."**[82]

Some of the Johannine additions are merely brief amplifications: the parenthetical translation of the terms **Rabbi** (v. 38), **Messiah** (v. 41), and

80. Hence, perhaps, Bultmann (*Gospel of John*) begins to find SQ only in this passage; but it patently requires the preceding one as preparation.

81. And much as with vv. 19–34 at v. 29, 4E again artificially breaks the originally continuous narrative of vv. 35–49 in two by a similar phrase at v. 43. Strictly speaking, more than one day is demanded by the source's account, if we press the datum of the late hour at the end of v. 39; but nothing is made of this until the present Gospel.

82. Like many redactional insertions, the colorlessness of v. 36, lacking new content, shows that it does not derive from tradition or source.

Cephas (v. 42).[83] Similarly, if the phrase **and the prophets** (v. 45) is Johannine, its insertion is perhaps meant to buttress the exegetical argument of the Johannine Christians against their rabbinic antagonists.[84]

Other changes are corrective:

a. Whether pre-Johannine or not, Jesus' question in v. 38a (**What are you looking for?**) now functions to test the purity of motive on the part of the new converts, a theme that will reappear in the redaction of several of the signs stories (4:48; 6:26). Contrast the simple question of desire in SG at 5:6.

b. Verse 50a interprets Nathanael's confession in v. 49 as an act of faith and questions the basis of that faith (again, just as in 4:48 and 6:26): **Jesus answered him, "Because I said to you, I saw you under the fig tree, do you believe?"** The second half of the verse prepares for the climactic addition of v. 51 by promising **You will see greater things than these.** The signs, of course, are hereby prepared for, but 4E has let his or her own addition of v. 51 have even more importance than they, so central and all-sufficient in SG.

c. Far more basically, the source's Christology is corrected. Specifically, the older identification of Jesus as Elijah—one of the three confessions expected from John's denials—is suppressed by the omission from v. 43. The reason for this suppression is not evident from the passage at hand. But on the basis of work by Dunn ("Let John Be John," 321–25), it appears that the Evangelist has a strong interest in denying that anyone, even the great worthies of Israel's past, "has ascended into heaven except he who came down from heaven, the Son of Man" (3:13). So, since Elijah is probably most remembered for his final assumption into heaven, the Evangelist must omit "Elijah" as a messianic designation used by the chain of witness; see further part 2.A. In its stead, and added to Nathanael's confession of Jesus as "King of Israel," is the **Son of Man** logion of v. 51, serving as climax to the passage. We need not try to exhaust what 4E understands by this title.[85] Here it sums up all that has been said in chapter 1 of Jesus' identity.

The obviously important assertion in v. 43—that **on the next day Jesus decided to go away to Galilee**—has no direct bearing on the present passage, apart from providing its division into two parts. Rather, it prepares for the passage to follow and belongs to the Evangelist's schematic use of geography, which we consider in part 2.F.

---

83. All using the same term—(*met*)*hermēneuesthai*—meaning literally "translated as by an interpreter."

84. As in Martyn, *History and Theology*.

85. It appears many times in the course of the Gospel, always Johannine and nearly always in contexts apart altogether from SG. It is evidently quite absent from SG but is possibly one of the oldest designations of Jesus in Christian tradition.

Thus, most of the Johannine redaction either consists of relatively minor explanations or introduces corrections and themes that can be understood only at a later stage in our investigation. But the major redactional change in the passage is the expansion of the portrait of Nathanael. (Apart from brief mention of his name and place of origin in the list in 21:2, he appears only here in the NT.) And while a number of broad Johannine themes lead out from it, the episode can here be treated in its own right.

In the source Nathanael was simply the last in the chain of witnesses that began with the Baptist and his two disciples. Perhaps he was the most vivid of the converts—on hearing of Jesus' village he doubts the christological claim Philip has made for him—but Jesus' word to Nathanael is hardly more remarkable than the renaming of Peter. If he is finally the mouthpiece for a climactic announcement of Jesus' identity, that is simply because he stands at the end of the chain; even the titles he uses in his acclamation of Jesus do not greatly add to what has gone before.

The Evangelist, on the other hand, has considerably enhanced this scene. In v. 48, which we took to be a Johannine insertion, Nathanael reacts to Jesus' acknowledging word to him by an astonished question (**How** [lit., "from where?"] **do you know me?**). This picks up from the tradition of his doubt in v. 46, but it asks a Johannine question, the source of Jesus' knowledge.[86] In fact, it is only with this insertion that Jesus' knowledge comes to our attention; nothing of the sort has yet appeared in SG.[87] But that Nathanael's question, whether still only suspicious or already incredulous, is theologically meaningful is clear from Jesus' reply: **even before Philip called** to him Jesus **saw** him, and presumably supernaturally knew him. Thus Nathanael, standing at the end of the conversions, elicits the uniqueness of Jesus' powers.[88]

By Jesus' unusual disclosure all Nathanael's doubts are overcome.[89] His confession (v. 49) becomes almost a surrender. Further, the double christological affirmation ("Son of God . . . King of Israel") that presumably capped the source's narrative is now but the occasion for a further and crowning word of Jesus. In v. 50 Jesus raises a question about Nathanael's

86. The question contains two characteristically Johannine terms, often used together—*pothen* ("from where?"; "whence?") and *ginōskein* or a synonym ("know"). See 2:9; 3:8, 10–11; 7:27–28; 8:14; 9:29–30; 19:9.

87. Not even in the present text of v. 42, where Jesus merely displays what must have been common knowledge of Peter ("You are Simon son of John"). It is only in the miracles that the pre-Johannine Jesus fully shows his special knowledge (e.g., 11:11; 21:6; perhaps 5:6).

88. There is very likely some significance in the detail (repeated in v. 50) that Jesus saw him "under the fig tree"—the typical place for a "true Israelite" to learn from the Word of God, perhaps—but we are given no clue in the redaction how it is to be understood.

89. This kind of rationale for conversion, based on a depiction of Jesus interacting with the candidate (e.g., in chaps. 5 and 9), is simply lacking in the source. There, faith springs automatically from hearing the announcement, "We have found . . . ," not from a direct encounter with Jesus.

faith and in v. 51 corrects his christology; these are themes to be developed by 4E at later points in the Gospel. Here it is primarily Jesus' twofold proclamation that stands out:

1. He promises **You will see greater things than these** (v. 50b).[90] If this had appeared in SG, it would have meant something like: You have had a hint of my clairvoyance and now you are about to see my truly messianic signs. Something of such a meaning holds in the Johannine context.

2. But that cannot be 4E's primary intent, for v. 51 goes on to explain the "greater things" Jesus has promised, using the form of a solemn declaration: **Amen Amen I say to you, You will see heaven opened and the angels of God ascending and descending on the Son of Man.** Whatever the origin of this saying in the Johannine tradition, its OT overtones are resonant. Nathanael—and through him a far wider audience, for the declaration is made in the second-person plural (as also in 4:48)—is to receive the divine revelation, rivaling and surpassing that of Jacob and the ladder. Building on the source's designation of Nathanael as a "true Israelite" (Israel is of course the name that Jacob receives from God) and his confession of Jesus as "King of Israel," 4E has made him the representative of a new and greater people of God. In contrast to the wily OT patriarch, in Nathanael—despite his earlier cynicism—and in those he stands for, **there is no guile** (v. 47d, presumably a Johannine addition).

We can name this section The Promise of a New Christological Community. The hint of a church implicit in the "We" of the pre-Johannine testimonials, each new convert to the next, is now a promise clearly given.

Before leaving this passage we must examine another element, and one that pulls the whole of chapter 1 together in its Johannine shape: that of seeing. The source had played on this word in a minor way: Jesus three times **saw** one or more disciples coming to him (vv. 38, 42, 47), twice disciples are invited to "Come and see" (vv. 39, 46). Prior to that John had seen Jesus coming to him (v. 29). Above all John twice testified that he "saw holy Spirit" and hence could testify to Jesus as "the Son of God" (vv. 32, 34).

The Evangelist builds on this germ of an idea to create a major theme. Jesus reveals to Nathanael that he "saw [him] under the fig tree" and promises that if this impels him to believe, how much more will he—and all Israel—"see greater things than these . . . the heavens opened and the angels of God ascending and descending on the Son of Man" (vv. 48, 50–51).

Suddenly the entire chapter, with the prologue, becomes an *inclusio*, a unity gathered together at beginning and end by the theme of seeing: "We

90. A similar promise is made in 5:20; also in 14:12.

beheld his glory" (v. 14c), and though "no one has ever seen God" yet "the only Son . . . has made him known" (which surely means at least "seen"— v. 18).

Analysis

In this section, perhaps because there is less anti-Baptist tendency motivating 4E than in section 1, the separation of redaction from an underlying source is easier.

• John's public testimony, instigated by the question of the priests and Levites, is complete; its consequences are now about to take effect and John is to fall from view. But it is 4E who has punctuated the transition to the disciples' conversion by inserting at the beginning of v. 35 the phrase **on the next day** (as at vv. 29 and 43), and adding, perhaps only for euphony, **again.** Thus John's **standing with two of his disciples** here, which originally only led into v. 37, becomes an event in itself, yet, with the insertion of v. 36, almost pointless. Where is John standing? (If time has passed, has the locale of v. 28 remained the same?) For what purpose? (Even in the present text it is his seeing Jesus again and repeating the Lamb of God testimony that matters, not his "standing.")

• Verse 36 forms a doublet with v. 29, and therefore is almost certainly a Johannine insertion here, palely imitating the pre-Johannine text.[91] What **the two disciples**[92] **heard [John] speak** in v. 37a was originally not a simple repetition for their benefit of the Lamb of God title but, by implication, either the whole of John's testimony, or at least its climax at v. 34 ("This is the Son of God"). That they left John and **followed Jesus** (v. 37b) was thus more understandable and natural in SG.

• There is a tension between Jesus' question in v. 38a and what follows: the question **What are you looking for?** goes unanswered.[93] It may be redactional, then, though it matters little. But the verse's introduction (**Jesus turned and saw them following**) is perhaps original to the source.

• The parentheses in vv. 38b, 41b, and 42b—all giving the Greek equivalent of Semitic words (**which translated says [or is] . . .**)—are obviously redactional and reflect a post-Jewish or at least monolingual situation that would fit better the circumstances of 4G than of the source (see 9:7). Otherwise, vv. 38b–42 derive directly from SG.[94]

---

91. John here simply "looked at Jesus passing," rather than "saw [him] coming to him" (for baptism); and the title "Lamb of God" is spoken without "who takes away the sin of the world." (Whether the latter was found already in the source or added by 4E, it evidently is not thought important enough to reiterate.)

92. The phrase is probably duplicated from v. 35, after the insertion of v. 36.

93. Unless the disciples' question in turn means, as a kind of reply, "[To know] where you are staying."

94. We note, for the future, these features: "Come and see"; literal compliance to the command ("So they came and saw"); specific detail of time ("about the tenth hour"); amplification of earlier datum ("Andrew, Simon Peter's brother, was one of the two who heard John and followed [Jesus]"—see v. 44). Is the rather graceless repetition of "stay" in vv. 38c–39 a sign of redaction? I can find no way of disengaging any of the three instances from the source; evidently all are original and yield two meanings, as we have seen, and much like the multiple uses of "follow" and "find" in vv. 37–43 (see in this section, pre-Johannine source).

• The phrase **the brother of Simon Peter** in v. 40 is redundant with data in v. 41 ("his brother Simon") and v. 42b ("Cephas, which means Peter"), and could be redactional. On the other hand, the redactor who prematurely alerts the reader to Andrew's more famous brother, using his full traditional name, could as well be the pre-Johannine author as the Johannine, a possibility we shall occasionally encounter.

• A sequence of testimony and subsequent conversion begins in v. 37 with John and Andrew (the latter as yet unnamed) and leads next to Peter (v. 41), then to Philip (v. 43b), and finally to Nathanael (v. 45), each new convert finding and testifying to the next. (The sequence follows a pattern: [a] finding an associate and testifying to him ["We have found . . . !"], [b] associate's question with the reply "Come and see," [c] the associate brought to Jesus, [d] Jesus' declaration concerning him. Occasionally some elements are missing: [d] and parts of [a] in Andrew's case; [b] in Peter's; and [a–c] in Philip's as the text now stands, but see just below.) But this sequence is interrupted by the first half of v. 43, which breaks the passage's obvious continuity into two scenes on successive days and prematurely prepares for Jesus' departure to Galilee following this episode; v. 43a is thus comparable to v. 28 and patently redactional.[95] When it is removed, the subject of the verb **found** in v. 43b is not Jesus but either Andrew or Peter. Then **Jesus** at the end of the verse was originally the subject only of **said,** and not of the verse's three indicative verbs, as now by strained syntax.

• There is reason to believe that in addition to inserting v. 43a, 4E has excised something from SG in this verse, the omission perhaps having occasioned the insertion. The fourfold pattern followed throughout the sequence is truncated here as the text now stands. According to that pattern we should expect to find a declaration to Philip of the form, "We have found [some messianic title]," followed possibly by a question on Philip's part, and then Philip brought to Jesus. Martyn ("Elijah," 33–54) has cannily demonstrated that the messianic title we should expect here and which the Evangelist has presumably chosen to suppress is Elijah; for when that is reinstated the three successive affirmations here of Jesus' messianic status correspond precisely to the three titles John denied for himself in the preceding section (1:20–21).[96] Conjectural reconstruction of material supposedly omitted by 4E is something we shall generally avoid in this study, but the evidence for Martyn's proposal is so compelling that we can adopt it with some confidence. At v. 43b, then, the source would have read: "And he [i.e., Peter, or possibly Andrew] found Philip [[and said to him, 'We have found Elijah!' And he led him to Jesus,]] and Jesus said to him, 'Follow me.'"

• In v. 45 the phrase **and also the prophets** (following **of whom Moses wrote in**

95. Neirynck (*Les synoptiques*) holds here as everywhere that 4E is dependent not on any pre-Johannine source, but simply on the Synoptics, in this case on the "calling of Simon Peter" in Matt. 16:16, 18. But nowhere do I find evidence of any Matthean redaction, only of the barest of traditions underlying the episode in Matthew. Not the Synoptics but some other earlier vehicle of the tradition lies behind 4G. See further excursus B.

96. And to the three *mis*interpretations of Jesus' status in the Synoptics (see on these verses, this part, sec. 1). If, at some point prior to SG, the three titles were understood to be in descending order of rank, once they have been applied explicitly to Jesus they become synonymous (see this part, p. 17).

the law) seems at first syntactically intrusive but contains what will appear to be the pre-Johannine use of singular verb with double subject (see 2:2) and so may stem from the source. There is reason to believe, however, that the last phrase of v. 47—**in whom there is no guile**—may be redactional, inserted along with the addition of v. 51 (see Johannine Redaction, just above).

● Verse 48, in a way replicating Nathanael's skepticism from v. 46, is most likely a Johannine insertion (so Martyn shows, "Elijah," 51 n. 85); it paraphrases the source's "found" with "called," assumes without preparing the reader that Nathanael had been under the fig tree, and contains a phrase akin to one that is characteristic of 4E (lit., "knowing from where").

● The double title in v. 49 is probably not due to redaction but provides a fitting conclusion of the new disciples' witness to Jesus.

● Verse 50 uses the technique of quoting an earlier saying of Jesus and raises the question of the proper basis of belief, both Johannine motifs.[97] Although **You will see greater things than these** finds a kind of fulfillment in 2:11c and the subsequent signs and so might be pre-Johannine, it seems designed chiefly to lead to the addition of v. 51 (Martyn, "Elijah," 43 n. 72).

● Verse 51 is a traditional saying, adapted and added by 4E: grammatically, its pronouncements are made not to the individual Nathanael but in the second-person plural, and it uses the Johannine formula (**Amen Amen I say to you**) and title (**Son of Man**).[98]

---

97. For the former, cf. 3:7; 16:16–19 (also 1:15, 30); for the latter, 4:48; 20:29.

98. The former is found in 4G twenty times (and five with a single "Amen") and the latter twelve times, always in the Johannine discourses and denoting Jesus (in contrast to the Synoptics where sometimes a distinction is made between Jesus and the supernatural figure).

The Signs of Jesus

The Signs in Galilee

In a word used only pejoratively in the Synoptic Gospels, and to some extent also in the Johannine redaction, the source describes Jesus' public activity, approvingly and exclusively, as his signs.[99]

The order of the miracles in the source is less certain than which stories it includes. But there can be no doubt of the first two: their original numbering survives even though now anomalous (2:11a; 4:54a); this may be true of a third episode as well (21:14). That the miracle of the loaves (6:1–14) followed these will be seen to be likely. These four are set in Galilee, while the rest of the signs take place in or near Jerusalem. Whether the pre-Johannine author, in arranging this material, had a primarily geographical schema in mind is not clear. There are editorial links between one story and the next that provide a coherent if rudimentary itinerary for Jesus—one that is more consistent and careful than, for example, Mark's series of mostly independent episodes that at many points are loosely strung together. But these links in SG are not stressed, and we certainly are not to think that they intend to present a total portrayal of Jesus' work. The author provides only a selection of Jesus' signs, but one sufficiently representative and varied for that author's purposes (20:30–31a).

99. It would be inappropriate at the pre-Johannine level, and probably even at the Johannine, to call the succession of Jesus' miracles his ministry, in the sense of the term in the Synoptics, for here we see Jesus not as one who "went about doing good and healing all those that were oppressed" (Acts 10:38), but rather displaying to his followers his messianic identity in the miracles. In SG, then, Jesus' ministry is one of revealing himself, and only in this sense a caring for human need. Further, we find little in the pre-Johannine source analogous to the Synoptic impression, given again and again, that the crowds, sometimes all the inhabitants of a region, flock to Jesus to be either healed or amazed by his miraculous power. The crowds in the source, as only occasionally in the Synoptics, have consistently and solely a christological intent in seeing Jesus. If people are fed and healed and and raised from the dead (as the stories once emphasized), those benefits have become at the immediately pre-Johannine level only byproducts of Jesus' christological self-disclosure.

J. M. Robinson (*Trajectories*, 236 n. 10) objects that since in SG these stories do not usually have symbolic meaning they ought to be thought of simply as "miracles." But in fact they have virtually nothing of the element of wonder (the strict meaning of "miracle"); rather they are powerful indications (that is, signs) of Jesus' messiahship, and nothing more.

48

SECTION 3 (2:1-11)
WATER INTO WINE

Pre-Johannine Source

It is almost univocally agreed by critics that 4E has taken the bulk of this story from a Signs Source of one kind or another. This uncommon consensus has two implications for us. First, it means that our separation of source from redaction in this passage (see Analysis in this section) can serve as a kind of benchmark for source analysis elsewhere in the Gospel. Second, it strongly suggests that the pre-Johannine source had a defined structure. For this episode marks **the beginning of signs,** while the story at the end of chapter 4 is **the second.** Because such enumeration is not to be found in the other miracle stories (with the possible exception of the miracle in chap. 21 [see this part, sec. 5]), many scholars agree that it must be pre-Johannine. The wedding at Cana, then, is the opening story of a narrative source.[100]

But then did the SQ perhaps begin only here, so that the pre-Johannine material in chapter 1 would have been drawn by 4E from some other tradition? Even the quickest reading of the story at hand suggests that chapter 2 is a continuation of the same pre-Johannine source as in chapter 1. This story cannot have been the very opening of the source, for it presupposes that Jesus has been introduced already and has a following; the disciples figure peripherally but nonetheless inextricably in the account. That the pre-Johannine form of 1:35-51 was in fact such an introduction is of course not absolutely necessary, but we could hardly hope to invent a better one; and it in turn presupposes the source material in 1:6-7, 19-34.

When the redactional phrases identified in the Analysis in this section are lifted out of 2:1-11, a complete story remains, and one more coherent than the present text of the passage.

2 ¹Now (on a Tuesday) there was a wedding at Cana (in Galilee), and the mother of Jesus was there. ²And both Jesus and his disciples were invited to the wedding.³ᵃAnd when the wine gave out[101] Jesus' mother said ⁵ᵇto the servants, "Do whatever he tells you." ⁶Now there were six stone water-jars standing there, each holding twenty or thirty gallons. ⁷Jesus said to them, "Fill the jars with water." So they filled them full. ⁸And he said to them, "Now draw some out and take it to the steward," and they did. ⁹When the

---

100. Some have held that such a source contained only the two or three episodes just referred to. So Heekerens, *Zeichen-Quelle.* And B & L assign these three stories to their hypothetical Document C.

101. Or, according to the longer reading (see Analysis in this section): "And they had no wine, for the festal wine had given out; then . . . ."

steward tasted the water changed into wine [he][102] called the bridegroom
[10]and said to him, "Everyone serves the good wine first, and when people
are drunk the poorer wine; but you have saved the good wine until now!"
[11]This [was] the beginning of the signs Jesus did[103] (and he showed [him-
self]), and his disciples believed in him.

Now at last Jesus takes center stage. In section 1 it was the Baptist who
was prominent, in section 2 the disciples. Jesus was no less important than
they; on the contrary, everything had to do with making clear who he was
and how his disciples assembled. But now his own miraculous work, the
heart of SG, begins.

What kind of story is this? To what literary category does it belong? We
have here an especially clear instance of what form critics call a *novelle* or
tale, and a miracle story in particular. Characteristically it is told with great
economy, yet with all the necessary components of such a story: the
situation is described, the need for a miracle made clear; instructions are
given and carried out; the miracle takes place and is attested by the
reaction of one or more witnesses. There is ambiguity in applying this, the
formal structure of a miracle story, to the Cana episode only when we try
to identify the final element: who is the real witness to the miracle—the
steward in v. 10 or the disciples in v. 11? Some would say that it cannot
originally have been the steward, for a story of this sort would not end with
a proverbial saying such as the one he utters ("Everyone serves the good
wine first . . ."). But we need not be so rigid in our definition of the forms
stories take.[104] The steward's words may contain some theological hint of
their own, as we shall see; but they also ratify the miracle. We do not have
to be told: Then Jesus changed the water into wine.[105] Rather, the fact of
the miracle is made clear indirectly but unmistakably in v. 9—**the steward
tasted the water changed into wine**—and his amazed words to the
bridegroom (v. 10) drive home the message. He is the witness to the
miracle, even if unwittingly. (It is not clear in the pre-Johannine story
whether or not the steward knows where the wine has come from—it is 4E
who specifies that.)

102. Evidently it is 4E who has reiterated the sentence's subject ("the steward") after the
long insertion within v. 9; in the source only the pronoun contained in the Greek verb ending
would be needed. On the phrase "water changed into wine," see the comment on v. 9.

103. Lit., "Jesus did this beginning of the signs. . . ."

104. Walter Wink points out to me that a number of miracle stories in the Synoptic Gospels end with sayings that, if not truly proverbs, have become proverbial in Christian tradition (e.g., Mark 4:41; 7:37; Luke 7:49; also Matt. 8:10). In the terminology of form criticism
the "tale" has been "invaded" by the kind of memorable declaration that characterizes another literary form than that obviously found here, namely, the Pronouncement Story.

105. Or even simply: The water became wine. A number of the miracles in SG are depicted indirectly (4:51–52; 6:11; and to some extent also the miracles in chaps. 9, 11, and
21); only 5:9 explicitly states that the miracle had occurred. With the source's reticence here,
contrast the Evangelist's later summary of the miracle in 4:46a: "he made the water wine."

What then of the disciples in v. 11c? We can suspect that in the oral tradition lying behind the source the story ended short of the whole verse and that the author of SG has added it as a redactional interpretation.[106] And this addition makes a radical change. We no longer have just a miracle story. Jesus is no mere wonderworker (what is technically called a thaumaturge); his miracles are not meant primarily to astound. The element of wonder, in fact, appears remarkably seldom in SG.[107] Rather, he performs a **sign,** an act in which he shows himself as Messiah (whether or not any of the middle clause of v. 11 derives from the source). In chapter 1 we only overheard the disciples' excited message, each one to the next: We have found the Messiah. Here at last we see them gathered together and acknowledging Jesus' public deed, not just as witnesses to a miracle but as exemplars of the only appropriate response to Jesus' sign, demonstrating his messiahship: they **believed in him.** Their earlier recognition now comes to full faith. Thus does this episode cap the preceding ones. Yet on the whole we have here not a culmination of sections 1 and 2 but a new beginning.

We are not actually told that in this particular deed the disciples recognized Jesus specifically as Messiah. But that is clear from what precedes in the source (now underlying chap. 1). It is the only conclusion to be drawn from the series of miracles that Jesus has now embarked upon and that will follow one upon another in the source. Presumably the source's readers already expected that the Messiah, when he came, would bounteously feed and heal and restore to life, and they needed only to be shown Jesus doing just that.[108]

If this episode in some way completes what was anticipated in the two preceding sections (e.g., as vindication of the trust the disciples show in Jesus) that is not stressed by the pre-Johannine author. This story is the **beginning** of the source proper, and points forward, not backward; what preceded is only preface. (In 4G, the matter is more complex; see Johannine Redaction in this section.) Thus on the one hand the word "beginning" implies that there is more to follow, a series of signs; and the fact that we still have "the second" and perhaps "the third" in that series (in this part, secs. 4 and 5) confirms that. But this "beginning" is also unique; it stands at the head of the series, as normative.

106. Not only was 4E a redactor, but the pre-Johannine author as well. It is simply for convenience that in this study we use "redactional" and "Johannine" interchangeably. The source's author would have added "and his disciples" here in v. 2 at the same time; see Analysis in this section, on that verse.

107. Only here, implicitly, in the case of the steward; and perhaps in the wondering questions of the crowd at 6:25 and 9:8. Here, just as elsewhere, nothing is made of the astonishing lavishness of the miracle: perhaps as much as 180 gallons (12 to 18 "measures") of wine.

108. The kind of argument over true messiahship, and especially whether Jesus had its credentials, that we find in the dialogues of 4G is altogether missing in the source.

It is undoubtedly to be taken for granted that this is an astonishing and marvelous new fact—of what theologians call eschatological, that is, ultimate, importance, signaling the arrival of the new age. But at most such meaning is only hinted at in the wonder of the steward: **You have saved the good wine until now.**[109] It will remain for 4E to draw out and elaborate the symbolism contained in that metaphor. For the source its chief significance is what the sign signifies, namely, Jesus' messianic status. If there is wonder in his appearing, in the "good wine" he provides, it only attests to who he is. This christological emphasis will be true of all the signs, and it is clear from "the beginning."

How did the source come by this story? Was it, like the other miracles we shall assign to SG, part of the Jesus tradition evidently available to the pre-Johannine author and finding expression also in the Synoptic Gospels? Clearly not. Of all the miracles, only this one lacks real Synoptic parallel or analogue. Conceivably it bears distant relation to elements of the Synoptic tradition—not to a story but to Jesus' saying about old wine in new wineskins.[110] As story the passage is altogether unique within the Gospel tradition and in this way is unlike all the other miracles in 4G, including even the raising of Lazarus.

Broer ("Jo 2,1–11") has shown that attempts to find the origin of the story in the OT are also insufficient, and he gives renewed plausibility to the proposal, made by Bultmann, that it stems originally from the Dionysus cult of Syria-Palestine. If that be the case, what significance would such provenance have for the meaning of the story in the context of SG? Evidently a christological one; that is, the story's "pagan" thrust would underscore the general purpose of the source. (For this reason it is less surprising that an otherwise purely Jewish document may have been influenced by Gentile religion. But in any case the dependence may have been unconscious, or quite indirect.)

We have here in the source a legendary account, possibly imitating the deed of a god (the Dionysus tradition of water-changed-into-wine), that displays his astonishing power and status. Just like Dionysus, Jesus shows who he is, what he can accomplish, and in that way reveals a kind of divinity, within the limitations of Jewish-Christian monotheism. (It will remain for 4E to break open these limitations, by showing Jesus' deed as a true theophany, a manifestation of his divinity equal to the Father's "glory" [v. 11]. This is a christological advance over SG that will incur the charge of ditheism from "the Jews" [5:18].)

109. Hinted at also perhaps in the portrayal of Jesus at a wedding feast, a common image of the messianic age.

110. Mark 2:22; Luke 5:37–39; *Gospel of Thomas* 47c. For a summary of such a theory, see *TGOS*, 34.

Thus the story could serve as the first and definitive sign of Jesus' messiahship. SG's summary and evaluation (v. 11), then, only explicates such an understanding: Jesus performed this feat, "the beginning of the signs," in order to show from the start who he was, to reveal himself and so to elicit his disciples' belief in him. Just as in an "aretalogy" of a god (the record of divine deeds that in this case would have expressed the miraculous tradition about Dionysus) so we have here in SG the analogous miracle story, one, however, that is not merely aretalogical but christological.[111]

This theory of the tradition's derivation, then, both underscores the meaning we had already found within the story and helps to account for it.

Johannine Redaction

2¹**And on the third day** there was a wedding at Cana (**in Galilee**), and the mother of Jesus was there. ²And both Jesus and his disciples were invited to the wedding. ³ªAnd when the wine gave out Jesus' mother said **to him, "They have no wine."** ⁴**Jesus said to her, "Woman, what have you to do with me? My hour has not yet come."** ⁵**His mother said** to the servants, "Do whatever he tells you." ⁶Now there were six stone water-jars—**in accordance with the Jewish rite of purification**—standing there, each holding twenty or thirty gallons. ⁷Jesus said to them, "Fill the jars with water." *Then* they filled them full. ⁸And he said to them, "Now draw some out and take it to the steward," and they did. ⁹When the steward tasted the water changed into wine—**and did not know where it came from, but the servants who had drawn the water knew**—the steward called the bridegroom ¹⁰and said to him, "Everyone serves the good wine first, and when people are drunk the poorer wine; but you have saved the good wine until now!" ¹¹Jesus did this beginning of the signs **at Cana of Galilee, (and he *manifested* his glory)**, and his disciples believed in him.

The pre-Johannine meaning of the story is still visible in the Evangelist's presentation. But by relatively minor changes it comes to have new meaning, and some of the earlier implications are qualified. We can most readily see both those effects in the closing verse of the story (v. 11). The Evangelist has added the middle clause, or at least changed Jesus' showing himself (to be Messiah) into a manifestation of his **glory**. This may seem a small enough change, but it transforms the verse, indeed the whole story. What was, in the source, a summary of the effect of the miracle on the disciples (they believe in him as Messiah) becomes, for the present Gospel's reader, a new evaluation of Jesus' act: in it he reveals his divine being, his glory.[112] The sign has become a christophanic, still more a theophanic

111. On the term "aretalogy" and the influence of Hellenistic religion on SG and 4G, see further part 2, n. 9.

112. One recalls the surely Johannine and important use of this word in the prologue: "We have beheld his glory, glory as of the only Son from the Father" (1:14b). But whereas that is a prospective summation of Jesus' earthly activity, in the first sign we are actually shown the display of Jesus' divinity taking place.

act, in which the invisible God makes himself known.[113] (The passage remains christological, and in a most heightened way, but soteriological and even eschatological implications appear.)

The Evangelist further calls attention to the theological reevaluation of the miracle, simply by emphasizing its locale in the final verse; we hear again that it took place **at Cana in Galilee**. This partly sets the stage for the break in the source about to be effected by the introduction of the great block 2:13—4:45; when the source is again taken up Jesus is brought back to the same place. But the geographical notice, only here in the signs, also affirms that this miracle is more than simply the first in a series; it is a signal event in its own right whose locale is therefore memorable.[114]

The minor insertion in v. 1 (if it was not merely a factual detail from the source) is puzzling: **On the third day,** evidently matter-of-fact, but hardly that for an Evangelist so little concerned with mundane details. It is sometimes interpreted as having symbolic meaning, recalling the resurrection of Jesus "on the third day." But that phrase is never used by 4E to date Easter. More likely, therefore, if it is Johannine, it is meant to conclude the series of four days that we saw now punctuates the originally unbroken account of the first disciples in chapter 1. If so, the whole series could be seen as constituting a week, the week of the new creation perhaps, culminating in the majestic epiphany of the wedding miracle.[115] The redaction has then highlighted a movement implicit already in the source: the miracle as confirming the disciples' discovery in chapter 1 that the new age has begun. But the Evangelist is not explicit about this, so the phrase must remain uncertain.

If a symbolic understanding of the story is not entirely assured in v. 1, it becomes so later on. We spoke just now of a new creation. In fact, neither that adjective nor its opposite is used, any more than in the source. But 4E underlines a contrast that was already present in the story—inferior and superior wine (v. 10)—by adding the reference in v. 6 to **the Jewish rite of purification** (lit., "the purification of the Jews"). Clearly this phrase is to be understood as establishing a contrast between Judaism and Christianity, the latter having now in 4E's time been forced to become a separate religion; this is reflected also in the contrast between ignorance and knowledge in v. 9. The water belongs to the Jewish cult; it is replaced by the wine of Christianity that Jesus provides. The steward, attempting to preside over the traditional customs, does not **know** where the good wine **came from,** but the **servants** know—those, that is, who recognize Jesus'

---

113. The same prologue ends: "No one has ever seen God; the only Son . . . has made him known" (1:18).

114. We postpone (to part 2.F) the question why 4E so emphasizes this Galilean venue, reiterating it both here and especially in chap. 4 (vv. 43, 45, 46, 47, 54).

115. As originally maintained by Boismard, *Jean 1:19—2:11.*

authority and follow his instructions. This kind of theological symbolism, evidently deliberate on 4E's part, is perhaps not wholly absent from the source, which may have hinted that the wedding feast, so often a symbol of the messianic age, had now begun. But besides adding explicit symbolism, 4E has sharpened the claim: Jesus represents not only the new age, come at last, but the new revelation superseding the old.

The Johannine additions to the source, as we have taken them up, happen to be arranged more or less in order of increasing intrusiveness within their pre-Johannine context. So far it is only the insertion in v. 9 (knowing whence the good wine comes) that noticeably disrupts the source's prose. The final and chief instance of Johannine editing to be considered, that in vv. 3b–4, is not syntactically disruptive at all; after the insertion 4E repeats the phrase at which the source had been interrupted and thus smoothly resumes it. Mary (she is not actually named in 4G) addresses first Jesus and then, following his reply and as the source is taken up again, the servants; the flow of the narrative is smooth.

But the sense of the passage is greatly disturbed by the content of Jesus' reply. Mary's words to him are a request for a miracle, implied at least when she calls attention to the lack of wine. Jesus first addresses her in a way that is both distant and strangely abrupt—**Woman, what have you [or your concern] to do with me?**[116]—and still further startles us by an assertion that seems altogether inappropriate: **My hour has not yet come,** as if Mary had meant to say anything at all about his hour, whatever it might be. This is not the only place where 4E suddenly changes the plane of discourse altogether, breaking for a moment out of the matter-of-fact tone of the narrative (see this part, sec. 4, Johannine Redaction, on 4:48, and in the Introduction, pp. 4–5). Here, as elsewhere, the story just as quickly resumes its earlier course. Although Jesus' words are surely to be seen as a refusal of Mary's request, yet, due to the resumption of the source in v. 5, they are not taken as such by her. Unperturbed, she directs the servants to heed Jesus' instructions (those had been her only words in the source, which lacked an exchange with Jesus altogether), and soon Jesus has amply provided the needed wine.

Clearly 4E makes a major claim on our attention by this striking insertion. Even at this point in our study we can understand it; such at least must be 4E's expectation of the reader when it appears without preparation so early in the Gospel. Its meaning is that the request for a miracle, even from Jesus' own mother, is inappropriate when compared to his greater purpose, the enactment of his "hour." As SG had portrayed it, Jesus' mission was simply to show himself, by means of the various signs,

---

116. A form of the Semitic phrase used in the Synoptics by demons protesting Jesus' imminent expulsion of them and also in OT in connection with Elijah.

as the Messiah.[117] But with 4E's intervention in this first sign we are given a correction of the older portrait; what matters above all is Jesus' death, for that is what his **hour** refers to. Jesus' working of miracles, even his self-manifestation in signs, is not his chief role to play. Rather, since at 4E's hand Jesus' miracle is an early manifestation of his glory, of which only the cross will be the full demonstration, his mother's request, though it will be met by Jesus, is premature.[118]

The time when Jesus will play his role **has not yet come.** There is a focal point, an "eschatological moment," in the story of Jesus as 4E presents it, and at this point in the Gospel it is still in the future. Note how the **not yet** of the declaration in v. 4 collides with the **now** of the older story (v. 10); into a passage that proclaims, however implicitly, the arrival at last of a historical turning point, another time scheme has been introduced. Yet the older view is retained. Having interpolated the corrective, 4E resumes the source. Jesus performs the sign—valid enough in the Johannine view, so long as the concept of sign is properly understood, that is, with 4E's qualifications of it in v. 11. It is not a miracle, even a christological demonstration, in its own right, but rather an occasion of divine self-disclosure.

On the basis of this passage we can say that 4E's relation to the source is a dual one. On the one hand that author respects SG sufficiently to retain its wording,[119] with the result that its text can readily be separated from 4E's redaction, which at points appears disjointed by comparison. Had 4E had a lower view of the source, she or he would have felt freer to rewrite it into a more finished work. On the other hand, 4E is willing at points to break with the source's theology, qualifying, even correcting it boldly. But what is modified does not appear to have been suppressed;[120] we can hear both its voice and 4E's, even when they differ. That is surely remarkable.

For SG, this passage finally began Jesus' public activity; it is the first of many signs. For 4E this is still true, but it seems now even more to conclude a section. It is not simply the **beginning** of Jesus' self-disclosures, as in SG. (The present Gospel breaks up the original series of miracles.)

117. Even if, as I think likely, an account of Jesus' death followed the signs in the pre-Johannine source, the cross was not portrayed (as it is in Mark) as Jesus' appointed path, his mission. Rather, even it is subordinated to the overriding christological purpose.

118. Miranda suggests (*Being and Messiah,* 104) that Jesus here shrinks from his death due to the tendency, in an otherwise profoundly independent work, to harmonize it with the Synoptics.

119. At the very least, 4E knows the respect paid to it by the pre-Johannine author's readers, so as not to dare openly to rewrite it.

120. A notable exception would be the disciples' assertion that in Jesus they had found Elijah, if (as it has been proposed) the source contained that datum; on 1:43, see this part, sec. 2.

Rather, that Jesus **manifested his glory** primarily brings to a climax the sections preceding it. The Inauguration of Jesus' Public Ministry is now complete.

Analysis

The redactional elements in the story are fairly clear:[121]

• **On the third day** (v. 1a) is perhaps a continuation of the scheme of days in chapter 1, playing no role in the story itself.[122]

• The composite place-name is possibly original (lit., **Cana-of-Galilee**), distinguishing this Cana from others, named in the OT and Josephus (see *IDB* 3:493). But such a datum would be unique in SG. Very possibly, then, "of Galilee" is Johannine emphasis (see further part 2.F, and compare Bethany-beyond-Jordan).

• The prominence, and even the presence, of "the mother of Jesus" is in any case unusual in Gospel miracles, but especially her being mentioned before Jesus (v. 1b), taking the initiative in requesting a miracle (v. 3), and presiding over the servants who will assist Jesus (v. 5). No doubt she has been introduced in the development of the tradition from its simplest form.[123] But it is clearly not 4E who has done this, for that author's insertion (v. 4) jars with the way she is otherwise portrayed, especially in vv. 3 and 5. The addition was made prior to SG or, possibly, by the pre-Johannine author him- or herself.

• That Jesus **and the disciples** are invited to the wedding (v. 2) but the verb used is singular is not a "grammatical unevenness,"[124] but a common enough construction in SG. Nevertheless, it may stem from the pre-Johannine author's having introduced the disciples (who play no role in the story proper) to prepare for their response in v. 11c, which is so important in SG.

• Mary's words to Jesus (v. 3b) with his reply (v. 4) jar sharply with the rest of the story: Jesus objects to his mother's implied request for a miracle, but then proceeds to perform it. And his words—**My hour has not yet come**—belong to

---

121. A far more extensive identification of redaction in this passage, and so the reconstruction of a much more rudimentary source, has been carried out by Busse and May ("Weinwunder")—e.g., they excise all mention of Jesus' mother, of the disciples, and of the miracle as a sign. On the basis of tensions perceived within the story and on the basis of a "syntactic-stylistic" examination of small sentence structure, their analysis leaves a very spare "unit": more or less 1a, 2, 3a, 6a/7a, 7bc, 8, 9a/g, 10ab, 10e/11b. Quite possibly something like this was the earliest form of the story, but it can hardly have been so meager in the source, for then the tensions within what is not included (e.g., vv. 3–5) go unexplained. Rather, the source had probably already expanded an earlier, rudimentary version of the story, so as to incorporate it into the series of signs; it is this immediately pre-Johannine version of the story, not the simplest and earliest oral form of all, that we seek to recover. See this part, n. 106, for other evidence of the source's author as redactor.

122. Alternatively, it has been suggested that the phrase means simply "on Tuesday," since that was perhaps a common day for weddings in ancient Judaism; if so, it could be part of the traditional story, characteristic of the source's interest in detail and having no theological significance such as it may have if 4E has introduced it (see Johannine Redaction in this section).

123. So Busse and May, "Weinwunder," 50.

124. Ibid., 38.

57

the overall Johannine interpretation of Jesus' activity.[125] 4E has evidently inserted vv. 3b–4,[126] requiring also the addition of "His mother said" in v. 5a as transition back to the source.

• **For the Jewish rite of purification** (v. 6) interrupts the Greek syntax of the sentence (not evident in most translations) and uses the generalizing Johannine phrase: (lit.) **of the Jews.** It may not be accidental that the word for "water-jars" here (*hydriai*) is the same as appears in a miracle by Elijah (1 Kings 17:12 LXX).

• The parenthesis in v. 9 (**but the servants who had drawn the water knew**), and also the preceding **and [he] did not know where it came from,** display the evidently Johannine themes of "knowing"—in particular knowing where something or someone is "from."[127] The obvious insertions both overload the sentence and jar subtly with v. 10, where the issue is not how the wine has appeared but its superior quality.

• Form-critically, the miracle story as such ends with the pronouncement in v. 10, which provides the astonished response that we expect. Then in v. 11a both its evaluation as **sign** and the sign's enumeration are redactional additions.[128] But they are *pre-Johannine* redaction, shaping the story to belong to Signs Gospel; similarly, the disciples' response in v. 11c.

• The middle clause of v. 11—**and [he] manifested his glory**—is evidently 4E's commentary on the first clause; or at the least **his glory** (*doxa*) is Johannine. In the latter case, it would have replaced some pre-Johannine object of the verb such as "himself " : not a theophany of Jesus' divine glory (as now in 4G), but a revelation to the disciples of his messianic identity.

• The reiterated geographical notice in v. 11a (**at Cana in Galilee**) is possibly due to a Johannine preoccupation.

SECTION 4 (2:12a; 4:46–54)
THE OFFICIAL'S SON RESTORED
TO LIFE

The clear reasons for thinking that in the source this story followed the miracle at Cana are found partly in the next verse in chapter 2 and partly in the story itself. On the basis of these data we depart for the first time from the present order of the Gospel, jumping to the end of chapter 4. In other words, apart from the addition of the prologue 4E has not till now altered the format of SG in a major way, but after the first sign withholds the second until the end of the major block, 2:13—4:45.

125. See just above, on the tension between "not yet" in this verse and "now" in the pre-Johannine v. 10.

126. There is text-critical support for this analysis. In some MSS a more clumsy and possibly authentic reading is found in v. 3a: "And they had no wine, for the festal wine had given out; then [Jesus' mother said to him . . .]." If this was original, once vv. 3b–4 have been added the text would be impossibly long and redundant, leading copyists to substitute the shorter version found in most MSS. (Here we have an example of the way text criticism and source criticism can be mutually helpful.)

127. *Pothen* in Greek, the same word used in 1:48 and in many other Johannine passages (3:8; 4:11; 7:27–28; 8:14; 9:29–30; 19:9). See this part, n. 24, on 1:26c.

128. As Busse and May rightly point out ("Weinwunder").

Pre-Johannine Source

2 ¹²ᵃAfter this he set out¹²⁹ for Capernaum with his disciples.

4 ⁴⁶ᵇNow there was a certain official whose son was ill in Capernaum. ⁴⁷(When he heard that Jesus [was] com[ing]) he went out to him (and begged him to come down and heal his son, for he was at the point of death): ⁴⁹ᵇ"Sir, come down before my child dies." ⁵⁰ᵃᶜJesus said to him, "Go, your son lives." And he went. ⁵¹Now as he was going down his servants met him and declared to him that his boy¹³⁰ was alive. ⁵²So he asked them the time when he had recovered, and they told him, "Yesterday at one o'clock the fever left him." ⁵³(So the father recognized that that was the time Jesus had said to him, "Your son lives.") And he believed, and all his household. ⁵⁴This was now the second sign Jesus did.

The notice in 2:12a leads obviously into the next pre-Johannine story— contrast the verse's odd irrelevance in 4G—and resolves the anomaly of this second sign now so artificially separated from the first. From Cana, in the hills of Galilee, Jesus makes his way down to Capernaum, on the northwestern shore of the Sea of Galilee. But he is met on the road by the father of a dying boy in Capernaum, and then and there effects a healing. The miracle is perhaps less stupendous in magnitude than the first, but it is none the less impressive. The boy is healed from afar, by the word of Jesus alone, and instantaneously.

The man is identified only as an **official**.¹³¹ What is noteworthy about him is his expectation that Jesus can heal his son (v. 49). We have not been told that Jesus has these powers, nor, as in Mark, that such news of him

129. Just as in the very roughly parallel story in the Synoptic Gospels (the healing of the centurion's servant, Matt 8:5–13 = Luke 7:1–10), so already in the pre-Johannine source the miracle was evidently worked from a distance; the man met Jesus between Cana and Capernaum as he was coming down from the wedding. The past tense that means "he went to Capernaum" in the present text of 4G, therefore, if original would have meant only that he began his journey (an "ingressive aorist"). Typically of SQ, the text reads literally, "He set out . . . , he and his disciples."

130. Some see the change in noun here (from *huios* to *pais;* but there is significant variation among the MSS, and cf. *paidion* in v. 49) as a sign of redaction. Rather, it seems to be the natural variation of the storyteller. In v. 53 Jesus' word (with *huios*) is repeated.

131. Or possibly a "nobleman" (*basilikos* is a rather general term). In the Synoptic version the man is a centurion—that is, an army officer—and this is taken by Matthew and Luke to imply that he was a Gentile; the story in their Gospels is an object lesson about Gentile faith (especially as he declines to come to Jesus out of unworthiness and asks him to "speak the word only and my servant [*sic*] will be healed"). If our pre-Johannine author knew the story in that form, he has removed all trace of it; the Gentile issue, so important in the letters of Paul and the Synoptics, is virtually absent from 4G and presumably from the source as well. It is far more likely that in its original form, or at least as known to SG, the man had not been identified as to nationality but could be presumed to be a Jewish official, living as he does in the Jewish town of Capernaum.

Dauer (*Johannes und Lukas*) seeks to show that the source in this pericope contains traces of Lukan *redaction*, not just tradition in common with Luke, and so must have depended on the Third Gospel more or less as we know it; but despite Dauer's painstaking analysis the evidence he cites (pp. 116–20) is so meager and the parallels are so remote that I find his argument unconvincing. See further pp. 217–18 in excursus B.

had spread. We are simply shown, as here, people expecting this ability in him. The instance of Jesus' mother (2:5) is a parallel.

After only a word from Jesus—**Go, your son lives**—the man complies at once. Whether he hears it as only a prediction or as a promise, or already trusts, we do not know. It will remain for 4E to underline this obedience on the man's part and to elaborate on it. For the pre-Johannine author there is evidently nothing extraordinary about it; this is the way that Jesus naturally is regarded. The christological claim here is implicit, but clear: Jesus is Messiah and people respond to his authority accordingly.

What shows that Jesus, by virtue of this dramatic healing, is Messiah? The title, of course, is not used; it had already been proclaimed of Jesus by the newly converted disciples in chapter 1. There we also saw that other titles were used synonymously with it; it is the office of God's unique agent, not any particular conception of it expressible in a single title, that was affirmed. But then what, here, reinforces Jesus' messianic status? Surely it is his word to the father, "Your son lives," identical to Elijah's word to the widow of Zarephath (1 Kings 17:23).[132] SG's identification of Jesus with the returned Elijah as a kind of messianic figure is explicit in chapter 1 (as reconstructed—see this part, sec. 2, on 1:43). Here it is subtly implied for any Jew familiar with the scriptures.[133]

But we have gotten ahead of ourselves. If the story wants us to take all this for granted, it nevertheless delights to portray at some length the process by which the participants understand that the miracle really has taken place. The official's servants meet him and announce the miracle; the boy is **alive** (lit., "lives"), just as Jesus had declared. This means, of course, not that he was still barely holding out against death but that he had been saved from death, restored to life. That becomes clear in the next verse, as the man asks when the boy had recovered[134] and learns the precise hour. The healing is seen as occurring in an instant; the fever breaks, and the boy's health is assured.

Even without v. 53a ("So the father recognized . . ."), which may be Johannine, it is to be understood by the reader from v. 52b that **yesterday at one o'clock** (lit., "the seventh hour" in ancient reckoning) was the time Jesus had spoken the healing word. If, on the other hand, the half-verse is *pre*-Johannine it makes this more emphatic, but does so, I think, inciden-

---

132. = 3 Reg. 17:23 in LXX.

133. The Evangelist suppresses this identification in chap. 1; here it is permitted, presumably just because it is not explicit. In all of the above, I am indebted to Martyn, "Elijah."

134. The usual translations—began to mend, improve, etc.—lend a more gradual note to the circumstances than the idiom I have used here. But there is nothing in the Greek corresponding to "began"; the phrase means literally "had it better," and I take it that here "better" (rather like the modern child's expression "all better") practically speaking means "well."

tally. For in SQ v. 53a would have had as its chief purpose something else, in fact, a double purpose: to reiterate still again the saving word of Jesus (already echoed in the servants' announcement) and to lead up climactically to the fact that the father **believed.** As at the first sign the disciples' prior trust in Jesus became full faith, so here with the official. He had sensed power in Jesus and had entrusted his son's ebbing life to him. We are not told whether this was an act of quiet faith or of desperation; apparently it makes no difference. What matters is that he now *becomes a believer,* and with him a community of believers comes into being—**all his household.** The faith in Jesus' messiahship spreads contagiously.

To complete the story the pre-Johannine author need only add an enumeration of the miracle (v. 54a). The **second,** like the first, is not a mere wonder but a christological **sign** that **Jesus did.**

Johannine Redaction[135]

2 [12]After this he *went down to* Capernaum with **his mother and his brothers and** his disciples, **and they remained there not many days.** [13]**And the Jewish feast of Passover was near, and Jesus went up to Jerusalem.**

[2:14—4:45]

4 [46]**Then he came again to Cana in Galilee, where he had made the water wine.** Now there was a certain official whose son was ill in Capernaum. [47]**(When he heard that Jesus** *had come*) from Judea to Galilee, he went out to him **(and begged him to come down and heal his son, for he was at the point of death).** [48]**Then Jesus said to him, "You people, unless you see signs and wonders, refuse to believe!"** [49]**The official said to him, "Sir, come** down before my child dies." [50]Jesus said to him, "Go, your son lives." **The man believed the word that Jesus spoke to him.** And he went. [51]Now as he was going down his servants met him and declared to him that his boy was alive. [52]*Then* he asked the time when he had recovered, and they told him, "Yesterday at one o'clock the fever left him." [53](**Then the father** *knew* **that that was the very hour when Jesus had said to him, "Your son lives.")** And he believed, and all his household. [54]This was now the second sign Jesus did **when he had come from Judea to Galilee.**

1. The Johannine author's adaptations of this story, while manifold, fall conveniently into two categories. The first has to do with *Jesus' itinerary.* This sign now comes as the climax, indeed the chief event, of a pointed withdrawal on Jesus' part **from Judea to Galilee.**[136] After a long sojourn in the south he comes again to **Cana in Galilee.** It was here that the

---

135. The import of 4E's preface to this story (4:43–45) must await consideration in part 2.F, on 4E's theological use of locale.

136. A quick glance at 4:3, 43 will bear this out, and the phrase "from Judea to Galilee" appears twice in the present passage (vv. 47a, 54b).

Evangelist left him in the source, and so when it is taken up again Jesus is brought back to the same place.

Rather, in the source he had already departed from Cana and was on his way down to Capernaum. The Evangelist backtracks slightly then, since that departure has been adapted to a quite different use in 2:12. In contrast to the source, the official now must come to Cana to find Jesus. The effect of this is that the distance from which the boy is healed is greatly increased. But it is not 4E's purpose primarily to heighten the miraculous element of healing-at-a-distance; rather, it is to connect what is about to happen, on the way down from Cana, to the first sign, done in that village. Thus the Evangelist adds, before taking up the source's account, **He came again to Cana in Galilee, where he had made the water wine** (v. 46a). This arrival is evidently important for 4E, as the subsequent insertions show: the man seeks Jesus **when he heard that [he] had come from Judea to Galilee** (v. 47a),[137] and this second sign is summarized at the end as accomplished by Jesus **when he had come from Judea to Galilee** (v. 54b).

The full implication of all these references to Jesus' withdrawal from Judea (the preposition used here each time literally means "out of") is not yet clear. But they can hardly be intended simply to preserve the original numbering of the sign; while it is true that among all the signs Jesus has so far done this is, strictly speaking, only his second that immediately follows a journey from Judea to Galilee, nothing was made of Judea as starting point in the first sign. Evidently intervening events have made the locale of this episode and the journey immediately preceding it especially significant. (Again, see further part 2.F.)

2. The second set of alterations that 4E makes has to do with *faith*. Paramount among them is the insertion of v. 48. In response to the official's plea for his son, Jesus suddenly addresses a nameless crowd and berates them for demanding dramatic evidence on which to base their faith: **You people, unless you see signs and wonders, refuse to believe.** The man has made no insistence whatever about faith; he certainly did not ask for a sign (see Introduction, A. The Johannine Riddle). Into the older story, then, 4E has interjected a wholly new note, and one that is oddly intrusive. (Who are addressed here? Is it the readers, familiar already with SQ? "Unless you read of wonders [that is, signs seized on as marvels in themselves], you are determined not to believe!") But startling as this outburst appears, the setting in the original story of the official is not lost sight of. This expostulation is made by Jesus **to him**, and as occasion for it 4E inserts (v. 47c) a paraphrase of the man's request still to come in the source (v. 49; or, if v. 47c was already in the source, 4E positions the

137. Some find dependence on the Synoptics, rather than on a peculiar pre-Johannine source, to be a sufficient explanation for the origin of this story, pointing out the similarity here to Luke 7:3. But I find the similarity too inexact to support any theory of dependence.

corrective in the midst of the official's request). So we are expected to focus on his response; he evidently stands as representative of those to whom v. 48 is addressed.[138]

The official then repeats his request (v. 49)—the greater vividness of his very words lends urgency now—and when Jesus has declared that the boy will live, 4E interrupts the older story once again, to tell us that **the man believed the word that Jesus spoke to him** (v. 50b). Thus is his trust in Jesus, at most only implicit before, brought to the foreground: he believes without any sign or wonder, *solely on the basis of Jesus' word*. The saying in v. 48, then, is to be understood as setting up a kind of test of human faith, a test that the official clearly passes. Thus Jesus' proceeding to work the miracle to which he had objected is altogether appropriate.

The further statement of the man's belief (v. 53b—from the source, following the dialogue with the servants) is not anticlimactic but a *ratification* of what 4E has already depicted; the official's leap of faith was itself justified and led immediately to the spread of faith.[139]

If the preceding half-verse (v. 53a) is a Johannine addition, it is made to stress this confirmation of the man's prior faith (**Then the father knew . . .** [that is, no longer merely recognized but displayed the Johannine theme of knowing]) and to emphasize that it was Jesus' word that he believed (**the very hour when Jesus had said to him, "Your son lives"**). Further, the repetition of Jesus' promise of life to the boy conveys that what he bestows is not simply physical recovery but salvation itself. If the half-verse is instead pre-Johannine, then 4E adopts it with these new emphases.

The story, thus, finds fundamentally new meaning in 4E's handling:

a. Chiefly, a sharp corrective of the source's theological center (the sufficiency of signs faith) is introduced. The urgency of this issue for 4E is expressed in the otherwise illogical conjunction "so" at the beginning of v. 48. In the face of a request for a healing, one that will prove to be a messianic sign, it is necessary that Jesus forcefully raise the question of valid faith.

b. The Evangelist also elaborates elements that were already contained in SG (trust on the basis of only a word from Jesus, vindicated in the detail of an instantaneous healing).

c. Finally, the locale has become a matter of prime importance to 4E, as

138. A test of *Galilean faith* in general (see v. 45) is sometimes understood as 4E's chief purpose here, but that is not yet clear (see in part 2.F). The only belief 4E is explicitly concerned with is that of the official. Possibly the words of Jesus here are traditional, even proverbial, and so fit the context so poorly. But in any event it is obvious that 4E has introduced them.

139. On the Johannine preoccupation with the relation of signs and faith, see further part 2.B. Also Schnider and Stenger, *Johannes und die Synoptiker*, 83–88.

well. The passage is now a portrait of Valid Faith in Jesus' Word on the part of a Galilean.

Analysis

Verse 2:12 was originally the transition not to the Temple Cleansing/Restoration, in vv. 13–22, but to the second sign, now in chapter 4. Recognizing this solves the anomaly of the verse as it now stands, a nearly pointless journey to Jerusalem in a Gospel where Jesus' itinerary is hardly casual or incidental. A good part of the verse, then, is Johannine:

• Perhaps in the first place the inclusion of Jesus' **mother and brothers** in v. 12a. Mary plays no further part in the miracles, and the brothers none at all. Some MSS lack a second "his" after "brothers," but show it after "disciples," suggesting that the family members have been added as a unit ("his mother and brothers"), maybe to flesh out this otherwise skimpy notice, separated now from its original sequel in 4:46b. The mother would have been taken from v. 1b of the preceding sign and the brothers added in line with the Johannine notice to come in 7:3–9.

• Also the whole of v. 12b (lit., **and they remained there not many days**), which is meaningless except as a makeshift transition to the Restoring of the Temple that now follows.

In analyzing the story of the official's son at the end of chapter 4 there are a few more problems to be solved than in 2:1–11, since evidently more extensive redaction has occurred; but the following is clearly attributable to the Johannine author:

• Verse 46a, by which 4E prepares to take up the source again, set aside at 2:12. With 4E's massive insertion Jesus had in the meantime been in Jerusalem (2:13—3:21), in "the land of Judea" (3:22–36), and in Samaria (4:1–42). Now he is brought back to Galilee. In fact he comes to **Cana in Galilee**, with the effect that the reader is reminded of the miracle Jesus had already done there.

• In v. 47a, that the official heard that Jesus had come **from Judea to Galilee** is undoubtedly Johannine, recalling for the reader the geographical framework begun in 1:43 (see on v. 54b, below). But just conceivably the first words of the verse (with present tense for Jesus' coming, not perfect) are traditional— **When he** (that is, the official) **heard that Jesus [was coming]**—as the loosely parallel form of this verse in Luke 7:3a may suggest.[140]

• Verse 47cd is also perhaps Johannine: **begged him to come down and heal his son, for he was at the point of death**—a paraphrase of the source's more vivid wording in v. 49b. But since it is unusual for a Johannine paraphrase to be inserted ahead of what is pre-Johannine, these two clauses could be from the source, anticipating the direct quotation in v. 49.

• Verse 48 (**Jesus therefore said to him, "Unless you see signs and wonders you will not believe"**) is clearly redactional. Like Jesus' reply to Mary in 2:4 it conflicts sharply with the context, both in grammar (second-person plural) and sense (the official has asked for no signs and wonders, or even to believe, and in

---

140. So Dauer, *Johannes und Lukas*, 72.

v. 49 he seems ignorant of this objection to his request; see also Introduction, A. The Johannine Riddle). (Van Belle ["Jn 4,48"], following Neirynck, interprets this verse as integral to the story and as having in mind the Synoptic story similar to this one, in which the centurion requests Jesus' healing-at-a-distance ["Say the word only . . ."]. Jesus' word here then criticizes the official for having faith inferior to the centurion's. But this fits the verse no better than the suggestion that it is not a criticism. Theories of Johannine dependence on the Synopsis generally must use the kind of uncontrolled imagination displayed in this example and ignore the sometimes small but telling differences that betray not literary dependence but the variation of parallel but distinct tradition.)

• The Evangelist has presumably supplied the indirect object and subject in v. 49 ("the official [said] to him"—*pros auton ho basilikos*) to avoid confusion after inserting v. 48.

• Certainly v. 50b (**The man believed the word that Jesus spoke to him**) is Johannine, interrupting the flow from Jesus' command (v. 50a) to the official's compliance (v. 50c) and, further, making the assertion of his belief in v. 53 somehow redundant.

• Verse 52a gives first mention of the details of the boy's sickness, but it does not appear to be a Johannine afterthought.[141]

• Possibly v. 53a (**So the father knew that that was the hour when Jesus had said to him, "Your son lives"**) is also redactional, if this is an instance of the Johannine theme of knowing (as in 2:9) and if the change in noun (from **official** to **the father**) is significant (compare **the man** in the inserted v. 50b). But here the verb may mean only "realized"; and the motif of an instantaneous cure, while explicit only here, is implied already in v. 52. So v. 53a is more likely pre-Johannine.

• In v. 54b the qualification that this sign had been done **when he had come from Judea to Galilee** is plainly 4E's addition, as in v. 47a. It attempts to preserve the source's original enumeration of this as the **second sign**, otherwise anomalous after the suggestion of other signs in 4E's inserted material (2:23; 3:2; 4:45). It also clearly plays a part in a Johannine geographical schema (see part 2, n. 140).[142]

SECTION 5 (21:1–14)
THE CATCH OF FISH

For this story, which I propose as the third sign in the source, we jump all the way to 4G's last chapter, and the reader will justifiably want some

141. Lindars ("Traditions," 112) thinks that the phrase "the fever left him" (see also Matt. 8:15, of Peter's mother-in-law) appears in the story too late to be original, and must be 4E's addition, like the sabbath notices in 5:9b and 9:14 (see this part, secs. 9 and 8, respectively). But the latter parallels are not very close; in those passages 4E clearly interjects the detail in order to introduce the topic of a new section ("Now that day was a sabbath . . ."). Here, by contrast, the datum of the fever leads nowhere but seems to be an accident of storytelling.

142. Some would see the enumeration both here and at 2:11a as entirely Johannine: 4E counts the first and second signs done by Jesus only "after coming out of Judea into Galilee." This suggestion resolves the tension within the two notices in question, but raises harder questions than the one it seeks to solve—namely, why 4E numbers only the signs done after such a journey, and in particular, why the feeding of the multitude is not numbered as the third in such a series.

evidence that we are not following an altogether whimsical path. There is such evidence, but from the outset it should be recognized that the assignment of this story to the source is more hypothetical than for the other miracles.

The uncertainties are due both to the character of the story and to its present place in chapter 21. It is now one of the accounts of Jesus' resurrection and not (or, on our hypothesis, no longer) a miracle story pure and simple. Further, chapter 21 is quite widely regarded as not part of the original Gospel.[143] So to suggest that one of the signs from the pre-Johannine narrative source has found its way to us by a sort of accident (the author of the appendix reclaiming the passage after 4E had discarded it) is more than some will find plausible; that it has been so radically transformed into a resurrection story will seem just as unlikely. Perhaps, then, we have here only a separate tradition that has been incorporated by whoever penned the twenty-first chapter, never part of SQ.

In the face of all these difficulties, a number of scholars hold nevertheless that this tradition very possibly belonged to the same source as the other signs.[144] It certainly seems to contain a miracle in form very like the others we are examining, especially when the evidently redactional elements are removed.

But if it derived from SG, why suppose that it came next after the healing of the official's son, especially since no trace of an original connection between 4:54 and 21:1 remains? There are two data that suggest this.

1. The more striking of the two is the notice in 21:14 that this was the **third** time Jesus manifested himself to the disciples, a statement anomalous in its present context: In a rough way the enumeration is correct, if the appearances of the risen Jesus in chapter 20 can be taken as "manifestations" and if we count the appearances to the disciples in 20:19–23 and 24–29 as the first and second;[145] but the anomaly is in the fact that neither of those appearances in chapter 20 was numbered. Why then is the third and only the third so treated?[146] Further, the notice unmistakably rounds off the story of the miraculous catch of fish, and brings the

143. But Reim ("Johannes 21") has boldly challenged that majority opinion.

144. Most recently Heekerens, *Zeichen-Quelle*. See also *TGOS*; B & L (their "Document C"); Schnackenburg 3:411. Pesch (*Fischfang*, 149) also considered it possible.

145. Strictly speaking there are in fact three appearances in chap. 20, not two, but one of them—the first—is to a lone woman, Mary Magdalene, and for this reason perhaps was not included in the enumeration.

146. It could be argued that the enumeration in 21:14 is merely a post-Johannine imitation of 2:11 and 4:54. But it is not enumerated as a sign, like those two, and it seems more likely that the datum is the vestige of an earlier use of this story. It is introduced simply by saying that "Jesus revealed himself again to the disciples" (21:1); with that heading, no such coda as v. 14 is needed.

narrative to a climactic end; yet in the next verse the scene of the risen Jesus with his disciples continues as if oblivious of the vestigial notice.

For these reasons we may suspect that this verse, together with the original story leading up to it, is left over from some earlier framework and that that framework was a series of miracle stories during Jesus' public life (and thus no Easter narrative) such as we find underlying chapters 2—11. (The Synoptic parallel to this episode is the miraculous catch of fish in Luke 5, devoid of any Easter context.) Was it not, then, perhaps originally the third episode in SQ?

2. The other datum suggesting an original context for this story in SG is a geographical one. In the present position of the story its Galilean locale is awkward—we hear of no return to Galilee on the disciples' part after the appearances of chapter 20, taking place in Jerusalem. But if, as it seems, SG had a simple but clear and straightforward geographical framework for the signs, this episode belongs more or less at the point we have reached in SG's framework. Jesus and the disciples are in Capernaum—we last heard that they were headed there—a fishing village on the Sea of Galilee. Shortly (at what is now 6:1) they will cross the lake for the miracle of the loaves. This episode of the fish, which sets out from land and returns there, thus fits naturally after the healing of chapter 4 and before the feeding of chapter 6. But we shall remember that this element in our proposed order for the signs remains only a more or less intelligent guess.

The story is clearly composite, as even a cursory reading of it will show, and there is widespread agreement that the following elements have somehow been combined: a miraculous catch of fish, the disciples' recognition of Jesus, and a meal in which he feeds them. In the second element, and probably also in the third, there is a connection with Easter, but not in the miracle story proper. And since a Synoptic parallel to the miracle story is found in Luke 5, which lacks any hint of a meal or reference to the resurrection,[147] we can speculate that either the post-Johannine redactor or, just possibly, 4E has found such a story in a miracle tradition/source and chosen to combine it for the first time with Easter traditions.[148] Can

---

147. Equally, the Lukan parallel to the meal elements here are found only in the resurrection context: Luke 24:41–43.

148. The Lukan author also has adapted the miracle to a particular use, i.e., the call of the disciples, a redactional theme altogether missing here. But to hold that both the Third Evangelist and the author of the pre-Johannine source have demoted an original resurrection story (as perhaps Mark with the epiphanic transfiguration story) to a pre-resurrection miracle, and done so in such different ways, stretches the imagination intolerably (so also Fuller, *Formation*, 148–52; Smalley, "John xxi," 287–88, disagrees). While very roughly parallel to our story here, the miracle in Luke 5 shows almost no verbal similarities to this one; evidently the two stories stem distantly from the same tradition, and have no more than that in common.

we readily separate the redactional elements, including the meal and recognition themes, from the miracle? It appears that despite a number of minor uncertainties we can (see Analysis in this section).

Because we are not sure that it is 4E who has adapted the story to its present form, but possibly a post-Johannine author, we shall refer to that writer simply as the Redactor. That the story stems from SG is also uncertain, but less so; we shall therefore provisionally speak of it in that way.

Pre-Johannine Source[149]

[[21 ([1]Then Jesus showed himself again to the disciples by the Sea of Tiberias; it happened like this:)[150] [2]There were [gathered] together Simon Peter and Thomas known as the Twin [or Didymos] and Nathanael from Cana and the sons of Zebedee (and two others of his disciples). [3]Simon Peter said to them, "I'm going fishing." They said to him, "We'll also come with you." They went out and got into the boat, and that night they caught nothing. [4]At daybreak Jesus was standing on the shore, [6]and he said to them, "Cast the net on the right side of the boat, and you will make a catch." So they did so ... and could no longer haul it in for the great number of fish. [7]So Simon Peter (girded up his clothes and) leapt into the water, [8b]for they were not far from the land—only about 100 yards off. [11][He] went ashore and hauled in the net full of large fish, a hundred and fifty-three of them; and even so the net did not break. [14]This was the third [sign] Jesus [did] (before his disciples) [or the third time Jesus was shown to the disciples].]][151]

Here then is another of Jesus' stunning miracles and, despite a number of minor questions, one that is coherent in form and consistent in story line once the evidently redactional elements are removed. Like the signs of chapters 2—11 in their pre-Johannine form, it is told with the now recognizably typical use of detail for its own sake. Presumably in SQ it takes place during Jesus' miraculous activity in Galilee, with no connection to the resurrection. And, also as usual, it is done not to meet human

149. Since this story, and a few others, does not certainly derive from 4E's narrative source and its position there is uncertain, it is enclosed in double brackets [[ ]].

150. Lit., "and he showed in this way"; the verb is the same as in the first half of the verse but here lacks an object.

151. On form-critical grounds, a somewhat sparer reconstruction can be proposed (as suggested to me in private communication by R. H. Smith). This would have a much simpler introduction (Peter and others go fishing . . .), lack some of the details we have included (153 fish, net not torn), and in particular Peter's taking the lead in landing the catch. Very likely the story once existed in this simpler, purer form. But if we think it at all likely that it was mediated via SQ, we recognize that some of the elements just excluded derive from that source as well, being characteristic of it (and not at all characteristic of Johannine or even Johannine-like redaction): the vivid but inessential details, the distinctive role of one disciple, and so forth. Conceivably, the story ultimately derives from Jesus' parabolic saying about the net (Matt. 13:47–48).

need—at most the disciples are frustrated by their fruitless night of fishing—but chiefly to display Jesus' power. It is a sign, then, by which once again Jesus showed himself to his followers. The first time was, of course, at the wedding in Cana, where it was the disciples, not the entire wedding party or even the steward and servants, on whom the sign had its full effect (2:11c). If in the second miracle (the official's son) the disciples did not figure centrally, their presence was nevertheless noted in the original introduction (2:12a). Here they come to the foreground, and the miracle is worked directly to their benefit. If we are right to guess that the present miracle came at this point in the source it is thus **the third time** that Jesus shows himself to them. (All this holds true whether or not v. 1 was to be found in the source and whatever the original reading in v. 14.)

Some of Jesus' disciples have gone fishing; their names and various details about them are vividly supplied. After a vain night Jesus sees the boat from the shore; there is no hint that he appears to the disciples, even that they see him. Rather, he perceives their predicament[152] and gives a directive. In contrast to the exasperated objection of Peter in Luke 5:5 ("We have toiled all night and caught nothing"), here the disciples unquestioningly follow Jesus' authoritative command. And immediately the miracle occurs: they cast their nets as directed—and can no longer lift them for the weight of fish they suddenly contain. Peter then impulsively goes ashore and from there hauls in the catch, too heavy to be lifted into the boat.[153] The miraculous catch is then at last described with vivid explicitness: the net is **full of large fish** (that is, none too small to be kept?), **a hundred fifty-three of them**. And **even so the net did not break**, a miracle within the miracle.

If the disciples' reaction to the miracle was originally recounted, it is hard to see why that would have been omitted without trace as the story became a resurrection appearance. On the other hand, if the story derives from SG, the disciples had already come to belief, and their response to the wonder is thus simply to be inferred. We need only hear in conclusion the by-now-familiar enumeration: this self-presentation of Jesus, whether or not expressly called a sign, was **the third**.

Was the source's story intended to be symbolic? Does the fishing expedition somehow stand for the mission of the church, the number of fish for a kind of perfection, or the unbroken net for the unity of Christians? I think

152. If v. 5 is from the source (we left that possibility open) it only makes this explicit: Jesus calls to them, "You have no fish, have you?"

153. Some would see him miraculously endowed with strength here, but that seems unlikely; such power belongs entirely to Jesus, as appears in the fact of the unbroken net. The element of the disciples' sharing in Jesus' miracle-working seems wholly absent from SG. The distance of the boat from land (100 yards) on a realistic level is excessive (the slope of the lake's floor being in fact not at all gradual), but from the source's point of view, which can hardly still be in touch with such geographical facts, it was "not far."

not, at the pre-Johannine level. The original story, with all its gratuitous detail, is wholly centered on the person of Jesus: it shows only his activity, his supernatural knowledge, the magnitude of his power. Not ecclesiological symbolism, then, but christological significance—everything points to that at the level of the source.

(Post-) Johannine Redaction

21 **[1]After this (Jesus** *manifested* **himself again to the disciples by the Sea of Tiberias);** *and he manifested [himself]* **like this:** [2]There were [gathered] together Simon Peter and Thomas *which means* "Twin" and Nathanael from Cana **in Galilee** and the sons of Zebedee **(and two others of his disciples).** [3]Simon Peter said to them, "I'm going fishing." They said to him, "We'll come with you." They went out and got into the boat, and that night they caught nothing. [4]At daybreak Jesus was standing on the shore. [5]**Jesus said to them, "Children, do you have any food?" They answered him, "No."** [6]And he said to them, "Cast the net on the right side of the boat, and you will make a catch." *Then* they did so and could no longer haul it in for the great number of fish. [7]**Then the disciple Jesus loved said to Peter, "It is the Lord!"** So Simon Peter, **hearing that it was the Lord,** (*put on* his clothes), for he was naked, and *threw himself* into the water. [8]**And the other disciples came in the boat,** for they were not far from the land—only about 100 yards off—**dragging the nets full of fish.** [9]**Then, when they landed they saw a fire laid and fish on it and bread.** [10]**Jesus said to them, "Bring some of the fish you have just caught."** [11]Then Simon Peter **also** *went ashore* and hauled in the net full of large fish, a hundred and fifty-three of them; and even so the net did not break. [12]**Jesus said to them, "Come and eat." And none of the disciples dared ask him, "Who are you?" for they saw that it was the Lord.** [13]**Jesus came and took the bread and gave to them, and also the fish.** [14]This was the third **time Jesus manifested [himself]** (*to* **the disciples) after he was raised from the dead.**

Two preliminary questions face us as we consider how the original story has been shaped into its present form in chapter 21. The first is the question of authorship and amounts in fact to a cluster of issues, some of them already mentioned: Is 4E the author of the chapter? or a successor? What is the author's purpose in attaching the chapter? How does it integrate with the purpose of chapter 20,[154] and indeed with the whole Gospel? These issues are both too intricate and too broad to be fully resolved here, but I have come to prefer the view, by far the dominant one,

---

154. Although the last two verses of chap. 20 were evidently not penned *de novo* by 4E but are mostly the conclusion of the source, they obviously are intended to conclude the original Johannine Gospel. It is therefore difficult to imagine how in any original plan 4E could have saved this miracle story, even when transformed into a resurrection appearance, to fall outside the framework summed up by those two verses. If chap. 21 is Johannine, then, it appears at most to be an afterthought; but more probably the chapter is a post-Johannine appendix. See further this part, n. 462.

that this chapter is post-Johannine. In any case, however, it is our task here chiefly to let the redaction within the passage speak for itself, from whosever hand it comes and of whatever larger pattern it is a part.

The second question is the extent to which we should assign symbolic meaning at this level of the story, even if not—as I hold—at the level of SG. The passage has been the occasion for many imaginative suggestions, partly because of the various details within it (some of them just noted) that can lend themselves to symbolic or even allegorical interpretation, partly because of its present character as a resurrection story. But I propose that in the ensuing interpretation we should use caution in attributing symbolism to the Redactor. Only those points by which that author seems deliberately to attract our attention, whether to details or to broader themes that might be symbolic, are confidently to be understood in that way.

The fundamental adaptation that the miracle of the fish has undergone is its transformation from a christological sign to a resurrection epiphany. This is clearest in the changes to the concluding verse (14). The event now takes place **after [Jesus] had been raised from the dead,** and Jesus' self-disclosure becomes the **third** instance that the risen Christ **was manifested to the disciples,** following the two such instances of chapter 20.[155] If v. 1 stems from SG, it also has nonetheless now acquired a new meaning—not the Messiah "showing" himself, his messiahship, to those ready to believe in him by means of a sign, but the risen Lord "manifesting himself" once again to his incredulous followers.[156] Despite the disjunctures of time and place with chapter 20, the reader can nevertheless understand chapter 21 as a continuation of the Easter story.

A number of redactional changes in the body of the story further this transformation, having to do with the theme of recognizing Jesus. Verse 4b interjects that **the disciples did not know that it was Jesus** as he stood on the shore. In view of what follows (v. 7) this cannot mean merely that the light was still too dim or their distance from him too great. Rather, Jesus appears to them, but in a form not yet recognizable. So the matter-of-fact statement from the source that he "stood on the shore," ready to direct the disciples toward the miracle, has now become a mysterious appearance important in its own right: even before he speaks they see him, we are to understand, yet do not know him. As we noted, there was no hint of this in SG.

---

155. Note the two passives used, in both cases uncharacteristic of SG which perhaps portrayed Jesus showing himself (2:11b) but nowhere the subject of a revelation. In references to the resurrection the source presents it as an act that Jesus himself accomplishes.

156. In this too the passage fits poorly after the appearances in chap. 20, where though at first mystified or even doubting, the disciples come to full recognition of Jesus, expressed in Thomas's words, "My Lord and my God!"

Verse 7 has undergone more intricate change. On our analysis it now consists of three redactional portions, breaking up the source, once a continuous sentence, into three parts. The first insertion (v. 7a) is the major one and is prefixed to the source's wording: now that the miracle has taken place (v. 6), **the disciple whom Jesus loved** (hitherto not mentioned in the story)[157] immediately recognizes Jesus and **says to Peter, "It is the Lord!"** The miracle is thus no longer chiefly a legitimating sign of Jesus' status but a disclosure of the stranger's identity as the risen Lord.[158] If we could know who the beloved disciple is understood to be, it would probably not be unimportant that it is he who discloses Jesus' identity, and that he discloses it only to Peter.

On thus **hearing that it was the Lord** (the second insertion), Peter responds in a dramatic way: First of all, it is **because he was naked** (the third insertion)—that is, stripped for work—that he clothes himself; that latter parenthetical remark decidedly changes the pre-Johannine meaning, which, if we understood it aright, meant not that he clothed himself but only that he girded up his clothing to go ashore. When, as in the source but now with a new impetuousness, he now **threw himself into the sea**— that more literal translation is demanded for the redacted text—it appears to mean that despite his shame, possibly because of his all-too-recent denials of Jesus, he seeks to go to Jesus and for that reason clothes himself. (It is also conceivable, but less likely, that Peter jumps into the water not despite his shame but because of it, in an unsuccessful attempt to avoid Jesus.) His original role of landing the net full of fish is for the time being lost sight of. **The other disciples** of v. 8 now assume that responsibility.

Finally, in v. 12b we hear: **But none of the disciples dared ask him, "Who are you?"** knowing that it was the Lord, a curiously illogical comment. Presumably it compresses two ideas into a single sentence: that Jesus' identity has now been unmistakably shown and that it nevertheless fills them with such awe that they cannot express any lingering question.

Even more striking than the introduction of the recognition scene is the addition of a meal provided by Jesus for his disciples, as sequel to the miracle and making of it only a sort of preparation. This equally contributes to the story's adaptation to the Easter setting.

The origin of the meal theme is disputed. A miracle like this one having to do with the gathering of food might generally suggest a meal, as would

---

157. Is he to be identified with one of "the two other disciples" of v. 2, or with one of "the sons of Zebedee" (in later tradition, of course, it is with John son of Zebedee), or do the mention of the beloved disciple here and the full list in v. 2 stem from different hands?

158. Whoever the redactor here, that writer conforms to the Johannine practice of using the arthrous title *ho kyrios* only for the risen Jesus. In the first half of the Gospel, this phrase occurs three times (4:1; 6:23; 11:2), and these are widely held to be post-Johannine glosses. Otherwise we find only the vocative *kyrie*, presumably not a theological title but an everyday term of respect ("Sir" or "Master").

even a casual acquaintance by the Redactor with a tradition of the risen Jesus eating with his disciples (cf. Luke 24:30–32 and 41–43, the latter involving broiled fish). But perhaps there was an already developed narrative of Jesus preparing a meal on the shore of the Sea of Galilee which the Redactor had at hand and with which the miracle story can be combined.[159]

Very likely we cannot satisfactorily settle this question, but we can identify the following additions to the miracle and recognize their effect:

1. It is probably the Redactor who has created v. 5, which skillfully asks about the fishermen's success, using a term meaning both fish and "food." Jesus shows by the form of his question that he knows their negative answer before asking; we are thus prepared for the disciples' need to be fed. Verse 9, led up to by the additions at the beginning and end of v. 8, then sets the stage for the eventual meal. After Peter has impulsively left the boat (now not because of the catch but in reaction to Jesus' appearance) **the other disciples** bring it to shore (v. 8a), **dragging the net full of fish** (v. 8c—with strained syntax; see Analysis).

2. Once they have landed they see preparations for a meal on the shore—**fish** (using a different term than in the miracle) **broiling on a fire, and bread** (v. 9). Then in v. 10, an apparent attempt to link miracle and meal, Jesus suggests that some of the catch be brought, presumably to augment the food already prepared. But while the command is directed to all, it is only Peter who complies (v. 11a, as the source is resumed), and for a moment the immediate sequel in the original story overshadows the meal: the catch is not merely a source of food but is itself a prodigy (v. 11bc, astounding quantity of fish, unbroken net). But the meal theme returns, as Jesus invites the disciples to come and eat (v. 12a), at which bidding they come both awestruck and perceiving (v. 12b). He then **takes the bread and gives it to them, and likewise the fish** (v. 13); because this language is reminiscent of the accounts of the Last Supper in the Synoptic Gospels it is just possible that here, as maybe also earlier in the canonical Gospel (6:11b), the meal is to be understood eucharistically. It certainly expresses the fellowship of the risen Lord with his disciples.

3. These two ways of adapting the original miracle story, then—by making it both appearance and meal—successfully produce a complex whole. Each of the three components of the finished passage is intertwined with the others: Jesus reveals his identity both in miracle and in meal; the meal is both an outcome of the catch and an Easter event; the wonder is not only in the catch of fish but also in the disciples' recognition of the

---

159. So Pesch (*Fischfang*), who attributes vv. 4b, 7–9, 12–13 to such a narrative and other verses (5 and 10, which show some redundancy with this material) to the Redactor. But according to our analysis, some of the details he attributes to the self-contained story of a meal (esp. parts of vv. 7–8) seem to belong to the original miracle.

risen Lord and fellowship with him. Whether we have here the redactional work of the Evangelist or, as is more likely, of a later editor, it has come to impressive effect.

Perhaps such a dense knot of ideas, so full of implication, is sufficient theological payoff to ask of any passage. But we cannot leave it without turning to the second question we raised at the beginning, namely, the possibility of hidden symbolic meaning, if only because it has so often been proposed for the story in its present form.

The usual suggestion is that certain details in the narrative are meant to instruct us about the church—either its mission, symbolized by fishing;[160] or its perfection, whether represented by a complete circle of disciples (the number seven), a perfect number of fish,[161] or the unbroken net.[162] These proposals are intriguing, and we cannot assert a priori that nothing of this sort was intended by the Redactor. But I find no indication of such interpretations in the redaction as we have uncovered it. Either they are based on elements already present in the source (the decision to go fishing and its initial failure, the number of fish, and so on) and not in any detectable way emphasized in the redaction—if anything such details are passed over—or the suggestions call on us to find the meaning of the passage in subtle and hidden clues (such as the unexpressed number of the disciples) by contrast with the two themes that are expressly underscored. Further, we may contrast the way some of the details in the miracle at Cana (2:1–11) are apparently interjected or pointed up just for their symbolism (the Jewish rite of purification, the good wine).

In looking for such meaning, then, we ought to focus on the total effect of the redaction[163] as the christological sign is transformed by the means we have seen into a resurrection epiphany: A miracle story that on our hypothesis 4E chose not to include in the body of the revised source[164] has been rewritten and reinstated at the end of the Gospel, whether by him or

160. C. F. Evans (*Resurrection*) sees this expressed in the disciples' decision to go fishing, and the mission as barren until directed by the Lord to the favorable side of the boat, when a perfect catch is then made.

161. According to ancient reckoning 153 is derived from the number 17 (itself the sum of two "perfect" numbers, 7 and 10) as follows: an equilateral triangle filled with dots, 17 dots to a side, contains 153 dots, that number therefore being called "triangular."

162. See, e.g., B & L, 485.

163. Of course we may be dealing here with a post-Johannine redactor, whose way of introducing symbolism may be different from 4E's. But we have seen reason to believe that in many ways that editor imitates the Evangelist's redactional style.

164. Just why 4E would have omitted it is not easily determined. But the most likely surmise is that it did not fit into the geographical schema, Galilee alternating with Judea, that the Evangelist imposes on the source's miracle stories. Four signs in Galilee are more than can be fit into that schema, evidently. But why this one of the four was omitted is a matter of conjecture only.

her or, more likely, by a later hand. Although it falls outside the original scope of the Gospel's conclusion (20:30–31),[165] it readily becomes a third appearance of the risen Jesus to his disciples, following the two recounted in 20:19–23 and 26–29.[166] But unlike them, here the temporal and spatial ligatures to what precedes are unclear—it takes place only **later** (lit., "after these things"), and while the locale is specified there is no explanation for the sudden shift of the disciples from Jerusalem to Galilee (not even one so minimal as that 4E provides in 5:1 [see this part, sec. 9]). The story too has a fuller, more circumstantial telling than the brief accounts in chapter 20.
. In various ways, then, this third appearance stands by itself, more distinctive, more vivid than the rest. In the midst of their everyday work Jesus appears to his disciples. They fail to know him until he displays his miraculous power; then he is seen as Lord and invites them to a meal. In other words, and here is the present story's primary intent, the Risen One Is Recognized by His People and Feeds Them. In the broad sense this is symbolic, and indeed ecclesiological.[167]

We have still to account for the role of the beloved disciple in the redaction. He is mentioned only in v. 7 but possibly is to be understood as one of the **two others of [Jesus']** disciples in the list in v. 2.[168] If both details are redactional and *post*-Johannine they perhaps were meant to prepare for the identification of the beloved disciple at the end of the chapter as not simply the witness behind the Gospel[169] but its author (v. 24). On the other hand if it is the Evangelist who has introduced the beloved disciple,[170] then here as elsewhere in the Gospel that disciple's role is primarily to contrast favorably with Peter's. It is he who realizes that the figure seen on shore from the boat is Jesus and who tells Peter **It is the Lord.**
This raises the question of the role of Peter in the redaction. While prominent already in the source, he is now given greater attention; he alone reacts to the stunning realization that it is the risen Jesus who speaks to them and consequently he hurls himself into the water, whether in

165. R. H. Smith (*Easter Gospels,* 177) in commenting on this passage notes that the "many other signs" of Jesus mentioned in 20:30 give the Redactor an opening for adding the chapter.

166. The appearance to Mary Magdalene—the first of all—is presumably not counted in this reckoning, either simply because she is a woman or (what may be the same thing) because only appearances to an official group are considered.

167. Compare Pesch, *Fischfang,* 148.

168. The total of seven disciples in this list, however it arose, can hardly be understood symbolically, since it is not explicit.

169. Such as in 19:35—whatever its derivation.

170. And possibly also if it is a later hand, who then would here be imitating the Johannine portrait of the beloved disciple.

impetuous need to go to Jesus or from fright, attempting to elude him. We observe how the beloved disciple and Peter, whose relation to each other becomes an issue in the second half of the chapter, function within the redacted story.[171] The recognition of Jesus was no element in the original story. But once it has been introduced it is the beloved disciple who realizes Jesus' identity; he tells Peter, who then acts in such a way that the rest of the disciples also come to perceive Jesus' identity. A chain of recognition has thus been depicted, not unlike the chain of witness in chapter 1.

Analysis

We saw at the beginning of this section that this story combines three distinct elements: a miracle story, a meal, and Jesus' epiphany. The latter two belong to the redactional level, serving to adapt the story to an Easter setting. So, despite the passage's complexity, in most cases we can readily separate the redactional elements from the miracle proper.

• If the verb translated "revealed" or "manifested" in 2:11b is pre-Johannine (see this part, sec. 3, Analysis), v. 1 here may be an editorial introduction present already in the source, with or without the rather superfluous clause at the end— lit., "and he revealed like this." Equally, the verse could be a later redaction. The verb can mean either revealed himself (i.e., as Messiah) or showed himself (as, e.g., risen from the dead).

• **The Sea of Tiberias** is another name for the Sea of Galilee, and possibly the pre-Johannine one; see this part, sec. 6, Analysis, on 6.1.

• The original list of disciples in v. 2 is hard to identify. Only **Simon Peter** and **the sons of Zebedee** (the latter uniquely here in 4G) are named in Luke 5, but **Thomas known as the Twin** is evidently traditional here as well (see 11:16). **Nathanael** is found also at the beginning of the narrative source (1:45–49) but oddly only here identified as **from Cana in Galilee.**[172] The phrase **two of his disciples** is also found in the source's introduction (1:35, applied, however, to followers of the Baptist). At what point have these various names been collected here? Why do we hear nothing of Andrew and Philip from the same introduction? Since these questions involve the identity of the Redactor and the chapter's relation to chapters 1—20 they are perhaps unanswerable. But on the basis of distinctiveness we can perhaps suppose that the first four phrases in the list are original to the source: Simon Peter, Thomas known as the Twin,[173] Nathanael, the

171. Presumably Peter's role here prepares for the scene that is about to follow the present story (vv. 15–19), a reversal apparently of Peter's three denials of Jesus a few days earlier. And similarly the figure of the beloved disciple is surely intended to introduce vv. 20–23, and especially v. 24. In this way the status of the two chief disciples—Peter and the nameless beloved disciple—is raised as an issue and, in a somewhat ambiguous way, settled.

172. The identification may therefore be a redactional addition here, in casual imitation of the widespread Johannine use of the phrase.

173. The diction (*legomenos* = "called") is akin to that in 5:2 and 19:13, 17, all pre-Johannine, as we shall see. But in those cases a geographic feature is introduced (using a common noun in Greek—"pool," "place") and then given a name: sometimes first in Greek,

sons of Zebedee. At some point, whether source or redaction, the purpose may simply have been to bring the number to seven, a good Jewish round number.

• Is there symbolism in Peter's announcement in v. 3 **(I am going fishing)** and his comrades' resolve to accompany him **(We'll also come with you)**? Is the verse therefore redactional? This approach begs the question. We can determine the answer to the question of symbolism, at each of the two principal stages in the narrative's development, only after we have distinguished those stages (tradition from redaction) on contextual grounds, that is, leaving ideological assumptions aside. For the present the brief exchange in v. 3 seems more or less in keeping with the source's narrative flow.

• Verse 4b—**yet the disciples did not know that it was Jesus**—collides with their unquestioning obedience in v. 6b and represents the first evidence of the recognition theme (Jesus' identity in the strict sense, as distinguished from the general question of his messianic status in SG). Recognition is exclusively an apparition motif.

• Verse 5 is ambiguous. If Jesus asks about fish (the word means literally only "food"), the question's function in the story would be to underline the fishermen's need for a miracle and so may have had a place in the source. In the Greek it is clear that the question expects a negative answer and thus might express Jesus' typically supernatural knowledge. But since the disciples' need has already been made clear to the reader (v. 3b), it is rather more likely that the verse is redactional and speaks in general of food, preparing for the meal.

• Jesus' directive in v. 6 and the disciples' compliance, eliciting the miracle itself, are the very heart of the miracle story and thus clearly pre-redactional.

• The complexity of v. 7 evidently indicates the Redactor's reworking of earlier material. The Greek wording in this verse and the next one is so disrupted (translators have mostly smoothed this over—see, e.g., on v. 8 in this subsection) that the two verses are clearly composite.[174] The first sentence **(Then that disciple whom Jesus loved said to Peter, "It is the Lord"**—v. 7a) introduces a new figure (even if he is to be identified with one in the list in v. 2), involves the recognition theme again, and plays no part in the miracle, quite clearly; likewise Peter's **hearing that it was the Lord** (part of v. 7b). The non sequitur of his clothing himself and jumping into the water (v. 7c) is notoriously puzzling. But if **for he**

---

always in Aramaic (with the adverb *Hebraisti*). By contrast, here (as also in 4:25) a Semitic name appears and is then given its Greek counterpart. Evidently, then, the pre-Johannine use of *legomenos* is more flexible than the Johannine formula "which translated means" (*methermēneumenos*), used only for a Greek equivalent of a Semitic original (see this part, sec. 2, Johannine Redaction, on 1:38, 41–42; see also 9:7; 20:16). Here it is not immediately clear whether the word following *legomenos* is a real Greek name ("Didymos," as with "Lithostrotos" in 19:13) or is to be understood only as a kind of translation conveying etymological meaning ("Twin," "Stone Pavement"). The matter is important, obviously, for any later translator: Should the name be transliterated or translated? On the analogy of 19:17, where no one has been tempted to transliterate "Place of the Skull" as *Kraniou Topos*, the second option is perhaps preferable. In either case, however, the term is a kind of name, and the participle should be translated not "meaning" but "called" or "known as." But at the Johannine level, evidently we should translate "which means Twin."

174. Pesch (*Fischfang*, 103–6) on the other hand takes the whole verse, along with v. 8, to be from the resurrection tradition and not at all part of the miracle.

77

was naked is removed from that last third of the verse as an insertion somehow related to the resurrection/recognition theme, a clear enough meaning emerges, rather different from the present one: In response to the catch and its great weight (v. 6b) Peter girds up his garments so as to leap overboard and wade or swim ashore. The Greek (*ton ependutēn diezōsato*) can mean either that he put on his clothes (the usual translation because of the presence of the redactional element of nakedness) or—as here proposed for the original version of the story—merely tucked them into his belt.

• Once Peter's jumping into the water in an attempt to land the catch (such it evidently was in the source) was changed to an abandonment of the catch because of Jesus' appearance (as in the present text), we must be told what otherwise was to be taken for granted, that **the other disciples came in the boat** (v. 8a).[175] The logical connection of this with the following clause (**for they were not far from the land** . . . [v. 8b], evidently a datum from the source) is decidedly strained. And the dangling clause (**dragging the net full of fish**) at the end of the verse[176] is intolerably awkward. But v. 8a and c are redactional, and the middle clause, including the detail of distance from the shore (typical of SQ), originally explained why Peter could jump overboard to land the catch (v. 7).

• Verse 9 has to do only with a meal, and probably so also v. 10, and both use a new term for fish.[177] They are not part of the miracle story, which has no hint of an appearance of the risen Jesus at a meal.

• Perhaps it is the Redactor who has repeated the name ("Simon Peter") in the present text of v. 11a, for clarity, after inserting vv. 9–10 between Peter's jumping overboard (vv. 7b, 8b) and his action here. The verb usually translated "went aboard" can also mean "went ashore," and so it must have been intended in the source, for now Peter is able to haul in the catch, which had been impossible for all of the disciples together from the boat.

• Many see the precise number of fish and the unbroken net in v. 11bc as symbolic and therefore probably redactional, a conclusion that does not necessarily follow. But, in any case, similarly precise details are often found in SG (2:6; 4:52; 5:5; 11:17), so that if the passage as a whole seems to be part of SQ we can expect that these details may stem from it. The number, however it arose in the tradition, vividly expresses the magnitude of the miracle, and the unbroken net adds to the wonder.[178]

• Verses 12 and 13 belong solely to the meal and recognition themes and ignore the miracle altogether.

• Except for the qualifying clause **after he was raised from the dead**, the final verse of the story (v. 14) may derive from the source. But more likely **was**

175. The word for "boat" here is slightly different from that in the source at v. 3.

176. At the end, that is, in the Greek; in an attempt at greater sense it is put second in most translations.

177. The connection between the two verses is loose, and attempts have been made to assign v. 10 to the source, as a directive by Jesus leading to the miracle's demonstration. But v. 11 does not fit with v. 10 as the usual compliance following such a directive.

178. And thus represents a slightly more developed form of the tradition than in Luke 5:6, where the nets were breaking. On the question of symbolism at the level of the source, see this section, end of Pre-Johannine Source.

manifested (the same verb as in v. 1 and 2:11b, but only here in the passive) is redactional; perhaps the source summarized the story as the third sign.

SECTION 6 (6:1–25)
FEEDING THE MULTITUDE;
CROSSING THE SEA

We return now to the body of 4G. Whether or not the miracle of the fish preceded, there is a strong case for supposing that not the healing of the lame man in chapter 5 but this episode, the feeding of the five thousand with its sequel, was the next sign in SG.[179] Indeed, a number of critics propose that even in 4G the order of chapters 5 and 6 should be reversed. The logical and geographical connections between chapter 5 on the one hand and both chapters 4 and 6 on the other are notoriously awkward. But a simple rearrangement of whole chapters creates about as many problems as it solves,[180] and in fact it is chiefly the connections among the three miracles in these chapters—that at the end of chapter 4 and those at the beginning of chapters 5 and 6—that cause the difficulties. If in the source the miracle of the five thousand (6:1–14) followed the official's son (4:46–54) and if 4E has inserted the healing of the lame man and its subsequent dialogue (chap. 5), then virtually all of the anomalies of the text's present arrangement are intelligible.[181] Prior to this reordering by 4E, the source would have displayed a smooth sequence: after the healing at Capernaum (end of chap. 4), and possibly after the extraordinary experience of the disciples fishing on the sea and ashore as well (21:1–14), Jesus and his disciples go across the sea for the next miracle (6:1, 3), and at the end return to Capernaum (6:17, 21).

179. Unless, of course, the source was comprised of only the three miracles that now retain their enumeration, as maintained by Heekerens (*Zeichen-Quelle*). But to make that feature the criterion for identifying the source's contents is tenuous. The second sign can keep its numbering only by a Johannine tour de force in 4:54b. To expect that any of the other signs would also still show an original enumeration fails to consider the radical degree to which they have undergone Johannine rearrangement. Numbers 1 and 2 are still in their original order, though separated. Number 4, which we are about to consider, now follows a later sign (the healing of the lame man in chap. 5, originally perhaps no. 7), and nos. 5 (Lazarus, chap. 11) and 6 (the blind man, chap. 9) are widely separated and probably inverted in order. Only the first two, then, and the second with some straining, can retain their numbers intact. Number 3, as we know, is a special case, and its number survives, if at all, only by an ingenious transformation and as afterthought to the entire Gospel. But the strongest evidence that the feeding of the multitude belonged to the pre-Johannine source is its structural and theological similarity to the first two stories; it too reveals to the audience who Jesus is, eliciting their proffered confession of faith, and thus clearly is not simply a miracle story but a sign. And even though the Jerusalem miracles (nos. 5–7) now take place in a far less receptive milieu, their original character as signs endures as well.

180. See *TGOS*, 55.

181. If the catch of fish originally separated official's son from feeding, then 4E has more or less replaced it with chap. 5.

Pre-Johannine Source

6 [1]After this Jesus went across the Sea of Tiberias. ([3][He][182] went up into the hill country and there he sat with his disciples.) [5]Looking up and seeing that a great crowd was coming to him, Jesus said [to the disciples], "Where shall we buy bread for these people to eat?" [7][They] answered him, "Half a year's wages would not buy enough bread for everyone to have even a crumb!" [8]One of his disciples (Andrew, Simon Peter's brother) said to him, [9]"There is a child here who has five loaves of barley bread and two fish, but what is that among so many?" [10]Jesus said, "Have the people sit down." Now there was a lot of grass there, so they sat down, the men alone numbering about five thousand. [11]So Jesus took the loaves and gave thanks and distributed them to the people sitting there, and also the fish, as much as they wanted.[183] ([12]And when they were full he said to his disciples, "Gather up what is left." [13a]So they gathered.) [13b]And they filled twelve baskets with what the people who had eaten left of the five barley loaves. [14]So when the people saw the sign he had done they said, "Surely this is the Prophet who is to come into the world!"

[15c]Jesus went away again, into the hill country by himself. [16]Now when evening came his disciples went down to the shore [17]and got into a boat and set out across the sea for Capernaum. [18]But the sea grew rough from a strong wind. [19]When they had rowed about three or four miles, they saw Jesus walking on the sea, and they were frightened. [20]But he said to them, "It's me; don't be afraid." [21b]And suddenly the boat was at the point of land they had been making for! ([22]The crowd, which was standing by the sea, saw that Jesus had not gotten into the boat with the disciples, [25]and when they found him on the other side of the sea they said to him, "Rabbi, when did you get here!?")

The episodes preceding this sign, whether or not they include the miraculous catch of fish, took place more or less in private, for the benefit of a small circle of people at most. Even in the case of the wedding feast there was no mention of the miracle's effect on the party as a whole. Now, however, we come to a public miracle, and one of astonishing proportions: from a handful of bread and fish a multitude is fed, so many that even a great sum of money[184] would not provide the most meager rations. Just as in varying ways in the other Gospels, here **the men alone** come to about **five thousand,** so that with women and children we probably are to think of at least three or four times as many. And finally, when all have been

---

182. If 4E took this verse from the source, the same writer is perhaps responsible for the present reiteration of Jesus' name, following the insertion of v. 2.

183. See this part, n. 202, for the possibility that a sentence something like "And they ate and were filled" (see 6:26) originally stood here; if so, 4E has replaced it with the phrase now at the end of v. 11 and postponed the original datum in order to introduce with it the ensuing dialogue (6:26–58).

184. "Half a year's wages" is a rough attempt to express the scope of the Greek's "two hundred denarii," a denarius perhaps representing about the daily wage of a poor laborer.

satisfied, **twelve baskets** of food remain. A miracle of extravagant abundance.

But our attention is not to rest on the statistics themselves, though as so often the source takes interest in giving them, nor even on the barely imaginable proportions of the miracle. In the Synoptic Gospels, the story has its climax in those matters, the number fed and the amount of food left over. But here the former datum is found buried in the body of the story (also, slightly differently, in Luke), and while the detail of the twelve baskets necessarily comes at the end of the meal, our account does not stop there but reaches its climax in the response of the crowd. Here, as before, the miracle is not merely a wonder, dramatic in its own right, but a **sign** expressing who Jesus is and eliciting faith on the part of the crowd of witnesses (v. 14).

This focus on the person of Jesus rather than simply on his deed is evident throughout the story. In contrast to the Synoptic accounts, here it is Jesus who recognizes the crowd's need (v. 5)—his question is rhetorical, as only 4E makes explicit (v. 6b)—and who himself distributes the bread to them (v. 11). As in most of the other signs the actual miracle is reported almost in an aside (**as much as they wanted**); the attention is rather on Jesus, the source of the food.[185] He stands everywhere at center stage. Fittingly, then, the conclusion of the miracle is an acclamation of Jesus by the crowd. If the sign was originally numbered like the first two or three, that datum has had to fall out in the Johannine rearrangement.[186] But in any case, it is a **sign** that Jesus has **done**, and solely because of it—**when the people saw it**—they profess their faith, as if in unison. No longer only the small band of disciples, or an individual household, but now thousands of people hail Jesus.

We are not actually told that they "believed," but that is to be understood from their declaration, **Surely this is the Prophet who is to come into the world!** It is a proclamation such as we have not heard since the chain of witness on the part of the first disciples. The title ascribed to Jesus has the very same force as the designations used in chapter 1. "The Prophet" is, of course, the third title denied of himself by the Baptist, and it is identical in reference to "the one of whom Moses wrote" in the words of Philip to Nathanael. Now, on the basis of the miracles we have seen at Jesus' hands, we can also say that the term probably includes the title "Elijah," for in the Jewish scriptures it is preeminently Elijah (along with Elisha) who in various ways turns dearth into plenty (1 Kings 17:8-24;

185. The element of his compassion as motive, in Mark and Matthew, is absent. Unless v. 12 is entirely Johannine, Jesus is shown similarly still in charge after the crowd has eaten.

186. Possibly this deed of Jesus' was identified as either the third or fourth of Jesus' signs (as I theorized in *TGOS*, 105), especially since it is still explicitly a "sign" (v. 14), unlike some of the other miracles that nevertheless are attributable to SG.

2 Kings 4:1–7, 32–37, etc.). Finally, the words **who is to come into the world** clearly mean that this title is to be understood messianically. Thus, at the culmination of Jesus' activity in Galilee (it is this both for the source and the present Gospel) he works this most stupendous sign and is recognized by all as the unique agent of God.

The sequel has obvious affinities with the walking on the water that follows the parallel feeding story in Mark and Matthew—a private event on the sea, the disciples' fear allayed by the appearance of Jesus, mention of his defying gravity. But the event here is not primarily Jesus' walking on water nor his calming their fright; rather it is his role in bringing the disciples to shore when they find themselves impeded by a storm on the sea.[187] It is told from their standpoint, not that of Jesus (as in the Synoptics), but he remains the focus of interest. Not itself a sign, it nevertheless forms a kind of coda to the Galilean signs, before those in Jerusalem begin. It also has the effect of bringing the disciples, whose place in the feeding was only ancillary, to the fore again. Further, it preserves the continuity of locale that we have seen as we move from sign to sign.

Jesus **[goes] away by himself,** and the disciples embark for the return to **Capernaum.** During their crossing a squall comes up, common enough today on that body of water. After they row a great distance but still have not reached the opposite shore,[188] they see Jesus, **walking on the water,** a kind of miracle-within-the-miracle, natural enough in view of his status. (Whereas the sea crossing is often seen as a miracle within the greater miracle of walking on water, here just the reverse is true.)

But this is not the point of the story, nor is the disciples' understandable fright identified, either as in Mark 6, Matthew 14 (at Jesus as a ghost), or Mark 4 (at their danger). Jesus simply speaks to them: **It's me; don't be afraid.**[189] **And immediately**[190]—by his word alone, evidently—the problem is solved; they have arrived at their destination. This, then, is the miracle, the sudden and unexplained landing on shore, displaying Jesus'

187. This passage has usually and carelessly been treated as another walking-on-the-water story, as in the Synoptics (see *TGOS*, 64–70, and now Heil, *Jesus Walking*). Its distinctiveness was first recognized, so far as I know, by Kiefer, "Two Types of Exegesis," 11, and developed more fully by Giblin, "Crossing."

188. The focus is not on their struggle against the wind, as in Mark 6, so much as on the distance achieved without reaching the destination. Nevertheless, the account has some of the elements also of the distinct tradition of the stilling of the storm (Mark 4:35–41 pars.), except that here Jesus is not with the disciples in the boat.

189. At the risk of making Jesus sound too colloquial here, I deliberately avoid the correct but sonorous "It is I" and especially "I AM," since in the source the words seem to have no revelatory quality (see also 18:5). Jesus makes known his presence, but not as an epiphany. The story's similarities to the pre-Johannine miraculous catch of fish are clear.

190. This adverb appears in the Synoptics of Jesus' act of calming the disciples' fear.

authority and power, and it aptly rounds off all his various signs that take place in the region of the sea.

If parts of vv. 22 and 25 should be pre-Johannine—and that is at most a tentative suggestion—they would provide, even for this subordinate event, a counterpart to the usual ending of the signs proper. The private miracle of crossing the sea directed our interest back to the disciples; now it is expanded to include the crowd and Jesus as well. It is finally his crossing of the sea that becomes central. Presumably, after the miracle of the feeding, the crowd are not so much baffled by Jesus' unexplained arrival in Capernaum as admiring. Their question, like the saying of the steward at the wedding feast (2:10), chiefly expresses wonder. It is not clear that the title "Rabbi" is meant to have christological impact; but here again, if this material stems from the source, the passage ends with our eyes fixed on Jesus, and not simply on his miracle.

Johannine Redaction

6 ¹After this Jesus went *to the far side of* **the Sea of Galilee, that is,** the Sea of Tiberias. ²**And a great crowd followed him, for they saw the signs he was doing on the sick.** ³**Jesus** went up into the hill country and there he sat with his disciples. ⁴**Now the Jewish feast of Passover was coming.** ⁵Then looking up and seeing that a great crowd was coming to him, Jesus said to **Philip,** "Where shall we buy bread for these people to eat?" ⁶**But he said this to test him, for he himself knew what he would do.**

⁷**Philip** answered him, "Half a year's wages would not buy enough bread for everyone to have even a crumb!" ⁸One of his disciples (**Andrew, Simon Peter's brother**) said to him, ⁹"There is a child here who has five loaves of barley bread and two fish, but what is that among so many!" ¹⁰Jesus said, "Have the people sit down." Now there was a lot of grass there, so they sat down, the men alone numbering about five thousand. ¹¹Then Jesus took the loaves and gave thanks and distributed them to the people sitting there, and also the fish, as much as they wanted. (¹²**And when they were full he said to his disciples, "Gather up what is left." ¹³Then they gathered**) and filled twelve baskets with what the people who had eaten left of the five barley loaves. ¹⁴Then when the people saw the sign he had done they said, "Surely this is the Prophet who is to come into the world."

¹⁵**Then, knowing that they were coming to seize him and make him king,** Jesus *withdrew* again into the hill country by himself. ¹⁶Now when evening came his disciples went down to the shore ¹⁷and got into a boat and set out across the sea for Capernaum. **And it had already grown dark and Jesus had not yet come to them,** ¹⁸and the sea grew rough from a strong wind. ¹⁹Then, when they had rowed about three or four miles, they saw Jesus walking on the sea **and approaching the boat,** and they were frightened. ²⁰But he said to them, "*I AM;* don't be afraid."

²¹**Then they tried to take him into the boat,** and suddenly the boat was at the point of land they had been making for!

²²**On the next day (the crowd, which was standing by the sea, saw that) there was only one other boat there (and that Jesus had not gotten into the boat with his disciples) but the disciples had left by themselves.** ²³**But other boats from Tiberias came near the place where they had eaten the bread [after the Lord had given thanks.]**¹⁹¹ ²⁴**Now when the crowd saw that neither Jesus nor his disciples were there they got into the boats and came to Capernaum, looking for Jesus.** ²⁵**(And when they found him on the other side of the sea they said to him, "Rabbi, when did you get here!?")**

[Vv. 26–71]

The Evangelist's insertions into these two stories are less disruptive than those we have seen so far: there are no sudden shifts in the sense of the story line, such as we saw at 2:4 or 4:48, and certainly no major transformation such as in chapter 21. But the stories find considerable new interpretation at 4E's hands all the same.

1. They now mark the culmination of Jesus' work in Galilee, to a far greater degree than in the source. There they seemed to be simply the last and greatest of several consecutive episodes set entirely in the north of Palestine, prior to Jesus' miracles in Jerusalem. But in the present framework Jesus has already worked in both south and north. The first six chapters reflect a repeated alternation between the two regions: in chapter 1, a deliberate withdrawal to Galilee; in chapter 2 an abrupt return to Jerusalem; in chapter 4 another emphatic withdrawal, followed in chapter 5 by yet another return to Jerusalem, where Jesus is presumably still to be found at the end of the chapter. So when in 6:1 he goes (lit.) **across the Sea of Tiberias,** it constitutes—however awkwardly conveyed—not just a crossing of the lake but a journey from Jerusalem in the south of Palestine to the far side of the sea in the north. The Evangelist underlines this by adding to the name of the lake, **that is, of Galilee.** It is to Galilee once again, then, that Jesus goes—and for the last time.

Furthermore, the double miracle story, quite unlike the others set in Galilee but very much like those done in Jerusalem, will in 4E's handling provide the occasion for an extended and increasingly tension-filled dialogue between Jesus and his audience (from v. 26). Thus, by its very setting after the schematic alternation of north and south in chapters 1—5, and with the help of the long discourse that follows the stories, the account brings to a momentous close Jesus' work among the inhabitants of Galilee.

To be sure, the Galileans are not expressly named—and as we shall see Judeans/"Jews" are present also (see this part, n. 195). But when we read here in v. 2 that **a great throng was following him because they saw** (lit.,

---

191. Or possibly, "made eucharist."

"kept seeing") **the signs he was doing on the sick** we are surely to imagine once again that earlier enthusiastic and lavish response to him in 4:45 ("When he came to Galilee, the Galileans welcomed him, having seen all that he had done in Jerusalem at the feast"; see also 2:23). If there is to be any criticism of this Galilean following, any suspicion of its trustworthiness—as of that in Jerusalem in 2:24–25—it is as yet no more evident here than in 4:45.

But just possibly we get a dark hint early in the story. The naming of **Philip** in the story of the feeding may suggest a flaw in Galilean faith. We first heard of Philip, as things now stand in chapter 1, in immediate connection with Galilee (1:43); now he is singled out as the addressee of Jesus' question about how to feed the crowd (v. 5), and he becomes spokesman of the disciples' exasperated objection (v. 7). Is Philip then the example of a Galilean failure to understand? So far nothing of that sort is clear, but it may be in part the purpose of the insertion of the parenthetical v. 6.

The second half of that insertion (**for [Jesus] himself knew what he would do**) clearly only seeks to guard against the reader's misinterpretation of Jesus' question; for the Johannine just as for the earlier author, it is not to be understood as having been asked out of any bewilderment or incapacity on Jesus' part. But in the first half of the verse we read that Jesus asked the question of Philip **to test him.** This is not the first time that the Johannine Jesus seeks to test someone. His jarring declaration to the Galilean official in 4:48 was also, without being so designated, a testing of his faith, a test that the official passes most notably. It looks here very much as if Philip, by his response to the explicitly labeled test ("Half a year's wages would not buy enough . . .!"), fails it.

It is perhaps for a similar reason that we are told (if not already in SQ) that it was **Andrew,** Philip's fellow townsman and Galilean, who while offering the suggestion of the loaves and fishes at the same time despairs of his suggestion: **But what is that among so many?**[192] Both Philip and Andrew, then, seem now to represent inadequate faith on the part of Galileans.

If these suggestions of imperfect faith are tentative,[193] it is clear from the

192. This question in v. 9 is evidently not a Johannine insertion, but in the context of the source the question does not express doubt so much as dramatize the miracle by pointing out the contrast between human resource and divine power.

193. Brown thinks that Philip and Andrew are not Johannine insertions but part of the tradition, since in Luke this event takes place in Bethsaida, which according to John 1:44 is Philip and Andrew's hometown. But this posits a common factuality lying behind assorted pieces of tradition that I am unable to rely on. None of the Synoptic Gospels names any of the disciples in this story, and as can be seen in the Analysis in this section, the naming of Philip here creates contextual difficulties. Just possibly, however, Andrew was a redactional addition by the pre-Johannine author.

85

way 4E handles the ending of the miracle of loaves that, finally, Galilean faith is greatly overdetermined and to that degree quite inappropriate. This effect is deftly accomplished by the insertion of v. 15a (**perceiving that they were about to come and take him by force to make him king**), which both underlines the contrast between human intent and Jesus' divine prescience and structurally alters the meaning of vv. 14–15 altogether. Verse 15 is now disengaged from what follows, to which it originally was the introduction (cf. 2:12), and becomes a definitive comment on what has just occurred in v. 14. The acclamation of Jesus as **Prophet,** in the source so authentic a response to the miracle, now is nothing less than an expression of the crowd's misunderstanding. Jesus must distance himself from this, so his departure "to the mountain alone" (see just below on the possibility of Mosaic typology here) is no longer simply an occasion for the disciples' embarking without him and so for the miracle on the sea, but becomes another deliberate withdrawal on the part of the Johannine Jesus.[194]

Again, at the end of the sea miracle, the Evangelist detaches what may have been its conclusion—the crowd's marveling question to Jesus—and makes of vv. 22–24 a new episode (**on the next day**). The crowd now are **seeking Jesus,** and on finding him their question (**Rabbi, when did you get here?**) becomes but the occasion for Jesus' solemn pronouncement in v. 26 (a thoroughly Johannine verse, so like 4:48 in its thrust): **Amen Amen I say to you, you seek me not because you saw signs but because you ate the loaves and were filled.** Whatever else this puzzling verse means, it conveys another criticism of the crowd's response to him. They have not adequately understood what he has done in their presence.

We cannot do justice here to the Johannine dialogue that follows. Suffice it to say this much about it: (a) The crowd's question in v. 30 ("What sign do you do, that we may see and believe?") obviously represents still a further misunderstanding on their part, whether well intentioned or not; (b) the dialogue depicts an increasingly hostile response to Jesus (vv. 41, 52) and finally "murmuring" and a falling away on the part of many even of his disciples (vv. 60, 66); (c) yet the crowd is never called Galilean; instead those who first **murmur** (v. 41) and then **dispute** (v. 52) in both cases are called **Judeans.**[195]

194. The verb used here (*anechōrēsen*) is not the one usually employed by the Evangelist in the pattern of Jesus' repeated retreats in the face of adversity or misunderstanding (*exerchesthai*), but in fact a more emphatic one, frequent in the Synoptics and only here in 4G.

195. The mention in v. 2 that the crowds "saw the signs (*sic*) that Jesus did on the sick" suggests the present arrangement of the Gospel, for only so has there been more than one healing (but see this section, Analysis, on vv. 2 and 5). Thus, we can imagine that not only Galileans (chap. 4) but also Judeans make up the crowd. The usual translation of this phrase is of course "the Jews," and that is the translation that in the end is demanded, but only after it is made clear to what extent the phrase represents for 4E an anti-Jewish stand on the one hand or a theological evaluation of humankind as a whole on the other, a condition that for schematic reasons 4G usually depicts as occurring in "Judea." See part 2.F.

2. So far we have pursued a single, albeit complex theme running through the two linked stories—the climax of Jesus' Galilean ministry and what it reflects in the response he finds. We need to backtrack now and pick up another thread, introduced into the texture of the passage by v. 4: **Now the Passover, the festival of the Jews, was at hand,** an editorial comment on 4E's part, quite extraneous to the original story but in the Johannine scheme of things not at all incidental to a proper understanding of it.[196] This is only one of several references in 4G to the festival of Passover, usually providing a date for some event which it seems important to associate with the festal season. A number of these references have to do with one and the same Passover, of course—that associated with Jesus' death. But in the course of the Evangelist's story that occasion is only the last of three distinct Passovers, and all of them are announced by a stereotyped formula (2:13; 6:4; 11:55): the Passover **was at hand** (*ēn engus*); and each time we are reminded that the feast belongs to the liturgical calendar **of the Jews.**

This particular Passover differs from the others. Whereas in the first and third instances Jesus goes to Jerusalem, here he does not, staying instead in Galilee until **the festival of Tabernacles.**[197] So all the more clearly does the notice that the Jewish—and Judean—festival is being observed at the time of this miracle reflect on the Johannine story's meaning. It may account for the appearance of Jews/Judeans later in the chapter; certainly it sets this story somehow in juxtaposition, and contrast, to the Jewish rite. (We are reminded of the Johannine insertion in 2:6: "according to the Jewish custom.") The miracle of the loaves becomes a kind of Christian feast,[198] and the bread Jesus gives is at least comparable to the unleavened bread associated with Jewish Passover.[199] The sign in SG, one more demonstration of Jesus' messiahship, has now become an event in the history of religions: Christianity Replaces Judaism.

3. But more still is involved here. If the source, as always, was con-

196. Lowe's suggestion (*Ioudaioi*, 116–17) that this verse, missing in a very few obscure MSS, is a post-Johannine gloss seems to me special pleading, to make good his view that all references to "feasts of the Judeans [*sic*]" are to be understood as having to do only with region, not with the Jewish people, since Jesus is often depicted as making his way to Judea at festal times.

197. At 7:2, where Jesus at first also remains away from the feast.

198. The overtones of eucharistic action in the verbs of v. 11 (as also in the Synoptic versions of the feeding of the multitude) perhaps suggest this, if the Johannine community, despite this Gospel's silence, knew the tradition of the institution of the Lord's Supper found in the Synoptic accounts of Jesus' last meal with the disciples. The English word "feast," with its connotation of a meal, is entirely apt here, since both Passover and the miracle center around a banquet. The Greek term *heortē* means only a time of celebration, a festival.

199. In fact, it will emerge that it is superior, as a glance at the discourse that follows, especially at vv. 27 and 35 ("the food which endures to eternal life," "I am the bread of life"), bears out.

cerned to depict Jesus' office by this story, that is also the intent of 4G, and on a deeper level. Who is Jesus that he can provide a better Passover? some of the crowd will want to know. Is he another **Moses?** Can he supply anything like the **manna** the patriarchs ate in their exodus? A negative answer, they imply, is obvious. But 4E's answer, while not obvious, is equally clear: Yes! In fact Jesus is greater than Moses and the bread he gives greater than manna. That is conveyed as follows:

a. Passover, as everyone knew, had its origin with Moses; if this miracle is somehow a Passover meal, then its author is somehow equal to Moses, who himself gave **signs** and promised that God would cause a **Prophet** like himself to appear one day. That much is probably implied in the source, in the acclamation of the crowd (v. 14). The Evangelist makes it explicit and central in v. 4. Whether or not the preceding verse is a Johannine addition, it probably is now intended to be understood with something of the same meaning—that is, as Mosaic typology:[200] **Jesus went up on the mountain and there sat down with his disciples.** "The mountain" is no longer simply the Galilean "hill country" of SG but the Christian Sinai. In that sense Jesus is Moses.

b. But that definition of his status, while valid, is inadequate. For one thing, **the prophet** like Moses is as ambiguous as all messianic titles; it can be understood in a political, or as 4E would say an earthly, way. So taken, it does not apply to Jesus at all. This fact is dramatically shown by the insertion in v. 15a; the crowd want to **seize** Jesus and **make him king.** Full of good intentions, they will only make their Messiah a prisoner of their nationalist aspirations. Insofar as Moses is in some way the prototype of such a Messiah (though David would more obviously be so),[201] in that way, Jesus is no Moses at all.

c. Further, the example of Moses is not only misleading, it is insufficient christologically; it is not exalted enough. That is the thrust of the verses that immediately follow the important pronouncement in v. 26. There 4E verges on the most daring christological claim we have so far encountered. The train of thought by which Jesus is shown leading his hearers runs something like this: Your interest in food is misplaced (v. 26); work instead for food that does not spoil (v. 27). You ask how; believe in me (vv. 28–29). You seek proof that God works in me and imply that no one can match the food given to your fathers in the wilderness (vv. 30–31). **Amen Amen I**

200. Or, to explain this technical term, as viewing Moses only as a precursor, a prototype, of the later and more important activity or character of Jesus.

201. The relative lack of Davidic typology in 4E (explicit only in 7:42, implicit perhaps in 12:34—see Ps. 110:4) is noteworthy; no doubt it reflects the form of messianic speculation peculiar to the Jewish community that the Johannine was in contact and conflict with, and probably reflects a late-first-century date as well, after most Jewish political hopes had been dashed in the defeat of the year 70.

declare to you, it was not Moses who gave you the bread from heaven (v. 32a). It is God (my Father) who gives you genuine, life-giving bread (vv. 32b–33).

The claim implied is clear, and receives express statement in the next paragraph: I am the bread of life (v. 35). Without the typology of Moses (and presumably a Jewish/Christian debate on christology) as background, 4E could hardly have made these claims. But God of course is greater than Moses, and God is Jesus' own Father. The bread Moses gave was God's bread; the bread Jesus gives is himself. Jesus is even greater than Moses.

4. In the somewhat simplified sketch just given of vv. 26–33 we passed over two further themes that lead us back to the miracle story and shed light on its Johannine redaction. The first is the possibility that something perish or be lost, as in the phrase the food that perishes (v. 27). The Greek verb used here (apollumi) means literally to be lost, hence to spoil, and refers to food that is transitory, as opposed to what is eternal. What is not clear in most translations is that precisely the same word is used by 4E in the one insertion in the miracle story still to be examined: Jesus directs that the leftovers from the feeding be gathered up lest anything be lost (v. 12c). If the first two-thirds of this verse stood in SG, they had to do only with the awesomeness of the miracle; Jesus' feast was unbelievably bountiful, yet even so the food itself is not to be wasted. So 4E's addition of v. 12c would seem simply to underline this. But the use of the same word here as later in v. 27 suggests still more. The loaves, as a sign of Jesus' true identity, are already the food that does not perish. They do not simply show who Jesus is—true enough—but they symbolically contain the salvation, the life, that he gives, that he himself is.[202]

5. The other theme still outstanding is the demand for a sign in vv. 30–31, in response to Jesus' implied claim to be the one sent by God: Then what sign do you do, that we may see . . . ? Our fathers ate manna in the wilderness. This only demonstrates what Jesus has said in v. 26; he has just done a sign and, like God himself, given them bread from heaven (v. 32). So to ask for a sign, understandable enough in the face of his tremendous claim, is to confirm that they do not seek him because they have seen signs. Their initial coming to him, which 4E—for the moment adopting the mentality of the source—could attribute to seeing signs (v. 2), in the end has proved shallow and blind. They can no longer see the

---

202. If on the other hand the whole of v. 12 is Johannine and has replaced a simpler pre-Johannine statement that "they ate and were filled" (those very words, found in all five of the Synoptic parallels to this story, appear now in v. 26), then 4E has partly paraphrased them in the opening words of v. 12a ("When they had eaten their fill . . .") and partly deferred them to express the later criticism of the way the crowd appropriated the miracle (v. 26). In that case too, then, we see 4E correcting and deepening the source.

multiplication of the loaves even as a sign (contrast v. 14a), still less as a sacrament of life itself.

6. We have looked at all of the Johannine changes in the feeding miracle, and seen how they lead us back and forth between the story itself and the opening of the dialogue that follows it. What we have not had occasion even to notice is the intervening story, the crossing of the lake. Presumably it has been retained largely because it was found attached in the source. But 4E might have omitted it, so it must serve some Johannine purpose. In fact, by the one insertion made into the body of the story 4E has highlighted the christological concentration already added to the feeding story. As the disciples are on their way to Capernaum, and before the storm blows up, we now learn of a need still greater than the physical one they are about to find themselves in; by the insertion in v. 17 we understand the disciples' need to have Jesus **come to them** and dispel the **darkness** that has overtaken them. The symbolic meaning of v. 17bc is clear and hints at the themes that will emerge in the ensuing dialogue from v. 26 onward (Jesus as the one whom God sends to the world in its need) and later in chapters 8—9 (Jesus as the "light of the world"). In the midst of the disciples' danger, if that is implied (it is clearer in the Synoptic parallels), it is no longer walking on the sea and bringing the disciples to land that constitutes Jesus' primary act, but his coming to them. At both these points in the story, 4E adds a new note; she or he inserts **and drawing near to the boat** (v. 19b) after the one pre-Johannine notice, and **they tried to take him into the boat** (v. 21a) before the other. If Moses appeared to the Israelites after coming down from Mount Sinai, here Jesus still more dramatically, in fact theophanically, Reveals Himself to His Disciples.[203]

Analysis

What are the redactional elements in this double story?[204]

• The overfull designation of the sea in v. 1—the Greek says literally "the Sea of Galilee of Tiberias"—is patently due to redaction. On the basis of 4E's very great emphasis on **Galilee** as a region (see 1:43; 2:1, 11; 4:3, 43, 45, 46, 47, 54, and part

---

203. The more or less colloquial meaning of *egō eimi* in the source—simply "It's me"—gives way to the divine "I AM."

204. This pair of stories has far closer parallels in the Synoptics than any of the other miracles in 4G. The feeding of the five thousand is found in all three and a feeding of four thousand in Matthew and Mark. In the former cases the miracle is followed by a walking on water which has a common if more remote origin with the sea crossing here in John 6. But we look primarily for evidence of redaction within the passage, all the while keeping the parallels in mind, rather than basing the analysis primarily on them.

2.F), the latter may be his addition to an original **Sea of Tiberias.**[205] See also 21:1, possibly pre-Johannine.

• The premature mention of **a great crowd** in v. 2, redundant with that in v. 5, and the summary of Jesus' activity as **signs**[206] **that he was doing on those who were sick** (the plural [if we may take it at face value—but cf. the unsupported plural in 2:23] presumably denoting the healings in 4:46–54 and 5:1–9a) suggest that the verse is Johannine.

• Some see v. 3 as inconsistent with v. 15, since we are not told in the meantime that Jesus came down from **the hill country** (lit., "the mountain"), and there is no counterpart to the verse in the Synoptic parallels. Possibly it is Johannine. But v. 15 may mean only that he withdrew still farther into the mountains (the Greek says "went away," not "went up into"). So the assignment of the verse is in doubt.

• Verse 4 parenthetically interrupts the story, with a dating like that in 2:13 and not directly relevant to the episode itself, and contains the Johannine phrase **the Jews** (as in 2:6).

• That Jesus and not the disciples, as in the Synoptics, recognizes the crowd's need to be fed and so himself asks **How are we to buy bread . . . ?** is due either to the distinctiveness of the pre-Johannine tradition or to the redaction of the source's author; that it is not a Johannine alteration is evident from 4E's need in v. 6 to explain parenthetically why Jesus should ask at all. The way **Philip** in v. 5 and **Andrew** in v. 8 are named is oddly inconsistent: both are known to us already from the source (1:40, 43), so after Philip is named here without introduction, it is strange three verses later to hear Andrew identified as **one of [Jesus'] disciples, the brother of Simon Peter.** Probably, in the light of v. 6 (see below) **to Philip** in v. 5 has replaced an original "to the disciples," and the subject of **answered** in v. 7 was then once simply "they." If so, the disciple in v. 8 was possibly nameless as well; the datum that it was Andrew, and Peter's brother, reads like an afterthought. But given the source's predilection for superfluous detail, the identification may be original and its redundancy with 1:40 due to the pre-Johannine combination of once-independent traditions. The phrase remains in doubt.

• The parenthesis of v. 6 is redactional, as in 2:9; although the source is aware of Jesus' supernatural knowledge, it tends simply to take it for granted, whereas knowing is an explicit Johannine theme.

• Jesus' directive in v. 12 to gather the fragments **that nothing be lost** is extraneous to the story. The whole verse (along with the compliance at the very

---

205. I come to this conclusion despite the fact that in Mark the name of the body of water is twice given as "the Sea of Galilee" (1:16; 7:31; paralleled in both cases, in Matthew). In fact, elsewhere in the Synoptics, and repeatedly, it is simply referred to as "the sea," and frequently when there has been no reference to it for some time. We seem to have in Mark, then, a traditional detail that is remarkable for its infrequency. Luke only once names the sea, calling it "the Lake of Gennesaret" (5:1; either a separate tradition or due to Lukan preference for the name also found in 1 Maccabees and Josephus). We might innocently suppose that the source would have shown the name most often used by us today and that it is 4E who has inserted the less-familiar Roman one ("of Tiberias"). But we see that modern convention is barely supported by ancient tradition.

206. Note the plural, never in SG until 20:30.

beginning of v. 13) may be 4E's addition; its opening clause is somewhat redundant with the end of v. 11. But that it is Jesus who orders the gathering of fragments (itself traditional) is possibly due to a tendency of the source, and likewise the immediate compliance; so perhaps only that last clause of v. 12 is Johannine.

• Verses 14–15 now provide a most Johannine conclusion to the miracle (see on these verses, Johannine Redaction, above), but in fact it is only the participial clause in v. 15 that makes them so: **perceiving that they were about to come and take him by force to make him king.** Jesus has divine perception, as in v. 6; the people respond to him inappropriately; and he eludes them. In the source, however, v. 14 would have provided the typical "choral ending" to the miracle, and v. 15b the transition to the sequel, which is distinct from the feeding but usually connected with it in the tradition.[207]

• The second half of v. 17 appears redactional: the statement that **Jesus had not yet come to them** (v. 17c) is odd, since the disciples have already set off in the boat without him. If it presupposes the miracle about to occur, nevertheless it somehow collides with the disciples' fear in v. 19. It is presumably a Johannine addition. The preceding **it had already grown dark** (v. 17b) is inconsistent with the disciples' sighting of Jesus in v. 19, and is probably Johannine as well,[208] added along with v. 17c, perhaps for theological symbolism.

• In v. 19, the disciples see Jesus both **walking on the sea** and **approaching the boat.** Only the former is paralleled in the Synoptic tradition; the latter seems likely to have been added, in line with v. 17c and the theme of christophany. The same would probably be true of v. 21a (**Then they tried to take him into the boat).**[209]

• The rest of the story proper (vv. 16–21) appears to be pre-Johannine, v. 21b providing the climax.

• Verses 22–25 are notoriously tangled but possibly contain the kernel of a conclusion to the pre-Johannine episode just examined, despite the extensive presence of what is widely held to be post-Johannine gloss.[210] As it stands, the passage introduces a new section (indicated by the Johannine phrase **on the next day,** just as in chap. 1), and in showing the crowds **seeking Jesus** it prepares for the discourse to follow (see v. 26). But in the source perhaps the crowd of the feeding episode—some of them anyway—discovered Jesus in Capernaum, and because they knew he did not cross the sea by boat they would then become witnesses to the miracle with their astonished question, **Rabbi, when did you get here?**[211] So, we remove the opening phrase of v. 22, and very likely the middle clause ("that there had been only one boat there") as well, together with the obviously related vv. 23–24—the issue of more than one boat being subsidiary and causing virtually all of the passage's unusual complexity. (Roberge, "Jean VI, 22–24," has shown

207. Heil (*Jesus Walking,* 75) believes that "by himself" (*autos monos*) may be Johannine, and cites 8:16, 29; 16:32. But the phrase itself does not occur there and is in fact found in Mark 6:47b. It seems, therefore, to be traditional.

208. Heil (ibid., 146) points out the chiastic structure of these two clauses, which—if deliberate—is surely Johannine.

209. For both these points, see ibid., 81, 147–48.

210. As the unusually high number of textual variants in these verses suggests.

211. The question "how?" would be more apposite.

that the solution to this complexity is more likely to be literary- than text-critical and independently concurs in our analysis, despite his failure to look for a pre-Johannine literary layer below the present text.)

The Signs in Jerusalem

Three stunning miracles remain to be considered—the healing of a man crippled for thirty-eight years (chap. 5); the giving of sight to a man blind from birth (chap. 9); and the raising of Lazarus, already four days in the grave (chap. 11). In each case the stories emphasize the duration of the predicament, and thus the acuteness of need. In this way they are not so very different from the Galilean signs: a whole wedding party without wine, a boy at the point of death, (possibly) a futile night of fishing, thousands in the wilderness with nothing to eat. As we have seen, and shall see further in these three signs, the primary interest at the *pre-Johannine* level is in the person of Jesus and what it means christologically—that is, about Jesus himself—that he can remedy such dire circumstances. Secondarily, it may also be important that people are saved from their infirmities, no matter how hopeless their case may appear. By contrast, as we shall see, *the Evangelist's* concern is considerably more complex.

How were the three stories arranged in the source? If the climax for the first group of signs—supplied by perhaps the most impressive one, the feeding of the huge crowd in chapter 6—is to find an analogue in this second group, the almost unimaginable Lazarus story would provide the original conclusion of the Jerusalem healings (as it now does in the Gospel) with the two healings quite possibly also in their present relative order. But the first two or three Galilean signs were probably to be seen as equally impressive; so it does not appear that building up to a dramatic high point is the pre-Johannine author's intent. Indeed the climactic impact of Lazarus's resurrection is due in large part to 4E's redaction. Further, as we find it in the Johannine framework, the Lazarus story is artificially placed,[212] and it appears that 4E has given it the position that in the source the Restoring of the Temple had (see this part, sec. 10). Thus, whereas originally (that is, in the pre-Johannine source) the latter provocative act of Jesus in the Temple was almost certainly what precipitated the official conspiracy against him, in 4G it is this miracle, the resurrection of Lazarus, that plays that decisive role.

It is more than just conceivable that the Lazarus story was in fact not the last but the first of the three Judean signs in their pre-Johannine form. It alone finds Jesus away from Jerusalem and accounts for a long journey

---

212. Jesus' curious response to the news of his friend's illness, namely, to stay longer where he was (11:6), is only explicable as a vestige of the story's setting at an earlier stage; see further, this section, Analysis.

(such as from Galilee to the capital): Lazarus was still alive, seriously ill, when word was sent to Jesus, but four days buried when Jesus arrived (details that appear to be pre-Johannine). Also, the story brings him only to Bethany, on the outskirts of Jerusalem. The healing of the blind man, if the original sequel to this story, takes place as Jesus is evidently still "on his way" (9:1—it is no longer clear where) but within reach of the pool of Siloam, on the periphery of the city. The story of the lame man's healing occurs in the vicinity of the Temple itself (5:2), that is, in the heart of the city. When the present order of the three stories is exactly reversed, then, there emerges a gradual and coherent pre-Johannine itinerary for Jesus from Galilee into the capital city, with the same topographic logic as we found within Galilee in the first group of signs. But, as with all questions of the arrangement of the pre-Johannine source, the order of these three is less certain, and less vital, than their substance.

None of these miracles is now numbered, or even designated as a sign; any such original identification would have necessarily disappeared in 4E's rearrangement and evaluation of Judea (see part 2.F). But they have the same effect on their audiences—however pointedly 4E has now qualified it—as the signs in Galilee, so that designation for them is still apposite.

SECTION 7 (11:1–45)
LAZARUS RAISED FROM DEATH

Pre-Johannine Source

11 ¹Now there was a certain [Mary] (and her sister Martha) of Bethany, ²ᶜwhose brother Lazarus was sick.²¹³ 3 So she [or the sisters] sent to Jesus²¹⁴ saying, "Master, your beloved friend is sick." ⁷He said to the disciples, ¹¹"Lazarus our friend has fallen asleep; ¹⁵ᶜlet us go to him."

¹⁷So Jesus came, and found him already four days buried. (¹⁸Now Bethany was near Jerusalem, about two miles away.) ³²When Mary saw [Jesus], she fell at his feet and said to him, "Master, if you had been here my brother would not have died." ³³So Jesus (when he saw her weeping) was angered in spirit and deeply troubled. ³⁴And he said, "Where have you laid him?"

213. B & L ingeniously propose this as the story's original opening, closer in format to the pre-Johannine 4:46. It is based partly on the highly complex textual problems in these verses, partly on the analogy of a possibly independent version of the story discovered by M. Smith (*Secret Gospel*). I adopt this reading, somewhat tentatively, since it resolves the otherwise hopelessly tangled problem of the source's view of the relationship among the three characters introduced at the story's opening. Smith's text of this story now seems to me, on balance, to be derivative from the Synoptics and 4G, and thus to have little bearing on the pre-Johannine source (contrast my preliminary view in *TGOS*, 87).

214. Only some MSS record the name here, but perhaps correctly; it would then have been omitted by other scribes as redundant after the insertion of v. 2ab—see Analysis in this section, on that verse.

They said to him, "Master, come and see." [38]So Jesus came to the tomb. Now it was a cave, and had a stone lying against it. [39a]Jesus said, "Take away the stone." [41]So they took the stone away. And Jesus (lifted up his eyes [43b]and) called out with a great cry, "Lazarus, come forth!" [44]The dead man came forth, bound feet and hands with cloths, and his face wrapped in a handkerchief. Jesus said to them, "Unbind him and let him go."

[45]Those who saw what he did believed in him.

From the milling crowds of Galilee (evidently, that is, after the feeding of the multitude and Jesus' crossing the sea) Jesus is urgently summoned to a bedside in a Judean village. The scene will become a kind of public event, as does each of the signs stories, but like the other Judean miracles it centers around the illness of an individual. Lazarus is **beloved** by Jesus, and by the disciples too—**our friend**, he says to them.[215]

The message sent is that Lazarus is **sick**, but Jesus prophetically declares to the disciples that in fact he has died (**fallen asleep**), presumably during the messenger's journey to Galilee.[216] Thus Jesus displays his supernatural—or should we not say simply messianic?—perception. Without delay he determines to **go to him**, presumably not merely from human sympathy or loyal concern, but because of what he can do.

When Jesus arrives in Bethany he finds an apparently hopeless situation. Lazarus is already **four days** dead and buried. If, according to Jewish belief, death was irreversible after three days, the scene is understandably one of grief and despair. Mary's words on Jesus' arrival, while expressing a kind of trust in his miraculous power to heal—implied already in her earlier message to Jesus—also convey that it is now too late: **If you had been here. . . .** All of this causes him to be **angered in spirit and deeply troubled**, whether purely from indignation at the display of human pessimism (as in Mark 5:39) or from a more eschatological rage at death's hold on humanity. Terms that once probably reflected miracle-working technique (lit., they convey frenzy and trembling)—also possibly looking up to heaven in v. 41—have thus been demythologized by the pre-Johannine author. Jesus' emotions now subtly hint at his messianic power even over death. We sense the discrepancy between limited human expectation and Jesus' impending act.

He asks to be taken to the tomb, directs that it be opened—no rival here to his own resurrection—and summons Lazarus from death. And he, spoken of now only as **the dead man**, that is, one who cannot return, comes forth! But he emerges from the tomb as if still held by it: he is

215. The Greek verb "loved" and the noun "friend" have the same root (*phil-*).

216. In the remotely related raising of Jairus's daugther in Mark 5 the same phrase is meant literally by Jesus, in contrast to death; but as 4E rightly understands in redacting the source it is here the common metaphor of death (cf. e.g., 1 Thess. 4:13).

bound feet and hands, his face still **wrapped in a handkerchief** as in burial. It is a minor miracle that he can come forth at all. Yet the true miracle has occurred; he is alive. Jesus only directs that they **unbind him and let him go.**

Who are those to whom Jesus gives these directions? Without difficulty we can imagine. The story that began quietly in a household has turned into a village event. And it is with a public response that the story ends. **Those who saw** [the sign Jesus] **did believed in him.** A miracle, yes, and a marvelous one; but for the pre-Johannine author only one more proof of Jesus' power and status, and thus the basis for faith in him.

This story, together with the wedding at Cana, has no obvious parallel in the Synoptic Gospels. Whence then did it arise? Unlike that first sign, this one need not seek its origin in non-Christian circles, for it seems likely to be a highly derived form of the parable Jesus tells (itself a narrative, of course) of the rich man and Lazarus (Luke 16:19–31).[217] It is notable, on the one hand, that only this parable has a named character and, on the other, that the Synoptics are totally silent on so noteworthy a miracle as the raising of Lazarus, hardly possible if it were a tradition from the lifetime of Jesus. The fact that the story, even in its simpler, pre-Johannine form, already shows "novelistic" touches and contact with other stories (e.g., the Lukan tradition of Mary and perhaps Martha) further suggests that it derives not from an actual event but is an early Christian construct, like a good deal of the Jesus tradition.

It has often been observed that the conversation having to do with resurrection in the Lukan parable ("though one should return from the dead") has a rough parallel in the discussion between Martha and Jesus, which we assign to the Johannine redaction. Can we then hold that the source's author, and not 4E, has received this tradition? Or shall we posit a Johannine dependence on Luke (or vice versa), which otherwise we have failed to find? The answer is the former: we have a pre-Johannine story of a raising from the dead that is somehow derived from the tradition underlying the parable in Luke. If 4E has added the element of a theological discussion of resurrection, it has no real parallel with the conversation between the rich man and Abraham in the parable's folk tale, but derives solely from elements of the miracle story the Evangelist takes over from the source. Just as the author of Luke will have elaborated the tradition, so 4E, along roughly parallel but quite unconnected paths.

---

217. As the development of a saying into a narrative this would not be unique in the Jesus tradition. The miraculous cursing of the fig tree (Mark 11:12–14, 20–21 par.), e.g., seems to have evolved from the parable of the barren fig tree (Luke 13:6–9).

Johannine Redaction[218]

11 ¹Now there was a certain sick man, Lazarus of Bethany, of the village of Mary (and her sister Martha). ²[It was Mary—who had anointed the Lord with myrrh and wiped his feet with her hair]—whose brother Lazarus was sick. ³*Now* (the sisters) sent to Jesus saying, "Lord, your beloved friend is sick." ⁴But when Jesus heard it he said, "This illness is not mortal but is for the glory of God, so that the Son of God may be glorified by it."

⁵Now Jesus loved Martha and her sister and Lazarus. ⁶So when he heard that he was sick he nevertheless stayed two days longer where he was.

⁷Then, after this, he said to the disciples, "Let us go into Judea again." ⁸The disciples said to him, "Rabbi, the Jews were just now trying to stone you, and you are going there again?" [Vv. 9–10]

¹¹He said these things, and after that he said to them, "Lazarus our friend has fallen asleep; but I go to awaken him." [Vv. 12–15ab]

¹⁵ᶜ"But let us go to him." ¹⁶Then Thomas, known as Didymos, said to his fellow disciples, "Let us go too in order to die with him."

¹⁷*Then* Jesus came, and found him already four days buried. (¹⁸Now Bethany was near Jerusalem, about two miles away.) ¹⁹And many of the Jews had come to Martha and Mary to condole with them for their brother. [Vv. 20–31]

³² Now when Mary came to the place where Jesus was and saw him, she fell at his feet and said to him, "Lord, if you had been here my brother would not have died." ³³*Now* when he saw her weeping and those who had come with her weeping Jesus was angered in spirit and deeply troubled. ³⁴And he said, "Where have you laid him?" They said to him, "Lord, come and see." [Vv. 35–37]

³⁸*Then* Jesus, again troubled within himself, came to the tomb. Now it was a cave, and had a stone lying against it. ³⁹Jesus said, "Take away the stone." Martha, the dead man's sister, said to him, "Lord, there will be a smell, for it is the fourth day." ⁴⁰Jesus said to her, "Did I not tell you that if you believed you would see the glory of God?" ⁴¹*Then* they took the stone away. And Jesus lifted up his eyes and said, "Father, thank you for hearing me. ⁴²I know you always hear me, but I spoke for the crowd's sake who are standing here, that they may believe that you have sent me." ⁴³When he had said this he called out with a great cry, "Lazarus, come forth!" ⁴⁴The dead man came forth, bound feet and hands with cloths, and his face wrapped in a handkerchief. Jesus said to them, "Unbind him and let him go."

⁴⁵Many of the Jews who had come to Mary and who saw what he did believed in him.

---

218. Since often two- or three-verse blocks of Johannine material now intersperse the source, we mostly indicate them only by verse numbers, in the interest of space and because we are chiefly concerned with the internal redaction of the source material.

A brief story, in the source no longer than the miracle of the loaves, has become an extended and complex narrative. Only a glance at its format shows how intricately the Evangelist has reworked it. Prior to v. 38 hardly a single sentence of the source stands next to another, and most have internal redaction as well. We must now account for this reworking.

The Evangelist has radically set this miracle off from the rest in several ways: (1) It is now preceded and followed by a deliberate withdrawal on Jesus' part from the heart of the Jewish nation (10:40; 11:54). This arrangement is roughly comparable to the way the last of the Galilean signs is now framed by notices of Jesus' movements with respect to Judea—6:1 (see 5:1) and 7:1. (2) It has become the last and greatest of Jesus' signs, climaxing his activity "in the world" (13:1, etc.). And (3) it has ceased to be a miracle in its own right; rather, it is the occasion for elaborate and climactic Johannine theological development. This has not taken place in ensuing dialogue such as we have found in chapter 6 (and will find again in chaps. 5 and 9), but is interwoven intricately with the story at every point.

So by means of its placement, as we have just seen, but still more as a result of the repeated insertions into it, the episode now primarily serves a theological function—it has become a prefiguring of Jesus' coming glorification. It has apparently replaced the Cleansing of the Temple as the original inciting event for the Jewish authorities' plot against Jesus (see this part, sec. 10, Johannine Redaction); and the raising that it recounts is now a preview of the resurrection of Jesus himself. What was once—that is, in SG—only one of several arresting messianic signs has become at 4E's hands the great bridge between the public ministry of Jesus and the account of his death and resurrection. Its internal redaction shapes it accordingly: Jesus' public career is characterized (as "the day"—v. 9), his destiny in Jerusalem is foreshadowed (vv. 8, 16), his work, which will end in death, is defined as glorification (vv. 4, 40c), authentic faith is further discussed (vv. 15, 27, 40b), and above all resurrection is reinterpreted (vv. 23–26).

If the hypothetical reconstruction of v. 1 we have adopted as pre-Johannine is correct, 4E has rewritten it to bring Lazarus to the fore—and possibly to introduce Martha into the story for the first time (then altering "she" in v. 3 to **the sisters**). The explanation in v. 2ab may be Johannine, but more likely it is post-Johannine; in either case its addition produces the redundancy of v. 2c.

In the Johannine Jesus' striking response (v. 4) to the news about Lazarus, his declaration that **this sickness is not mortal** qualifies the source in what is now v. 11. On one level he makes a prophecy, or rather a divine pronouncement, of the story's eventual outcome: Not that Lazarus will not die, but rather that he will die—and will be brought back from death to life. But on a deeper level this declaration is a corrective, as its continuation makes clear: Do not think (Jesus implies) that anything earthly, that is, my attachment to Lazarus, or even something so important as Lazarus's resurrection, comprises the center of what is about to occur. Rather, **it is for the glory of God**; it will be a divine event, a disclosure of God's very self. And as any reader of the Gospel knows, the glory of God is to be seen chiefly in the glorification of Jesus. Thus 4E adds, by way of paraphrase, **so that the Son of God may be glorified through it**. What is about to take place, then, will be a sign (though that word does not appear) in the deepest Johannine sense, the prefiguring of Jesus' own death and resurrection.

The chief means 4E will use to convey this complex message is the dialogue between Jesus and Martha in vv. 21–27. The editorial comment of v. 5 now prepares for it: **Now Jesus loved Martha and her sister and Lazarus**. Martha takes center stage and her special relationship to Jesus is established. But Jesus is still only on his way to Bethany, so in the meantime that journey becomes for 4E the occasion of extended dialogue between Jesus and his disciples (vv. 6–16).

Verse 6 seems pointless on any factual level—**Now when he heard that [Lazarus] was sick he nevertheless**[219] **stayed two days longer where he was**. After the reminder in the preceding verse that Jesus loved Lazarus, this deliberate delay can only appear arbitrary. Perhaps it is designed in part to deepen the miracle story's dramatic tension. But chiefly it is an unavoidable consequence of the Johannine rearrangement of the source: whereas Jesus was originally at least two days' journey from Jerusalem— the datum **already four days buried** requires this—as the Gospel now stands he is merely **across the Jordan** (10:40). Most notable, however, is the way that once again the reader is led not to focus on the level of earthly events, even miraculous ones, as represented by Lazarus, but on the higher drama of which Jesus himself is the center. Where (in the source) Jesus is about to say, "Let us go to him," the present Gospel anticipates and adapts: **Let us go into Judea again** (v. 7). The running theme of Jesus' ambiguous relation to Judea is thus reintroduced. In v. 8 Lazarus is lost sight of altogether, and instead events in earlier chapters (8:59; see also 10:39) are recalled by the disciples, who thus play the Johannine role of those who fail to understand: **"Rabbi, the Jews were just now trying to stone you, and you are going there again?"** (v. 8). We note in passing how casually *Judea* is taken to denote *the Jews;* the region and the people are treated as if interchangeable and coterminous.[220]

The unreality of this exchange on any matter-of-fact plane is evident in

219. Or perhaps even "accordingly." Many versions ignore the blatant *tote men* of the second clause.

220. As we shall see in part 2.F, this is possible because in Greek there is no distinction between Jew and Judean, between Judea and Jewry.

Jesus' puzzling and revelatory reply to the disciples (vv. 9–10). Evidently Jesus' hour, the **day** in which he can **walk**, is now closer at hand.[221] The point here, though, is the difference between Jesus who acts in **the light of the world** and those who **stumble** in darkness; this is typical Johannine dualism and gives a hint of the coming conflict between Jesus and those in whom **there is no light.**

In v. 11, with telltale awkwardness of transition (**He said these things, and after that he said to them . . .**), the Evangelist takes up the source momentarily ("Lazarus our friend has fallen asleep") and adds the christological **but I go to awaken him.** This last might conceivably derive from the source, but as a prior announcement of the intent to perform a miracle it would be unique there. It seems instead designed only to evince the misconstruing literalness of the disciples (vv. 12–13), where once again attention is not at all on Lazarus, or even on Jesus' ability to save him, but on the proper understanding of Jesus' word. "Fallen asleep" just as surely meant "died" in SG as it does in 4G; but the metaphor becomes in 4E's hands still another example of the disciples' misappropriation of Jesus' meaning (as with Nicodemus and "born again" in chap. 3). Jesus must therefore finally speak **plainly: "Lazarus is dead"** (v. 14).[222]

The misunderstanding cleared up, Jesus can **rejoice** in Lazarus's death and in his own absence, because it is not to be viewed as an event in itself but as the occasion for the disciples, just now so uncomprehending, to **believe** (v. 15a), that is, to understand.[223] Finally the source's brief report (parts of vv. 7, 11, and 15) of Jesus' words on hearing that Lazarus was ill is exhausted by 4E ("Let us go to him"—v. 15b).[224] Once again it is transformed—into an ironic pointer to Jesus' approaching fate. This is accomplished by the addition of Thomas's response, expressing either courageous resolve or bitter resignation: **Let us go too in order to die with him** (v. 16).[225]

Whether v. 18 was to be found already in the source or is a Johannine insertion, it now leads from the next statement in the source to v. 19 in which the Evangelist has introduced **many of the Jews** (from Jerusalem,

---

221. See 12:23 ("The hour has come for the Son of Man to be glorified"), and contrast 2:4 and 7:6 ("not yet").

222. Adverbial *parrhēsia* is a common Johannine term (see 7:4, 13, 26; 10:24; 11:54; 16:25, 29; 18:20; as against only five instances in the rest of the NT). Here it contrasts pejoratively with the subtle way Jesus can teach those who readily understand him. A similar connotation of inappropriateness is found in 7:4; 10:24; and 11:54. Contrast Marrow, *"Parrhēsia,"* 442.

223. Compare and contrast SG's view of belief on the basis of signs as it is voiced in that document's conclusion, 20:30–31a.

224. Because of the insertions 4E has introduced this with the conjunction "But."

225. The origin of this notice may be simply 4E's creative imagination. She or he gives Thomas another minor part at 14:5, and a major one in 20:24–28.

presumably) who **had come to condole with the sisters.** This prepares for the eventual conflict with the Jewish authorities (vv. 47–53). That will be instigated in v. 46 by **some** of those who appeared in v. 19. The Evangelist also introduces **Martha** once again ahead of Mary, to lead into the all-important Johannine block that follows (vv. 20–31).

In the Lazarus story of the source, Mary was the principal and possibly the only interlocutor with Jesus. But evidently the Evangelist knows something of the tradition, found in different form and with Lukan redaction in Luke 10:38–42, in which the two sisters figure (on vv. 21–27, see Analysis in this section; on vv. 28–29, see just below). Thus it can be used as a means of introducing the purely Johannine dialogue between Jesus and Martha on the subject of resurrection. Martha goes out to Jesus, while Mary stays at home (v. 20). Here there is no critical comparison of Martha's busyness with Mary's quieter response as in Luke; on the contrary, Martha, while not always understanding properly, becomes a kind of exemplar of the believer who is led by Jesus to deeper faith.[226] She approaches Jesus with confident trust in his ability to heal—**Master, if you had been here my brother would not have died** (v. 21). The same words, from SG, will soon be used by Mary, but here they lack any sense of despair or rebuke, for Martha goes on to hint that **even now** it is not too late to hope for a miracle, so great is Jesus' influence with God, the sole author of resurrection: **whatever you ask of God, God will give you** (v. 22).

On one level Jesus proceeds to affirm Martha's expectant trust: **Your brother will rise again** (v. 23). But whatever she may have hinted in v. 22, she now takes Jesus' promise literally (a frequent Johannine technique)—**I know that he will rise again in the final resurrection** (v. 24). This evokes the central pronouncement of the dialogue, and indeed of the whole Lazarus episode as 4E has re-created it: **I am resurrection and life** (v. 25a). So we now are dealing not simply with a marvelous raising of Lazarus or even a preview of Jesus' own resurrection. Rather, we learn the underlying meaning of both events. That Jesus can raise Lazarus, and will rise himself, means that he himself is the source of resurrection[227] and life; in short, that he *is* salvation. Christology, then, both is radically heightened and gives way to soteriology.

The heart of the dialogue has been reached, but not its end; the theme of faith resumes. It is by faith that the life Jesus is, and therefore gives, is appropriated: **The one who believes in me . . . will in no way ever die**

---

226. She reappears in v. 39, however, with a literal and unbelieving attitude, needing Jesus' reminder of v. 40.

227. This is but an extension, albeit a radical one, of the source, where Jesus promised that he would raise himself (2:19).

(vv. 25b–26a). Martha's faith is then put to the test—**Do you believe this?** (v. 26b). To this she replies with a confession in Jesus that sounds like something from SG, so singly christological is it: **You are the Christ, the Son of God who comes into the world** (v. 27b—compare the crowd's affirmation of Jesus in the source at 6:14). But against the background of what precedes it, it is clear that this climax to the scene is not just an acceptance of Jesus' true messianic status. Martha's initial faith in Jesus' signs has matured into both an understanding of his saving work on earth and a commitment to it; the confession is prefaced with the assertion, **Yes, Lord, I have come to believe** (v. 27a).

If vv. 28–31 are Johannine, as I maintain, yet they are not especially important theologically; rather, they bring the story back to the point in the source where 4E had left it. Yet the first two of those verses (vv. 28–29) contain a number of gratuitous details, some of which derive again from the Martha/Mary tradition reflected in Luke 10.[228] Then in v. 30 we find the artificial explanation we can attribute to redactional invention: Jesus' whereabouts ("Jesus had not yet come to the village . . .") must be accounted for to allow the successive meetings with the two sisters and for the chorus of the *Ioudaioi* in what follows. In v. 31 the latter begin to take on an ambiguous character; they had come out of human empathy to mourn with Mary, and they follow her to share her grief, but now mistake her going out, **supposing** that she is going to the tomb. This hint of misunderstanding on their part seems designed to prepare for the division among them in vv. 36–37.

With vv. 32–34 4E at last resumes again SG's account, only inserting for Mary a repetition of Martha's coming **to the place where Jesus was** (v. 32a) and introducing the fellow mourners into v. 33. The Evangelist allows the pre-Johannine story here to speak for itself. The grief of Jesus— in that verse so beloved by Bible memorizers for its brevity: **Jesus wept** (v. 35)—had no doubt been suggested by the traditional notice of his intense emotion (v. 33b); the present writer thus reinterprets it, and it now serves to elicit the divided comment of **the Jews** in vv. 36–37. They marvel at his humanity (**See how he loved him**—is this also to be seen as a misunderstanding on their part?), but **some** question his power, referring to the miracle, in chapter 9, that now precedes this one in the Johannine arrangement: **Could not he who opened the eyes of the blind man have kept this man from dying?** It is probably due to 4E's subtle skill that they imagine that Jesus could have healed Lazarus before he died, which in a

228. E.g., the details that Martha summons Mary "quietly," telling her that "the Teacher is here and calling for you," and the notice that Mary "rose quickly" to go to him.

different context would be an act of faith, but not that he can bring him back to life—and thus they do not believe in Jesus at all.

The Evangelist takes up the source's story once more in v. 38. A parenthesis characteristically repeats the last detail in the source prior to the insertion of vv. 35–37: Jesus was **deeply moved again**. Thus the somewhat ambiguous pre-Johannine reference to Jesus' emotion is clarified. The source then runs to its climax, with but two more interruptions, both of them bringing to completion Jesus' prophetic declaration in v. 4 ("This illness is not mortal; it is for the glory of God, so that the Son of God may be glorified by means of it"):

1. At Jesus' command to open the tomb (v. 39a) Martha is now made to object (v. 39bc), reflecting once more a lack of understanding on her part that Jesus can in fact perform the miracle, or rather a failure to understand that in it she would, as he had originally declared, **see the Glory of God** (v. 40). The condition for this vision, as was made clear in Jesus' dialogue with her, is that she **believe**.

2. Almost the opposite relation between seeing and believing, or rather hearing and believing, is expressed in the second insertion (vv. 41b–42). Jesus' lifting up his eyes, if pre-Johannine, suggests to the Evangelist no longer a wonderworking act, as presumably in SG, but a prayer. Jesus knows that the miracle is about to take place and so thanks God for hearing him; we are reminded of Martha's words in v. 22—"Whatever you ask from God, God will give you." Lest this reflect too low a christology, the Johannine Jesus goes on to explain (as it were for the reader's benefit) that of course God always hears him (v. 42a). So what he has just said about believing and so seeing the glory of God is **on account of the people standing by—that they may** [hear his word and so] **believe**. They will believe not only in the glory of God (as if that were insufficient!) but in Jesus as the one God has **sent**. So the christological program that was announced in v. 4 is now completed, for in this sign not only the Father but also **the Son** is truly **glorified**.

Having said this (v. 43a), Jesus proceeds to call Lazarus forth from death, in effect to work his resurrection. The story is complete and, alongside the intricate Johannine reworking, retains its original power and meaning. Only in the sequel has the Evangelist changed the course of events. **Many of the Jews who had come to Mary** (he specifies) **believed** (v. 45a); **but** (he adds) **some of them went away to the Pharisees and reported to them what Jesus had done** (v. 46). The act of resurrection, for 4G *the* Demonstration of Jesus' Glory as Divine Son and Savior, is at the same time to nonbelievers a blasphemous claim to usurp God's authority. So in its present position it leads inexorably to Jesus' execution. The ministry of Jesus is over, his passion has begun—in contrast to SG, where at this point (originally held by the Temple Cleansing, not the Lazarus sign), the Culmination of the Signs preceded the actual beginning of the passion.

Analysis

Separation of source and redaction in chapter 11 is more difficult than in any of the other miracle stories. And among all the narrative material its only rivals in this respect are the accounts of the Baptist's preaching (1:19–34) and the trial by Pilate (chaps. 18—19). It is my contention that this is so largely and perhaps entirely because of the special interest 4E had in redacting these passages and the intricate way that the original narrative and its considerably Johannine reinterpretation have consequently been interwoven. In this case we have a matter-of-fact, though hardly ordinary, story—with considerable detail about Lazarus's illness and burial, the mourning for him, and Jesus' manner of raising him. It is thus not so very different in character (or even length, as we observed above) from the other pre-Johannine miracles we have examined. On the other hand, the chapter now "bristles with Johannisms all the way through," not only in style and theme[229] but still more in method: the death of Lazarus is nearly lost sight of for great sections of the chapter in favor of theological discussions of resurrection and christology.

The result is that in its present form the miracle, while still concretely depicted, stands in odd tension with the intervening discourses, filled as they are with lofty, abstract teaching. The passage is not wanting in unity or dramatic power—quite the contrary—but to me it seems clearly to be the complex and skillful product of a very Johannine redaction upon a distinctly pre-Johannine story.[230]

Since this passage is so unusually complex, then, analysis will leave a number of questions of detail unanswered.[231] Nevertheless it is not impracticable. A few details have already been footnoted in the reconstructed text of the source. The broader separation of elaborate Johannine redaction from an original miracle story proceeds as follows:

• Verse 2ab, with its reference to an event not yet narrated (12:1–8), is evidently redactional.[232] The insertion now separates v. 2c from v. 1 (in the form of it we adopted—p. 94).

• Verse 4, deflecting interest from the circumstances of the story onto a theological plane (**for the glory of God**), is patently Johannine in both style and content.

229. As Lindars (*Behind 4G*, 55) means by that phrase.

230. Lindars (ibid., 58) insists that because this story is so skillfully composed "it is not to be expected that it might be carved up [*sic*] into a pre-Johannine story overlaid with Johannine touches." I find this conclusion a non sequitur, and in any case the redaction involves more than "Johannine touches."

231. Thus Nicol (*Sēmeia*, 26) chooses simply to identify those verses within which the source is found, along "with J[ohannine] additions": vv. 1–6, 11–17, 33–44. I believe that a more detailed separation is possible and that it is not altogether to be confined to the verses Nicol lists.

232. But more likely post-Johannine than Johannine. It uses *kyrios* of the pre-resurrection Jesus and speaks not to the reader hearing the story of Jesus as if for the first time but to the one who has heard it over and over: "It was Mary, you remember, who would later anoint [lit., *who anointed*] the Lord."

• Verse 5 also represents a late, apparently Johannine, stage in the story's evolution, since both Lazarus and Mary, the latter not even named, have been overshadowed by Martha, in preparation for the great block of Johannine material in vv. 20–27.[233] The notice that **Jesus loved . . . Lazarus** is in itself a neutral element as to provenance but, since it is redundant with the sister's message in v. 3, would most likely be redactional.

• Verses 6–10 arbitrarily heighten the story's suspense and again direct our attention away from the miracle: Jesus' delay of two days (v. 6) in going to Lazarus is capricious,[234] and it occasions a discussion with the disciples about the decision to go to **Judea**—to the place of **the Jews**—and to work there in **daylight**. The entire block of verses is Johannine.

• The awkward first part of v. 11 (**He said this, and then he said to them . . .**) is obviously redactional—a conclusion to the Johannine insertion of vv. 6–10 has been prefixed to the older introduction to a pre-Johannine remark. The latter now follows, namely, the middle clause of v. 11: **Lazarus our friend has fallen asleep.**[235] The last clause of the verse (11c: **but I go to awaken him**) appears to be 4E's insertion again: it uses the Johannine phrase, "I go . . . in order to . . ." (see, e.g., 14:2, 12; 16:28), and Jesus announces beforehand the miracle he will perform (6:6; 9:4). The original sequel to v. 11b is perhaps now the last clause in v. 15 (**Let us go to him**); it has been set off from what originally led up to it by the Johannine block (vv. 12–15a), displaying the disciples' misunderstanding of Jesus' intent. The Evangelist brings the whole scene, now more preoccupied with Jesus' fateful return to Judea than with Lazarus, to an end with Thomas's utterance in v. 16. Jesus' original response to the message from Bethany, then, though scattered, is recoverable from vv. 11b and 15b: **Lazarus our friend has fallen asleep; let us go to him.**[236]

• That Lazarus is referred to in v. 17 simply by a pronoun in the Greek is anomalous only after the Johannine insertion of v. 16.

• As to origin, both vv. 18 and 19 are uncertain, but to different degrees. Specifying Bethany's distance from Jerusalem in v. 18 is typical of SG. It may be pre-Johannine, then, intended in the source as an indication of Jesus' itinerary. By itself v. 18 does not seriously interrupt the story's flow. But with v. 19 added it does, so the condolers are redactional; and their description as *Ioudaioi* clearly indicates 4E's hand.

• Verses 21–27 constitute a self-contained theological dialogue between Jesus and Martha that quite obviously has been added as a whole by 4E. But it demands

233. 4E is perhaps responsible for every mention of Martha in the chapter, in which case we should need to omit from the source the last phrase in v. 1, together with *the sisters* and the plural participle *saying* in v. 3 (and to read in the last case an alteration of *she sent*). We have allowed for this possibility.

234. It was evidently necessitated, because of the pre-Johannine *four days* of Lazarus's burial, by 4E's present geographical framework: Jesus now comes to Bethany not from Galilee, as evidently in the source, but only from across the Jordan (10:40).

235. It displays supernatural knowledge on Jesus' part, taken for granted in SQ, and contains the common metaphor of sleep for death (as used by Paul, for instance, in 1 Thess. 4:13).

236. Introduced by v. 7a: *He said to the disciples.*

an introduction: not only the insertion of Martha's name in v. 19 but the notice (v. 20) that she went out to Jesus when she heard of his coming.[237] Verse 20, and especially the contrast it contains between the attitudes of the two sisters (Martha goes out to greet Jesus, Mary quietly remains in the house), is closely akin to the tradition in Luke 10:38–42, where Martha is the more prominent sister (though not the more highly praised). The question then arises whether it was 4E or the predecessor who was responsible for combining it with the Lazarus story. I find no clear answer. But because only Mary is prominent in the source, both up to this point and later on in the story, the Lukan Martha/Mary tradition seems not to have penetrated very far into the traditional miracle story and probably for that reason should be attributed to 4E. Provisionally, then, I attach v. 20 to the Johannine scene that follows it. Similarly, v. 28 now seems to be Johannine—Martha brings Mary onstage and herself fades from view (to reappear fleetingly and in-congruously in vv. 39b–40).

• Verses 28–30 are Johannine too, providing transition back to the original story and Jesus' encounter with Mary in v. 32.[238] The sisters' respective meetings with Jesus form a doublet; but while the scene involving Martha has been modeled roughly on the source's account of Mary and Jesus, the Evangelist has inserted into both the fiction of a private meeting with Jesus outside the village. Originally he simply came to the village, where **Mary saw him,** and together—and by now with other townspeople, we understand—they went to the tomb. Thus I find the pre-Johannine continuation of the story only in v. 32bc.

• Verse 31 is more of 4E's creation, to bring "the Jews" onstage (see just above on v. 19), in preparation for vv. 36–37.

• In v. 32a, **when [Mary] came to the place where Jesus was** is syntactically cumbersome alongside the following participial clause (lit., **seeing him**) and pre-sumably redactional, as its content confirms. Possibly it has caused the original object of "saw" to be changed from "Jesus" to simply "him."

• Mary's expostulation in v. 32c (**Lord, if you had been here my brother would not have died**) is clearly pre-Johannine, representing a trust in Jesus' wonderwork-ing power (not unlike the words of Jesus' mother in chap. 2 and of the official in chap. 4) that has now turned to despair. They have been imitated by anticipation in 4E's portrayal of Martha at v. 21, but there they led on to a kind of hope that is lacking here.

• Verse 33ac is pre-Johannine. That is, **and those who had come with her** (also) **weeping** is 4E's addition, taking up from their introduction in v. 31. So it is Mary's saying and tears alone, or perhaps also the fact of Lazarus's death, that originally occasions Jesus' anger in v. 33c and leads on to his question in v. 34 and its answer.

• Jesus' grief for his friend (v. 35) is surely redactional, interrupting the connec-tion between vv. 34 and 38 and showing an emotion somewhat at variance with that

237. See 4:47, either Johannine or somehow the basis for 4E's imitation here.
238. Martha summons Mary, who goes "to the place where Jesus was"; it is explained in an afterthought that he had still not come to the village. The identifying and multiplying of locations in and around the village (this meeting place on the outskirts, the house) is a Johan-nine dramatic device.

in v. 33.[239] It is designed chiefly to occasion the very Johannine portrayal of "the Jews" and their reaction in vv. 36–37, where they are now detached from the events and divided among themselves.

• The phrase **deeply moved again** in v. 38 is a reminder of Jesus' emotion in v. 33, necessary after the Johannine insertion of vv. 35–37; it is therefore redactional.

• Martha's objection and Jesus' reassurance in vv. 39b–40 again interrupt the flow of the narrative (Jesus' command in v. 39a/immediate compliance in v. 41—a typical pattern in SG). Martha, whose presence at the tomb has not been accounted for, again overshadows Mary; her objection evinces Jesus' word in v. 40. The latter **(Did I not tell you that if you would believe you would see the glory of God?)** is a typically Johannine reminder of an earlier saying, shifting the plane from the miracle about to take place onto the theological level of divine revelation and— most uncharacteristic of the source—suggesting that Martha's faith is a necessary precondition to belief in what Jesus is about to accomplish.

• Possibly SG contained the detail that Jesus **lifted up his eyes** (v. 41b), as part of his thaumaturgy, and continued with the words **and called out . . .** in v. 43. But Jesus' gesture now leads into the very Johannine prayer of vv. 41c–42 and so it may be redactional as well. In any case, the dependent clause almost at the beginning of v. 43 **(when he had said this)** is redactional, needed to resume the source.

• What shall we make source-critically of the often-noted similarities (and differences too) between this story and the account of Jesus' own burial and resurrection in chapters 19—20? Details in v. 44 raise this question, though it is not confined to them. The overall parallel is an important one for 4E, as his or her placing of this miracle shows: the raising of Lazarus is now the preview of Jesus' resurrection, and as such appropriately occasions the extended teaching about those events that now intersperses itself throughout the miracle story. Has 4E therefore created or elaborated the parallels? Probably not, for most of them are either unavoidable, given the common subject matter, or only apparent.[240] There is little reason, then, to postulate deliberate assimilation in the Lazarus story to the death and resurrection of Jesus. So we can take v. 44 (where, as we noted, several of the details paralleled occur) to be entirely pre-Johannine.

• Verse 45 now leads into the Johannine sequel to this momentous passage, that

---

239. Most translators harmonize these two verses. In v. 33 the Greek verbs seem to mean "angered and disturbed." On the contrast between this sense and an earlier one in the tradition, see the comment on this verse, in this section, Pre-Johannine Source.

240. That a *stone* covered the tomb in both stories (here we take elements of chaps. 19 and 20 together) is surely traditional, based on Jewish practice and found also in the Synoptics with different words. The same terms are used in the case of Lazarus and Jesus for "tomb" and "burying" (lit., laying out) and for removing the stone, but they are all the common words to be expected. The tombs, however, are described differently: in chap. 11 a natural *cave*, in chap. 19 a *new tomb*, that is humanly cut out of the rock. Both Lazarus and Jesus were *bound* for burial, but in different ways—Lazarus's *hands and feet* with *cloths*/Jesus' *body* and using *spices* and evidently *cloths* (a different word) only to cover his body as it lay on the stone slab prepared for it. In both cases the *soudarion* is mentioned, for the napkin or handkerchief used to cover the head, though presumably it is the standard Greek term for the Jewish practice; but it was *wrapped around* Lazarus's *face* and had been *upon* Jesus' head. (See further, this part, sec. 19, Analysis, on 20:7.)

is, to the decision by the Sanhedrin to put Jesus to death (11:47–53). But the verse appears to contain the conclusion to the original story. The mourners, **the Jews who had come to Mary,** are Johannine as in v. 19 (Martha). The by-now-familiar choral ending of the pre-Johannine miracle is then simply the statement: "Those who had seen what [Jesus] did believed in him." Presumably they are simply the villagers whose presence can be assumed.

The reader who has worked through the intricacies of this analysis deserves at last a summary of our results, a view of the forest after foraging in the trees. Also, the one who has only glanced here before delving into the meaning of the passage has the right to know what we have found. In fact, a coherent and recognizably pre-Johannine miracle story emerges, as the translation (given in Pre-Johannine Source in this section) can show. It has been repeatedly interrupted with a great variety of Johannine insertions, some brief and some of considerable length, but more often than not these can readily be lifted out of the original narrative.

Only a few questions were left unanswered. The major one, but itself not of great moment in the long run, is the extent to which various traditions had already been combined before 4E took up the story. I believe one can represent the evolution of the story, as it has interwoven those traditions, roughly according to the following stages:

1. A dead man, presumably identified as Lazarus and possibly as friend of Jesus, is raised.
2. This takes place in Bethany, the village of a certain Mary.
3. She is the sister of Lazarus.
4. Also of Martha.
5. Martha is favorably contrasted with Mary.

Where in this list shall we draw the line that separates 4E from the source? Certainly after the first three stages and possibly after the fourth as well. (We have allowed the possibility that Martha was named in the source, but have doubted that she had any prominence prior to 4E's redaction.) Thus the Johannine stage appears to begin at least by stage 5, and just possibly the line should be drawn between stages 3 and 4.

Following Bultmann, I once held (see *TGOS*, 189–95) that the episode of Jesus and the Samaritan woman, or rather the pre-Johannine form of it, was to be found in the source and, I suggested, between 11:15 and 17. It is the only episode in the tradition that spoke of a journey between north and south (albeit now in the opposite direction to that demanded at the pre-Johannine level). Moreover, it contains the datum that Jesus, at the Samaritans' behest, "stayed there two days," which I took possibly to be a clue explaining Jesus' stay of "two days where he was" in the present form of the Lazarus story (v. 6).

But further reflection has convinced me that the suggestion does not work.[241]

241. The present smooth transition between vv. 15 and 17 (even though now interrupted by the redactional parenthesis of v. 16) lacks all indication—such as a repetition of Jesus' name in v. 17—that an intervening passage has been removed. At the pre-Johannine level a stay of two days in Samaria, when Jesus is already en route to Lazarus, is even more anomalous than is 11:6 now at the Johannine level.

Yet the *Vorlage* of 4:4-42 resembles SQ in some respects even though it is not readily separated from its present Johannine form. In literary method and detail of plot (e.g., in v. 6) it bears a relation to the signs.

SECTION 8 (9:1-8)
A BLIND MAN SEES

Pre-Johannine Source

9 1As he was leaving he saw a man, blind from birth [sitting and begging]. 6He spat on the ground and made clay of the spit and anointed the man's eyes with the clay 7and said to him, "Go, wash in the pool of Siloam." So he went and washed, and returned able to see. (8So those who had seen him before as a beggar said, "Isn't this the man who used to sit and beg?!")

This is the briefest of the source's miracles, not called a sign in 4G. But despite its great brevity it adequately and effectively tells its story of Jesus' self-demonstration. The opening redactional phrase that connects it with whatever originally preceded (lit., "As he passed along . . .") is looser than is usual in SG, sounding more like the transitions between stories in Mark. But it is quite possible that the participle has a sharper meaning, like that proposed in the translation above, especially if this passage followed the raising of Lazarus; it would then mean "And as he was leaving Bethany . . . ."

The pool of Siloam, while not the actual site of this episode, is the locale with which it is remembered, and only a slight familiarity with the topography of Jerusalem would therefore place the healing between the raising of Lazarus at Bethany outside the city, on the one hand, and, on the other, the still remaining miracle story, that of the lame man in chapter 5 at another pool, next to the Temple itself.

The circumstances of the miracle are quickly sketched: a blind man, congenitally blind and probably forced by his infirmity to a life of begging, is encountered by Jesus. He does not ask to be healed, nor are we to imagine that Jesus goes to him chiefly from compassion. The man's state is not so much an occasion of human need as an opportunity for God's Messiah to show himself—to those who will witness what takes place, and above all to the reader. The generous deed, then, is not just a miracle but in fact a sign. Yet it is accomplished in the most materialistic way possible. Much like any ancient wonderworker Jesus makes a salve of spit and dust and applies it to the man's eyes. This, however, does not directly restore his sight. Instead, we are to gather that it is the command Jesus gives and the man's unquestioning compliance, both so typical of SG, that accomplish the healing: **"Go, wash"; so he went and washed . . . and came back able to see.** Not for the first time, then (see esp. 2:1-11 and 4:46-54), the actual cure takes place offstage.

We are like those in v. 8 who **beheld** the result; we recognize the deed from its consequence. The man who **used to sit and beg,** and presumably had to be led about, is now able to make his own way. Just as at 2:10 (and perhaps 6:25), the astonished question of the witnesses (**Isn't this the man . . . ?**) attests to the sign Jesus has done. Attention subtly shifts from the cure itself to amazement at its worker. A fuller ending, spelling out belief on the witnesses' part, may have been truncated in 4E's adaptation; but possibly not—in scarcely more than three or four sentences Jesus is shown revealing himself once again.

Johannine Redaction

9 ¹As he was leaving he saw a man, blind from birth. [Vv. 2–5] ⁶**When he had said this,** he spat on the ground and made clay of the spit and anointed the man's eyes with the clay ⁷and said to him, "Go, wash in the pool of Siloam" (**which translated means 'Sent').** *Then* he went and washed, and returned able to see. ⁸**The neighbors and** those who had seen him before as a beggar said, "Isn't this the man who used to sit and beg?!" [Vv. 9–41]

At 4E's hands the healing of the blind man—in its pre-Johannine form a self-contained story—becomes only the first scene, and in a way the least important, of a seven-scened drama.[242] But as with chapter 6 we shall concentrate primarily on the Johannine insertion into the story itself, the somewhat intricate exchange between the disciples and Jesus in vv. 2–5.

Although the detail of blindness **from birth** at the end of v. 1 is almost certainly pre-Johannine, with the disciples' question presupposing it 4E now sets the stage for the drama that is to follow: **Rabbi, who sinned, this man or his parents, that he was born blind?** (v. 2). The parents are thereby introduced, and also the question whether the man is "a sinner"— and by implication Jesus' involvement with a sinner. All of this will presently become of central importance (vv. 16, 24, 34). But here at the start Jesus altogether rejects the question's validity (**It was not that this man sinned, or his parents**—v. 3a) and just as in the Lazarus story treats the human predicament as existing only for a theological end (. . . **but that the works of God may be manifest**—v. 3b). Though couched now in Johannine terms and thus to be understood in a Johannine way, this is not so very far from the story's understanding in SG; miracles are not events important in themselves, but only as they display theological truth. What distinguishes 4E's understanding, in which even Jesus' messianic status is no longer central, is Jesus' oneness with the Father; the meaning remains christological, but now in a way entirely inseparable from the activity of God. It is therefore striking that in the present case this activity will be

---

242. Martyn (*History and Theology,* part 1) shows how skillfully 4E has created this drama, reflecting explicitly the recent expulsion of Christians from the synagogue.

manifest **in him,** that is, in the blind man: by his paradigmatic coming gradually to full belief in Jesus, and so to salvation, he will be still more an expression of God's work.

The text of v. 4 is problematic, but if with the majority of critics we take the more difficult reading as original—*"We* must work the works of him who sent *me"*—a redaction-critical explanation of the anomalous mixture of pronouns suggests itself. The Evangelist has taken an independent and traditional logion about Christian mission ("We must work . . . while it is day; the night is coming when no one can work"; see Analysis, in this section) and because it speaks of working has attached it to v. 3b ("that the works of God may be manifest"). But then, in accord with that declaration, the verb **work** in the pre-Johannine logion must be qualified in two ways: it is **the works of [God]** that must be accomplished, and God is identified as **him who sent [Jesus].** With these phrases inserted, the saying is no longer concerned primarily with late-first-century Christian mission but becomes chiefly christocentric; Jesus declares that he must do what the Father intends. The healing of the blind man, like the raising of Lazarus, is an expression of Jesus' own divine mission.

Yet the clash of pronouns, according to the above explanation an accident of 4E's adapting the traditional saying, may serve a purpose of its own in the Johannine intent and refer still to the mission of the Johannine church. Martyn *(History and Theology)* has suggested that there is a two-level drama running through the Gospel, in which the latter-day Christian situation of 4E's time is superimposed, rather like a photographic double exposure, on the story of Jesus. Here, then, perhaps the mission incumbent on the church in the original logion still obtains, so long as it is seen as identical to the mission of Jesus himself: "We (that is, the Johannine church) must work the works of [God] who sent me (that is, Jesus)."

Since in this particular case it is the restoring of light to one who is in darkness, 4E can add v. 5, building also on the day/night theme in the logion: **While I am in the world, I am the light of the world.** Jesus' mission is limited in time, but of eternal significance; on the one hand he does only the works of the Father, yet on the other can solemnly declare himself to be the Light by which the world lives (see 8:12). In form, this is another of the great "I AM" sayings; as to content, we are reminded of the Gospel's prologue ("The light shines in the darkness . . ."; "the true light that enlightens every one"—1:4–5, 9; see also 11:9–10; 12:46).

With one small exception, the only Johannine redaction within the body of the source's story is the insertion of vv. 2–5. And the exception relates to it: namely, the parenthesis in v. 7, symbolically interpreting the name **Siloam** by giving, probably falsely, its etymology. The man, of course, was in effect **sent** by Jesus to the pool, but on a more important level 4E's

111

intent is surely to reiterate that *Jesus* is the one sent by God,[243] just as we saw in the redaction of the logion in v. 4; and it is chiefly in this way, beyond his eventual belief in Jesus, that the work of the Father is **manifest in the man.**

Finally, as with all of the Judean miracles, and also the last Galilean one, 4E elaborates what appears to be the original choral ending, so that it becomes the opening of a new scene (vv. 8–12) involving the man healed and the miracle's witnesses. But the latter become a mixed group with 4E's insertion of **neighbors** in v. 8a, alongside the probably traditional witnesses to the miracle,[244] and thus we are not surprised that they soon argue among themselves over the fact of the healing: **Some said, "It is he"; other said, "No, he is like him."** In a similar way the identity of Jesus is debated by the Pharisees in the third scene of the drama (v. 16).

It is beyond our reach to lay out the thought of the entire chapter, the seven-scened drama that so clearly reflects conflict between Christians and Jews in 4E's time. Suffice it here to observe on the one hand that most of the themes there interwoven—sinner/"from God," sight/blindness, discipleship, faith—somehow find their origin in the source's story, and on the other hand that 4E has transformed what was originally a *healing* (understood, to be sure, as christological sign) into a gradual account of the blind man's *conversion* to full Belief in Jesus' Divinity.

Analysis

Chapter 9 is another passage in which a miracle story—in this case as short and simple as the raising of Lazarus is (even originally) long and detailed—has provided the basis for a major Johannine drama. Here, however, the miracle is concluded before the major Johannine expansion begins. Within the story itself there is very little of the extended dramatic delay we found in the Lazarus story; separation of redaction from source is therefore considerably easier.

• Although the connective phrase in v. 1 (**As he passed by**) follows tolerably well after the last verse of chapter 8, it is a locution occurring only here, and is common in the Synoptics. It appears to stem from the source and then as now to indicate a literary seam. Since we learn later (v. 8) that the blind man **used to sit and beg,** much like Bartimaeus in Mark 10 and in another story with similarities to this one (the lame man in Acts 3) it is possible that the source gave that datum here and that 4E has deferred it, perhaps to call greater attention to the phrase **from birth,** the basis of the brief theological debate to follow (vv. 2–5). But this detail

243. In the source this designation was reserved for John the Baptist.

244. At the pre-Johannine level the witnesses would have been more or less neutral, certainly not raising any objections, and when they see the man healed they would display by their astonished question incipient belief in Jesus' messianic power. By contrast, 4E's insertion of "the neighbors" perhaps adds a note of disbelief, even scoffing, if it reflects the experience of the Johannine late-first-century community which found its neighbors, who ought to be sympathetic, in fact hostile to them and their movement.

itself is not Johannine; it reflects the source's interest in factual circumstance, it is not otherwise taken up in the redaction, and the same words appear in Acts 3:2.

• That Jesus' **disciples** appear in v. 2 might suggest the hand of the pre-Johannine author, for whom they are usually at least in the background. But although they do not figure in the Johannine drama that follows, their asking a theological question—**Who sinned, this man or his parents, that he was born blind?**[245]—is surely typical of the Evangelist; and Jesus' answer to it in v. 3 provides the basis for vv. 4–5, which leave behind the blind man and his condition altogether. Verse 4 sounds like a traditional logion ("We must work . . . while it is day; night is coming when no one can work") imported by 4E and then expanded with the insertion of "the works of him who sent me" (so Pancaro, *Law*, 67–68).

• We thus find the source again in v. 6, after the Johannine resumptive phrase **having said these things**. The miracle now follows quickly and it is complete even though very brief. If the Evangelist's insertion of vv. 2–5 has displaced a notice depicting Jesus' approach to the blind man (as has sometime been suggested, since otherwise v. 6 is rather abrupt after v. 1) that omission by 4E would be virtually unique in the Johannine redactional method so far as we can tell from analysis of the other stories.

• The parenthetical explanation in v. 7 ("which means Sent") is redactional, as in 1:38, 41–42; 20:16. So too is the present form of the neighbors' response to the healing (beginning in v. 8); but even this latter just may contain a vestige of the earlier account's ending. The subject in v. 8 is compound—"The neighbors [not previously mentioned] and those who had seen him before as a beggar." As we suggested, perhaps "the neighbors" has been added to set the stage for the division among the spectators in v. 9. But the traditional detail of the man's former way of life is quite possibly pre-Johannine (as we saw, on v. 1); and so perhaps the astonished question in the second half of the verse (like that in the possibly pre-Johannine 6:25) was to be found in the source (**Isn't this the man who used to sit and beg?!**), as confirmation of the healing and implicit confession of what it shows about the healer.

SECTION 9 (5:2–9)
A CRIPPLED MAN WALKS

Pre-Johannine Source

5 ²**In Jerusalem by the Sheep [Gate]**[246] **there is a pool, known as Bethesda in "Hebrew,"**[247] **having five colonnades.** ³**In these there usually were lying a crowd of the sick—blind, lame, paralyzed.** ⁵**Now there was there a certain**

---

245. The view implied by the question is, however, reiterated by "the Jews" in the Johannine v. 34 ("You were born in utter sin").

246. The arguments for and against this interpretation of the ambiguous reading here (the Greek gives only an adjective ["of Sheep"] with no noun) are presented by Lindars, *Gospel of John*, 211–12.

247. NT Greek does not distinguish between the Hebrew and Aramaic languages, but in every case in 4G the latter is clearly meant by the term *Hebraïsti;* see BAGD.

man who had been crippled for thirty-eight years.[248] [6]Jesus saw him lying there and (knowing that he had been there a long time) said to him, "Do you want to be well?" [7]The crippled man answered him, "Sir, I have no one to put me into the pool when the water is flowing; when I am making my way someone else gets in ahead of me." [8]Jesus said to him, "Get up, take up your mat, and walk." [9]And immediately the man was well, and he took up his mat and began to walk.

At first sight this passage, of the seven miracles we have examined, seems the least susceptible of theological interpretation. But a closer look is more rewarding. The story's factuality is striking, by which I mean not its historicity but the attention it gives to circumstantial detail: a specific place in Jerusalem as setting; a habitual gathering place for crowds of invalids, carefully identified and described. With the same focus on the concrete a particular sick man is singled out.[249] Perhaps we are to understand that Jesus heals him as the most needy (**crippled for thirty-eight years**). Even if the middle clause of v. 6 ("knowing that he had been there a long time") is 4E's later addition—and it could as well reflect a pre-Johannine interest—we are hardly to suppose that it was by mere chance that this man is the one healed. Just as elsewhere in SG, however, there is no indication here that compassion is a factor in Jesus' act; his question to the man reflects challenge as much as human concern: **Do you want to be well?** At the same time, we note that unlike the Synoptic healing stories, here a prior question as to the man's faith is entirely missing. If anything he has lost hope; his reply is one of resignation: Of course I want to be healed but it is no use. Nevertheless, Jesus immediately gives the instructing command, and just as immediately the miracle takes place (v. 9a).[250] The man's very act of compliance demonstrates both the healing and his trust in Jesus' word.

Thus, as usual, Jesus dominates the story, both by his initiating the healing and by directing its occurrence. And he heals by his word alone. Display of his power to make the man **well** motivates the story.[251] We should perhaps imagine, therefore, that the original story ended with a

248. B & L suggest that the number is symbolic (perhaps of Israel's years of wandering in the wilderness) and so added by 4E. But this is unlikely, since no attention is called to it, as the Evangelist usually does. Rather, the number seems to be typical of the source's interest in such gratuitous details for their own sake.

249. Curiously, his specific illness is not given; presumably (on the basis of v. 7) he was severely crippled—hence our translation in v. 5. which literally speaks only of his "illness."

250. The statement ("And immediately the man was well") is common in the Synoptics but found only here in SG (but see the presumably instantaneous healing of the official's son, at a distance, in 4:46–54). Elsewhere we infer the miracle from its effect, as we could here too (v. 9b).

251. While the verb "to heal" is not used, the adjective *hygiēs* appears twice—first in Jesus' question (v. 6), then almost unnecessarily in v. 9.

statement to the effect that the man, or witnesses, believed. And even as now without a characterization of Jesus' deed as a sign[252] it is clearly just such a demonstration of Jesus' power and therefore identity.

There is reason to think that this episode was the last of seven signs in the pre-Johannine source (see this part, The Signs in Jerusalem). If so it provides no particular climax in the portrayal of Jesus' self-authenticating miracles, for they all convey the very same thing: he is the Jewish Messiah, and faith in him is virtually demanded by this portrayal. This episode, then, would have led immediately into the source's conclusion (20:30–31a), when these collected miracles constituted a Signs Source in the narrow sense. Later, as I believe, but still prior to the Johannine redaction, that source was combined with an independent passion narrative; then this last sign would have been followed by the so-called culmination of the sign.

Johannine Redaction

5 ¹**After this there was a feast of the Jews, and Jesus went up to Jerusalem.** ²In Jerusalem by the Sheep [Gate] there is a pool, known as Bethesda in "Hebrew," having five colonnades. ³In these there usually were lying a crowd of the sick—blind, lame, paralyzed. ⁵Now there was there a certain man who had been crippled for thirty-eight years. ⁶Jesus saw him lying there and knowing that he had been there a long time said to him, "Do you want to be well?" ⁷The crippled man answered him, "Sir, I have no one to put me into the pool when the water is flowing; when I am making my way someone else gets in ahead of me." ⁸Jesus said to him, "Get up, take up your mat, and walk." ⁹And immediately the man was well, and he took up his mat and began to walk. **Now that day was the sabbath.**

The story itself is almost devoid of internal redaction, possibly totally so. The opening verse, by which the Johannine author sets the stage for the tense drama that will follow the miracle, is as spare an editorial transition as can be imagined: Jesus abruptly goes again **to Jerusalem** for **a feast.** We are reminded of 2:13, but here the feast is not even named. The placing of the story at this point in the Gospel—between two Galilean signs—is arbitrary and must belong to a larger Johannine schema (which we shall explore in part 2.F). Here we note that it is to a feast of **the Jews** that Jesus goes. That stereotypical Johannine phrase will recur several times in the ensuing drama, to identify those who oppose Jesus, even "persecute" and "seek to kill" him.

The Evangelist's redaction begins with the last clause of v. 9. As an afterthought we learn that Jesus has healed on the **sabbath** and thus, as

---

252. Which, if it had been in the pre-Johannine text, 4E will have eliminated here, as at 9:8, so as to go immediately into the ensuing scened drama.

"the Jews" point out to the man who had been healed, his carrying his mat is "unlawful" (v. 10).[253] The man cravenly insists that he is only obeying orders, and so the attention of the inquiry (for that it has become) shifts to the authority of the one who gave these orders. As often in Johannine redaction, Jesus' magisterial words—**Take up your mat and walk**—are twice quoted (vv. 11–12; see also 4:50–53). In a quick succession of scenes Jesus first reveals himself to the man (v. 14), and the man then turns informer on Jesus to the authorities. Consequently they accuse Jesus himself of doing work on the sabbath. Finally, and this is the goal of the redaction, Jesus identifies his work with that of the Father (v. 17), and the basis for a full christological and soteriological debate between Jesus and his opponents is set. Thus has 4E adapted a relatively simple story displaying Jesus' messianic power into an occasion for putting into the mouth of Jesus a definitive judgment on the conflict that surely separates the Johannine community from the orthodoxy of the synagogue that has recently expelled it. A late-first-century issue—Jesus' Equality with the Father—is depicted as arising in the lifetime of Jesus.[254]

Analysis

● Verse 1 ("After this there was a feast of the Jews, and Jesus went up to Jerusalem") is clearly Johannine framework, as, for example, in 2:13; 6:4; and 7:2. The miracle story begins with v. 2, where the stage is set for the healing.[255] Too much has been made of the shift of tenses in vv. 2–5: even with 4E's addition of v. 1 the passage reads smoothly enough.[256] The giving of the place's Semitic name[257] is to be distinguished from the typically Johannine translation into Greek (as, for example, in 9:7).[258]

● On text-critical grounds the legend in vv. 3c–4 ("waiting for the moving of the waters . . ."), which are lacking in the best MSS, are a post-Johannine addition, presumably attempting to explain the ambiguity of v. 7.

● Jesus' **knowing that [the lame man] had been there a long time** in v. 6 could be a Johannine insertion (so Schnackenburg), but it just as likely indicates the supernatural knowledge that SG attributes to Jesus (as, e.g., in 11:11). His taking

---

253. Much as 4E adds again in chap. 9 (vv. 14–16), but there not so centrally to the drama.

254. Here, as in this part, sec. 7, I am in debt to Martyn, *History and Theology.*

255. B & L think the traditional story begins only in v. 5 and that vv. 2–4 stem from the later Johannine redaction. But while the lame man himself does not appear till v. 5, vv. 2–3 are hardly Johannine (see *TGOS*, 49–50; also Duprez, *Dieux guérisseurs*, 134).

256. Punctiliar *ēn* ("there was," that is, on a particular occasion) in vv. 1 and 5; continuous present in v. 2 (indicating an enduring state); and habitual imperfect in v. 3a.

257. Whatever its correct form; the Copper Scroll of Qumran perhaps now adequately resolves the debate in favor of *Bethesda.*

258. The diction is subtly different. The Johannine phrase is "which means . . ." ([*met*]*hermēneuomenos, -etai*), the pre-Johannine "which is called . . ." (*legomenos*). See this part, n. 173. The pre-Johannine phrase reappears in PQ at 19:13 (where, however, the name is given bilingually), 17, 20; 20:16.

the initiative for the healing by his question (v. 6c) is similarly not essential to the basic story, yet reflects an interest of the source (as in 6:5) more than a Johannine one.

● Only in v. 9c (**Now that day was a sabbath**) do we certainly find 4E's hand. The detail sounds traditional enough, but unlike its Synoptic analogues it here has no part in the miracle story proper; it has been added by 4E to introduce the contentious debate between "the Jews" and Jesus that now issues from the healing. As it stands, the first half of chapter 5 comprises a drama of five scenes, leading in v. 19 to an extended discourse by Jesus.[259]

We have now completed analysis of the narratives in the first half of the Gospel that seem most likely to have been based on an earlier source. It is possible that in some form one or two other traditions—that concerning *Nicodemus* in 3:1 and *Peter's confession of Jesus* in 6:67–70[260]—were found in the same source. We have already suggested (this part, end of sec. 7) that the episode of the Samaritan woman (4:4–6, etc.) also stemmed somehow from SQ, in a way and a location no longer discernible. But in each case the pre-Johannine form is not readily lifted out of the present context, and so at the risk of possible incompleteness we omit treatment of them here. (See further, this part, sec. 14, for elements of the passion tradition similarly not susceptible to redaction criticism.)

259. Attridge ("John 7:1–36," 164–66) holds with Bultmann that the whole of 5:2–16 derives from a pre-Johannine source, citing what he takes to be parallels in the Synoptics of healings that contain a scene of controversy with the authorities over Jesus' words and deeds; but in fact in none of the alleged parallels is the controversial detail (here, that is was the sabbath) introduced only after the healing takes place. Attridge goes on convincingly to connect parts of chap. 7 to the Johannine material beginning at 5:9b, but this only means that they belong to the same Johannine stage of these two obviously complex chapters.

260. The phrase "the Holy One of God," and possibly a response from Jesus about "[the] devil," has parallel with the Synoptic accounts. See *TGOS*, 195–96.

117

Jesus' Death and Resurrection

It is possible that the source underlying the narratives of chapters 1—11 was simply an articulated gathering of miracle stories with at most an introduction telling of John the Baptist's testimony and the first disciples' conversion. In that case we have now exhausted those stories, and so we move from narrative material believed to stem from a Signs Source (SQ), in the narrow sense that Bultmann gave the term, to narrative with equal evidence of an underlying source, but a different one, the Passion Source (PQ).[261] Almost certainly the two bodies of material were once separate, as their contrasting genres indicate: a collection of miracle tales on the one hand and a continuous narrative of Jesus' death on the other.[262]

It is my contention that in fact these two sources had been joined together before 4E made use of them.[263] That is, while clearly deriving originally from quite distinct bodies of tradition—gathered together for different reasons, and one or both probably existing for some time as independent works—they were already combined into a single work, a primitive Gospel, by the pre-Johannine author. But this has not always been accepted by critics who otherwise are in some agreement with my source analysis. It will be one of our concerns in excursus A to examine the arguments for and against a pre-Johannine combining of sign and passion sources. (More basically, the question what constitutes a Gospel will also need to be considered there.)

So now we do not assume that we are dealing with the same source as heretofore. In beginning to look at the pre-Johannine account of Jesus' death and what led up to and followed it, we must start over again. So we make no prior assumptions about what might be pre-Johannine here. Rather, we shall look to discover only what is clearly redactional, and

261. This source also was identified by Bultmann in his commentary (p. 637), but so far as I can tell he nowhere gave it this name. In speaking of it in this way we follow D. M. Smith, *Composition,* 44. See Introduction, n. 14.

262. But see p. 136, on the possibility that the redaction of the passion tradition into its pre-Johannine form was impelled by the very existence of SQ.

263. Hence the designation I use: not simply Signs Source (SQ) but Signs Gospel (SG). Haenchen ("Literatur," 303) suggested some years ago that the narrative source of 4E was a Gospel, a kind of "coarsened Mark" (see further, this part, n. 514).

therefore probably Johannine, on the basis of internal contextual evidence.[264] But there is one difference: we can also now use as basis the Johannine characteristics already known.

The contacts in 4E's passion story with the Synoptic Gospels are well known, and so it will be useful as we go along to note the major similarities and differences among these accounts. Here again it appears plain that the parallels are not to be explained as the result of Johannine literary dependence on one or more of these Gospels—there is no evidence of Synoptic redactional elements in 4E's version of the passion story—but stem rather from the use of common tradition. But since it is likely that the author of Mark made use of an already existing passion source, and possible that the Lukan writer had at hand another such source, it will also be helpful from time to time to compare those sources with the corresponding pre-Johannine one.

Finally, we shall also be looking along the way for evidence that might emerge and bear on the question of an integrated narrative source underlying 4G—for example, is the christology in the pre-Johannine passion material like that in the signs or not? what of the role of the disciples? and so forth.

The Culmination of the Signs

As 4G now stands, it is only from the arrest of Jesus at the beginning of chapter 18 that the traditional account of his passion runs without major interruption. The arrest is now preceded by the long Farewell Discourse of chapters 14—17, on general consensus an almost wholly Johannine construct. But those chapters, whatever their background in the tradition, have clearly been inserted into a traditional narrative setting which, much as they overshadow it by their bulk, remains evident in chapter 13, namely, into the story of the Last Supper. In addition, two episodes in chapter 12, the Anointing of Jesus in Bethany and his Entry into Jerusalem, belong to the passion tradition as well. Further, the accounts of the Sanhedrin's Conspiracy against Jesus (at the end of chap. 11, now as sequel to the raising of Lazarus) and the Restoring of the Temple, though radically displaced by the Evangelist to chapter 2, are usually and properly regarded as part of the same tradition.

Thus, both on internal grounds and by analogy with the other Gospels it is evident that the passion story does not start only in chapter 18. So we begin with the stories belonging to what Dodd (*Tradition*) has usefully

---

264. The same care was in fact taken in the source analysis published in *TGOS*. Some supposed that there I set out hoping to find a single pre-Johannine source with both signs and passion, but in fact the evident integrity of the two bodies of material was an unexpected discovery.

named the Prelude to the Passion. The two (or really three) narratives we consider under the above heading belong to this loose collection of stories, along with the Anointing, the Entry, and the Last Supper. But in the pre-Johannine editorial use of this material, as it becomes part of PQ (and quite possibly of SG, the combined source used by 4E) these two have the function of joining signs and passion, due to the role played by the "Explanation" now found at 12:37–40. They thus are taken up into the signs material, in one sense, with backward reference—both have to do with Jesus' signs (2:18; 11:47c)—and become as much its climax as the beginning of the passion story. Hence the title (The Culmination of the Signs) given to this first subdivision of the passion material.

But before examining the first of them, a word about the term "passion." In using it we do not imply any particular interpretation of Jesus' death, especially as sacrificial or atoning, but mean it only as a familiar designation of the events surrounding his death. It will be our task to try to see how both the pre-Johannine and the Johannine authors understood that death; but that it involved Jesus' suffering (the basic sense of "passion") is obvious, so we can use the term with no more than that connotation.

SECTION 10 (2:14–19)
JESUS RESTORES THE TEMPLE

Virtually all scholars[265] accept that at the pre-Johannine level this story was not among the early signs, as it now appears in 4G, but stems from the passion tradition, perhaps at its beginning.

Pre-Johannine Source

2 14And in the Temple he found sellers of oxen and sheep and doves, and money-changers sitting at their business. 15And making a whip of cords he threw them all out of the Temple—the sheep and the oxen—and he poured out the coins of the money-changers and overturned their tables, 16and to those who sold the doves he said, "Take these things out of here. Do not make (my Father's) house a place of business." (17For [or As] it is written, "Zeal for your house will consume me.")[266] 18And (they)[267] said to him,

---

265. Except for those who defend the historicity of this dating, either holding that Jesus twice cleansed the Temple, accepting the Synoptic dating as also accurate, or rejecting the latter and treating "John's" report as the correct one. In both cases the data are being used, I maintain, for purposes they cannot support.

266. It is not at once obvious whether it is Jesus who here cites scripture—as the use of the first-person singular might suggest—or the author, as in 12:14 and 19:24, 28, 36. But in view of the tension with the preceding verse and the citation of scripture elsewhere in PQ it is likely that the quotation is the author's comment, as the punctuation shown expresses.

267. The Evangelist's insertion of "the Jews" here may have displaced a naming of Jewish authorities such as variously appear in the Synoptics. Alternatively, the subject of the verb is implied, as suggested here, simply indicating those directly affected by Jesus' actions.

"What sign do you show us for doing these things?" [19]Jesus answered and said to them, "Destroy this sanctuary, and in three days I shall raise it up."

This story, told with few details in Mark and more sparingly still in Matthew and Luke, finds denser form in this version. Only here are we told of **oxen and sheep**, Jesus' use of a **whip**, and that he **poured out the coins**. The still brief account (essentially vv. 14–16) is yet almost overloaded and, if read too closely, illogical. But this seems due not to redaction but to the evident urgency of the storyteller to include as much in small compass as possible. Thus, Jesus' words in v. 16 clearly apply to all and not only to the pigeon-sellers, as strictly they appear to; similarly **threw them all out** (v. 15) includes as object more than the sheep and oxen. And the word for money-changers in v. 14 shifts, probably only to provide variety in the next verse,[268] and not because of harmonization with the Synoptics.[269]

The effect is one of intensity, and it culminates in the authoritative command of Jesus: **Do not make [this] house a place of business.** This echoes the loosely messianic prophecy in Zech. 14:21 ("There shall no longer be a trader [lit., Canaanite] in the house of the Lord of hosts on that day").[270] There is a hint of christology also in the phrase **my Father,** if it stems from the source.[271] The act itself hints at least of christological meaning: Jesus as the Messiah, who comes in culminating judgment to purify the Temple. But the effect given so far is mainly one of prophetic criticism.

Everything so far pertains to vv. 14–16, which seem to have come directly to the pre-Johannine author from tradition. But in v. 17, while the theme of prophecy persists, a new dimension appears, no doubt the contribution of the source's author; hence I take the verse not as a continuation of Jesus' words in v. 16, as it could be construed—Jesus himself giving scriptural basis for his act—but as an editorial comment on what has gone before. Jesus' action in the Temple is to be seen as not only a prophetic action in itself but now also a *fulfillment of prophecy;* he did these

268. From *kermatistēs* to the synonymous term *kollybistēs* in v. 15, whose *kerma* Jesus pours out.

269. We find only such parallels between this Gospel and the other accounts as might be expected in two versions of the same tradition: "in the Temple," "drove out those who sold," "overturned [but using a different verb] the tables of the money-changers," "those who sold doves." In most cases these similarities appear alongside the kind of variations that are to be expected in diverging oral tradition.

270. Compare and contrast the Synoptic use of Jer. 7:11 ("robbers' den") and Isa. 56:7 ("a house of prayer for the nations"), the one phrase more radical than 4G in its criticism, the other more idyllic in its vision of the future Temple.

271. This wording, though not found in Zechariah, is very possibly traditional, as frequently in Matthew and Luke (esp. 2:49). It has a kind of Johannine ring, but 4E's more usual phrase is absolute: "the Father." See further, this part, sec. 15, Analysis, on 18:11c.

things in accordance with what **is written**. The event is part of a larger purpose, and as always such a biblical citation conveys a messianic claim.

But the prophecy cited (from one of the so-called Passion Psalms, 69) says still more, for it points to Jesus' approaching death. (All of the notices of prophecy fulfillment have to do with that.) The alteration of the psalm's perfect tense ("Zeal for thy house has consumed me") to future here makes this clear. The very act, then, by which Jesus asserts his prophetic and messianic authority (his **zeal** for God's **house**) will lead also to his own destruction. The play on the word **consume** is most skillful: Jesus is "absorbed" in a compelling mission—and in the process will be "devoured" by it.[272]

We come, then, to the reaction to Jesus' deed (v. 18) whether on the part of those driven out of the Temple (as an indefinite "they" would suggest) or on the part of religious authorities (specified as in the Synoptics). Presumably it takes the form of a reasonable demand that Jesus justify his action: **What sign do you show us for doing these things?** The tone may be angry, but the insistence is understandable in view of Jesus' provocative, even scandalous act.[273] The witnesses to the Cleansing of the Temple want only evidence of Jesus' right to do these things (see also Mark 11:28).

But the source has now another sign in mind, and the greatest one. Building on the prophecy of Jesus' death implied in v. 17 (**will consume me**), the pre-Johannine author uses for Jesus' answer to the request a traditional and surely independent logion associated with the Temple: **Destroy this sanctuary and in three days I shall raise it up** (v. 19).[274]

This gives an altogether new dimension to the story. For the pre-Johannine author, while alluding to the Temple that Jesus has just cleansed, the saying clearly speaks of another "sanctuary." The logion uses a different noun in Greek, and so by a wordplay Jesus can now be understood to speak of his own body. The sign promised in response to the request, then, will be his own *resurrection*—the **three days** make this clear. He will accomplish this himself (**I shall raise it up**); otherwise it would not be a sign that he would **show**. In this document, then, as in no other

272. On this use of OT "testimony" see further part 2.D (Source, 1).

273. If this passage marks the continuation of a Signs *Gospel* and possibly the very transition from miracles to passion, nevertheless the meaning of **sign** here (as legitimation) is somewhat different from its use in the miracle stories (as messianic proclamation) and this difference presumably reflects the distinct traditions originally lying behind the signs and the passion materials respectively. Even if Jesus has already clearly shown his messianic authority in the miracles, his new stance as reformer of the Temple raises the question of his legitimation.

274. The Synoptic version of this saying, used in a different context (the hearing before the high priest: Mark 14:58 par.) and alluded to elsewhere (Mark 15:29; Acts 6:14), is: "I will destroy this sanctuary . . . and in three days I will build another. . . ." There Jesus is depicted as claiming to be the destroyer and replacer of the Temple (*allon . . . oikodomein*); here he promises to restore (*egeirein*) what others destroy.

122

known to us,[275] Jesus' resurrection becomes his own act, a sign he performs, and his greatest one, consummating his entire work.

The theological consequences of this scene can hardly be overstated. It tells us that Jesus' authority, his messianic self-presentation, has yet to be shown in its greatest extent. We shall see who Jesus is only in the event that crowns the passion narrative. While the demand for a sign is thus met only with the promise of a future event, it is nevertheless met, in contrast to the Synoptic traditions paralleling this theme.[276] In this way the author has transformed the tradition, in which the demand for a sign and even the term "sign" itself are viewed in a way that is wholly illegitimate. Here, by contrast, the demand is taken as appropriate, and the concept of sign becomes a culmination of the whole of PQ and possibly of a combined SG: the resurrection that brings the story to a close is not simply God's act, vindicating his Messiah, but the greatest deed of the Messiah himself. In that fullest sense it is a sign, *the* sign.

In the source, then, the episode is more than a Restoration of the Temple; it is also, and chiefly, a forewarning and a foretaste of what lies ahead. The death of Jesus is something done by humans to Jesus (**Destroy this sanctuary** . . .);[277] to that Jesus' climactic self-resurrection will be his messianic response. Thus, for the pre-Johannine author, Jesus appears still more magisterial here than in the Synoptics (so Richter, *Studien*, 286) and in this respect moves in the direction of the otherworldliness of the Johannine Jesus.

On the level of developing plot this event, as the prophecy cited in verse 17 suggests, will be the cause of Jesus' downfall. It is thus likely that in the source it was this deed that immediately provoked the decision of the Jerusalem authorities to put Jesus to death (11:47–53). But then what preceded this episode? If we are dealing with a PQ in the strict sense, the logic of geography would seem to dictate that Jesus' Entry into Jerusalem (12:12–15) come before this Temple scene, as variously in the Synoptics.[278] But since as it stands that story can hardly have initiated an independent and extensive account of the passion,[279] the Anointing at

275. Here, uniquely in the NT, is the active voice with Jesus as subject employed of the resurrection, which even the occasional intransitive ("rise") in a few places elsewhere in the NT does not rival. The Evangelist borrows this idea in 10:17–18: "I lay down my life that I may take it again. . . . I have power to take it again."

276. E.g., "No sign shall be given to this generation" (Mark 8:12).

277. The force of the imperative ("Destroy . . .") could be conditional: If you destroy . . .; but in the context it seems to be more affirmative: When you destroy this sanctuary (or even Since you will destroy . . .) I will raise it up.

278. Mark's rather more tortured itinerary for Jesus on the days surrounding this event is evidently the byproduct of his redaction, and not traditional. See this part, sec. 13, Analysis.

279. It begins: "The next day a great crowd heard that Jesus was coming. . . ." Even if the time reference is not original, some other introduction to the story than this is needed.

Bethany (12:1–8) may have originally preceded it. Even now the anointing story is sonorously introduced in a way that might have once opened a passion narrative: "Now six days before the Passover, Jesus went to Bethany. . . ." We can imagine, then, that at an earlier point in the development of this connected narrative the order was as follows: Anointing, Entry, Temple Restoration, Conspiracy, Last Supper.[280]

But when the passion story is joined to the signs (and whether by 4E or the predecessor) Jesus was already in Jerusalem, at the end of those miracles. Thus, an arrival at Bethany, such as we find in 12:1 (in Mark the same notice serves to bring Jesus to the city's vicinity for the first time), would be superfluous.[281] Furthermore, after the stunning and untroubled sequence of messianic self-disclosures that the signs comprise, there is need of an event preparing for and explaining the sudden rise of the official opposition to Jesus that so quickly would destroy him. It is thus conceivable that such an editor, in putting signs and passion alongside each other, would lift out the Temple Restoration, which as we saw contains a foreordination of Jesus' destruction (2:17), and the officials' subsequent plot and put them at the juncture between the two collected narratives, signs and passion. In that case the order that we are pursuing—that of these events as they now appear somewhat scattered in 4G—happens to follow that of the earlier SG:

Temple Restoration
Officials' Conspiracy
Anointing
Entry into Jerusalem
Supper

This order is far from certain, but we can note how well the Temple Restoration would serve as transition from signs to passion. It shows Jesus in a new role, a provocative one that understandably raises opposition; the self-disclosing Messiah appears but now also challenges and offends. At the same time the story prepares for what is to follow both by predicting its outcome, and even the necessity of it, and by promising—as a culminating sign—the resolution to the theologically unacceptable death of the Messiah.

Johannine Redaction

2 [13]**And the Passover of the Jews was near, and Jesus went up to Jerusalem.** [14]And in the Temple he found sellers of oxen and sheep and doves, and money-changers sitting at their business. [15]And making a whip of cords he threw them all out of the Temple—the sheep and the oxen—and he poured

---

280. On the Anointing, see further this part, sec. 12.

281. Even if, as we posit, the concluding sign was not the raising of Lazarus in Bethany itself.

out the coins of the money-changers and overturned their tables, [16]and to those who sold the doves he said, "Take these things out of here. Do not make my Father's house a place of business." [17]**His disciples remembered** *that* it is written, "Zeal for your house will consume me." [18]And **the Jews** said to him, "What sign do you show us for doing these things?" [19]Jesus answered and said to them, "Destroy this sanctuary, and in three days I shall raise it up." [Vv. 20–22]

The Evangelist has more drastically altered the original setting of this passage, whether it comes from an integrated SG or a separate PQ, than any of the miracle stories (with the exception—if chap. 21 is Johannine— of the catch of fish). What appears to have been its original association with the passion story, and perhaps its position as the opening episode, is now held, in 4E's reordering, by the Lazarus story, and this event in the Temple has been brought all the way forward to chapter 2; there it abruptly follows the first miracle in Galilee—and presumably is meant both to parallel and contrast with it. This rearrangement necessarily entails that Jesus go **up to Jerusalem** from Cana (v. 13), with the hastily mentioned motivating explanation that **the Passover of the Jews was at hand,** the first of several Johannine notices of Jewish feasts. After the miracle at Cana, which in 4E's hands contains the symbolism of Christianity replacing Judaism, this act of Jesus in the Temple at Passover time becomes all the more dramatic: he purifies the very center of the Jewish cultus at one of the most solemn moments in its liturgical year, and this he does as the very first of his acts in Jerusalem.

Similarly **the Jews** are shown in a negative light. It is they who now insist on a sign from Jesus (v. 18a). What was a not inappropriate demand in the source becomes most inappropriate here. For in 4E's eyes, as will be implied in 2:23, the Temple Restoration itself is a sign (a Judean counter-part to the one at Cana, now just before it); so to ask no sooner than it is done what sign Jesus can do is to fail altogether to understand what he has just done. The theme of misunderstanding informs also their response in v. 20 (wholly 4E's addition) to the saying about the sanctuary in v. 19; taking Jesus' promise to "raise it up again" literally, **the Jews then said to him, "This Temple took forty-six years to build . . . ."**[282] So 4E explains, pointing up the misunderstanding: **but he spoke of the sanctuary of his body** (v. 21); this only makes explicit the saying's meaning in the source, where it presumably had been taken to be correctly understood by Jesus' hearers.

As foil to the Jewish failure to perceive, 4E twice introduces **the disciples.** In v. 17a we hear that they **remembered** (presumably at that very

---

282. The origin of this remark is obscure and its accuracy, or even meaning, difficult to estimate. See, for example, Lindars's commentary, *Gospel of John,* 143.

time) the prophecy in Psalm 69. The relation of this notice to what surrounds it is awkward and unclear, but coming just before the first insertion of *hoi Ioudaioi* the mention of the disciples points a contrast between their own perception and the Jewish failure to perceive.

There may be a future reference as well, to judge by the second and longer mention of the disciples' remembering (v. 22ab): **Now when he had been raised**[283] **from the dead his disciples remembered that he had said this.** ... In sharp distinction with the presumably permanent failure of "the Jews" to understand Jesus' saying (that it had to do with the resurrection) the followers of Jesus, who had so recently come to believe on the basis of the miracle at Cana, are before long to be led to further faith and understanding: **Now when he had been raised from the dead ... they believed the scripture and the word Jesus had spoken** (v. 22ac). Note here how Jesus' **word** (v. 19) is placed on a par with holy writ, presumably with the particular prophecy they had **remembered** in v. 17 but perhaps with the scriptures generally as well. And whereas they evidently had no more understanding than "the Jews," they are given the benefit of a delay in time and the new perspective provided by the resurrection; no such advantage accrues to "the Jews."

Thus does 4E transform the theme of resurrection found already in the source. What was there a future, culminating sign now becomes for the reader almost a present fact; or, put differently, the time of the resurrection is read back into that of the Temple Restoration at the start of Jesus' public activity. And the sign given is no longer only the eventual resurrection, but Jesus' act in the Temple itself. All of this is portrayed against the contrast between uncomprehending "Jews" and perceiving disciples. This Sign for the Jews in Jerusalem, then, contrasts with that given just prior to it for the disciples in Cana. Furthermore, it becomes for the reader an actualization of the goal of Jesus' ministry; at almost its beginning, his necessary death is in view.[284]

Analysis

Except for those who would defend the historicity of an early date in Jesus' career for the Temple Restoration it is generally agreed that 4E's placing of this story in chapter 2 is artificial and that in the tradition it was closely associated with the events that led up to Jesus' death.

• Verse 13, abruptly taking Jesus from Galilee back to the south (much as 1:43 accomplished a shift in the opposite direction, and precisely the way 5:1 will bring Jesus suddenly to Jerusalem), seems obviously to belong to the series of Johannine redactional notices that form a geographical schema quite distinctive of this Gospel

283. Note 4E's use of the passive voice, the usual way of describing the resurrection in the NT, in contrast to the striking active ("I shall raise it up") in the source. See this part, n. 275.

284. This was already hinted at in Jesus' speaking to his mother of his "hour" that was still to come (2:4).

(see also 6:4; 11:55; etc.). Whether it has displaced a notice of Jesus' whereabouts in the source will depend on the question what if anything originally preceded it (see pp. 123–24). But the opening of v. 14 adequately locates the story: **in the Temple.**

● Some have found in vv. 15 and 16 tensions with the rest of the brief story,[285] but they seem to me overly subtle, reflecting not redaction but only the idiosyncrasies of this account.

● Verse 17, which breaks the flow of the story, is clearly editorial, containing the Johannine theme of the disciples' remembering (again in v. 22 and 12:16) and interpreting the foregoing event in the light of scripture. But the element of scriptural fulfillment is common in PQ,[286] and very likely the verse, without the opening phrase (**his disciples remembered**), is a pre-Johannine comment. In that case it either began with the present *hoti*, meaning "for" rather than "that," or an original "as" (*kathōs*) has been displaced by 4E's addition of the disciples' remembering.[287] The outright quotation of Ps. 69:9 here stands in slight tension with the saying of Jesus in v. 16, with its mere allusion to Zech. 14:21c, and some have therefore attributed v. 17 entirely to Johannine insertion. It seems more likely that the tension is due to pre-Johannine redaction.

● The question to Jesus in v. 18 and his saying on the Temple by way of reply in v. 19 are not part of the Temple Cleansing episode in the Synoptics, and so the question arises whether it is 4E who has combined these traditions. But in Mark the material separating the question (11:27–28) from the Cleansing (11:15–17) appears to be redactional, so that 4E's tradition very likely contained both Jesus' act and the question then understandably put to him. His reply in v. 19 was in some form undoubtedly once an independent logion, but the question demands an answer and so the combination with the Restoration story seems to be pre-Johannine.

● That it is **the Jews** in v. 18 who ask for a sign is Johannine, but their question is evidently from the source.[288]

285. B & L, following Bultmann. They point, e.g., to the fact that the word for "money-changer" in v. 15, different from that in v. 14, is the one used in Mark and Matthew, and posit harmonization with the Synoptics at some point or other. Direct dependence by 4E on the Synoptics in this story has been asserted by Selong, "Jn 2, 13–22." But as appears in the exegesis of the source, there is insufficient basis for these judgments.

286. In the so-called Triumphal Entry, with much the same diction as here ("as it is written"—12:14–15), and in the execution of Jesus, with a heightened formula that more urgently connects scriptural preparation and fulfillment in the events of the passion ("so that the scripture might be fulfilled"—19:24, 28, 36). The variation in this formula, as between its simpler form used twice in the "prelude"—Temple Restoration here and Entry—and the heightened form in chap. 19, is perhaps due to an originally distinct provenance of the stories constituting the prelude on the one hand and the passion account proper on the other. The simple form appears also in the source at 1:23 and is seven times imitated by 4E in the first half of the Gospel (6:31, 45; 8:17; 10:34; 12:16; see also 7:38, 42). The fuller form is used by 4E at 15:25 and 17:12 and probably it is Johannine also at 13:18.

287. Just this use of *hoti* occurs also at 12:16 when 4E there refers to the source's phrase "as it is written" two verses earlier.

288. On the analogy of the authorities' question in the Synoptic sequels to this story ("By what authority do you do these things [*tauta poieis*]?") and because the request for Jesus to "show" a sign also has Synoptic parallel (Matt. 16:1), we can suppose that something of that

127

• The change of word for Temple in Jesus' reply in v. 19 is not necessarily an indication of 4E's hand. *Naos* may refer more narrowly to the Temple sanctuary itself, in distinction to the wider precincts *(hieron)* in vv. 14–15 (so Brown). In any case Jesus' words seem to be a saying introduced by the source's author.

SECTION 11 (11:47–53, 12:37–40)
THE OFFICIALS' CONSPIRACY
AND ITS THEOLOGICAL EXPLANATION

(Until now we have left open the question of a combined SG, and we shall again in secs. 12–20. But these two episodes can only be understood, I hold, if they were part of such a joining of SQ and PQ prior to 4E's redaction. So here we assume the conclusion reached in excursus A.2.)

Pre-Johannine Source

In 4G, far more than in the Synoptic Gospels, we hear often of the intent of the religious authorities in Jerusalem to seek Jesus' death, and usually in 4E's summary (e.g., 5:18; 7:1, 25; 10:31). But this passage, by its length and literary complexity, appears to contain the tradition, unique in the Gospels, actually recounting the scene. It now awkwardly follows the raising of Lazarus, and evidently due to the Evangelist's arrangement. It probably provided the original sequel to the Restoration in the Temple at the beginning of PQ.

11 [47ac]So the chief priests assembled the Sanhedrin and they said, "This man does many signs. [48]If we leave him alone in this all will believe in him and the Romans will come and destroy our nation." [49ab]Now one of them, Caiaphas, who was high priest that year, said to them, [50bc]"It is expedient (for us)[289] that one man die instead of the people lest the whole nation perish." [53]So from that day they formally determined to put him to death.

As part of the introduction to an independent PQ this plot by the Sanhedrin carries its own justification (mistaken, of course, from the standpoint of the traditioners of Jesus' passion): by restoring the Temple and performing "many signs," Jesus has threatened the authorities' standing and perhaps Jewish survival itself. But when passion is joined to Signs Source—that is, when the theological problem of Jesus' death is addressed, and specifically its conflict with the view in the signs stories that faith in Jesus is inevitable for those who witness the signs—then a definitive explanation for the officials' rejection of Jesus, their *failure* to believe in his signs, is needed by the reader. This 12:37–40 provides (see Analysis, Explanation, in this section).

---

sort was to be found here in the source, and very possibly just the wording we have. (In that case the similarities in the Johannine 6:30 suggest that there this pre-Johannine usage has been imitated by 4E.)

289. Some MSS read "for you" here and some omit any such phrase.

12 37Although he had done so many signs they would not believe in him
38—so that the word of Isaiah the prophet might be fulfilled, when he said:
"Lord, who has believed our report, and to whom has the arm of the Lord
been revealed?" 39Therefore they could not believe, for again Isaiah said:
40"He has blinded their eyes and hardened their heart, lest they see with
their eyes and know with their heart and turn, and I heal them."

Conspiracy

The gist of the first account (11:47–53) is that **the Sanhedrin** meets and
on the advice of the **high priest Caiaphas** conspires to have Jesus killed.
The vexed historical question whether the Jewish authorities (here the
initiative is the **chief priests'**) in fact had the legal capability to carry out
the death sentence themselves is beside the point. Accurately or not, what
is asserted by the pre-Johannine community is that the members of the
Sanhedrin (though not, of course, "the Jews" generally or even the Pharisees, as later in 4G) were deliberately responsible for Jesus' execution;
they **formally determined to put him to death.** The stage is thus set for
the passion to follow.

The impression the author wants to give about how and why Jesus'
death was agreed upon is clear. It is Jesus' **many signs**[290] and the response
they elicit from the people that must be stopped: the Baptist's mission,
that all might believe (in Jesus) (1:7c), is in process of realization. In
voicing their fear the Sanhedrin unwittingly bears testimony to Jesus' wide
reception.

The motive for putting an end to Jesus' activity is thus at base in no way
political; with the popular recognition of Jesus as Messiah (such an interpretation of the signs is not stated here but implied) it is the religious
authority of the Jewish leaders that is threatened.[291] Yet this is rather
different from the religious objections to Jesus in 4E's later situation (see
this section, Johannine Redaction).

But, of course, under Rome even the priestly religious authority had
political connotations. It was charged with maintaining the peace. And any
popular movement under a widely acclaimed leader—such as the
Sanhedrin imagines about to emerge from Jesus' miracle-working activity,
indeed his performing of messianic **signs**—is politically dangerous as well.
For then **the Romans** [might] **come and destroy** [the Jewish] **nation,** such
as it was under this most recent of the foreign empires successively ruling
the Palestinian Jews. The "nation" here means literally an ethnic identity,

290. While it is usually 4E who speaks of signs in the plural, we find this phrase at one
other point in the source (20:30). A generalizing summary here too, originally at the introduction to PQ, would be most appropriate. See also 12:37.

291. In the miracle stories a political understanding of messiahship is equally missing;
there is only the theological interest in demonstrating that Jesus is the one to be called
Messiah.

not any fully political expression. But what had happened to Israel under the Assyrians and was almost accomplished against Judah, first by Babylon and then Syria—namely, not so much political defeat as genocide, the disappearance of a people—could happen again. This expectation would not actually be fulfilled in the catastrophe of the year 70, nor even 135, but in the mid-first century it was a real enough fear.

Caiaphas, who as **high priest that year** was most directly answerable to Rome, is clever. It is the popular acclamation of Jesus that is the real threat to the Sanhedrin, but one cannot punish or suppress that. In any case, it is Jesus whom the authorities, or some of them, need to dispose of. So without raising the question of Jesus' legitimacy (or at least explicitly rejecting it, as in the later Johannine portrayal of the Jewish leaders) Caiaphas simply builds on the fear of his colleagues, suggesting, as the only wise and fair move, and thus ensuring that the national disaster they have envisaged does not occur: **It is expedient for us that one man die instead of the people** (who can argue with that?) **and the whole nation not perish.**

There is no suggestion of soteriology, no hint that Jesus dies on behalf of the people, and certainly not for their sins, but only that he, after all the cause of the trouble, be sacrificed to protect the nation's future. He will die **instead of the people.**[292] It is a simple matter of survival. **So from that day**—the day, presumably, on which Jesus purified the Temple[293]—**they formally determined to put him to death** (lit., "they took counsel to kill him").

Explanation

The Sanhedrin knew that Jesus **had done . . . many signs** (see 11:47c), but their action showed clearly that nevertheless **they would not believe in him.** The author has simply to state that fact, in a summary very close in style to 20:30–31a which had originally ended SQ (it later became the conclusion to SG, the combined account of signs and passion). This is accomplished by v. 37 (less only the phrase "in their presence").

But the fact must be explained, and the method to be used at several points in the passion account is first applied here (v. 38). The OT prepared for this circumstance, and thus made it both inevitable and understandable. Isaiah had experienced the same problem as the pre-Johannine author. Why have none, he plaintively asked, **believed our report?** to any of them **has the arm of the Lord been revealed?** (v. 38b = Isa. 53:1). And this cry on his part is of course no longer remembered for its own sake, in the context of eighth-century Israel, but is seen instead as explaining the

292. The preposition *hyper* has only this meaning here; see further, Johannine Redaction, for the Johannine sense.
293. Hence the same connective ("So") also in v. 47.

conspiracy against Jesus' life, despite his self-demonstration as Messiah. It was **so that the word of the prophet Isaiah might be fulfilled** (v. 38a). This concept, like the citation formulas in the passion account, both *explains* the officials' decision to put Jesus to death and *requires* it: (a) It expresses the divine necessity as the reason for the otherwise inexplicable failure of the Sanhedrin to believe. And (b) the conspiracy against Jesus was made in order—one might say only in order—to complete what had been foreordained. In the next verse (39a) the author repeats and paraphrases: **It was for this reason** [*dia touto*] **that they** *could not* **believe.** What seemed a deplorable, a tragic fault in the Sanhedrin becomes instead their unwitting working out of God's will; their decision is not really their own at all, though no exoneration is thereby implied.

Then a second prophecy is cited, just as at the climax of the passion narrative itself (19:37) and in almost the same way: **And again Isaiah said** (v. 39b). The passage used is one found at a number of points in early Christian tradition,[294] the prophecy of the "hardening of hearts" (Isa. 6:10). Once more it explains that "they" (here, that is, the members of the Sanhedrin) were *prevented* from believing; their eyes were blinded and their heart hardened **in order that they not see with their eyes and perceive with their heart and turn and** [God] **heal them** (v. 40). What has now transpired, just as what will quickly follow, is theologically tolerable—because it had to occur.

This passage, then, originally formed the bridge between signs and passion. It comes just after the beginning of the passion material, that is, after Jesus' provocative act in the Temple and the Sanhedrin's response. These events explained the death of Jesus at the beginning of the earlier form of the passion tradition, when it was independent of the signs. But now Restoration and Conspiracy have become the culmination of the signs (which are mentioned in both passages), and only here does the passion fully begin. The tension between the success of the signs (even the Temple Cleansing is seen in that way) and the final apparent failure of Jesus' career, signaled first of all by the Conspiracy, must be accounted for. After two or three further messianic events (the Anointing at Bethany, the Entry into Jerusalem, and perhaps the Last Supper), the death plot's unfolding begins in Jesus' Arrest.

Johannine Redaction

11 **47***Then* the chief priests **and the Pharisees** assembled the Sanhedrin and they said, **"What are we to do?** *For*[295] this man does many signs. **48**If we leave

---

294. See this part, n. 308. In wording it is considerably different, and presumably altered, from both the Masoretic Text and the Septuagint.

295. This conjunction (*hoti*) can have several quite different functions; it was originally only the indication of a direct quotation, as also in v. 50 where now it means "that."

him alone in this all will believe in him and the Romans will come and destroy **both our [Holy] Place and** our nation." [49]Now one of them, Caiaphas, who was high priest that year, said to them, **"You know nothing at all, [50]nor do you understand** *that*[296] it is expedient (for us) that one man die instead of the people, lest the whole nation perish." [51]**He said this not of his own accord, but being high priest that year he prophesied that Jesus would die on behalf of the nation. [52]And not on behalf of the nation alone but in order to congregate the dispersed children of God into one.** [53]*Now* from that day they formally determined to put him to death.

(Since the Evangelist makes only one redactional change within the text of 12:37–40—inserting the phrase "in their presence" in v. 37—and adds a single comment at its end, we need not reprint the text here. See p. 129.)

Conspiracy

Whether 4E here takes up again a discrete PQ, not used since chapter 2, or—more likely, I would hold—continues to rely on a source that contained both signs and passion, the original order of events is now considerably rearranged: It is the raising of Lazarus that causes the Sanhedrin to act, and the Temple Restoring has been put to different use. This placing of the account of the Conspiracy as the immediate sequel to the Lazarus episode tells us primarily about 4E's understanding of the latter—it is Jesus' greatest miracle, the one that epitomizes his "many signs" and so his greatest offense to the authorities. But the rearrangement also transforms the effect of the present story. At last the *religious* threat that Jesus has posed repeatedly throughout the first half of the Johannine Gospel comes to a head; the authorities fear that "all will believe in him," as is shown happening already in the source and in the present Gospel in consequence of the raising of Lazarus. Any political relevance is now secondary—it has become meaningless from the vantage point of 4E's time near the end of the first century; after the catastrophe of the year 70, the anxiety that "the Romans will come and destroy **our [Holy] place**"[297] is now only ironic, yet it shows that in some sense the Sanhedrin was correct in its fear.

That the religious dimension is uppermost for 4E is apparent also in the introduction of **the Pharisees** (v. 47), anachronistically, as party to the official council. In the time of Jesus they would have had, as a group, no role in the Sanhedrin, whereas in 4E's time they represent perhaps the only Jewish leadership that survived the revolt against Rome. It is to the Pharisees, then, that some of the witnesses of Lazarus's raising now report (v. 46), thereby now setting in motion the convoking of the Sanhedrin. As usual they here represent the enemies of Jesus who yet are baffled by him

296. See the preceding note.

297. "The nation" survived in a sense—but see below on v. 51—so 4E adds this phrase, in a "both . . . and" construction, to retain a kind of accuracy.

(**What are we to do?**) and who wholly lack wisdom, as even their own leader Caiaphas declares: **You know nothing at all, nor do you understand** (vv. 49c–50a).[298]

The major Johannine change in the story, apart from the new setting as sequel to Temple Restoration, is the commentary (vv. 51–52) added to Caiaphas's word of advice. If the Sanhedrin unwittingly testifies to Jesus, as already in the source ("this man performs many signs"), even more does Caiaphas become a witness, indeed a prophet, of Jesus' death and the effect it will have. And Caiaphas too, it is emphasized, is unaware of what he says; no credit for the truth he utters is to be accorded him: **He said this not on his own part but being high priest that year he prophesied;** he is only a channel of divine inspiration.

As v. 51 understands Caiaphas's word, his "prophecy" introduces a new dimension. Beyond the political expediency of the saying and even the religious concern of 4E's Pharisees, Jesus' death here gains a theological significance—that he will **die for the nation;** and here "for" at last means clearly "on behalf of." (As intervening events had shown, any original hope that Jesus' death "instead of the nation" would avert an open conflict with Rome had proved to be in vain. True, the nation, or part of it, had survived; hence—as we just saw—4E's insertion of "both our [Holy] Place and." But the national protection hoped for by the Sanhedrin had not obtained.) The Johannine view of Jesus' death is not fundamentally salvific but rather revelatory (see part 2.D), but there is the hint of the former element, both here and in the addition of the phrase "who takes away the sins of the world" to the traditional Lamb of God title (1:29; see this part, sec. 1).

Verse 52 in turn goes beyond v. 51 as a further extension of the Johannine commentary on Caiaphas's advice. And in view of its clear resonance with two other important Johannine passages (10:16 ["other sheep . . . not of this fold"] and 17:21 ["that they all may be one"]) it adds a dimension that is of some importance to 4E. The death of Jesus is thus not so much sacrificial (**on behalf of the nation**) as in a broad and non-institutional way ecclesiological: Jesus died **not for the nation only** (and perhaps not ultimately for that purpose at all) **but to congregate the dispersed children of God into one.** Wholly without knowing it the Sanhedrin and Caiaphas interpret for us the meaning of the death they are bringing about as a constituting of the Christian church. (See p. 135.)

Quite remarkably, then, the story of the Conspiracy climaxes the official opposition to Jesus that now runs through the public ministry of Jesus in 4E's portrayal—beginning with the Baptist's testimony in chapter 1 and

---

298. It is not the Pharisees as such who are so characterized by Caiaphas, but the whole council; yet their inclusion appears to lend it this futility, in 4E's view. "The chief priests and Pharisees" here (v. 47) have the same stereotyped function as the Pharisees alone elsewhere.

Jesus' first appearance in Jerusalem (2:13–22). But in addition it points ahead not only to his death, as in the pre-Johannine level, but to a special theological understanding of it. Caiaphas's unconscious prophecy of Christian truth has eclipsed even the Jewish authorities' pivotal decision. The passage looks forward—perhaps beyond the period in which 4E and her or his reader are living—to the time of the New People of God.

This narrative, of course, is solely about Jesus; yet it does not directly depict him at all. In this respect it resembles some of the scenes in the dramas 4E has created, for example, that in chapter 9 involving the blind man. But in the end 4E brings Jesus into view again (v. 54). Just as at several points earlier in the Gospel, so here as well Jesus responds to the official action against him by withdrawing: **Jesus therefore no longer went about openly among the Jews but went away from there. . . .** The intent of this notice is obviously not to portray prudence or any other biographical trait on Jesus' part, but to show christologically that whatever transpires—even the solidification of all the ecclesiastical power in the Jewish world against him—he is in command.[299]

Explanation

The source's explanation for the official plot has lost that role in 4G. For 4E provides another, and more extensive, explanation, not given after the account of the conspiracy but before it, in the raising of Lazarus. It is as if self-evident that the Sanhedrin will condemn Jesus to death after the provocative deed in Bethany, particularly with so many of "the Jews" looking on as spies. They report to the authorities (11:46)[300] and the Sanhedrin is accordingly convoked (11:47).

Thus 4E could either omit the pre-Johannine explanation of the conspiracy or give it another place and function. Obviously the latter path is taken. This passage no longer has the function of bridging signs and passion—at least not in the straightforward way that SG used it, namely, to join two previously distinct documents. The predecessor made a slight shift of material in forming this bridge, so that Temple Restoration and Conspiracy become the culmination of Jesus' work of signs (having once belonged to the passion tradition more or less as "prelude"). The Johannine writer makes a much greater shift, in the same direction, including all of the "prelude" in the public ministry of Jesus (chaps. 1—12), as well as the great body of teaching and dialogue that has been added. Now the "explanation" bridges Public Ministry and Private Revelation; it explains

---

299. See further part 2.F, on this verse and the theological use of geography in Jesus' itinerary.

300. Only the Pharisees are named; the drama outlined here has nothing to do historically with Jesus' death in ca. A.D. 30, but rather with the circumstances of Jewish persecution of the Christians in 4E's day, when presumably only the Pharisees were in command.

why Jesus turns from "the world" to extensive teaching of his disciples in private (the Farewell Discourse at the Last Supper). It therefore explains not just that some officials failed to understand and believe in Jesus' signs but that—except for the disciples, on whom he now focuses all attention— the whole world (symbolized by "the Jews") did not believe, in other words that Jesus' work had been a failure. The whole of chapter 12, after the Johannine version of the accounts of the Anointing (vv. 1–8) and the Entry (vv. 12–16), accomplishes this.

The explanation has of course become ironic, for in fact many of the Jews believe in him, as 4E tells it (the continuing response to the raising of Lazarus—12:17–18), so that the Pharisees can say, confirming their fear and the plot based on it: "You see, you can do nothing; look, the whole world has gone after him" (v. 19). And, still more, "Greeks" appear and seek Jesus (vv. 20–22); these are perhaps no more than dispersed Jews, fulfilling Caiaphas's "prophecy" (but see pp. 280–81, 293). In any case their arrival signals that Jesus' work is done and the passion must begin (v. 23).

Jesus teaches about his coming death and is once again misunderstood by "the crowd" (vv. 24–36a). So, for the last time, he withdraws and hides (v. 36b), and the Evangelist finally presents us with the traditional explanation (vv. 37–40), adding only that "Jesus had done so many signs" **in their** [that is, the crowd's] **presence,** in other words before the world. Just as, on its own scale, this explanation once divided in two the unified SG— coming immediately after the Conspiracy—so now it is the watershed for the Johannine work, at almost the end of chapter 12. The separation is no longer between persuasive messianic proofs and paradoxical suffering, but between ministry in the world, which fails, and disclosure of the truth to the disciples, which succeeds. Only after that is completed (chaps. 14– 17) does 4E resume the narrative and present the death of Jesus. But just as the latter is his glorification, so to the pre-Johannine "explanation" 4E adds that, while the world could not see and believe, Isaiah—whose "prophecy" made this acceptable—**said this because** already in his day he saw [Jesus'] glory and spoke of him (v. 41).

And even then some of the authorities believe, but not openly (vv. 42–43). So Jesus' last word to the world is one of judgment (vv. 44–50). While the world's rejection of Jesus puts him at the mercy, in one sense, of the authorities, and forestalls his work, yet he can now turn to the fashioning of the true community. By contrast, by its own failure, in this redacted explanation the World only Judges Itself.

Analysis

Conspiracy

• All accounts agree that **the chief priests** (v. 47a) were central to this episode in Jesus' passion, but there is divergence as to other participants: Mark, followed by

135

Luke, includes "the scribes," Matthew instead speaks of "the elders of the people." 4G has also **the Pharisees,** which is both historically anomalous and on literary grounds redactional, connecting v. 47a with the Johannine verse that now precedes it ("but some of them went to the Pharisees . . ."). That **the Sanhedrin** was convoked (it is named only here in 4G, against several times in the Synoptics) seems to be traditional; though not common to the Synoptic summaries of this episode, it figures—often translated "council"—in the Synoptic notice of the official intent to dispose of Jesus (Mark 14:55 par.) and in the Jewish trial in Luke 22:66–71.[301] The leaders' bewilderment in v. 47b **(What are we to do since . . . ?)** is probably Johannine in style and point of view (as Schnackenburg suggests).

• The assignment of vv. 47c–48a **(and they said, "This man performs many signs; if we let him alone in this all will believe in him")** to the pre-Johannine level does not depend on the question whether we are dealing here with the continuation of a combined signs and passion source (SG) or only the start of a still-separate PQ. If the former, of course the phrase "many signs" summarizes all that has preceded, taking the plural phrase from the original conclusion of SQ (20:30a). And the feared result (the expectation that if he is not stopped "all will believe in him")[302] could not be more apt here; with the Temple Restoration both as provocation and a promise of the most dramatic sign of all the present story would serve as the pre-Johannine bridge to the passion from the signs. But even if this passage is the original introduction only to an independent passion narrative, PQ, and only later to become part of SG, in the earlier context these words would supply the best opening for such a narrative. They are not traditional but redactional on the part of that community, which here reveals what very likely was in time the impetus for adapting the passion tradition to their circumstances: It is just Jesus' messiahship, on the basis of so **many signs,** that forced the question why he who did them should have died as he did. (It would then be but a small step, of course, to combining SQ with this passion narrative.)

• The officials' further argument in v. 48b for the need to destroy Jesus **(the Romans will come and destroy our [Holy] Place[303] and nation)** is possibly traditional, but containing as it does ideas and phrases unique both in SG and 4G it is difficult to assign. In a way it collides with v. 48a, adding a political fear to the mere threat to their own authority felt by the officials. If the Evangelist has added

301. The source will not describe a formal trial by the Sanhedrin; the interrogation at night by the high priest suffices. (Mark also has this tradition, but has made it into a formal if irregular meeting of the Sanhedrin. It is noteworthy that there is no trace of this Markan redaction in 4G; see my article "Jesus and Peter," esp. 373–74.) Rensberger, "Politics," lists a number of political elements in 4G that, he holds, reflect a late-first-century and studiedly anti-Zealot form of resistance to Roman rule: "king of the Jews," Romans at Jesus' arrest and only they mocking and scourging Jesus, Pilate's fairness (in some passages), his taking the responsibility for Jesus' death, and—of present significance—the lack of a Jewish trial scene. All of these, I claim, stem from the pre-Johannine, and thus pre-A.D. 70, layer in the Gospel. (But Rensberger's thesis is not contradicted by this observation; 4E has clearly chosen not to expunge these elements while adding other elements alongside them, for example, Pilate's weakness or the final responsibility for the crucifixion placed on "the Jews.")

302. Paraphrasing the pre-Johannine definition of the Baptist's mission in 1:7c.

303. It is widely agreed that the unqualified noun here (*topon*) is used as a technical term and means the Temple in Jerusalem.

it, it is purely ironic, a prediction-after-the-fact. But the "fact" is only the destruction of the Temple, which almost certainly preceded the completion of the Gospel by more than a decade, whereas the Jewish nation survived—all too palpably from the standpoint of the Johannine Christians. So it appears that only "both the Place and" has been added, and that the loss of nationhood was original; only the latter is mentioned in Caiaphas's words, v. 50.

• The naming of **Caiaphas** in v. 49ab is surely traditional (see Matt. 26:3), and most of his words can be assigned to the source. Only the initial aspersion of his colleagues (vv. 49c–50a: **You know nothing at all; you do not understand**) will be the familiar Johannine polemic. The rest of v. 50 (**It is expedient that one man die in place of the people** . . .) belongs with v. 48b, as we saw, and so stems from the source.

• The explanatory and parenthetical v. 51 (**He did not say this of himself** . . .) is clearly Johannine both in format (see for instance 4:2; 6:6; 9:22–23) and diction ("of himself"—5:19; 15:4; 16:13; compare the still more frequent "of myself").

• Verse 52 (**And not for the nation only** . . .) contains still further reflection on v. 50, a clearly redactional qualifying postscript.

• The original account concluded sonorously with v. 53.

Explanation

Bultmann proposed that 12:37–38 stemmed from SQ, coming just before the closing (20:30–31a). Schnackenburg (2:411–13) disputes this, pointing out that such an arrangement would be quite anomalous (especially, we might add, since SQ as such did not countenance the failure of the signs to convince and lead to faith). He treats the passage, together with the revelatory discourse that follows it, as entirely Johannine.

I now would take a middle position.[304] The passage fits poorly in its present context, as the final Johannine summary of Jesus' public ministry, for it speaks only of Jesus' signs and not also of his teaching (now far more prominent than the deeds). And its view of the signs, that simply faith on their basis is the proper response to them, is the pre-Johannine one. These verses, then—together, I also hold, with vv. 39–40—most probably stem from the source, but were penned *only when signs were combined with passion* and functioned along with the Temple Restoration and the Officials' Conspiracy as the transition between the two sources. This bringing together of two quite different traditions would have required just such a theological justification as this. Or, to put it differently, the problem raised and answered here (namely, how the messianic worker of signs could have been executed by official decision) is what demanded the juxtaposing of the passion tradition with SQ in the first place. And the answer given here is that found at several points later in the passion story, especially in the crucifixion scene: Jesus' death was foretold in biblical prophecy (read with Christian eyes) and therefore *had to take place*.

---

304. Contrast *TGOS*, 199. I am influenced in what follows by the argument of D. M. Smith, "Setting," 90–93. Among other things, Smith points out the difference between this generalizing notice about the response to the signs, with no immediately preceding sign story, and the usual Johannine summaries (e.g., in 2:23; 3:2; 7:31; 9:16; 10:41).

I propose then that the most likely position for this passage originally (that is, in the pre-Johannine stage) is just at the point we have reached, following the account of the official Conspiracy against Jesus and seeking to explain it.

• The passage is framed by two clearly Johannine sentences, vv. 36b (Jesus' departure) and 41 (Isaiah as witness to Jesus' "glory"). If this paragraph originally followed 11:53, the verb's subject in v. 37 is still understood to be Jesus even when separated from v. 36b (**Jesus said these things and went away and hid himself from them**).

• A generalizing summary begins (v. 37, much as in 20:30–31a): **Although he had done so many signs before them they would not believe**[305] **in him.** The only Johannine element here is the phrase "before them." It fits the present context of Jesus' having just spoken to the crowd. In the source, following the officials' conspiracy, it is inappropriate, for the signs were always performed, as 20:30 understands, "before his disciples,"[306] and the officials were not themselves their audience. Yet the official failure to believe is notable, so that is what is asserted.

• To introduce the prophecy, v. 38a uses a version of the common scriptural quotation formula appearing later in PQ:[307] **that [the word of Isaiah the prophet] might be fulfilled [which says].** . . .

• Two proof texts from Isaiah are now linked to explain the Sanhedrin's plot (vv. 38b, 40). In both of them the prophet is taught by God to accept rejection of his message, and each is used elsewhere in early Christianity to account for nonacceptance of its good news.[308]

• At first glance the former (v. 38b, from Isa. 53:1) might appear to have been inserted by 4E,[309] intended to pair summarily the teaching of Jesus (**our report**) with his miraculous deeds (**the arm of the Lord is revealed**), a combination that would reflect the Johannine view of Jesus' ministry. But in v. 37 there was no mention of the teaching ministry—only Jesus' signs. And here it is not Jesus but the author who speaks through Isaiah. Then "our report" must be the pre-Johannine account of Jesus' signs, simply paralleling after the manner of Hebrew poetry the revealing of "the arm of the Lord." The first citation, then, is validly assigned to the source.

• Verse 39 makes the logic of v. 37 explicit and bridges the two quotations: **Therefore they could not believe, for again Isaiah said:** . . . Its mentality views

305. The imperfect *episteuon* seems to have something of this sense; lit., "they were not believing."

306. But the latter phrase does not argue by analogy for the originality of "before them" here, since the Greek preposition in 12:37 *(emprosthen)* is different from that used in this concluding summary *(enōpion)*.

307. Found variously worded in 19:24b, 28b, 36–37, the latter bringing together two prophecies, as here. Faure's early attempt ("Zitate") to separate source from Johannine redaction primarily on the basis of these biblical citation formulas has been discredited (partially by Smend, "Behandlung"); he did not allow for Johannine imitation of the source nor raise the question who it is that cites scripture—see part 2, n. 74.

308. See Rom. 10:16 (Isaiah 53) and Mark 4:12 par., Acts 28:26–27 (Isaiah 6).

309. That is, just the reverse of Bultmann's view *(Gospel of John)* that 4E added vv. 39–40; see the following note.

the authorities' failure to believe in a non-Johannine way—invincible ignorance rather than culpability.

• The second quotation (v. 40), paraphrasing Isa. 6:10,[310] is found also in the Synoptic Gospels, though in a totally different context (namely, the explanation for Jesus' speaking in parables, Mark 4:12 par.). Here the theme of ears and hearing is lacking,[311] since only seeing signs is what this passage summarizes. It too, then, was original to the source.

The Prelude to the Passion

SECTION 12 (12:1-8)
JESUS IS ANOINTED AT BETHANY

Pre-Johannine Source

12 ¹Six days before Passover Jesus went to Bethany where Lazarus was, (the dead man) whom Jesus had raised from the dead.[312] ²So they prepared a supper for him there, and Martha served, and Lazarus was one of those who ate with him. ³Mary took a pound of costly pure ointment and anointed Jesus' [head] and began to wipe his feet with her hair. And the house was filled with the fragrance of the ointment. ⁴But Judas Iscariot, one of his disciples (who kept the money chest), said, ⁵"Why was this ointment not sold for a year's wages and given to the poor?" ⁷So Jesus said, "Let her alone. [She has done it (or It is)] for the day of my burial. (⁸The poor you have with you always, but you do not always have me.)"

That this episode may have come next in SG appears from the minimal but logical indications of Jesus' movements at the pre-Johannine level (contrasting with the more intricate and artificial Synoptic order).[313] After 12:37-40, the anointing effectively moves the story along the same theological path: Just as the officials' disbelief is inevitable, even predetermined, so as to account for its part in Jesus' death, just so too his messianic designation now becomes a foreshadowing of his death.

The Temple Restoration and the subsequent Conspiracy of the Officials tie the passion to the signs. Now the passion itself, or rather its actual

---

310. Bultmann (*Gospel of John*) rejected this for the source, since it exactly conforms to neither LXX (as does v. 38b) nor to the Hebrew text. But in fact other OT quotations in the source have such a mixed reading. See Freed, *Quotations*, 87-88, on this text.

311. Suggesting again that it is not 4E who first introduced this citation; see above on v. 38b.

312. The connective (*oun*) at the beginning of this verse and of v. 3 is probably the Johannine particle meaning "then"; but in vv. 2 and 7 it appears to be pre-Johannine, in its more common sense of "so."

313. In a once-separate PQ it may have come first of all, as we suggested earlier (this part, sec. 10, Pre-Johannine Source). The fuller than usual opening ("Six days before Passover") is then accounted for. The author who combined signs and passion would then have moved the Temple Restoration and the Officials' Conspiracy (with its Explanation provided) to a point preceding this event so as to provide the necessary transition.

prelude, begins. Both preceding events were set in Jerusalem. Now, as **Passover** is approaching, Jesus goes out to the nearby village of **Bethany.** The reason is to be found in his connection with the household of **Martha** and **Mary,** and in particular with **Lazarus,** who give him **a supper.**[314] But the author is probably more interested in the theological overtones of the drama. Lazarus is he **whom Jesus had raised** and thus is now **one of those who ate with [Jesus]**; the miracle of his resurrection is reaffirmed. Also contained in this brief reminder of Jesus' power is the theme of *death*, evidently as a hint of what awaits Jesus: Lazarus is identified as one, literally, **who had died** and who had been raised **from the dead**; two terms for death are used. The same emphasis appears in Jesus' words in v. 7: Mary's action is somehow related to the time of *Jesus'* **burial.** And if v. 8 is original it intensifies that very note: **You do not always have me.** In several ways, then, the story casts a dark shadow over what lies ahead, but at the same time hints at the promise of the same reversal of Jesus' death as followed that of Lazarus.

Chiefly, however, our attention is drawn to the person of Jesus. He is here **anointed,** perhaps on the **head,** and the messianic overtones, however implicit, are evident. It was entirely appropriate that he be so extravagantly—shall we say royally?—treated: **a pound of costly pure ointment,** worth **a year's wages,**[315] filling **the house with [its] fragrance,** his **feet** wiped by Mary with her hair. The objection to the waste (only the Synoptics call it this) is reasonable but it is rejected; thus here it has become **Judas Iscariot** who makes it,[316] not an indefinite "some" (as in Mark) or "the disciples" (as in Matthew). Even the genuine need of **the poor** is secondary to Jesus. Him they will not always have; his fate is now all-important. Alongside the foreshadowing of Jesus' death, then, there is—not a theology of the cross, certainly no Johannine theology of glory, but a christological concentration on the figure of Jesus. We saw suggestions of this in the pre-Johannine Temple Restoration, where there was

314. We are not told here that Lazarus is brother of Mary, or that Martha is her sister (elements whose place in the pre-Johannine tradition we saw to be fluid, this part, sec. 7, end of Analysis). But unless the plural subject of "prepared a supper" is meant to indicate an indefinite "they," we may suppose that Martha and Mary, and perhaps also Lazarus, are Jesus' hosts.

315. Lit., "three hundred denarii." In Mark the datum has been heightened ("*more* than 300 denarii"), just the reverse of the relation of the detail in John 6:7 ("two hundred denarii would not suffice . . .") to that in Mark 6:37, as often at the level of tradition.

316. But besides supplying this detail, the tradition may also preserve an older datum about Judas from before the time of his betrayal, namely, that he was the treasurer among the disciples and further that they kept a "money chest" in which evidently funds for the poor were collected—a rare bit of early and quite possibly factual information. (It can hardly be Johannine, since the present Gospel, apart from this notice, shows no interest whatever in the economic conditions within the community—see 4E's portrayal of what some of the disciples mistakenly "supposed" in 13:29!)

also the element of forewarning. Here both dimensions are more sharply drawn.

Johannine Redaction

12 ¹Six days before Passover Jesus went to Bethany where Lazarus was, (the dead man) whom Jesus had raised from the dead. ²*Then* they prepared a supper for him there, and Martha served, and Lazarus was one of those who ate with him. ³Then Mary took a pound of costly pure ointment and anointed Jesus' feet and began to wipe his feet with her hair. And the house was filled with the fragrance of the ointment. ⁴But Judas Iscariot, one of his disciples, **the one who would betray him,** said ⁵"Why was this ointment not sold for a year's wages and given to the poor?" ⁶**He said this not because he was concerned for the poor but since he was a thief and, having the money chest, he would take whatever was put into it.** ⁷*Then* Jesus said, "Let her **keep it** for the day of my burial. ⁸For the poor you always have with you, but me you do not always have."

We considered that this passage may once have opened an independent PQ. If it is 4E who for the first time combines signs and passion sources, he or she has then placed the official plot, and preceding it the instigating raising of Lazarus, before the Anointing. But more likely signs and passion were already joined (SG), and apart from replacing Temple Restoration with the Lazarus story the Johannine author has simply retained the source's order. The only alteration 4E makes in the story's context is to expand it by creating brief scenes—before and after the Anointing and again after the Entry—in which the reaction of "the Jews," both the masses and the officials, is described. It is in these that we find 4E's understanding of the Anointing and the events that surround it.

The first of these scenes is 11:55–57, following the brief notice of v. 54 (Jesus' withdrawing in the face of the Conspiracy that ensued from his raising Lazarus). **The Passover of the Jews was at hand** it begins—a typically Johannine statement (see 2:13; 6:4; 7:2), replicating the opening of the pre-Johannine anointing story about to begin. The feast becomes in 4E's hands the occasion wherein **many went up to Jerusalem;** they do so in advance of the feast ostensibly **to purify themselves** (v. 55), but for 4E's purposes their real function is to constitute the crowd who wonder whether Jesus, since he has withdrawn from official opposition, will stay away from the feast (v. 56). All are under orders to report any knowledge of Jesus' whereabouts to **the chief priests and Pharisees . . . so that they might arrest him** (v. 57), but at this point the crowd's attitude is not yet clear. They stand in the midst of a polarity, between the quiet but commanding figure of Jesus and the menacing leaders bent on his destruction. They are perhaps meant to represent as much the great body of Jews in the late-first-century Johannine context as those of Jesus' time; certainly the

141

portrayal of a systematic effort to find Jesus by any means (an element lacking in the Synoptics) would reflect the persecution of Christians of a later day.

Jesus *is* about to come to the feast, as 4E will presently tell us, quite openly and indeed with a display of authority (12:13–15). But before that Entry the private scene in Bethany takes place. There was a slightly different treatment of this motif (will Jesus come to the feast?) in 7:1–14.

The Johannine alterations of the source within the Anointing itself are for the most part minimal. It may be that in v. 3 "head," if that was the source's reading, has been replaced by **feet**. This would have been done to downplay any messianic connotation in Mary's gesture. For 4E, Jesus is the only begotten Son of God, not merely Messiah; the messianic language of the source is retained, but in the discourses it is deepened and replaced with a far higher christology. And this sonship is based in a preexistence going back to the beginning of time. Thus an anointing that designates simply messiahship and is performed at the end of Jesus' life becomes wholly inadequate.[317]

The Evangelist underscores the inappropriateness of Judas' objection to the waste of oil by adding the reminder **who would betray him** in v. 4. The only major Johannine redaction in the passage is the creation of v. 6: the notice that Judas' concern was not, in fact, **for the poor,**[318] but rather personal greed. As the treasurer among Jesus' followers,[319] and **a thief,** he stood to suffer from the loss of a potential contribution of great size to the resources under his control. These pejorative details are unique to 4G, and reflect the tendency in the development of tradition to blacken Judas's character. The Evangelist's interest seems not solely to explain how a follower of Jesus could have betrayed him, but chiefly to give a negative example to readers, one that contrasts with the appropriateness of Mary's act.

A final change within the original story is made in v. 7. If in the source, as we surmised, Jesus declared that in some sense Mary anointed him in advance for his burial, this conflicts with the way 4E will expand the actual burial scene following Jesus' death in 19:39–40 (see this part, sec. 18, Johannine Redaction). Thus a statement of proleptic yet accomplished fact (**Let her alone; she has done it** [or **it is**] **for the day of my burial**) must be changed to a directive for the future: **Let her keep it for the day of my burial.** As often in Johannine redaction, Jesus' time is not yet.

Once the episode is over, 4E again adds a scene describing the people's

---

317. The change to "feet" could also be intended to provide beforehand a counterpart to Jesus' washing the disciples' feet in chap. 13.

318. The expression used echoes 10:13, the hireling who "has no concern for the sheep."

319. This detail, as suggested in the reconstructed source, may be pre-Johannine.

response to Jesus and what he does (vv. 9–11). This, more than the anointing itself, seems to be 4E's chief interest. We hear now of **a great crowd of the Jews**[320] who **learned** (lit., "knew") **that he was there** and accordingly **came** (v. 9a). The people's wondering whether Jesus would come to the feast in the earlier scene has now become an eagerness to see him, and an eagerness on the part of a considerably larger group. Further, they come to Bethany **not only on account of Jesus but also to see Lazarus whom he had raised from the dead** (v. 9b). They evidently want to see and believe in Jesus' greatest sign, so confirming the worst fear of the Sanhedrin (11:47b–48a). The fact that so **many of the Jews** were seeking Jesus and Lazarus leads the authorities to extend their death plot to include Lazarus, since he is the occasion for many who are **going away and believing in Jesus** (vv. 10–11). (Thus, once again, Jesus' situation is combined with Lazarus's, whose resurrection implicitly foreshadowed Jesus'.)

The Evangelist, then, has subordinated the source's mounting drama— the fate awaiting Jesus—to a continuing preoccupation with the Jewish response to him, and in this case that response is portrayed as yet another result of the last and greatest of the signs. Already on account of that raising, and not solely the one Jesus would later accomplish for himself (the chief sign in the source), **many** among the Jewish community are becoming Christians. The standard against which "the Jews" of 4E's own time are found wanting is clear. Properly, all who see that Jesus is not simply the anointed one of Jewish expectation but Believe in Him as Resurrection and Life will come thereby to Christian faith. Whereas, then, the source emphasizes Jesus' death in this passage, even above his messiahship, 4E points our attention beyond Jesus' death to its sequel and, still more, to the response on the part of latter-day believers.

Analysis[321]

Critics differ in separating tradition from redaction in this passage, but there can be little doubt that it stems in some form from PQ (or SG). With Schnackenburg I continue to maintain that most of the story's details are pre-Johannine,[322] but I allow that uncertainty attaches to some of the individual elements.[323]

320. Or possibly "*the* great crowd . . . ," according to many MSS. In that case it refers not only to the "many" of 11:55–56, who are "from the country," but to others as well, and must mean more or less "the majority of the people."

321. The rather different analysis implied by Holst ("Anointing," 435–46) fails to distinguish between Johannine and pre-Johannine redaction of the tradition and so is not very helpful here.

322. Versus B & L, who see detailed Johannine redaction, the main purpose of which is conflation with the Synoptics.

323. Here again Dauer makes a prodigious attempt (*Johannes und Lukas*, 126–206) to demonstrate that the pre-Johannine source is derived from the present text of Luke. See further, this part, excursus B.

• The precise dating of the story—**six days before Passover** (v. 1a)—contrasts with 4E's more general formula ("the Passover of the Jews was near") in 2:13 and 6:4, and, just three verses before the present passage, 11:55. Similarly, in v. 1b the identification of Bethany as the place **where Lazarus was, the dead man**[324] **whom Jesus had raised,** is awkward coming from 4E, in whose arrangement that story has just been told. By contrast, in an independent PQ some such initial identification of the tradition would be needed, and in a combined SG the reminder of a passage probably separated from this one by a number of scenes would be appropriate.

• In the Lazarus story we found reason to suspect that the contrast between Mary and Martha, and possibly all mention of Martha, was 4E's addition, serving as a vehicle for Martha's dialogue with Jesus. But here, though Mary again plays the fundamental role, the notice that **Martha served** (v. 2b) is quite natural to the **supper** prepared for Jesus. That **Lazarus was one of those who ate with him** (v. 2c) either is a version of the tradition that Jesus and Lazarus were close friends or seeks to confirm the factuality of his resurrection. In either case, it is probably pre-Johannine.

• The overfull description of the oil used by Mary to anoint Jesus (v. 3a) has appeared to some to be redactional. It is possible, however, that post-Johannine assimilation to Mark has occurred, since some important MSS lack one of the two words for the oil here ("nard") and, in their text of Mark, some of the other common terms. In any case, the retention of vivid and rare phrases in the tradition is not surprising and is not to be attributed to Johannine reworking.

• How shall we account for the variation, among the four Gospel accounts (of what seems to be one tradition), as to the part of Jesus' body—his feet or his head—that Mary anointed? (The question is of more than casual importance, since a quasi-messianic interpretation of the text may depend on it.) Mark 14:3, followed closely by Matt. 26:7, tells of an unnamed woman who "poured ointment" over Jesus' "head." Luke 7:38 (in a differently placed but perhaps parallel story) reads that a sinful woman wetted Jesus' "feet" with her tears and "wiped them with her hair" and kissed his feet and "anointed" them. Here, in v. 3b, we read that Mary **anointed Jesus' feet and began to wipe his feet with her hair.** There seems to be no redaction here; rather, the source would appear to be in touch with a brief version of the tradition behind Luke, only the circumstances and the woman's identity and character varying.

But there are clues that all is not so simple. In 4G, there is the redundant repetition of "his feet," not by itself very troubling but suggesting the possibility that an older reading has been changed, one involving the mixed reading of "head" and "feet."[325] Unless we suppose Johannine assimilation to the Synoptic Gospels

---

324. This phrase is found in many important MSS, and its omission by scribes as redundant is easier to account for than its insertion, so I take it to be probably original to the text of 4G.

325. In Luke, a bit later in the story, Jesus contrasts the welcome Simon, his host, has given him with that of the woman: "You gave me no water for my feet, but she has wet my feet with her tears; you gave me no kiss, but . . . she has not ceased to kiss my feet; you did not anoint my *head* with oil, but she has anointed my *feet* with ointment" (7:44b–46). There is evidently a more complex tradition history behind this story than at first appears.

(which elsewhere we have never found tenable), the most likely way to account for 4E's text here is to suppose that a mixed pre-Johannine (and pre-Lukan) tradition—"anointed his *head* and wiped his *feet* with her hair"—has been de-messianized by 4E to give the present text.[326]

• That vv. 4–5 portray Judas and only him objecting to the lavish waste is entirely understandable as a development of pre-Johannine tradition, but the verse is textually uncertain and seems overloaded; possibly then the last phrase in v. 4 **(who would betray him)** is Johannine.[327]

• The parenthetical explanation of Judas's reason for speaking (v. 6) is typical of 4E with respect to both form (compare 11:51, in the preceding section) and content (13:29). The syntax in the sentence's second half is awkward and overloaded (lit., "but because he was a thief and having the money chest . . . "); just possibly the second phrase here is traditional and was found in the source at the end of v. 4, helping to explain the detail of giving to the poor in v. 5. It is then picked up by 4E and made the kernel of the invented v. 6.

• In vv. 7–8 Jesus answers Judas in words that, typically of SG, parallel the Synoptics closely yet differ in various ways as well. But both verses are in themselves problematic. Verse 7 is baffling: How is the ointment just wasted to be "kept" for the day of Jesus' burial?[328] Perhaps in the source the thought was, as in Mark, that the preparation for burial has here taken place; then 4E has sought, with partial success, to play that down in the light of what he will narrate later on. Provisionally, then, at v. 7 the source reads: "Let her alone. [She has done it (*or simply* It is) for the day of my burial."[329]

• Some see v. 8 as an unnecessary afterthought and, since a number of MSS lack it, hold it to be a post-Johannine gloss, harmonizing with Mark and Matthew. On the other hand, it may be original, some later scribes having omitted it, perhaps to suppress "You do not always have me." The possibly pre-Markan form of the saying[330] suggests that it may have been found in the source and provided Jesus' chief answer to Judas's objection. But, as with several elements in this story, we

---

326. If anointing of the feet were original in the tradition and only Mark (and Matthew) altered it to "head" and omitted the wiping of Jesus' feet altogether (perhaps to remove the suggestion of too intimate an act on the woman's part), then why the indications in Luke and perhaps also behind 4G of the mixed reading? If Holst ("Anointing") is right that originally the (unidentified [but possibly sinful?]) woman wetted Jesus' feet with her tears—and this makes better sense of her wiping the feet—the tears would perhaps have been omitted if signs and passion were joined, since the woman is now identified with Mary whose brother had been raised from death and her tears would then be inappropriate.

327. Culpepper (*Anatomy*, 23) points out this phrase as one of a number that by their point of view betray the hand of the Evangelist.

328. The construction, an elliptical purpose clause, is typically Johannine: "[the foregoing was done] that she may keep it. . . ." On the other hand, the thought is close to that of Mark and Matthew ("my body for burial"). And 4E would hardly introduce a forward reference (to Jesus' burial) here since in the Johannine redaction others will provide an elaborate preparation of Jesus' body for the grave at a later point (19:38–42).

329. So also Schnackenburg.

330. Without Mark's intrusive middle clause ("And whenever you will you can do good to them").

145

must leave the verse in doubt; it seems not to be Johannine but either pre- or post-Johannine.

SECTION 13 (12:12-15)
THE MESSIAH ENTERS JERUSALEM

Pre-Johannine Source

12 ¹²**The next day a great crowd (that had come to the feast) heard that Jesus was coming into Jerusalem, ¹³and they took palm branches and went out to meet him, and began to shout "Hosanna! Blessed is he who comes in the name of the Lord, the King of Israel!" ¹⁴And Jesus found a young ass and sat upon it, as it is written, ¹⁵"Fear not, daughter of Zion; behold your king comes sitting on the colt of an ass."**

If nothing major in the source's account of this scene has been lost, it is far briefer and thus more christologically pointed than the same story in the Synoptic Gospels, particularly because it lacks the circumstantial preparations for the entry that Jesus makes in the other accounts. Much as the conversion of the disciples at the beginning of SQ progresses spontaneously, almost automatically, so here Jesus is first welcomed by **a great crowd** who go out to meet him as he merely approaches the city. Having, as it appears, just been anointed in Bethany on the previous evening, he is hailed with a shout of praise (**Hosanna!**) and as the **blessed** one, the one who at last **comes in the name of the Lord.** Thus does the crowd greet him with words of messianic designation (from Ps. 118:26), and the source's author makes this meaning explicit by adding **even the King of Israel,** just the acclamation that was made by Nathanael to cap the first disciples' chain of recognition (1:49).

Curiously it is only when he has thus been recognized, without provocation on his part, that Jesus engages in the symbolic act of riding into the city on a lowly donkey; he simply "found" the animal, without prior arrangement and almost in response to the acclamation. Thus he acts in explicit accordance with scriptural expectation: **as it is written.** The prophecy itself is cited as a final theological affirmation: **Fear not**[331] . . . **your king comes. . . .**[332]

While the Synoptic versions end with the messianic acclamation, here it is the fulfillment of prophecy—reiterating the messianic title (**your**

---

331. The passage in Zech. 9:9, from which the rest of the quotation comes, has "Rejoice" here. "Fear not" seems to stem from a similar passage in Zeph. 3:14–16. No doubt the conflation is unconscious, and the note of reassurance rather than joy may reflect the somber tone pervading the passion story in its pre-Johannine form.

332. B & L think that vv. 14–15 represent a different stage in the development of the story than vv. 12–13. This may be true, but at some earlier point than the source: both elements are found combined in Mark, and while that Gospel lacks the explicit citation of Zechariah, Matthew has it. The uniqueness of the present version is only in the order of the two elements (acclamation by the crowd before Jesus mounts the donkey, not afterward as in Mark).

King)—that completes the story. (The element of humility in the original prophecy has largely dropped out.) This theme of divine necessity pervades PQ, as we have begun to see. The event is indeed a Messianic Entry, but at the same time only part of a drama that must run its course.

Johannine Redaction

(Since 4E has evidently made no changes internal to this pericope, it need not be printed again here.)

The Evangelist strangely blunts the immediacy of this story—Jesus acclaimed by the crowd and fulfilling messianic prophecy—by adding (v. 16) that **at first his disciples did not understand these things.** The intent of this notice is not to display their ignorance or deliberately play down the source's theological statement, but, evidently, rather to say that everything Jesus did must be understood, can properly be seen, only in the light of what is still to come: **But when Jesus had been glorified, then they remembered that these things had been written of him and had been done to him.** There is, undoubtedly, a kind of historical accuracy in 4E's perspective; it was only in retrospect that the original disciples could understand all that had happened. The source, like most other Gospels, presented the story of Jesus as if entirely clear to the participants at the time, though it also hinted that each event is only part of a story making sense as a whole and from the standpoint of the outcome. If 4E overtly emphasizes this latter point of view, it is not out of concern for historical accuracy, to be sure, but theological validity. And, we can ask, precisely what is that point from which all is to be understood? In the Restoring of the Temple it is Jesus' resurrection, though the death is in view as well. Here just the reverse may be true: Jesus' glorification seems to refer primarily to the crucifixion (see further, part 2.D), with the resurrection, which is more traditionally the reference of the term "glorified," not far removed.

In vv. 17–19 the Evangelist adds a final crowd scene—but not by way of response to the triumphal Entry (whose effect has already been put off by v. 16 until a later time). Rather, we find a still further outgrowth of the raising of Lazarus. In fact, we now learn (v. 18) that **the crowd** that **went out to meet him** and hailed him (vv. 12–13) did so as a result of the report, the **witness,** of those who had seen "Lazarus . . . raised" (v. 17). Presumably that report had already been conveyed, but we are reminded once again that the people **heard he had done this sign.**

The sequence of events is confused, and the cast of characters complex—if one looks closely there seem to be three distinct crowds of believers that 4E identifies[333]—but the effect is clear, and it causes despair

---

333. The first crowd mentioned is that of 12:9, many of whom are becoming converts. The second is that of 12:12, and like the first they are made up in part of the "many" of 11:55–56 and their faith is displayed in v. 18. The third, mentioned only at the end but harking back to an earlier time, is made up of the witnesses to the Lazarus sign and their faith is self-evident.

in the officials: **The Pharisees then said to one another, "You see that you can do nothing; look, the world has gone after him"** (v. 19). Some take **the world** here to be used in the distinctive Johannine sense of humankind arrayed against God, but on the lips of the officials it seems to mean only the same as "all" in 11:48, the entire Jewish nation. The fear expressed there by the Sanhedrin had been well founded; it has begun to appear that Everyone Believes in Jesus.

Analysis

In Mark the order of the events preliminary to the passion—the Entry and Temple Restoration somewhat earlier in the story and separated from the Conspiracy and Anointing—is evidently of the Markan author's devising. In contrast to that contrived itinerary, the sequence now found in 4G is simple and appears to have been taken over from the source. This episode would have directly followed the Anointing, vv. 9–11 being obviously 4E's insertion.

• The phrase **the next day,** while sometimes a Johannine insertion, in v. 12 is more likely to be pre-Johannine (as in this context also in Mark 11:12; Matt. 27:62); after the supper of the preceding episode it is entirely natural. That the crowd here is the one **that had come to the feast** is Johannine in 11:55, but possibly traditional here. In any case the source would have named **a great crowd** (so Matt. 21:9) and perhaps identified it as **having heard that Jesus was coming into Jerusalem.**[334] This would be the source's first mention of such a following, necessitated by the story at hand. (By contrast there are several prior references to crowds in the present Gospel, as we have seen.)

• Verses 13–15 continue without evidence of redactional addition[335] and display the similarities to, and especially differences from, the Synoptics that one would expect in a parallel but distinct version of the tradition.

• Verse 16 is Johannine explanation (as in 2:17, 22), and vv. 17–19 comprise the third of the crowd scenes with which 4E has framed the Anointing and Entry stories.

SECTION 14 (13:1–20)
THE LAST SUPPER

Various attempts have been made to analyze 4G's intricate and patently composite narrative of Jesus' meal with his disciples prior to his arrest. Undoubtedly it is based in part on traditional material—specifically, the unique tradition of the foot-washing, which possibly derives from PQ. I earlier suggested the verses in chapter 13 most likely to contain vestiges of

334. Here and in the next verse there are verbal similarities to the pre-Johannine wording in the pericope of the official's son of chap. 4: "hearing that Jesus was coming," "went out to him and...."

335. Schnackenburg thinks "and the King of Israel" at the end of v. 13 is an added comment, and so it is, clarifying the acclamation that precedes it, but it is likely to have been added at the pre-Johannine level. For 4E Jesus' kingship is not at all an Israelite one (6:15; 18:36), even though "Israel" is sometimes used in 4E in a positive sense for "the Jews."

this pre-Johannine account (*TGOS*, 155–57). But the material has evidently been so greatly rewritten, perhaps more than once—as, for example, the overloading and redundancy in vv. 1–3 seem to show—that reconstruction of the source now seems too tenuous to be practicable. Thus an interpretation of the pre-Johannine form of the story is no longer possible.[336] And while on the other hand a number of Johannine themes can be perceived in chapter 13, they now are so intricately interwoven with the earlier traditions that our understanding of the chapter's meaning cannot be informed by redaction-critical study. (See Addendum.)

The same is true of other narrative elements here and there in the Gospel which by Synoptic analogy could derive from PQ, namely, Jesus' *predictions of Judas' betrayal* (6:70–71; 13:18 [with the familiar formula of OT prophecy quotation], 21–30),[337] of *Peter's denials* (13:38), and of *the disciples' "scattering"* (16:32b); elements of the Gethsemane tradition— *Jesus' soul troubled* (11:33; 13:21a), his *tears* (11:35), his *prayer to the Father* about *his "hour"* (12:27b), *"Arise, let us be going"* (14:31b); possibly the *institution of the Eucharist* (6:51c, 53). (See this part, end of sec. 9, for unrecoverable matter in the signs tradition.)

We therefore jump now to that point in 4G where, after the massive addition of the purely Johannine Farewell Discourse (chaps. 14—16) and High Priestly Prayer (chap. 17), the ongoing PQ reappears in recognizable form—we jump, that is, to the beginning of chapter 18.

The Passion[338]

SECTION 15 (18:1–12)
JESUS IS ARRESTED

Pre-Johannine Source

18 ¹Jesus went out with his disciples across the Wadi Kidron, where there was a garden. ²Now Judas his betrayer also knew the place, since Jesus often gathered there with his disciples. ³Therefore Judas brought a troop of soldiers, and guards from the chief priests, and came there with lanterns and torches and weapons. ⁴ᶜSo Jesus said to them, "Who is it that you want?" ⁵They said, "Jesus the Nazarene." He said to them, "I'm he." ¹⁰So

---

336. Schnackenburg, who believes that 4E's source material certainly contained a simple account of the foot-washing, also declines to isolate the basic narrative in the present passage, and instead makes a "synchronic" analysis of its various components. Segovia's article, "John 13 1–20," gives a thorough survey of all modern analyses of the chapter and argues that at most a separation between Johannine and post-Johannine layers can be made.

337. With Luke's tradition, the source here sees the activity of Satan in Judas's act.

338. I have found Dauer, *Passionsgeschichte*, helpful in revising my earlier analysis. Unfortunately he does not examine any of the episodes of the prelude and carries out his analysis only from this point to 19:30, stopping short of the burial.

Simon Peter, since he had a sword, drew it and struck the slave of the high priest and cut off his right ear. And the slave's name was Malchus. ¹¹So Jesus said to Peter, "Put back your sword; shall I not drink the cup the Father has given me?" ¹²So the soldiers and their captain and the guards seized Jesus and bound him. [*The disciples flee.*]

Unless 4E has suppressed it, the locale of the Last Supper was not specified in the source; but presumably it took place in Jerusalem. At its conclusion Jesus may originally have said, "Rise, let us go hence" (as now so anomalously at 14:31), and the present passage would have followed immediately. Jesus and his disciples leave the walled city and cross the **Wadi Kidron** (i.e., the small valley to the east, formed by the stream of that name that flows in the rainy winter months). They go to **a garden** (corresponding to "the place called Gethsemane" in the Synoptic Gospels?) on the slopes of the Mount of Olives. Jesus' intent is not stated, only the fact that he **often gathered there with his disciples.** Ominously, we learn this only in connection with **Judas** who **also knew the place** (v. 2); our attention focuses on the impending betrayal. It focuses, that is, on such portrayal of Judas's treachery as we find in 4G. There is nothing at this point in the source corresponding to the perhaps redactional account of Judas's bargain with the authorities in Mark 14:10–11 pars., and certainly no trace of the fuller legends found in Matt. 27:3–10 or Acts 1:16–20.

The betrayal is told with stark brevity. Judas is not identified by the patronymic found in 13:2, 26, but only as Jesus' **betrayer.** Nevertheless he **knew the place,** presumably as one of the disciples (see also 12:4), but that association evidently is past. He acts now as an outsider who happens to have more or less confidential information; this, apparently, is the force of "also" at the beginning of v. 2. And so he brings the police, both Roman and Jewish. Motive and means are not given, only the awful fact that Judas, a former disciple, is directly responsible for Jesus' arrest. His part in this is greater than in the Synoptics. He not only shows the authorities' agents where to find Jesus and identifies him for them; he acts as their organizer and leader (he **brought a troop of soldiers and guards**). And they come prepared, with lights and arms.

Jesus does not resist—presumably because, as PQ makes clear at various points, he dies in fulfillment of scripture; it must take place. He simply asks their mission; perhaps he knows it already and his question is almost rhetorical: "Who is it that you are looking for?" On hearing their reply he simply acknowledges that he is their man: "I'm he." By contrast, Peter responds with impulsive, perhaps desperate resistance; he attacks a member of the band with his sword.³³⁹ The **high priest's slave . . . named**

---

339. That this form of the tradition attributes the otherwise anonymous act of resistance to Peter is hard to explain. Has the Synoptic version suppressed Peter's name out of reverence? Or is Peter singled out in this version to credit him with an act of loyalty? In any case, Jesus' word to Peter is no more than an implied criticism, hardly a rebuke.

Malchus is presumably one of the Temple guard. Jesus restrains Peter from further resistance, pointing out that **the cup** awaiting him is unavoidable. The spiritual struggle of the Synoptic scene in Gethsemane ("Father . . . let this cup pass from me") is missing, only the equanimity of its outcome appears; with the phrase that the cup was **given** by **the Father,** the acceptance by Jesus of divine necessity is all the clearer.

Thus the inevitable takes place. Jesus is **seized** and **bound** by the guards; Judas, having played his role, no longer leads. Jesus will now be turned over to the high priest. But very possibly at this point in the original account we would have been told that the disciples flee, as Jesus had predicted. Except for Peter and an unnamed disciple in the next scene they do not reappear till after the resurrection.

In the source, then, this scene—like most to follow—is told flatly, "factually." The meaning is in the story—or rather despite it. Like Jesus, the author accepts what must be, understands its necessity. There is no pathos here as there is in Luke, nor obvious irony such as Mark shows.

Johannine Redaction

18 ¹**When he had spoken these things** Jesus went out with his disciples across the Wadi Kidron, where there was a garden **which he entered with his disciples.** ²Now Judas his betrayer also knew the place, since Jesus often gathered there with his disciples. ³*Then* Judas brought a troop of soldiers, and guards from the chief priests **and from the Pharisees,** and came there with lanterns and torches and weapons. ⁴*Then* Jesus, **knowing all that would come upon him, came out and** said to them, "Who is it that you want?" ⁵They said, "Jesus the Nazarene." He said to them, "*I am* [he]." **Now Judas, who betrayed him, was standing with them.** ⁶**Now when he said to them, "I AM,"** they drew back and fell to the ground. ⁷Now again he asked them, "Whom do you want?" And they said, "Jesus the Nazarene." ⁸Jesus answered them, "I have told you that I am he. If you want me, let these men go" ⁹to fulfill the word he had spoken, "Of those you gave me I did not lose one." ¹⁰*Then* Simon Peter, since he had a sword, drew it and struck the slave of the high priest and cut off his right ear. And the slave's name was Malchus. ¹¹*Then* Jesus said to Peter, "Put back your sword; shall I not drink the cup the Father has given me?" ¹²*Then* the soldiers and their captain and the **Jewish** guards seized Jesus and bound him.

After the long insertion of chapters 14—17,[340] 4E here returns to the source, which is now followed to its end without major interruption. The narrative is tied to the preceding block of discourses simply by prefixing the brief phrase (only two words in Greek), **When he had spoken these things.**

---

340. This block of four chapters was probably not inserted all at once. Chapter 14, with its now false ending to the discourse, seems to represent an earlier stage in the construction of Jesus' last words to his disciples than do chaps. 15—16 (Beutler, *Habt keine Angst*), and the prayer of chap. 17 is evidently of still another character and origin.

The redundant phrase at the end of v. 1 after mention of the garden—
which he entered with his disciples—is apparently made to stress Jesus'
initiative, and his solidarity with his followers, to prepare for his interces-
sion for them in vv. 8b–9. That the Jewish guards now come both from the
chief priests **and from the Pharisees** (v. 3) is probably designed to relate
the episode to the Jewish leaders in 4E's own time, as in the account of the
plot against Jesus (11:47) and earlier in the interrogation of the Baptist
(1:24): the persecutors of late-first-century Christians are identified as
sharing in Jesus' capture.

By far the most important enhancement 4E makes in this story is in the
portrait of Jesus' stance in the face of those who are about to put him to
death. He is in no way at their mercy, but rather entirely in control of the
course of events. This was perhaps implied in the source; now it becomes
explicit. Thus **he knew all that would befall him,** and far from being
surprised and overtaken by his captors he **came out** to meet them, asking
to know their business (v. 4ab). If, as we supposed (just above), the source
already showed him yielding to them without resistance, this now becomes
an act of sovereignty; they have power over him, but only because he
allows, indeed himself precipitates, the arrest. Thus the *oun* is no longer
"So" as in PQ, Jesus responding to their arrival, but the Johannine
historical *oun* ("Then"), Jesus coming out entirely of his own will.

All this is clearest in 4E's radical handling of the word Jesus says in
giving himself up. Originally it meant only "I am he," like the "It's me" in
the pre-Johannine episode with the disciples on the sea (6:20). But even
more than there the simple acknowledgment now comes in 4E's hands to
have theophanic impact. Jesus utters the I AM of Hebraic divine self-
disclosure and of the Johannine revelatory discourses. The effect on his
hearers, accordingly, is staggering: **When he said to them, "I AM," they
drew back and fell to the ground** (v. 6), a reaction that includes not only
the police but **Judas his betrayer** as well; for he also **was standing with
them,** with whom he now belongs (v. 5b). All those who dare come before
Jesus, then, are laid low by the power of his utterance. In unwitting
contrast to the Synoptic scene of Gethsemane it is not Jesus who undergoes "prostration in the dust of the garden" but rather his captors (so
Brown, "The Passion," 128). The christological import is clear. Richter is
right to see here 4E's "answer to Jewish polemic against [the] messiahship
and divine sonship" of Jesus (*Studien*, 86).

Jesus necessarily repeats his question ("Who is it that you want?"), and
the same answer is given (v. 7). This might seem designed merely to
resume the more realistic pre-Johannine account of the arrest, into which
the drama of Jesus' self-disclosure was an intrusion. Yet before that return
to the source, Jesus repeats also his response—a typically Johannine
device (see 4:50–53)—and then something of its original meaning returns:

152

I have told you that I am he. Having identified himself, he directs that they seize only him and **let these men go** (v. 8). Jesus thus takes care of his own, a common Johannine interest, probably accounting for the insistence in vv. 1–2 that Jesus be viewed in company with the disciples. But even here the attention is more on Jesus, his power and foreknowledge, than on what he accomplishes for the disciples. Thus in an editorial aside 4E tells us (v. 9) that Jesus spoke in this way **in order to fulfill the word he had spoken** earlier. The promise that he would guard all those given to him, that none of them would be lost (6:39; 17:12), is kept. And as we have seen before (2:22), Jesus' word is for the Johannine author what a prophecy of scripture is for the predecessor; in both cases the word uttered reaches fulfillment, thereby making sense of what has taken place. With this high claim 4E evidently replaces the tradition of the disciples' flight; from the perspective of a later time Jesus' own are saved by him from apostasy already in his lifetime, even in the midst of his own arrest.

Thus it is not what happens to Jesus—his betrayal and arrest—but what he shows of himself that 4E would drive home: his Sovereignty in the Face of His Enemies. And this is a consequence of his divine sonship; accordingly, we are reminded that his own, just as in the source the cup that he must drink (v. 11c), were **given** to him by **the Father** (v. 9b).

Analysis[341]

• In v. 1 only the connective **When he had spoken these things** (meaning most of the contents of chaps. 13—17!) is clearly redactional. But the last clause (**which he entered with his disciples**) also may be an insertion, since it is redundant after what is already implied and is one of three references to the disciples, in company with Jesus, within the first two verses.[342]

• Verse 2 is redactional; the verse is designed to explain Judas's actions in v. 3. But is the redactor in question 4E or the predecessor? That Judas **knew the place** on the surface sounds Johannine, but as it means only "was familiar . . . " it is hardly an instance of the theme of supernatural or faith-inspired knowledge typical of 4E. The identification of Judas as Jesus' betrayer was from the hand of the Evangelist in 12:4, but there the phrase was a fuller explanation serving as forward reference ("the one who would betray him"), not simply a label as here (lit., "the betraying-him-one"). And the same phrase is found also in Mark 14:44 = Matt. 27:3 (and see Luke 22:21—contrast Mark 3:19; Luke 6:16). The phrase appears in most MSS of 4G at v. 5, where it is perhaps 4E's imitation of the pre-Johannine label here. Finally, without 4E's mention of the disciples' presence with Jesus a second time in v. 1, the explanation in v. 2b (**for Jesus often met there with his disciples**) is not pleonastic. The phrase appears to be pre-Johannine.

341. For Johannine tendency in the present passage, see Richter, *Studien,* 74–87.

342. The stylistic datum toward the end of this verse (*autos* in compound subject with singular verb: (lit.) "which he entered, he and his disciples") is not by itself decisive. It is pre-Johannine at several points in the miracle stories, but we cannot take for granted the integrity of the signs and passion sources, and in any case 4E could have used it here by imitation.

153

• The designation of those Judas takes with him in v. 3 seems overloaded; **and from the Pharisees** is surely 4E's insertion, as at 11:47.[343] But the inclusion of a Roman **troop of soldiers** is hardly due to Johannine tendency, which seeks to shift responsibility as much as possible from the Roman to the Jewish authorities. While mention of **lanterns and torches,** emphasizing the darkness in which Jesus' betrayal takes place, may be symbolic for 4E (13:30),[344] there is no reason to suppose that the detail is invented; following on the supper of chapter 13 it is circumstantial: the arrest would clearly have been at night.

• Jesus' foreknowledge in v. 4, while not unthinkable in PQ, can hardly be anything but Johannine, if only because of its general form ("knowing all things"— see 13:3; 19:28). Dauer may be right that Jesus' *going out* to meet his betrayer is Johannine as well. But the question **Who is it that you want?** would be entirely natural in the source, even if a similar question is possibly Johannine in 1:38.

• That Jesus identifies himself (v. 5a) by the phrase *egō eimi*, so important in the discourses, is not necessarily Johannine; just as occasionally in the Synoptic Gospels, here it means simply "I'm he," without theophanic significance.[345] But it becomes the basis of 4E's christological elaboration in vv. 6–8.

• If v. 5a is pre-Johannine, the notice that **Judas his betrayer was standing with them** in v. 5b is probably not the vestige of a traditional identifying kiss by Judas, as has been suggested. There is no hint of that poignant detail here; rather, the half-verse is a Johannine addition to include Judas in what follows.

• Verses 6–8a are highly characteristic of 4E; they show the dramatic Johannine elaboration of a matter-of-fact saying ("I'm he") from the source and also make Peter's action in v. 10 anticlimactic.

• In the second half of v. 8, Jesus' protection of his disciples, thus saving them from the sin of abandoning him, could be the result of developing tradition. But at an earlier point in the story the source very possibly contained a prediction of the disciples' flight (16:32b; see this part, sec. 14); then vv. 8b–9 here, which subtly contradict it, would appear to be 4E's substitute for a pre-Johannine fulfillment of that prediction a few verses later. In that case what we now have here is the fulfillment of the Johannine Jesus' prediction that the disciples would not be lost (6:39; 17:12). Verses 6–9 as whole are thus redactional.

• The distinctiveness of v. 10 is, I think, due to developing tradition and not deliberate redaction: it is **Peter** who cuts off the slave's ear,[346] and the slave is named **Malchus.** The particle *oun,* originally logical ("So"), becomes the historical idiom ("Then," as in v. 4—see this section, Johannine Redaction) to connect 4E's added material (vv. 6–9) to the source, resumed here.

---

343. See this part, sec. 11, Analysis. Dauer *(Passionsgeschichte)* attributes all mention of Jewish officers to 4E, but the Synoptic tradition (Mark 14:43 = Matt. 26:47) had agents of the "chief priests" going with Judas, and "the slave of the high priest" (in Greek, the same word as "chief priest") figures in all versions of the story.

344. So Brown, "The Passion," 127.

345. One important MS (Codex B) reads "I am Jesus," which is hardly original but correctly understands the force of the pre-Johannine phrase prior to its interpretive development in the following verses.

346. And his *right* ear (see Luke 22:50). It is no clear mark of redaction that an unusual verb is used for drawing the sword.

• Possibly Jesus' word to Peter in v. 11c has been retouched by 4E—the phrase **which the Father** [sic] **has given me** has a Johannine ring—but the rough parallel in Mark 14:36 ("Father . . . this cup") suggests that it is traditional.

• In v. 12, which completes the episode, only **from the Jews** could be redactional.

• If the source originally reported the flight of the disciples, as seems likely on Synoptic analogy, it would have come at this point.

SECTION 16 (18:13-27)[347]
WITH PETER AT THE
HIGH PRIEST'S HOUSE

Pre-Johannine Source

18 ¹³**And they led him first to Annas, for he was the father-in-law of Caiaphas, who was high priest that year.** [[²⁴**So Annas sent him bound to Caiaphas.**]] ¹⁵**Now Simon Peter and another disciple followed Jesus. That disciple was known to the high priest, and he went into the courtyard of the high priest along with Jesus,** ¹⁶ᵃ**but Peter stood outside at the door.** ¹⁹**The high priest (asked Jesus about his teaching.** ²⁰**Jesus answered him, "I have taught in the Temple where all are gathered;** ²¹ᵃ**why do you ask me?")** [The **high priest said to him, "If you are the Christ, tell us,"**[348] **and he said, "If I told you, you would not believe." . . . And Jesus said, "Do you say, 'You are blaspheming' because I said that I am the Son of God?"**] ²²**When he had said this one of the guards standing there struck Jesus a blow and said, "Is that how you answer the high priest?"**

[[¹⁶ᵇ**So the other disciple, the one known to the high priest, went out and spoke to the doorkeeper and brought Peter in.** ¹⁷**And the maid who was doorkeeper said to Peter, "Are you one of this man's disciples too?" He said, "No, I'm not."** ¹⁸**Now the slaves and guards had made a fire, since it was cold, and were standing and warming themselves. And Peter also stood with them and warmed himself.**]] ²⁵ᵇ**So they said to him, "Are you also one of his disciples?" He denied it and said, "No, I'm not."** ²⁶**One of the high priest's slaves, a relative of the one whose ear Peter had cut off, said, "Didn't I see you in the garden with him?"** ²⁷**Again Peter denied it. And immediately the cock crowed.**

Realizing that our rearrangement is hypothetical, nevertheless on its basis we find a coherent pre-Johannine account, readily distinguishable from 4E's redaction and free of the strange inconsistencies in the canonical order.

347. See my article of a similar title, dealing chiefly with the passage as "a test case for the question of the relation between Mark's and John's Gospels."

348. The present form of this material, from chap. 10, presupposes that Jesus is speaking to a group of Jewish officials, not simply to the high priest. So possibly the original at this point had different pronouns. Alternatively, the high priest uses the official "we."

The arrest, as we saw, was somewhat overshadowed by the horror of Judas's betrayal and the drama of Peter's attempt at resistance; so when Jesus is finally seized (v. 12) the event is told very briefly and leads without pause into the present episode. Having bound him, the police take him to the Temple authorities. That they go **first to Annas** is not explained, but we can suppose that tradition has supplied this detail; Annas is not only of the high priestly family but presumably himself a former high priest.[349] He recognizes the importance of this arrest and immediately hands Jesus on to his son-in-law **Caiaphas,** the actual **high priest that year** (as we learned earlier, in the account of the Official Conspiracy). It is Caiaphas, then, who interrogates Jesus in the source, as we should expect. The scene is not presented as a formal trial, certainly not in the presence of the Sanhedrin, as Mark has shaped the tradition;[350] yet the proceeding is official enough in its outcome.

We have had to surmise how the hearing before Caiaphas was depicted prior to 4E's redaction. Jesus at first wonders why the high priest must ask about what is plainly public knowledge, **his teaching.** Then, when the question of his theological identity is bluntly put, Jesus declines to give a direct answer. As in the Lukan tradition, he observes that were he to answer, the high priest **would not believe.** For the source, the only relevant response to Jesus' messiahship is faith. Thus the juridical question put to Jesus **(If you are the Christ, tell us)** is inappropriate, for it is asked not from a desire to believe but rather to condemn. If the menacing circumstances did not show that, Caiaphas's role in the earlier meeting of the Sanhedrin (11:47–53) would make it clear. Together with that whole council, Caiaphas "did not believe in him, though he had done so many signs before them" (12:37). Jesus' initial evasiveness is not cagey or self-protective, but realistic; Caiaphas could not and would not react to the information that Jesus is **the Christ** in the way that that fact requires, namely, by believing in him.

But evidently Jesus does then acknowledge his divine sonship, as in all the Synoptics, and gains thereby the charge of blasphemy. This reaction on Caiaphas's part is both predictable and ironic; even in the source—as so much more clearly in 4G—Jesus is no ordinary Jew, subject to the laws of religion, but himself the Son of God, and therefore incapable of blaspheming. His question (**"Do you say, 'You are blaspheming,' because I said that I am the Son of God?"**) thus patiently raises the issue of the charge's inappropriateness. But it is misunderstood as disrespectful, and so he is struck by one of the guards (v. 22).

349. See Luke 3:2, Acts 4:6, where, however, he is taken to share the high-priestly office with Caiaphas.
350. Donahue, *Trial,* 63–98.

The image of Jesus projected by this story is one of authority and almost invulnerability, despite the fate that awaits him. He does not yet "preside" over the events that lead to his death, but he is calm and confident. What is taking place must take place, and so it is acceptable.

Jesus is not entirely alone during the hostile interrogation; an unnamed disciple has managed to follow him into the courtyard and apparently observes his mistreatment by the authorities. He then goes out and brings Peter in, presumably with the hope of somehow giving support to Jesus. But if so, the gesture is cruelly ironic. Just as Peter's impetuousness at the time of the arrest was inappropriate, so now even more does he fail his master, cravenly denying all connection with him. Three times he is asked if he is a disciple. It is not clear whether the questions put to Peter expect a negative or a positive answer, but in any case they express sufficient suspicion to elicit flat denials from him; twice he says, **No, I'm not:** to the doorkeeper (v. 17) and to the slaves and guards standing at the fire (v. 25). Finally the question is more pointedly accusatory, coming from the one Peter has made an enemy: **Didn't I see you in the garden with him?** (v. 26—see v. 20), and **again Peter denied it** (v. 27a).

The contrast with Jesus' fearless candor is evident.[351] But there is another contrast that is still more striking—between Peter's threefold denials here and the Baptist's threefold profession in chapter 1. We have not established the integrity of the source underlying that story and PQ, but it is remarkable that in the pre-Johannine form of both accounts there is so close a parallel.[352] Strictly speaking the Baptist disclaimed that he was the Messiah; but his three negative answers to the questions put to him are a forthright profession of Jesus' messiahship and are made honestly, selflessly. So the author can tell us that he "bore witness." By contrast Peter truly **denied**, and his mendacity was entirely self-serving. It fulfills Jesus' prediction (13:38b), as the cock crow reminds (only) us (v. 27b).

Johannine Redaction

18 [13]And they led him first to Annas, for he was the father-in-law of Caiaphas, who was high priest that year. [14]**It was Caiaphas who had counseled the Jews that it was expedient for one man to die on behalf of the people.** [15]Now Simon Peter and another disciple followed Jesus. That disciple was known to the high priest, and he went into the courtyard of the high priest along with Jesus, [16]but Peter stood outside at the door. *Then* the other disciple, the one known to the high priest, went out and spoke to the doorkeeper and brought Peter in. [17]And the maid who was doorkeeper said to Peter, "Are you one of

---

351. Whereas Peter twice says, "I am not" (*ouk eimi*), Jesus repeatedly has declared, "I AM" (*egō eimi*)—so Foster, "John Come Lately," 118.

352. There are other parallels between the source in chap. 1 and in chap. 18; see this part, n. 361.

this man's disciples too?" He said, "No, I'm not." ¹⁸Now the slaves and guards had made a fire, since it was cold, and were standing and warming themselves. And Peter also stood with them and warmed himself. ¹⁹Then the high priest asked Jesus about **his disciples and** his teaching. ²⁰Jesus answered him, **"I have spoken openly to the world;** I have always taught **in the synagogue and** in the Temple where all **the Jews** are gathered; **and I have spoken nothing in secret.** ²¹Why do you ask me? **Ask those who have heard what I spoke to them. You will see**³⁵³ **that they know what I said to them."** ²²When he said this one of the guards standing there struck Jesus a blow, saying "Is this how you answer the high priest?" ²³**Jesus replied to him, "If I have spoken wrong, testify to the wrong; but if right, why do you strike me?** ²⁴*Then* Annas sent him bound to Caiaphas, **the high priest.**

²⁵**Now Simon Peter was standing and warming himself.** *Now* they said to him, "Are you also one of his disciples?" He denied it and said, "No, I'm not." ²⁶One of the high priest's slaves, a relative of the one whose ear Peter had cut off, said "Didn't I see you in the garden with him?" ²⁷Again Peter denied it. And immediately the cock crowed.

The Evangelist's reworking of this story is of two kinds—rearranging and recasting.

1. Rearrangement within the passage takes place at two points:

a. The delivery of Jesus to Caiaphas is postponed, moving the original sequel of v. 13 to its present place as v. 24. This has the effect, no doubt intended, of making one hearing into two, thus *intensifying* the Jewish determination to destroy Jesus. We are shown only the first hearing, now undertaken by Annas (with the various anomalies we note in the Analysis); apparently we are to think of it as a preliminary investigation, supposing that Caiaphas completed the proceeding (or at least ratified Annas's finding) during the time of Peter's second and third denials. This of course entails no diminution of Caiaphas, whose earlier role is recalled in 4E's inserted v. 14 (usefully filling the original place of v. 24). If Annas, acting for his son-in-law, found Jesus culpable, and especially if Jesus ended by confounding him, this could be taken to apply also to the high priest himself in 4E's conception.

b. The Evangelist moves forward the first of Peter's denials so that each of the two hearings is to be thought of as simultaneous with the denials. This emphasizes the *contrast* between Jesus' steady and presiding presence and Peter's helpless cowardice. Whereas Peter had originally been kept offstage during the hearing, waiting outside the door, now he is brought in beforehand (with attendant confusion in vv. 15–16) so that his first denial is meant to precede, or more likely coincide with, what takes place between Annas and Jesus. When Jesus has been sent on to Caiaphas the denials resume.³⁵⁴

353. This, I think, is the force of the Greek *ide* (lit., "behold").
354. The separation of vv. 16b–18 from vv. 25b–27 requires the reiteration in v. 25a.

Apart from this displacement, there is no evidence of Johannine redaction in the denial half of the combined material. Not even the "other disciple" is identified, though in view of the close parallel with the beloved disciple and his relation to Peter in the account of the empty tomb (20:1–10), we can imagine that the faceless figure here is to be imagined as that Johannine character, acting as it were incognito. Or, to think of it another way, perhaps this traditional disciple was somehow a model of the beloved disciple's portrayal in chapter 20 (and also chap. 21).

c. A third kind of rearrangement altogether involves the interchanges between Jesus and the high priest, which have been separated altogether from this event at the end of Jesus' life and now appear in chapter 10, as part of the long dialogue in the Temple on the feast of Hanukkah. They involve "the Jews" in general. The conditional form of Jesus' answer to the question of his identity has now given way to factual: **I told you, and you do not believe. The works that I do in my Father's name, they bear witness to me; but you do not believe** (10:25–26a). Similarly, the question of blasphemy becomes the occasion for an attempt to stone Jesus, that is, a foreshadowing of the trial and execution that finally destroyed Jesus. The Evangelist has replicated Jesus' explicit self-disclosure, coming only at the end of his life in the source, as an event repeated again and again in 4G.

2. It is in the reshaping of the hearing before Annas that 4E's editorial hand is most evident. The questions and challenges put to Jesus in the pre-Johannine account having been mostly removed, at this point we hear only in summary that Annas, acting as if high priest, **asked Jesus about his disciples and his teaching** (v. 19). We supposed that the source read here only "about his teaching." If that could barely have meaning then, it now is obviously fitting; the Johannine Jesus teaches, even more than he performs signs. The addition of "his disciples' builds on the fact that in the source the disciples are almost always in the background of the signs, a role that 4E sometimes enhances (e.g., Philip in chap. 6, Thomas in chap. 11). And in the latter-day Johannine situation the disciples stand for the Christian community, here investigated by the Jewish authorities as much as Jesus himself and his activity were under scrutiny at the end of his life some sixty years earlier.

Still more than in the source, the commanding figure throughout this scene is not the high priest but Jesus. His answer in v. 20 greatly expands what we imagined the source to contain; it has now become an overt statement of his authority and integrity. He has **spoken openly to the world,** has **said nothing in secret;** his teaching has been **always in synagogue and in the Temple,**[355] **where all the Jews gather.** The double

---

355. Michaels ("Temple Discourse," 200) suggests that this summary phrase brings together the synagogue discourse in chap. 6 and the Temple discourse in chaps. 7—8, both Johannine constructs. If the source already spoke of Jesus' teaching in the Temple, as in the Synoptic account of the arrest, then 4E has added the mention of synagogue teaching, depicted in 4G only at the Johannine level.

phrase perhaps reflects once again the Johannine two-level technique: Jesus, in his lifetime teaching in the Temple, and the church, once the Temple was destroyed, working within the local synagogue. In fact, of course, 4E has just portrayed Jesus teaching at length more or less in secret (chaps. 14—17). Evidently 4E would like to claim both that Jesus teaches his own, teaches them in fact what the world cannot understand, and that he also reveals to the world the truth that only he can reveal. In short, Jesus stands both as the revealer to the world and as the special source of truth for the church.

And his seeming defense is really a counter-challenge to those who would question him: **Why do you ask me? Ask those who have heard what I have said. You will see that they know what I have said** (v. 21).[356] Jesus is not answerable for his practice; that responsibility is properly filled by his followers, ostensibly his contemporary disciples, in fact the Christians of 4E's own time. This answer now occasions the physical abuse that the traditional account contained (v. 22). But again Jesus keeps the upper hand, for he has the last word, challenging Annas to justify this impropriety in accusing him. Jesus thus turns the tables on the rebuke in v. 22b: **If I have taught wrong testify to the wrong** (v. 23a). And he leaves Annas with the unanswerable question, . . . **but if the truth, why do you strike me?** (v. 23b). In frustration and helplessness Annas turns Jesus over to Caiaphas (v. 24), just as the latter will soon send him to Pilate (v. 28). In this passage, then, as 4E reconceives it, Jesus the Revealer Interrogates His Questioners.

Analysis

This passage contains a number of difficulties of logic and sequence, just the sort of aporias that would suggest redactional adaptation. But critics are far from unanimous as to the literary history of this story, so the solution proposed here, while it seems to me to stand up in the face of recent analyses,[357] must be regarded as more tentative than in some other passages in the passion story.

Two stories, perhaps originally distinct, are interwoven here—*Jesus' hearing* before the high priest and *Peter's denials*—and it is primarily their present arrangement that causes the various difficulties. (1) As it now stands the hearing is conducted not by the high priest Caiaphas but by his father-in-law, Annas (v. 13), with only the suggestion of a second hearing by Caiaphas (the otherwise pointless v. 24). The authority conducting the hearing is nevertheless referred to several times simply as "high priest" (vv. 15–16, 19, 22), and there is confusion about where both the hearing and the denials take place, that is, whether in the house of Annas or of Caiaphas. (2) In the case of the denials, Peter's wait at the door (v. 16a)

356. Knowing is, of course, another Johannine theme, and in particular knowing and understanding what Jesus has said.

357. Notably by Dauer *(Passionsgeschichte)*, Schnackenburg, and B & L, all of whom resist the hypothesis that 4E has rearranged the source's sequence of events in this passage.

is curious, followed immediately by his admission to the house (v. 16b). The identification of the "other disciple" as "known to the high priest" in consecutive verses (15–16) is odd, as various textual attempts to eliminate the redundancy show. And the preparation for Peter's second denial—his "standing and warming himself" at the fire with the soldiers (v. 18b)—is now separated from the denial itself (v. 25b), requiring the mechanical repetition of v. 18b in v. 25a.[358]

The most satisfactory solution to all these difficulties, I propose, is that they stem from 4E's rearrangement of the source.[359] Such a hypothesis rightly causes some hesitancy, not to say skepticism, on the part of critics. Yet with two rather simple transformations a coherent source becomes separable from 4E's redaction, that redaction itself becomes explicable (the key test), and the resulting structure is roughly the same as that in Mark 14:53–72.[360]

The two rearrangements are these: (1') Verse 24, which now leads nowhere (though it can be seen to serve a makeshift purpose), would originally have followed v. 13; Jesus is thereby led "first"[361] to Annas, who immediately sends him on to his son-in-law, the actual high priest, for the hearing. (2') Peter's entry into the high priest's courtyard and his first denial (vv. 16b–18) would originally have followed the hearing (vv. 19–22) and immediately preceded the second and third denials (vv. 25b–27); thus Peter waits at the door during the interrogation, and the "other disciple known to the high priest"[362] then goes out for him, perhaps because he sees Jesus mistreated (v. 22).

On the supposition that 4E has made these rearrangements (for reasons detailed above, see Johannine Redaction), then, source and redaction can be distinguished as follows:

358. C. A. Evans ("Warming") notes that there is a similar repetition in Mark 14:54, 67, and suggests that it stems from the oral tradition and so finds its way into both the Markan and the Johannine accounts. The parallel is more tenuous than Evans supposes—only in 4G is there a verbatim repetition, whereas in Mark there is simply an allusion to what had been said—and I believe that the parallel is really only coincidence.

359. This way out of the difficulties presented by the text was perceived in antiquity, as the rearrangements in various MSS show. These cannot be held to be original (still less reflecting the pre-Johannine form of the story), but they suggest that it is the order in the canonical text that has produced the problems and thus they can lead us to the points where the rearrangements may have occurred.

360. That is, in both versions the hearing is completed before any of Peter's denials, as is also true in Matt. 26:57–75. Luke 22:54–71 shows just the reverse order, the denials before the hearing, but the two episodes are equally distinct. To be sure, the Markan order is only analogous to that proposed for 4E's source here, and not identical. More preparation for the denials (in particular, Peter's warming himself at the fire with the guards) appears in the Markan account of the hearing than in what I propose as pre-Johannine, and the manner by which Peter finds his way into the courtyard is different: in the pre-Johannine source it involves the "other disciple" peculiar to that tradition. Thus, as usual, we seem to be dealing not with dependence but with similar yet evidently only parallel traditions. The Synoptic evidence is useful to us as analogy, not as direct evidence; but it is useful all the same.

361. This word is now all but pointless. For a close structural analogue (whatever it means) to this and other details in a pre-Johannine narrative, see on 1:35–42 (p. 37): "followed Jesus," "standing," two disciples (one of them unnamed), "first."

362. If this figure is a Johannine creation, as some hold (see this part, n. 365), the redundancy of vv. 15–16 is unexplained.

• Verse 13 is a pre-Johannine continuation of the sentence begun in v. 12,[363] and v. 24 follows naturally after it. Only the unnecessary appositive phrase at the end of v. 24 (**the high priest**) is redactional. Verse 14 appears to be a Johannine cross-reference,[364] evidently filling the gap left by the removal of v. 24.

• In both source and present Gospel, just as in the Synoptics, Peter's denials are in some way combined with the hearing, and although—according to our hypothesis—in the source they do not occur until after the hearing, the stage must now in some way be set for them (as in Mark 14:54). Two of Jesus' disciples—Peter and "another disciple"[365]—follow him, but only the latter gains entrance to the high priest's house (vv. 15–16a).

• The hearing before Caiaphas (vv. 19–23) now takes place. I have been persuaded that 4E has considerably rewritten the original account,[366] making its recovery difficult. In v. 19 the indirect and compressed form of the high priest's question to Jesus—**concerning his disciples and his teaching**—is an editorial summary of all the interrogations Jesus has undergone in the Johannine scenes of conflict with "the Jews" in the first half of the Gospel.[367] Likewise Jesus' words here (vv. 20–21, 23) betray 4E's hand, both in diction ("openly"/"in secret," "the world," "all the Jews") and tone (Jesus' command of the situation: his regal attitude, especially in v. 21, and his authoritative logic in v. 23, in both cases returning the high priest's questions with his own).

• But some vestiges of the original hearing evidently remain. The slap given Jesus by one of the soldiers (v. 22a)—and possibly also the accompanying rebuke (v. 22b)—seems clearly part of the pre-Johannine story. But what of the words spoken on this occasion? Here the analogy of the Synoptics may be of help. For on their account of the arrest of Jesus, his remark ("Daily I was in the Temple teaching and you did not seize me"—Mark 14:49 pars.) has a strong echo here with v. 20 ("I have always taught . . . in the Temple"). Possibly, then, this detail is traditional.[368]

• Further, elements now to be found in *chapter 10*, and identifiable because of

363. If the source gave a notice of the disciples' flight which 4E has omitted (see this part, sec. 15), there was nevertheless no break in the connection between arrest and the present hearing; v. 13a implies the same direct object (Jesus) as that expressed in v. 12.

364. See 11:2 for the same form of editorial aside ("It was . . . who . . ."). Contrast the briefer, pre-Johannine reminder at the end of v. 13.

365. Is this disciple to be taken as the beloved disciple? (so Neirynck, "Other Disciple"). If so, mention of him could be a Johannine addition. But more likely the nameless figure is a traditional detail as in 1:35–39, possibly understood by 4E subsequently as the beloved disciple (or even used as the basis for her or his creation of this figure).

366. See Fortna, "Jesus and Peter," 380–81. Contrast *TGOS*, 117–22.

367. Michaels ("Temple Discourse") persuasively shows that this is true of the synagogue discourse in 6:26–59 and the Temple discourse in 7:14—8:59.

368. In the source Jesus has hardly taught; not at all in the signs, if that was already attached to the passion, but once very pointedly in the prelude to the passion, namely in the Restoration of the Temple—just the precedent needed for this question in the pre-Johannine high priest's interrogation and Jesus' answer about the Temple. The disciples do figure in the signs stories, but their role there would hardly be the subject of questioning here. Oddly, then, the source may have mentioned Jesus' teaching and not the disciples, and it is 4E who has created the double phrase.

their parallels in the Synoptic accounts of the high priestly trial, may have come originally from the source at this point, and then were removed by 4E to the earlier setting. In 10:24–25 we find: "If you are the Christ, tell us . . ."; " . . . I told you, and you did not believe" (see Luke 22:67).[369] And in v. 36 (also v. 33), the admission of divine sonship and the consequent charge of blasphemy (see Mark 14:64 pars.) is perhaps original. It is not foolhardy, then, to suggest that these fragments can help us imagine how the source once read.

● Peter's denials—all three together—would have followed in the source. Verse 16b resumes the brief preparation already laid. The nameless disciple, presumably on seeing Jesus struck, goes out and persuades the doorkeeper to let Peter in. This occasions the first accusation and Peter's curt denial (v. 17).
● Verse 18 sets up the second denial. Peter joins a group of slaves and soldiers warming themselves at a fire. They immediately make the same accusation, and Peter again denies it (25b).[370] The first half of v. 25 has been inserted by 4E to bridge the connection broken by that author's rearrangement.
● The third accusation and denial follow (vv. 26–27a), and the source's account ends with the fateful cock crow (v. 27b).

SECTION 17 (18:28—19:16a)
JESUS IS TRIED BY PILATE

Pre-Johannine Source

18 ²⁸ᵃSo they led Jesus from the house of Caiaphas into the Pretorium; it was early morning. ²⁹Pilate said, "What charge do you bring against this man?" [The Jewish leaders answered, "He has made himself out to be king."] ³³So Pilate called Jesus and said to him, "Are you the king of the Jews?" [³⁷ᵇJesus answered, "You say I am a king." *Perhaps a second question, to which Jesus remains silent.*] ³⁸ᶜHe said to them, "I find no crime in him, ³⁹but it is your custom that at Passover I release one man to you. Do you want me to release 'the king of the Jews' for you then?" ⁴⁰They shouted back, "Not this man but Barabbas!" Now Barabbas was an [insurrectionist]. [*Pilate asks what he should do then with Jesus.*] 19 ⁶ᵃᶜThe chief priests and the guards cried out, "Crucify him! crucify him!" Pilate said to them, "I find no crime in him." [*They call again for Jesus to be crucified.*] ¹³So Pilate took Jesus out and sat down in the judgment seat in the place know as the Stone Pavement,[371] or in 'Hebrew' Gabbatha. ¹⁴ᵃIt was Friday, about

---

369. Michaels, "Temple Discourse," 211. The difference in tense and mood in Jesus' reply compared to Luke (where it is conditional: "If I tell you, you will not believe") is perhaps due to Johannine redaction. In the source, Jesus has not explicitly said who he is, as he repeatedly does in 4G.

370. The indefinite "they" here, though not intolerable in its present context, becomes simply a natural extension of the subject of v. 18 when v. 25b is restored to what we hold to be its original place.

371. For this translation of the pre-Johannine formula *legomenon*, see in this part, n. 173. The Greek phrase evidently does not translate the Semitic name that follows; the text simply gives both names as attaching to the same place.

twelve noon. [[[¹Then Pilate took Jesus and had him whipped. ²And the soldiers wove a crown of thorns and put it on his head and put a purple cloak on him, ³and they came up to him and said, "Hail! the king of the Jews!" and they hit him.]] ¹⁶ᵃSo [Pilate] then turned him over to them to be crucified.

The above is offered as a reconstruction of the pre-Johannine text, as with every passage we analyze. The points at which it is based mainly on surmise are indicated by the brackets. We shall be wise to remember that in view of 4E's heavy reworking of the entire passage the reconstruction is especially hypothetical. Nevertheless a distinct and coherent narrative emerges and can be interpreted.

The passage constitutes one continuous scene, taking place—until the final sentencing—inside the military residence known as the **Pretorium**.[372] If the detail in 18:28b (the refusal to enter the Pretorium) were pre-Johannine, a slight possibility, it would have suggested to 4E the alternation between indoors and out that the present Gospel displays, but thereafter the narrative in no way indicates such a pattern prior to 4E's redaction. Once Jesus has been summoned (v. 33), the trial progresses with both accusers and defendant present together before Pilate. The identity of those who bring Jesus before the governor is not clear at first, but it emerges (19:6) that they are **chief priests and guards;** presumably these guards are those "from the chief priests" who functioned at the arrest (18:3, 12) and again at the high priest's house, and the chief priests themselves have then joined them to press the charge. We cannot be entirely sure what their accusation is or just what transpires in Pilate's interrogation of Jesus, but the general charge of political agitation is evident.

In Pilate's questioning Jesus it is apparent that he is not convinced of Jesus' guilt; thus, perhaps in the interest of justice, he proposes to compromise by treating Jesus as a political prisoner and as such to pardon him (**release "the king of the Jews"**). When this proves wholly unacceptable to the Jewish authorities, he hands the problem over to them (if our surmise about what originally followed v. 40 is correct). They insist that Jesus be executed, and despite his persisting opinion that there is no case against Jesus, Pilate consents. Thus Pilate turns out not so much fair-minded as uninterested, and motivated only by the wish to avoid a clash with the chief priests. In fact he goes out of his way to satisfy them; he formally condemns Jesus in public[373] and personally oversees the ritual castigation

---

372. Thus this source carefully locates the scene. In Mark it evidently takes place outside, since crowds appear, but that is not so clear.

373. We are to understand this from the act of sitting "in the judgment seat" at the place whose name means The Pavement.

and presumably also the derision that precede execution.[374] It is clear that the Jewish leaders play a critical part in all of this, but there is no question of the Jewish people, or even a crowd representing them, calling for the death of Jesus.[375]

Throughout, the impression we get of Jesus is only indirect. He says virtually nothing in the trial and thereafter is at the mercy of both Roman and Jewish authorities. Nothing of the sovereignty of the Johannine Jesus appears, consistent as that might be with the messianic worker of signs, and perhaps with Jesus' role in the house of the high priest (see this part, sec. 16). Presumably this section of the account had an origin distinct from others (scarcely based on eyewitness) and was only combined with them by the pre-Johannine author. The way this part of the narrative justifies Jesus' death is not to show him less a victim but, as we might expect, to prove in the next episode that all this had been foretold.

A distinctive mark of the account is its careful citing of details of time and place: early morning, Stone Pavement/Gabbatha, Friday at noon—in every case pointedly told for their own sake—and not merely in passing, as usually in the Synoptics. Such narrative vividness is the same as in the miracle stories.

Johannine Redaction

Scene 1

18 [28]*Then* they led Jesus from the house of Caiaphas into the Pretorium; it was early morning. **And they themselves would not enter the Pretorium lest they be defiled and might not eat the Passover.** [29]Pilate **thus went out to them and said, "What** charge do you bring against this man?" [30]**They answered and said to him, "If he were not an evil-doer we would not have handed him over to you."** [31]**Then Pilate said to them, "Take him yourselves and judge him according to your law." The Jews said, "It is not allowed us to put anyone to death,"** [32]**so that the word of Jesus, which he spoke signifying by what death he would die, might be fulfilled.**

Scene 2

[33]*Then* Pilate **went back into the Pretorium and** summoned Jesus and said to him, "Are you the king of the Jews?" [34]**Jesus replied, "Do you say this of**

---

374. The text reads literally that Pilate "whipped him," but we are surely to take this in the causative sense expressed in the translation above. Hahn ("Prozess," 38) holds that the Evangelist was the first to combine scourging and mocking. More likely it is the contribution of the narrative source, and reproduced by 4E.

375. If, as seems most likely, it was solely or predominantly the Roman power that in fact brought about Jesus' death, already in the tradition, then there is a tendency, accurate or not, to implicate the Jewish officials. They plot Jesus' death and force Pilate to carry it out. Thus, even in a combined SQ and PQ, an apologetic for belief in Jesus' messiahship on the part of Jews, there is no attempt to spare the leaders of the nation in the time of Jesus. Perhaps in the pre-Johannine community's Jewish context there was a good deal of tolerance for criticism of the establishment, at least in the past.

yourself or do others say it to you about me?" [35]Pilate answered, "Am I a Jew?! Your nation and the chief priests have handed you over to me. What have you done?" [36]Jesus answered, "My kingdom is not of this world. If my kingdom were of this world, my guards would fight lest I be handed over to the Jews." [37]Then Pilate said to him, "Then you are a king?" Jesus answered, "You say I am a king. For this I was born and have come into the world: to bear witness to the truth. Everyone who is of the truth hears my voice." [38a]Pilate said to him, "What is truth?"

Scene 3

[38b]When he had said this he went out again to the Jews and he said to them, "I find no crime in him, [39]but it is your custom that at Passover I release one man to you. Do you want me to release 'the king of the Jews' for you then?" [40]They shouted back, "Not this man but Barabbas!" Now Barabbas was a robber.

Scene 4

19 [1]Then Pilate took Jesus and had him whipped. [2]And the soldiers wove a crown of thorns and put it on his head and put a purple cloak on him, [3]and they came up to him and said, "Hail! the king of the Jews!" and they hit him.

Scene 5

[4]And Pilate went out again and said to them, "Look, I am bringing him out so that you may know that I find no crime in him. [5]Then he brought Jesus out, wearing the crown of thorns and the purple garment. And he said to them, "Behold the Man!" [6]Now when they saw him the chief priests and the guards cried out, "Crucify him! crucify him!" Pilate said to them, "Take him yourselves and crucify him, for I find no crime in him." [7]The Jews answered him, "We have a law and by that law he ought to die, for he made himself the Son of God."

Scene 6

[8]Now when Pilate heard this phrase he was greatly afraid, [9]and he went into the Pretorium again and said to Jesus, "Where do you come from?" But Jesus gave him no reply. [10]Then Pilate said to him, "Will you not speak to me? Do you not know that I have authority to release you and I have authority to crucify you?" [11]Jesus replied to him, "You would have no authority over me unless it had been given to you from above. Therefore he who hands me over to you has the greater sin."

Scene 7

[12]At this Pilate sought to release him, but the Jews cried out and said, "If you release this man you are no friend of Caesar's. Anyone who makes himself a king denounces Caesar." [13]*Then* hearing this Pilate brought Jesus out and *seated him* in the judgment seat in the place known as the Stone Pavement, or in 'Hebrew' Gabbatha. [14]It was *the preparation* [*day*] of Pass-

over, about twelve noon. **And he said to them, "Here is your King!"** [15]**Then they cried out, "Take him away; take him away! Crucify him!" Pilate said to them, "Shall I crucify your king?!" The chief priests answered, "We have no king but Caesar."** [16a]*Then* he turned him over to them to be crucified.

We have come here very nearly to the heart, in a sense to the climax, of the Johannine author's Gospel. This is the last and greatest of the scened dramas that 4E creates from the narrative material available.[376] In it the Johannine polarity between God and the world—dramatically represented here as a polarity between Jesus, inside the Pretorium, and "the Jews" outside—comes to a head. Pilate is but the go-between, the foil for this tension. Jesus, though at the mercy of "the Jews," yet is sovereign over all that takes place. He does not directly confront them, or they him; his separation from the world, begun at the end of chapter 12, is especially evident here, just before he departs from it altogether.

The trial, over which Pilate presided in the source, here becomes a contest in which Jesus and "the Jews" are the major forces, and Pilate is reduced to the status of a pawn. On the one hand the power the chief priests held over him in the traditional account ("Not this man but Barabbas," "Crucify him!") is now made explicit. On the other, Jesus quietly waiting within the Pretorium commands all that takes place.

As scene 1 (18:28–32) begins, "they" lead Jesus from the Jewish authorities to the Roman. The pronoun presumably referred to the guards originally, taking up v. 24. But the Evangelist has a different conception, which emerges in v. 28b. Those who bring Jesus before Pilate are now all Jewish, at first perhaps only the leaders or their representatives, but by v. 38b "the Jews" in general. For, we learn, **they would not enter the Pretorium**—this datum becomes the pretext for the alternation of scenes outside and within the official residence—**so that they might eat the Passover.** The latter is clearly intended as heavy irony: Just at the moment when "the Jews" are bringing about the death of him who is Lamb of God, the Bread of Life, they are careful only to preserve themselves from cultic defilement for their Passover meal.[377]

As a consequence, Pilate **went out to them** (v. 29a). Far from merely consenting to let them appear before him, he—the representative of the power of Rome—indulgently seeks them out in order to inquire what their complaint might be. The question of v. 29b (**What charge do you bring**

---

376. The drama in chap. 9 is almost comparable in scale and importance, as the ministry of signs, the first half of the Gospel, is drawing to a close. It thus has a position and a function similar to the Pilate drama in the Gospel's second half. The drama here has a carefully conceived symmetry, as Ehrman, "Trial," has shown.

377. See also the tragic irony in their eventual disclaimer of all Jewish loyalty ("We have no king but Caesar"—19:15) as Jaubert, "Pilate," shows. (The nonhistoricity of this portrayal of the Jewish people must be kept in mind, in view of the anti-Semitism the Gospel has occasioned.)

against this man?), taken probably from the source where it had a purely procedural function, now becomes his first act of condescension to the Jewish protagonists, and the rest of the scene is entirely Johannine.

For his pains he is met with insolence: **If this man were not an evil-doer we would not have handed him over to you** (v. 30). But Pilate's question has been answered. Jesus is presumably guilty only of a Jewish transgression; the charge is not documented but presented as if already proven. So Pilate tries to throw the case back to Jesus' accusers: **Take him yourselves and judge him by your own law** (v. 31a). A note of impatience is evident, but it is ineffectual and his attempt to sidestep the case is without success. We are to understand from their reply—**It is not lawful for us to put anyone to death** (v. 31b)—that Jesus had already been judged by Jewish law and found guilty of capital crime, but the Jewish authorities lack the capability to carry out the execution. The will is there, clearly, but a legal technicality prevents them. In a final comment (v. 32) 4E sees this as no happenstance. On the contrary a facet of the divine plan is in process of enactment: though now out of sight and jurisdictionally subject to the Jewish and Roman powers, Jesus is in control. For he himself had predicted **by what death he would die,** the Roman death of being "lifted up" on a cross (3:14), and that prophecy is coming to pass. So understood, the death itself—despite all the unjust conniving of the Jewish and Roman rulers—will be not abasement but exaltation.[378]

Pilate now goes back into the Pretorium for the first confrontation with Jesus (scene 2: 18:33–38a). He begins authoritatively enough—he **summoned** Jesus (a verb probably derived from the source)—but soon he will be shown to be at Jesus' mercy, merely an audience for Jesus' first speech and one who even so fails to understand. In the preceding scene 4E had perhaps suppressed an originally political charge ("he has made himself out to be king"), in favor of a view of Jesus as **evil-doer,** transgressor of the Jewish law, a view more relevant to 4E's own time. ("Evil-doer" is perhaps the epithet that their Jewish opponents hurled at the Johannine Christians.) In any case Pilate now raises the political charge (v. 33—**Are you the king of the Jews?**); he is not yet suspicious of treason so much as curious about Jesus' theological status. The Johannine Jesus will soon dismiss the title altogether, but first he turns the questioning back onto Pilate. The title "King of the Jews" just now on Pilate's lips suggests the hint of messianic belief on his part. Jesus therefore asks, **Do you say this on your own account, or have others spoken thus to you about me?**

---

378. The motif of the fulfillment of Jesus' word as prophecy, paralleling and rivaling fulfillment of scriptural prophecy, is a distinctively Johannine one. See 2:19, 22; 18:9; also the power of Jesus' word in 18:5–8. This motif represents a signal alteration of PQ, where scripture alone has the power to determine future events and to explain them to discerning believers.

(v. 34). But the fantasy of Pilate as incipient Christian—a fantasy, of course, only on our part; Jesus, as 4E portrays him, is merely playing with Pilate—is quickly dispelled. The title was only an ethnic one, and Pilate is no **Jew** (v. 35a).

Pilate rephrases his question, prepared now almost to accept Jesus' word for it: **What have you done?** (v. 35c). Jesus' reply (v. 36) not only denies the authorities' charge but also corrects the underlying christological assumption: his **kingship** is not a political one, of the Jewish people, **of this world; it is not in any sense from here.** But this denial implies no limitation, no deficiency in Jesus' messiahship; he commands forces that, if he chose, could forestall his fate: **My servants would fight that I might not be handed over to the Jews** (v. 36b).

This last phrase is puzzling. As Pilate has just said (v. 35b), **Your own people** [or **nation**] **and the chief priests**[379] **have handed you over to me.** How is Jesus still to be "handed over"—or betrayed (the same in Greek)— and by "the Jews"? In historical reality (what earlier in v. 36 4E calls "this world") the final power rests with Pilate. Any Jewish betrayal leads finally to a Roman decision; at most "the Jews" are only an instigating factor in Jesus' death. But the Evangelist speaks of Jesus being **handed over to the Jews,** as if they will play the final role of judge, even executioner.

The reason for this strange impression lies in 4E's theological purpose here. From that perspective Pilate's role is entirely secondary; it is "the Jews" who are portrayed as finally holding the power over Jesus and bearing the responsibility for his condemnation, even his execution. (We must remind ourselves that this wholesale assigning of responsibility for Jesus' death has no basis in fact; see this part, n. 377.) Such a presentation of Jewish responsibility here is not yet clear. But before the Pilate trial is over, the same verb ("hand over"/"betray") will be used again, and to convey more explicitly both the historical and the theological meanings we have just distinguished (19:11, 16a).

In the pre-Johannine account of the interrogation by Pilate, Jesus scarcely spoke. Now he wholly dominates, and Pilate cannot follow what he says. Seizing on Jesus' threefold use of the phrase "my kingship" (v. 36) he asks: **Then you are a king?** (v. 37a). But in what were once perhaps his only words to Pilate (***You** say that I am a king*), Jesus further dissociates himself from the idea of rule. The Evangelist portrays Jesus' purpose instead, and exclusively, as *revelation:* **For this I was born, and for this I have come into the world, to bear witness to the truth. Everyone who is of the truth hears my voice** (v. 37c). Pilate cannot begin to understand. In

---

379. Perhaps this double phrase is another instance of the two-level drama (Martyn's phrase, *History and Theology*) that 4E creates—the chief priests as Jesus' opponents belonging to the context of the historical Jesus, and the Jewish people, thought of as a block, to the situation of the Christians in 4E's time.

cynicism or deliberate ignorance—he clearly does not "hear Jesus' voice"—he asks, **What is truth?** (v. 38a), and the episode has ended.

With scene 3 (18:38b–40) the original negotiation between Pilate and the Jewish authorities, laid aside by 4E after v. 29, is resumed. The Evangelist has only prefixed v. 38b, in which Pilate **again** goes out **to the Jews.** That he now insists on Jesus' innocence, an element taken up from the source, is not entirely in keeping with 4E's portrait of Pilate. But the further pre-Johannine detail, found only here among the Gospels, that Pilate himself reminds the crowd of the Passover amnesty (**It is your custom . . .**), is included, presumably because in the light of all that has gone before Pilate will now be seen not shrewdly seeking a compromise (as apparently in SG) but trying to please "the Jews": **Is it your will . . . ?**[380] That Barabbas, whom they call for in place of Jesus, is a **robber** (v. 40)— 4E has perhaps supplied the word—reminds the reader of Jesus' teaching in chapter 10 about the robber who supplants the true shepherd. In choosing him, "the Jews" reject the one who bears the very mercy and protection of God—just as in remaining "outside" and refusing to be in Jesus' presence, for the sake of their Passover, they have rejected the true Paschal Lamb.

With scene 4 (the scourging of Jesus—19:1–3) the Johannine author creates a kind of structural interlude that heightens the symmetry between the three scenes that precede and the three that follow.[381] In both halves there is the same arrangement (one scene of Pilate with Jesus, framed between two with "the Jews"). Here the alternation, Pilate's going in and out of the Pretorium, is broken, the deadlock between Jews and governor postponed (and, incidentally, the imbalance of scenes—two with Jesus, four with "the Jews"—preserved), by the public spectacle of Jesus' scourging and mocking.[382] The Evangelist has taken this episode from the end of the source's account and interpolated it here. In this portrayal, Pilate's intent is evidently to humiliate Jesus in the hope of thereby placating "the Jews." That course will fail, but in the process Jesus is crowned and hailed as "king." This both highlights the irony of what is transpiring and prepares for the scene to follow.[383]

There (scene 5: 19:4–7) all parties in the drama come together. But Jesus and "the Jews" do not actually confront one another, even if Pilate intended that they should. In place of the question—in the source not so

380. The same phrase occurs in the source, but there it represents only the governor's diplomacy, since the Privilegium Paschali had become a Jewish right.

381. Respectively, acts 1 and 2 in Ehrman's schema ("Trial"). See this part, n. 376.

382. Strictly, we must imagine this as taking place inside the palace (see v. 4), but 4E does not think to take Pilate inside after scene 3, thus retaining to some degree the public setting of the source. Are we then to see it taking place in both domains?

383. As Brown has shown ("The Passion," 130).

much weak as uninterested—"What then shall I do with Jesus?" Pilate announces that he will bring Jesus forth to demonstrate again that he is innocent (v. 4).[384] (This is meant to demonstrate neither Pilate's strength nor his fairness, but rather emphasizes the irony of the proceeding; knowing Jesus to be innocent, Pilate nevertheless in the end helplessly consents to his execution. Note how different in purpose this is from Luke's threefold exoneration.) Jesus then comes out (note 4E's choice of the active voice) pitifully dressed as a mock king, and is heralded by Pilate: **See the man.** The words are ambiguous (as everything the Johannine Pilate does): on the one hand, "Here is the miserable fellow," forced into a masquerade, hardly capable of guilt; on the other hand and of course unintentionally, "Behold the archetypal human being," uniquely a king (v. 5).

But again the attempt fails. The Jewish authorities, now in Jesus' very presence, only insist on his death, and in so many words (v. 6a). Pilate, still reluctant to condemn an innocent man, would leave the dirty work to "the Jews": **Take him yourselves and crucify him** (v. 6b). This can hardly be intended at its face value, in view of 18:31 (**It is not lawful for us to put anyone to death**). Instead it hints at the theological claim, wholly lacking in factual truth, that 4E would impress on us, namely, that it is somehow "the Jews" who finally kill Jesus. This claim is dramatized in their response (v. 7b)—**We have a law, and by that law he must die.**

Then follows a statement of the reason Jesus must die,[385] meaningful only if "the Jews" are Jesus' court of sentence: His theological offense to Judaism (in the period when 4E was writing) is simply that **he has made himself Son of God** (v. 7c), and so is anathema.

With this a new dimension has been raised, new at least to Pilate's mind, and he hurries in to Jesus in order to pursue it (scene 6: 19:8–11).[386] If Jesus is charged with claiming to be not just king but "Son of God," the question of his origin (so important throughout the Gospel) must be dealt with: **Where are you from?** (v. 9b). On a realistic level Pilate asks this out of heightened fear—whether religious or merely political (v. 8b); on a deeper one, Pilate is but the mouthpiece of the Evangelist's theological

384. Added by 4E, this with the pre-Johannine 18:38 and 19:6 will bring the number of statements of Jesus' innocence to three, as in Luke; but the way and the reason this is done here have nothing to do with the Lukan redaction, as some would hold. See this part, n. 398.

385. This can be seen either as a continuation of their words to Pilate ("he must die since he . . .") or 4E's interpolated comment to the reader ("[They held this] since . . ."). But the effect is the same.

386. The strict separation of Jesus and "the Jews" from one another, that the alternation of scenes—now outside, now inside the Pretorium—was meant to ensure, broke down in scene 5. There Pilate was outside, speaking with "the Jews," but 4E contrived that Jesus come forth. Now, that scene over, Jesus is apparently inside again, and Pilate must go in to question him.

inquiry. But Jesus has already implied the answer (**For this I was born, and for this I came into the world** . . . —18:37), and in any case Pilate would not understand. Accordingly here Jesus keeps silent (v. 9), evidently the only traditional element in this scene. But that silence aggravates the authoritarian in Pilate: **Don't you know that I have power to release you and power to crucify you?** (v. 10).

So, in his second speech to Pilate, Jesus calmly explains that all power is **from above**—an answer, also, to the question of his own origin—and adds, **Therefore the one who has handed me over to you has the greater sin** (v. 11). This last is anomalous. Pilate obviously had not raised the issue of moral responsibility for Jesus' death; but clearly 4E is preoccupied with the question. Jesus' reference is not entirely clear, but in the end (as we saw, just above, on 18:36) it can only refer to the Jewish leaders, Caiaphas as perhaps their representative.[387] Pilate at least acts with the legitimate right of the state, Jesus implies. "The Jews" have no such excuse; they directly oppose God. If Pilate is not exactly sinless, theirs is a monstrous sin.

Scene 7 (19:12–16a) follows as a logical consequence of Jesus' words (**On the basis of this** [or "From that moment"]) and Pilate seems all the more convinced of Jesus' innocence. His second encounter with Jesus, then, has come nearer to converting him, or at least to making sense to him, than the first. But in this final scene he is shown passive and powerless; he **sought to release him,** but was quickly intimidated. "The Jews" threaten to expose him as disloyal to the emperor, in the menacing phrase **not Caesar's friend** (v. 12a). With this they at last take up the political charge against Jesus—**Anyone who makes himself a king denounces Caesar** (v. 12b), now accusing Pilate as well.

In his cravenness Pilate has almost totally capitulated. Immediately **on hearing these words** he reenters the Pretorium (we were—carelessly—not shown him coming out for this brief exchange) and then emerges for the last time, bringing Jesus with him for the formal act of condemnation.

That it was not merely a Friday (the weekly **[day of] preparation** for the Sabbath) but the preparation **of Passover** (v. 14a) heightens the irony of what is about to take place. And instead of the scourging and mockery that originally came here, 4E has provided a fitting climax to the theological drama. We know that Pilate can no longer resist the demand for Jesus' death, yet still again, and now unequivocally (he can hardly be making fun of the Jews), he proclaims Jesus Messiah. He enthrones him on the

---

387. While on a superficial reading the reference here might seem to be to Judas, especially in light of the singular ("the one who has handed me over"), the Johannine words Pilate spoke in 18:35 make it clear that the Jewish authorities are meant: "Your own people and the chief priests have handed you over to me." And it is to them that he will soon hand Jesus back! (19:16a).

judgment seat (if so we may suppose from the context—the verb *kathizein*, originally intransitive [to sit], can have the transitive sense [to seat]) and declares to them, **Behold your king** (vv. 13–14). This only provokes another cry for Jesus' death, with the near-hysterical shout, **Away with him, away with him!** (v. 15a). As if to elicit their final act of self-condemnation, Pilate asks, **Shall I crucify your king?**

The **chief priests,** speaking for the nation, then make the terrible renunciation of all messianic hope: **We have no king but Caesar** (v. 15c—see this part, n. 377). Having already spurned Jesus as Good Shepherd and Paschal Lamb, they now finally reject him as Messiah. So, in conclusion of this fateful drama, Pilate hands Jesus over **to them** to be crucified (v. 16), and in 4E's rearrangement[388] this can mean only that "the Jews" carry out Jesus' crucifixion. The historical reality, that it was the soldiers and ultimately the power of Rome that played this role, is overshadowed by 4E's theological insistence.[389]

The Johannine author's intensive treatment of this episode has radically altered it, making it profoundly ironic. What had been Pilate's trial and condemnation of Jesus has become instead Pilate's trial *by Jesus.* Still more, now "the Jews" are judged by their attempt to judge Jesus. The Evangelist's polemic against "the world"—represented of course by Pilate but ultimately and definitively by "the Jews"—is now explicit: The World Condemns Itself.

Analysis

This scene, or rather this many-scened drama, is widely recognized to be thoroughly Johannine in its present format, the most highly reworked passage in 4E's passion narrative. But its many affinities with the parallel accounts in the Synoptics suggest the outlines of the pre-Johannine narrative, and in most places 4E's hand is so clearly evident that we can go a good way toward identifying her or his additions and so discover what lies behind them.[390]

388. Wherein it is this final scene of Pilate's with "the Jews"—and no longer the soldier's scourging and mockery—that immediately precedes the delivery to execution.

389. In which "the Jews" represent the world. Note the final uses of the verb usually translated "hand over." In v. 11 the subject is evidently "the Jews" in their delivery of Jesus to Pilate, where, however, they are seen as having "the greater sin." Here in v. 16 it is used of them in just the other way, and with still greater effect: those to whom Pilate hands Jesus over for execution. Note that in another way the Lukan author accomplishes much the same effect—Pilate delivered him "up to their will" (Luke 23:25).

390. Dauer (*Passionsgeschichte*, 146) only lays out the "building blocks" the source contained here. But his results, although achieved by a somewhat different route, are in most respects one with ours. Ehrman ("Trial") separates redaction from tradition purely by comparison of 4G with the Synoptics. The result is not unlike what we find, but using this method Ehrman has no way of distinguishing pre-Johannine redaction from Johannine and thus sometimes attributes to 4E what on our view is the product of the earlier author. (Thus, e.g., he asserts [p. 125] that the Evangelist creates the notices of place and time in 19:13–14, since they are not found in the Synoptics. More likely these stem from the pre-Johannine redaction.)

The overall format of the story is quite evidently 4E's. There are seven scenes, arbitrarily defined by Pilate's shuttling back and forth between "the Jews" outside the Pretorium (scenes 1, 3, 5, and 7) and Jesus inside (scenes 2 and 6), with the scourging of Jesus artificially placed at the center (scene 4). Much of the content of these scenes is dialogue that is obviously Johannine—between Pilate on the one hand and either "the Jews" or Jesus on the other. But in several cases the situational kernel and even some of what is said seems to come from the narrative tradition, by loose analogy with the Synoptics.

• Scene 1 (18:28–32) begins with the pre-Johannine opening of the Pilate trial, which follows smoothly from the preceding episode: early in the morning "they" take Jesus from the house[391] of Caiaphas to the Pretorium, where Pilate is in residence (v. 28a). The verb's subject is presumably the Jewish Temple guard, the Roman militia of the arrest having disappeared. So it is arguable that the source showed them, as now, refusing to enter the Pretorium **lest they be defiled and might not eat the Passover** (v. 28b). But since there is no Synoptic counterpart to this note,[392] and since it serves mainly to provide the pretext of Pilate's moving in and out of the palace, setting up the multiscened drama, it is more likely Johannine. The expression **eat the Passover** is found only here in 4G but in all the Synoptic accounts of the preparations for the Last Supper (see n. 392). Perhaps 4E has derived it from his or her source in that context; but in any case its use here is peculiar to 4G.

• That Pilate **went out to them** (v. 29a) is certainly redactional, but his question in v. 29b (**What charge do you bring against this man?**) is probably original.[393] In that case the source's answer on the part of those who brought Jesus has been replaced by the Johannine conversation now to be found in vv. 30–31.[394] Their response in v. 30 ("if he were not a doer of wrong [*kakon*] . . .") recalls the Johannine hearing before Annas just concluded ("if I have spoken wrong, testify to the wrong") and portrays them as insolent toward Pilate. And his suggestion (v. 31a) that they settle the matter themselves, even if politically plausible, seems designed to transfer responsibility for Jesus' death to "the Jews," a major Johannine tendency, as we shall see. Their disclaimer of all ability to carry out an execution (v. 31b) appears to serve the same purpose, clearly implying that they would have put Jesus to death if they could. It occasions the characteristic Johannine comment in v. 32 (**This was to fulfill the word Jesus had spoken . . .**, recalling 12:32–33).

• Scene 2 (18:33–38a) sets out from the traditional account: Pilate interrogates

391. Presumably this noun is to be supplied. Literally the Greek reads only "from Caiaphas's" (*apo tou Kaïapha*).

392. Only the phrase "eat the Passover" (Mark 14:12 pars.), which is hardly more than the common idiom.

393. Mark 15:4: "See how many things they charge against you." The verb in Mark has the same root (*katēgor-*) as 4G's noun.

394. But it is just possible that a displaced vestige of "the Jews' " answer to Pilate's question in the source has survived in 19:12b: the datum that Jesus "makes himself out to be king" (see also Luke 23:2). Dauer (*Passionsgeschichte*) holds that this was the gist of the pre-Johannine charge against Jesus, and Pilate's opening question to Jesus (now in scene 2) bears this out.

Jesus on the charge of sedition ("Are you king of the Jews?"—verbally identical to Mark 15:2a pars.).[395] This hardly follows from what 4E has made of scene 1, and thus is all the more likely pre-Johannine. Possibly Jesus' original answer is now to be found toward the end of the scene in v. 37b (**You say I am a king**—see Mark 15:2b pars.: "You have said so"). But the rest of the scene is patently Johannine creation: that Pilate goes **into the Pretorium again** (v. 33a); Jesus' counter-interrogation of Pilate (v. 34) with the latter's defensive and lame reply (v. 35); that Jesus "treats Pilate to a course in Johannine theology"[396] (vv. 36, 37cd); and finally Pilate's vain attempts to understand (vv. 37a, 38a).

• In the third scene (18:38b–40) 4E first takes Pilate **out again to the Jews** (v. 38b). Thereafter, however, the source is followed: Pilate declares Jesus' innocence (v. 38c) and, apparently knowing that this will be unacceptable, proposes as alternative the custom of the Passover amnesty in Jesus' case (v. 39). But the accusers instead respond[397] by choosing **Barabbas** (v. 40a). His description as **robber** (v. 40b) would seem to be a Johannine touch (see 10:1, 8), and if so it may have replaced an earlier term such as "insurrectionist" (see Mark 15:7; Luke 23:19).

• Scene 4 (19:1–3) interrupts the interchange between Pilate and the authorities (to be resumed in v. 6), with the result that one continuous episode is spread over two scenes (nos. 3 and 5), the scourging and mocking now interposed. The content of this Johannine interruption is wholly pre-Johannine, however, clearly having come originally from the end of the Roman trial. The Evangelist does not even add after scene 3 that Pilate reentered the Pretorium—for reasons we noted (see Johannine Redaction in this section)—though we must surmise that from v. 4.

• In scene 5 (19:4–7) Pilate goes **out again** and reiterates his opinion that Jesus is innocent (v. 4).[398] He then brings Jesus out to "the Jews," decked in the mocking regalia of scene 4, and speaks the ironic *Ecce Homo* (v. 5). All this is

395. This standard phrase represents the only use in the preliterary Synoptic tradition of the expression "the Jews," so widespread in 4G. It was just beginning to be used editorially by the Synoptic evangelists, as so very often by 4E. Mark 7:3; Matt. 28:15; Luke 7:3; 23:50; in each of these cases there is no parallel in the other Gospels.

396. Winter, *Trial*, 89.

397. Brown and Dauer (*Passionsgeschichte*) have convinced me that "cried out again" here need not be taken literally, as an incongruity suggesting the omission of an earlier demand from the crowd, but means simply "shouted back."

398. Much has been made of the fact that in both 4G (18:38; 19:4, 6) and Luke (23:4, 14, 22), Pilate three times declares Jesus innocent, and in each Gospel the source seems to have had only two such announcements, 4E and the Third Evangelist having added another. This raises the question whether 4E (or even SG) is dependent on Luke as we know it, a possibility we have until now rejected. In fact I believe the parallel to be merely coincidental: (a) The wording of the announcements is different as between 4G and Luke, and whereas in Luke it varies, in 4G it does not. (b) Neither in 4G, nor in anything pre-Johannine, do we find the same arrangement of the declarations as in Luke (in one case following the trial by Herod, peculiar to Luke). (c) The threefold exoneration has a different function in Luke, where it seems to reflect knowledge of criminal procedure ("no crime deserving death"—23:22), whether Roman or Jewish, on the part of the Lukan author and possibly to prove the justice of Jesus' treatment at the hands of Rome, altogether different from the Johannine portrayal of Pilate—see this section, Johannine Redaction, on this scene. (d) Only in Luke is the fact of the threefold declaration made explicit (23:22).

distinctively Johannine.[399] Now, as a response to this sight (v. 6a), the source's cry for Jesus' crucifixion (v. 6b) and Pilate's reassertion of his innocence (v. 6d) follow. The intervening clause (v. 6c—**Take him yourselves and crucify him**) appears to be 4E's tendentious invention. The same is true of v. 7,[400] which has very possibly displaced a second cry for Jesus' death (now in v. 15a).

• The sixth scene (19:8–11), the second between Pilate and Jesus, is wholly Johannine, as our commentary on the redaction has shown. The only exception may be the mention of Jesus' silence (v. 9c), which has a parallel in the Synoptics, though with different wording. This may be the vestige of a second question to Jesus in Pilate's original interrogation (after 18:37).

• Scene 7 (19:12–16a) brings the drama to a close with the pre-Johannine account of Pilate's sentencing of Jesus in vv. 13–14a.[401] The Evangelist has framed it with two more exchanges between Pilate and "the Jews" (v. 12 and vv. 14b–15, respectively).[402] The second of these has evidently replaced the original scourging and mocking episode, now removed to scene 4. Pilate's delivery of Jesus to the soldiers to be crucified (v. 16a) would have followed.[403]

SECTION 18 (19:16b–42)
JESUS IS EXECUTED AND BURIED

Pre-Johannine Source[404]

19 [16b]So they took Jesus [17](and carrying the cross himself he went out) to what was known as the Place of the Skull,[405] which is called Golgotha in 'Hebrew,' [18]where they crucified him, and two others with him, one on either side. [19b]And there was written, JESUS OF NAZARETH, KING OF THE JEWS. [20c]And it was written in 'Hebrew,' Latin, and Greek.

[23]When the soldiers had crucified Jesus they took his outer garments and divided them in four parts, one to each soldier, also his tunic. But the tunic was seamless, woven from top to bottom; [24]so they said to each other,

399. It may have replaced an original response by Pilate to the demand for Barabbas: "Then what shall I do with Jesus?" (see Mark 15:12 pars.). This would have led up to the pre-Johannine cry for Jesus' crucifixion, now in v. 6b.

400. With the phrase "according to our law," see 18:31 ("judge him by your own law"). For the charge of "making himself Son of God," see 5:18; 10:33.

401. In v. 14a 4E has probably added "of the Passover" to "the day of preparation" (which then originally simply meant Friday; see 19:31a and the Synoptic parallels). While the source, along with the parallel tradition, knows that the crucifixion took place roughly at Passover time (see 18:39), the identification of the precise day here (and in 18:28 and 19:31b) is redactional, just as in a different way in Mark 14:12.

402. In both cases, as we have seen, 4E perhaps uses a pre-Johannine element: "makes himself a king" in v. 12 and the repetition of the call for crucifixion in v. 15a.

403. It has been noted that there is no mention again of Barabbas here, in contrast to the Synoptics. Just possibly 4E has omitted this. But it is more likely that it was implied in the verb "took" (= chose) in 19:1 (so Brown).

404. Quite independently of each other, both Broer (*Grab Jesu*) and I have reconstructed vv. 31–42 of the following text with virtually identical results.

405. Lit., "to the place called 'of a skull.'" The Aramaic name means the same.

"Let's not tear it but instead toss to see whose it will be"—that the scripture might be fulfilled which says, "They divided my garments among them, and for my clothing they cast lots." [25a]So that is what the soldiers did. [28]After this, that the scripture might be fulfilled, Jesus said, "I thirst." [29]There was a bowl of vinegar there, so they filled a sponge with the vinegar and putting it on a stick[406] they held it to his mouth. [30]And when he had received the vinegar Jesus said. . . .[407] And bowing his head he breathed his last.

[[[25b]Now standing by Jesus' cross were his mother's sister, Mary wife of Clopas, and Mary Magdalene.]] [31]Since it was Friday, lest the bodies remain on the cross on the Sabbath, they asked Pilate that their legs be broken and that they be taken away. [32]So the soldiers came and broke the legs of the first and then of the other who had been crucified with him. [33]But when they came to Jesus and saw that he was already dead, they did not break his legs, [34]but one of the soldiers stabbed his side with a spear and at once there came out blood and water. [36]For these things took place so that the scripture might be fulfilled, "His bone shall not be broken," [37]and again another scripture says, "They shall look on the one they have pierced."

[38]After this Joseph of Arimathea, a disciple of Jesus, asked Pilate that he might take Jesus' body down,[408] and Pilate consented. So [they][409] came and took down his body, [40b]and they bound it in burying cloths with (the) spices, [[[39d]about seventy-five pounds.]] [41]Now in the place where he had been crucified there was a garden, and in the garden a new tomb in which no one had yet been buried. [42]So since it was Friday and because the tomb was nearby they buried Jesus there.

This long passage, while falling naturally into several paragraphs, yet has the dramatic unities of time and place. Even Jesus' burial takes place **nearby,** and the only clue to the passage of time is the reminder (v. 31, possibly v. 42; see 19:14) of the approaching Sabbath. After the fixing of Jesus' condemnation at noon in the preceding passage, there is no marking of time, such as the hours that Jesus hung on the cross in the Synoptic accounts.

What distinguishes this passage most from the parallel versions is the

---

406. The Greek reads "on hyssop," but the text is very possibly corrupt.

407. On the possibility that the source gave the "cry of dereliction" ("My God, my God, why hast thou forsaken me?"), see this section, in the commentary on the Pre-Johannine Source, on Ps. 22:1.

408. The verb used repeatedly of removing Jesus' body from the cross (*airein*) can mean "take away," "take down," or simply "take," as will appear in our translation.

409. A number of MSS have this reading, quite baffling in its present Johannine context. Just possibly it is original and stems from the source. (Understandably it was then changed to "he" by the majority of scribes.) It would have referred to Joseph and unnamed helpers, possibly the women of v. 25b, and before the insertion of v. 39 by 4E would have led on to the plural subjects of vv. 40 and 42.

repeated and explicit fulfillment of OT *prophecies*—that is, of individual verses, most often from the Psalms, taken as prophetic. We encountered such citation earlier, in the Temple Restoring, the Messianic Entry, and the explanation for the Conspiracy against Jesus, but now the formula used is always the more pointed form: **in order that the scripture might be fulfilled.** (This is the formula used so often in Matthew, but curiously never there in the passion narrative after the triumphal entry, even though the whole passion tradition is studded with implicit allusions to OT.) Here is the heart of the passion narrative's rationale; the whole painful story is to be understood as no more and no less than the necessary fulfillment of prophecy. All had been foreordained and (to those with the eyes of faith) written beforehand. If the use of scripture is, to us moderns, naive and forced, it is simply in accord with first-century exegetical method.

The pre-Johannine author uses three explicit allusions to scripture, in the space of only ten verses. The *first* (vv. 23–24) is the dividing of the garments (Ps. 22:18), and here—unlike the Synoptics—the psalm is quoted. The tradition has been elaborated to provide the fullest possible fulfillment of it. The two lines, originally in synonymous parallelism (**garments/clothing**), are treated as discrete prophecies, each matched in the story of Jesus: (outer) garments divided/clothing (i.e., tunic) apportioned by lot.[410]

The *second* instance, Jesus' thirst (vv. 28–29), is unique to this Gospel, and the prophecy itself is not cited—we hear only that this happened **so that the scripture might be fulfilled.** But the author obviously builds on the tradition of the offering of vinegar, found in all the passion accounts, and seems to have in mind Ps. 69:2 ("For my thirst they gave me vinegar to drink"). The word for "fulfilled" is unique here and may reflect 4E's retouching (see this part, n. 426), but the sense is undoubtedly original.

The *third* instance (vv. 31–36), with paired citations (as also in 12:38–39), is again peculiar to this tradition. It includes an elaborate description of the custom of breaking the legs of those crucified, presumably to hasten death, and adds to it[411] the stab of the spear. It quotes first Exod. 12:46 = Num. 9:12 (a regulation concerning the Passover lamb)[412] and then, for the spear wound, Zech. 12:10.

The intended effect of this concentration of OT *testimonia*, as they are

410. Matt. 21:2–7 (the animals at the entry into Jerusalem) shows the same kind of literal fulfillment, with the odd consequence of Jesus somehow riding on two donkeys at once.

411. The tradition appears to be composite, since only the breaking of the legs is led up to by v. 31. The second citation's introduction reads rather like an afterthought ("And again another scripture says . . ."). This joining may have occurred prior to the writing of the source, or it may be the pre-Johannine author's contribution.

412. Or, less clearly, Ps. 34:20 ("Not one of [his bones] is broken"). Bultmann (*Gospel of John*) proposes that the source originally quoted the psalm and that 4E has adapted it to the passage from Torah—an interesting but unverifiable suggestion.

called, is apologetic—that is, they justify the shocking fact of Jesus' innocent and degrading death. It was unavoidable, indeed inevitable, ordained by divine necessity; therefore, it is not only theologically tolerable but in fact necessary and appropriate.[413] There is no interest here in either the horrifying tragedy or the ennobling example of Jesus' death. The various details that might be so understood—for example, Jesus' carrying his own cross (if pre-Johannine) and the trilingual sign, the offering of vinegar, the presence of the women, or the mutilation of the body—seem intended not to lend a note of emotional intensity, but of mere factuality. That note is especially evident in the first clause of v. 25: **So that is what the soldiers did.**

For that reason, this is not strictly a *passion* narrative, an account of suffering. The choice of OT passages cited might seem to tend in that direction, for they all have to do with righteous suffering, and in one case (if the reference to Exodus is correctly assigned) even sacrificial death. But the apologetic purpose dominates; nothing is made either of these soteriological hints or of a theology of the imitation of Christ.

If Jesus spoke any words in this portion of the source, apart from the prophetically necessary "I thirst," they have not survived 4E's redaction. His few utterances earlier in PQ are in a way christologically significant—they all call attention in some way to himself. But here the focus is on the need to make his death theologically comprehensible, to present an apologetic that is compatible with christology.[414] The barest christology ("King of the Jews") is of course stated, but at most still in a paradoxical way. If SG contained the so-called cry of dereliction (Mark 15:34), it would have been understood as an enactment—almost a fulfillment—of Ps. 22:1. In that case, despite its ironic power, 4E has suppressed it (as also the Lukan author); it was too discordant with the Johannine theology of the cross as glorification. It is just possible, then, that it was originally to be found in the pre-Johannine version of the crucifixion tradition.

There is a minor anomaly at v. 31. If 4E has introduced **the Jews** as subject of the request **that the bodies not remain on the cross on the Sabbath,** what was the original subject? The women of the preceding sentence (according to our reconstruction) may have been meant, for 4E would probably not have discarded any mention of specific Jewish authorities; or perhaps there was only a deliberately indefinite "they." Who-

413. But the perception that this Friday was not simply understandable but in itself Good will come only with 4E (in none of the Synoptics is it so perceived). The *titulus* is not a proclamation of good news (Jesus reigning from his cross) but an ironic christological claim. On the source's use of OT citations and the interpretation of Jesus' death in general, see further part 2.D.

414. It will remain for the author of Mark (as earlier Paul) to see in the death of Jesus, so unthinkable an end for the Messiah, the very heart of Jesus' messiahship and (unlike Paul) to depict it in Gospel form.

179

ever it was, those making the request clearly did not know, as the reader does, that Jesus had died already.

But the request of v. 31 was only partially carried out by the soldiers; as yet there has been no taking away of the bodies "so that [they] not remain on the cross on the Sabbath." But the Synoptic tradition of Joseph of Arimathea's petition, although ignorant of the preceding episode (e.g., knowing nothing of the issue of bodies to be removed because of the Sabbath), is skillfully introduced to complete the story. Joseph in effect repeats the request to Pilate, who now explicitly gives permission (having apparently only ordered the soldiers in the preceding story). So Joseph (and the women?) take down Jesus' body (the question of the criminals' bodies is no longer in view) and proceed with its careful burial.[415]

The account once again is simple, matter-of-fact. Joseph, **a disciple of Jesus,** perhaps together with the women, respectfully takes down Jesus' body and prepares it for the tomb. It is wrapped **in linen cloths,** having evidently been first embalmed **with spices.** The lavish supply of these, if it was specified in the source—equal to **about seventy-five pounds** in modern terms[416]—is probably intended as indication of the devotion of these loyal followers of Jesus.

Providentially perhaps, there is **nearby** a fitting burial place: **a garden** and in it **a new tomb where no one yet had been buried.** In the tradition, Jesus is buried there out of appropriate convenience. But the author of the source, combining this story with the crucifragium and thus introducing the element of haste in view of the approaching Sabbath, adds (v. 42) **because of the day of preparation and.** The addition is not so much redundant as conclusive.

So ends the story of Jesus' life; but of course not the source, for the death of Jesus, and his burial in particular, are only the prelude—the necessary and preordained preparation—for the climactic account of the resurrection.

Johannine Redaction

19 [16b]*Then* they took Jesus [17](**and carrying the cross himself**) he went out to what was known as the Place of the Skull, which is called Golgotha in

---

415. There has not been Johannine or post-Johannine accommodation to the Synoptics here, as sometimes suggested. The Joseph tradition shows no hint of verbal contact with those versions. The closest parallels are with the Lukan tradition: "the [day] of preparation" (Luke 23:54), " a tomb where no one had [ever/yet] [lain/been laid]" (Luke 23:53b), "myrrh and [spices/aloes]" (Luke 23:56). Yet even in cases of identical meaning the wording is different; e.g., "tomb" (*mnēma/mnēmeion*), "linen [burying cloths]" (*sindōn/othonion*), "myrrh" (*myron/smyrna*). (Here I must therefore differ with Bailey, *Traditions,* who holds that 4E used Luke in this material and elsewhere.)

416. One hundred Roman *litras,* according to the Greek text. It is characteristic of SG to give the datum of the amount.

'Hebrew,' [18]where they crucified him, and two others with him, one on either side, and Jesus in the center. [19]And Pilate also wrote a "titulus" and placed it on the cross. And there was written, JESUS OF NAZARETH, KING OF THE JEWS. [20]And many of the Jews read this titulus, for the place where Jesus was crucified was near the city. And it was written in 'Hebrew,' Latin, and Greek. [21]Then the chief priests of the Jews said to Pilate, "Do not write 'the King of the Jews' but that he said, 'I am King of the Jews.'" [22]Pilate replied, "What I have written I have written."

[23]Now when the soldiers had crucified Jesus they took his outer garments and divided them in four parts, one to each soldier; also his tunic. But the tunic was seamless, woven from top to bottom; [24]so they said to each other, "Let's not tear it but instead toss to see whose it will be"—that the scripture might be fulfilled which says, "They divided my garments among them, and for my clothing they cast lots." [25a]*Then* the soldiers did this.

[25b]*But* standing by Jesus' cross were **his mother and** his mother's sister, Mary wife of Clopas, and Mary Magdalene. [26]**Then Jesus saw his mother and the disciple whom he loved standing by, and he said to his mother, "Woman, this is your son."** [27]**Then he said to the disciple, "This is your mother."** And from that hour the disciple received her into his family.

[28]After this, that the scripture might be accomplished, Jesus—**knowing that all was now finished**—said, "I thirst." [29]There was a bowl of vinegar there, so they filled a sponge with the vinegar and putting it on a stick they held it to his mouth. [30]And when he had received the vinegar Jesus said **It is finished.** And bowing his head he breathed his last.

[31]**Then,** since it was Friday, lest the bodies remain on the cross on the Sabbath—**for that Sabbath was a high holy day**—the Jews asked Pilate that their legs be broken and that they be taken away. [32]*Then* the soldiers came and broke the legs of the first and then of the other who had been crucified with him. [33]But when they came to Jesus and saw that he was already dead, they did not break his legs, [34]but one of the soldiers stabbed his side with a spear and at once there came out blood and water. [35]**And he who saw it has testified, and his testimony is true, and he knows that he speaks truly, so that you may believe.** [36]For these things took place so that the scripture might be fulfilled, "His bone shall not be broken," [37]and again another scripture says, "They shall look on the one they have pierced."

[38]After this Joseph of Arimathea, a disciple of Jesus—**but secretly for fear of the Jews**—asked Pilate that he might take away Jesus' body, and Pilate consented. *Then* [they] came and took away his body. [39]**And Nicodemus, who at first had come to him by night, also came bringing a mixture of myrrh and aloes, about seventy-five pounds.** [40]**Then they took the body of Jesus** and they bound it in burying cloths with the spices, **as is the custom of the Jews to bury.** [41]Now in the place where he had been crucified there was a garden, and in the garden a new tomb in which no one had yet been buried.

⁴²*Now* because of the **Jewish** day of preparation and because the tomb was nearby they buried Jesus there.

We can most readily discern 4E's reinterpretation of the source by noting how two themes run through this passage as it stands before us in the canon.

1. The first has to do with *sovereignty.* The note struck in all the Gospels (to a lesser extent in 4E's source) at the Triumphal Entry into Jerusalem is here sustained throughout the entire story, uniquely among the Gospels; hints of a similar tone are found also in Luke's passion story. Beginning with the Johannine account of the arrest Jesus commanded the scene, and both the Jewish hearings and the Roman trial became occasions for displaying his authority over the worldly powers. Now even in his death, the Evangelist repeatedly drives this home:

a. Jesus **went out** to Golgotha freely, **carrying the cross himself** (v. 17). Whether or not these details derive from the source, in their Johannine context they remind the reader of Jesus' saying: "No one takes [my life] from me; I lay it down of my own accord" (10:18). His procession to Golgotha is calmly magisterial.

b. The addition of the redundant emphasis that, of the three crucified together, Jesus was **in the middle** (v. 18) is evidently designed to stress his centrality in the drama as a whole.

c. The Evangelist elaborates the tradition of the *titulus,* to the effect that it was Pilate himself who had it written and affixed to the cross. Pilate thereby proclaims Jesus king, refusing to say—what was perhaps in fact the case—that the placard was intended only as a derisive reminder of the charge on which Jesus was convicted (vv. 21–22; see also (a) just below).

d. Further, there is the royal burial, lavish in its proportions (v. 39)[417] and properly carried out (**as it was the custom of the Jews to bury**— v. 40b).

e. But above all, it is the redaction in vv. 28–30 that displays Jesus' sovereignty: He dies **knowing that all was now accomplished**—contrast the Markan, and just possibly pre-Johannine cry of dereliction. He expresses his thirst so as to **accomplish** the scripture.[418] And his last word is a triumphant and consummating declaration: **It is accomplished.**[419] In all

417. A detail possibly from the source ("about seventy-five pounds" of embalming spices). There it connoted generous loyalty; now, in the broad Johannine context, regality (cf. Ps. 45:8). Meeks, in a private communication, has suggested that this burial, with its outlandish quantity of spices, is depicted by 4E derogatorily, meant to represent another example of Jewish misunderstanding. This is an interesting possibility, but I find no clue—such as 4E so often gives—that it is intended.

418. The verb is perhaps due to 4E's slight alteration of the source (from "fulfill"), and is a cognate of that used in what precedes and follows it, as our translation seeks to show.

419. There may be Johannine irony here, a double-entendre: Both "It is over" (that is, Jesus' life) and "It is completed" (all he came to accomplish).

these ways, and without obliterating the pre-Johannine elements of the story, 4E contends that Jesus dies, even as he lived, at the mercy of nothing and no one, not even a divine necessity, but freely and victoriously completing his work on earth. The threefold use of the root "accomplish" drives this home.

2. The second theme extends the *conflict between Pilate and the Jews*, from the preceding section.

a. That Pilate himself had the *titulus* written and placed on the cross (v. 19a) occasions the objection by **the chief priests of the Jews** (v. 21). Pilate's forthrightness in placarding Jesus' title is an affront to the world, as represented by the officials, for it was shown **near the city** so that **many of the Jews read it**, and it was written "in all the pertinent languages of the Empire" (v. 20; in the phrase of Brown, "The Passion," 132).

b. Again, it is now **the Jews** who confront Pilate with their scruple against leaving the bodies on the cross during the Sabbath, and particularly on Passover (v. 31). This can scarcely be out of respect for the executed. Thus the Jews stand in contrast to Joseph, who makes a similar request, not out of religious punctiliousness but loyalty to Jesus. He is identified in such a way as to make this contrast clear: "a disciple of Jesus," **but secretly for fear of the Jews** (v. 38).

c. Something of this polarity between the Jews and the faithful, while not involving Pilate, is reflected also in the figure of **Nicodemus**, whom 4E introduces into the story of the burial. Originally a representative of uncomprehending Judaism (3:1–10), Nicodemus here has become a devoted follower, a former "ruler of the Jews" now lending generous aid to Joseph (vv. 39–40).[420]

Beyond these major themes there is a quite different kind of adaptation in the story that involves the women at the cross (v. 25). This is the only Johannine rearrangement in the passage, and by the addition of vv. 26–27 it has become a scene in its own right, standing at the center of the whole passage.[421] The women and their humanity now stand in contrast with the

---

420. In the meantime Nicodemus had called for justice on the part of his fellow Jewish leaders in deciding about Jesus and had been scorned by them for it (7:50–52)—an episode that represents a midpoint in his developing portrayal.

421. Brown (pp. 910–12) analyzes the present passage (19:17–42) into seven discrete scenes, which he diagrams as symmetrically arranged. While the division into paragraphs or even scenes is mainly evident in the text, I find no redactional basis (with the exception of the present scene) for attributing to 4E a detailed structure of the kind Brown suggests. (Contrast the explicit Johannine seven-scened drama of the trial before Pilate.) For example, 4E in no way indicates that in the last section Jesus' being taken down from the cross is to be thought of as balancing his being lifted onto it in the first, for even though earlier in the Gospel Jesus' death is described as being "lifted up," it is not so there. And the verb usually translated "taken down" here literally means only "taken," in contrast to the explicit depiction of the act of lowering the body in Mark 15:46 = Luke 23:53. Here we have an illustration of the way redaction criticism can lend precision (in this case, or as corrective) to the interpretation of the Johannine intent.

183

soldiers' uncaring cruelty, as the usually untranslated *men/de* construction hints: "Then whereas the soldiers did all this, by contrast his mother and . . . were standing by the cross." Since **the mother of Jesus** is not found in the parallel passion accounts, it is likely that the Evangelist has introduced her here, at the end of Jesus' life, and in so doing has deliberately balanced her role in the wedding at Cana, at the beginning of Jesus' revelatory activity in the world. There Jesus told her that his **hour [had] not yet come;** here she reappears to signal that what Jesus had come into the world to accomplish is at last being completed.[422]

The added episode involving **the disciple whom Jesus loved** (vv. 26–27) that now fills out the notice about the women is of obvious Johannine importance, but its meaning must be determined as part of the broader question of the beloved disciple's significance in the Gospel as a whole.[423] In any case, however, Jesus' family—his mother and brothers— were not portrayed especially favorably earlier in the Gospel (2:4; 7:3–5), but here his mother and her newly adopted son comprise the community who remain faithful to Jesus at the end and—perhaps—the germ of the Johannine church.

Some mention must also be made of the striking addition in v. 35—the eyewitness verification of the blood and water from Jesus' side. This dense comment is of obvious importance, but it is so self-contained, in no way using elements in the source, and its assignment (whether to 4E or a later hand) is so problematic, that we can say nothing about it here with confidence.

The death of Jesus, understood not as debasement to be explained but as glorification to be announced, is fundamental to the whole of the Johannine Gospel, but nowhere to the extent and with the clarity it attains here. What began in PQ as an apologia for the death of Jesus, the Messiah scandalously but necessarily crucified, has become in the Evangelist's hands a proclamation of the Consummation of Jesus' Work on Earth.

Analysis

From the elaborate revision 4E has given the Pilate trial we come to the account of Jesus' end, which runs largely in its pre-Johannine form. Most of the Johannine changes amount to minor retouching.

• That Jesus **went out carrying his own cross** (v. 17) may betray 4E's image of Jesus as independent and self-possessed throughout the passion events (contrast the episode of Simon of Cyrene in the Synoptics). But the detail could equally be

---

422. I express my debt to a former student, Anne C. Gable, for this imaginative perception. This symmetry might also explain 4E's moving the notice of the women forward, so as immediately to precede and thus prepare for Jesus' death.

423. See further, this part, sec. 19, Johannine Redaction, on the pre-Johannine materials, apparently from 4E's narrative source, that may have contributed to the present image of the beloved disciple.

due to the distinctiveness of the pre-Johannine narrative tradition, displaying no more than the willing acceptance by Jesus of what is in store for him.

• **And Jesus in the center** at the end of v. 18 is slightly redundant with what precedes and probably an instance of Johannine emphasis. The placing of the two fellow victims (**one on either side**) is surely traditional (see Mark 15:27 and Matt. 27:38); if it jars subtly with the soldiers' actions after Jesus' death, coming only third to his body to break the legs (vv. 32–33), the result is due to the combining of traditions.

• That **Pilate also wrote a "titulus" and placed it on the cross** (v. 19a) overlaps with the second half of the verse (**Now there was written . . .**) and is probably Johannine redaction, preparing for the insertion of vv. 21–22. Similarly v. 20ab, the publicity of the *titulus*.

• The Jewish reaction to Pilate's act (vv. 21–22, along with v. 20) resembles one of the scenes of the trial drama and is surely Johannine (as the phrases "many of the Jews" [v. 20a] and "the chief priests of the Jews" [v. 21] show). But the detail that the notice of accusation (only 4E uses the technical Latin term *titulus*) was trilingual (v. 20c) is exceptional; it seems rather like an insertion in its present context. It has probably been taken up from the source.[424]

• The particle *oun* ("So," "Therefore") is used frequently in the source, often expressing the sense of causality and inevitability running through it. In v. 23, however, it cannot have any such logical meaning, especially with the removal of vv. 20–22. It seems there to have the idiomatic historical sense ("Then," "Now") and to be the Evangelist's insertion, as at a number of other places.

• The mention of women at the foot of the cross, while traditional, is abrupt in v. 25, probably originally coming after v. 30. It has possibly occasioned the first clause of v. 25 (= v. 24d in the Greek text) as a summation prior to 4E's insertion of vv. 25b–27.[425] Verses 26–27 appear to be wholly Johannine, and also the mention of **Jesus' mother** in v. 25 (see just above, end of Johannine Redaction).

• Verse 28 is overloaded. Jesus' **knowing that all was now finished** is undoubtedly Johannine.[426] The rest, together with v. 29, is the traditional element of the offering of vinegar.

• Jesus' utterance in v. 30 (**It is finished**) is the Evangelist's; see n. 426. If this last word from the cross has replaced another in the source (such as the Markan "cry of dereliction"), it has left no trace.

• Verse 25b (= v. 25 in the Greek text), about the women, would originally have come next.

• The Evangelist has undoubtedly specified the subject with which v. 31 opens:

---

424. A somewhat different version of the same details is found as a variant reading at Luke 23:38. There it is usually taken as a scribal assimilation to this phrase in 4G, but because it is not word for word identical, possibly it is another example of the many points at which the Third and Fourth Gospels share traditions.

425. As the *men . . . de* construction connecting the clause to v. 25b suggests: "Whereas the soldiers . . . by contrast his mother. . . ."

426. Possibly also Johannine is the choice of the verb *teleiōthēi* to express the fulfillment of scripture in the next clause; it is a cognate of the term 4E inserts both here in v. 28a and again in v. 30. The source may have read *plērōthēi*, as at v. 24 and elsewhere, but with much the same meaning.

Then the Jews . . . ; originally it would have been indefinite, perhaps implying the women in what is now v. 25. The cumbersome explanation (**for that Sabbath was a high holy day**) is also 4E's, in accord with the Johannine dating of the crucifixion on the eve of Passover (see n. 401, on 19:14).

• Possibly the **blood and water** from Jesus' side (v. 34b), which has no obvious connection with the "prophecy" cited in v. 36, is redactional. It is usually seen as a theologically inspired Johannine addition;[427] but the phrase seems nevertheless traditional in origin, remembered as a supposedly factual detail. Certainly the accompanying offstage comment verifying the datum (v. 35) is Johannine.[428]

• The tradition of the *crucifragium* (vv. 31b–37), unique to 4G, has been smoothly joined to that of Jesus' burial (vv. 38–42), found in all the canonical Gospels; the parallelism of vv. 31a and 38 (two distinct expressions of concern for the removal of Jesus' body) shows this. The joining is obviously redactional, but pre-Johannine.[429]

• In v. 38 the qualification of Joseph of Arimathea's discipleship (**but secretly for fear of the Jews**) is anachronistic and surely Johannine. The awkward addition of **Nicodemus's** part in the burial (v. 39) is also Johannine elaboration,[430] together with the doubling and resumptive first clause of v. 40 (**Then they took the body of Jesus**). The clause **bringing** [sing.] **a mixture of myrrh and aloes . . .** (v. 39b), while possibly traditional (slightly different in the Synoptics), does not fit grammatically in the source; perhaps the specified datum **about seventy-five pounds** has been transferred from the source at the end of v. 40b.

• The fact that **they bound** [Jesus' body] **in burying cloths with (the) spices**[431] (v. 40b) is pre-Johannine, the plural subject possibly including with Joseph the women previously mentioned. The explanation in v. 40c (**as is the custom of the Jews to bury**) is altogether Johannine.[432]

• The historical anomaly of a Jewish tomb **near** a Roman place of execution (v. 41) need not concern us; the detail, including the location of the tomb in **a garden,** is unique to 4G and traditional. From v. 42 it is obvious that haste and so a nearby tomb were demanded by the approaching Sabbath.

• In v. 42 **on account of the Jewish day of preparation** is redactional, but only

427. Whether anti-docetic (Jesus was truly an earthly human being, with blood in his veins) or sacramental (the blood and water symbolic of Eucharist and Baptism, respectively).

428. The phrase "that you may believe" in v. 35 is reminiscent of 20:31a, which I take to be the ending of the pre-Johannine source (see this part, sec. 20). But here the verb "believe" is used absolutely, the basis for belief is different altogether than in the source's summary, and the emphasis on "you" ([*kai*] *hymeis*) is found only here.

429. So Broer, *Grab Jesu*, 219–20, 230–33.

430. Ibid., 234–35. It still seems to me likely that 4E drew the tradition about Nicodemus from his or her narrative source, but not necessarily that a part of 3:1 once appeared at this point in the source (as I held in *TGOS*, 132–34).

431. The definite article is either 4E's insertion, along with v. 39, or means something like "the necessary spices."

432. There are some similarities in this account to the burial details in the pre-Johannine Lazarus story (chap. 11), but gratuitous differences as well. We have here two independent traditions, quite patently, each with its own style. There may have been some slight assimilation between them as they come together (see sec. 19, Analysis, on 20:7) but nothing more than that. See this part, n. 240.

Jewish (lit., "of the Jews") is Johannine; the rest is the comment by the pre-Johannine author, "the day of preparation" meaning simply Friday, as in v. 31 (and see Luke 23:54).

The Resurrection

SECTION 19 (20:1–22)
THE EMPTY TOMB; JESUS APPEARS

Strictly speaking, there is no place in the Fourth Gospel for resurrection stories, since the ascent or exaltation has already taken place [in the crucifixion]. Nevertheless, and doubtless in deference to Christian tradition, [4E] supplies three [such stories], to which a fourth has been added . . . and in all of them traditional elements lie side by side with what is characteristically Johannine.

So wrote C. F. Evans ("Resurrection," 116), and we can concur, adding only that the Christian tradition to which 4E defers is evidently the narrative source. Evans's tally of resurrection stories appears to count only the three *appearances* (to Mary Magdalene [vv. 11–18], to the disciples [vv. 19–23], and to Thomas [vv. 24–29]), with the scene in chapter 21 being the added fourth. But this is not entirely accurate, for the story of the *empty tomb* (vv. 1–10) is surely to be counted as a resurrection story even though Jesus does not appear. So in chapter 20 alone there are four stories, of which, as we shall see, the first three derive in some form from the source. The Evangelist has added the Thomas episode, and either that author or a later redactor has appended the appearance to some of the disciples in connection with the miraculous catch of fish in chapter 21, as a fifth story.[433]

Pre-Johannine Source

20 **¹Early on Sunday**[434] **(while it was still dark) Mary Magdalene [and . . .] came to the tomb and saw the stone taken from the tomb. ²And she [or they] ran and came to Simon Peter and told [him], "They have taken the Master from the tomb, and we don't know where they have laid him." ³So Peter went out, and they came to the tomb. ⁶ᵇAnd he went into the tomb and he saw the burying cloths lying. [And he wondered.] ⁹For as yet they did not know the scripture that he must rise from the dead. ¹⁰So [he] went home again.**

¹¹Mary was standing outside the tomb, weeping. As she wept she stooped to look into the tomb, ¹²and she saw two angels in white sitting (one at the head and one at the feet) where Jesus' body had lain. ¹³ᵃAnd they said to

433. To that, of course, the rest of the twenty-first chapter continues as sequel.
434. Greek: "on the first of the week."

187

her, "Woman, why are you weeping?" [14a]She turned away, and saw Jesus standing! [15a]Jesus said to her, "Whom are you looking for, [16]Mary?" She said to him in 'Hebrew,' "Rabbouni!" [17]Jesus said to her, "Do not cling to me, but go to my brothers and tell them [. . .]. [18]Mary Magdalene went and announced to the disciples, "I have seen the Master." [*The disciples disbelieve.*]

[19]When it was evening and the doors were shut where the disciples were, Jesus came and stood in their midst and said to them, "Peace to you." [20]And he showed them his hands and his side. Therefore when the disciples saw the Master they were overjoyed. [22]And he breathed on them and said to them, "Receive holy Spirit."[435]

Three brief resurrection stories, then, economically told according to the source's usual style, and showing both parallels with the Synoptic Gospel versions and the accustomed differences. The reconstruction contains some guesswork, since the Johannine redaction of the passage is more than a retouching, but we can have greater confidence in it than in some other passages (e.g., the Baptist's testimony).

In the first account, the episode of the empty tomb has at some point been simplified to include only **Mary Magdalene** of the tradition's women but—uniquely—expanded to include also Peter,[436] with the result that there is a kind of progression within the story. The effect of Mary's discovery of the opened tomb is consternation, as her haste to tell Peter and her message to him show. There is no thought of resurrection yet, no one appears to announce it, Jesus is not seen. This is true even when Peter comes and finds the tomb not only open but empty. But the discarded cloths hint at something. Peter at most only wonders, but the reader is given the clue. Like the crucifixion, the empty tomb is to be understood as foreordained: according to "the scripture" **he must rise from the dead.** But since Peter and the others neither know nor understand this **yet** (the implication is that soon they all will know), he returns home, and Mary stays mourning not only Jesus' death but now also his disappearance.

The story is followed by an episode originally independent of the first, for there is now no indication of abandoned cloths in the tomb, just as there had been no hint of what Mary will now see. In place of the cloths, or rather **where Jesus had lain,** are seated **two angels in white.**[437] Their

---

435. For this form of the phrase, see this part, n. 51, on 1:33.

436. Wink's suggestion ("Sexual Politics," 177–82) that Peter (and, he would hold, also the other disciple now introduced in v. 2) appears in the story to replace the technically unreliable witness of women with that of men is plausible (see also Luke 24:11). But when only Peter is added, as apparently here, it is just as likely that his function is not "sexual politics" but rather a matter of Peter's apostolic status (sexual politics of another sort, perhaps). See further this part, n. 456.

437. See Mark's "young man sitting . . . in a white robe," Matthew's "angel . . . his garments white as snow," Luke's "two men . . . in dazzling apparel."

presence signals that something extraordinary is afoot, as does their question, apparently rhetorical, why Mary grieves. She does not sense this, however, but turns away—and there Jesus is, standing before her. He addresses her by name, asking ironically what her mission is. His speaking to her makes an answer on her part unnecessary. Her recognition is instantaneous (contrast John 21:4; Luke 24:16): **Rabbouni!** The title she uses presumably has the same force as our translation of *kyrios* in all three episodes: **Master.** It is personal rather than technically christological. Nonetheless it conveys not only Jesus' followers' devotion to him but also his authority, for evidently Mary falls down before him to embrace his feet (see Matt. 28:9) or in some other way elicits Jesus' word: **Do not cling to me.** He overrides her joy to send her to his **brothers**—a locution, probably traditional, used of the disciples only here in 4G. Whatever she was instructed to say to them, if explicitly anything,[438] it is surely comprehended in her words: **I have seen the Lord.**

Mary's role so far is noteworthy. She first saw that the tomb had been opened; she alone saw the angels and then Jesus himself; and twice she carries the message, first to Peter, then to all the disciples. But a final episode remains, for presumably her good news was doubted by the disciples, certainly it was not fully understood. (We cannot be sure whether this is a reflection on her or on them.) So by a kind of minor miracle—**the doors were shut where the disciples were**—Jesus appears to them and demonstrates his identity (**his hands and his side**). This dispels their disbelief, and they rejoice to **see the Master.**

And in a final act he completes what had been foretold of him in SQ (or at the very beginning of an SG). By revelation the Baptist, the witness God had sent, had announced: "This is he who [will] baptize with holy Spirit" (1:33). That baptizing, that bestowal, is here depicted as a single two-part act, for not only does he explicitly grant the Spirit, but by his breath (= spirit in both Semitic and Greek)—the breath of him on whom from the beginning the spirit had descended—he also conveys that spirit: **He breathed on them and said to them, "Receive holy Spirit."**

The impact of the three episodes is clear. Each of them ends with a dramatic proclamation: **He must rise from the dead / I have seen the Master / [You now] receive holy Spirit.** Jesus is not held by the tomb, he *has risen*, as the scripture promised. Indeed he himself had promised it, and in particular that he would *raise himself* (2:19).[439] Jesus' greatest sign,

---

438. Either something in the source has been replaced by 4E's addition of v. 17c ("for I have not yet ascended . . .") or, as we have speculated, it said simply, "Go . . . and tell them," that is, what she had seen.

439. This striking use of the active voice, whether with transitive or intransitive verb (i.e., "raise" or "rise")—in contrast to the usual passives ("is raised," "is risen")—is unique to the pre-Johannine resurrection narrative.

then, has taken place, as the disciples joyfully recognize. And their receipt of holy Spirit that until now only Jesus himself had possessed climaxes all.[440]

So ends the source's narrative. Only a brief closing follows (this part, sec. 20).

Johannine Redaction

20 [1]Early on Sunday while it was still dark Mary Magdalene came to the tomb and saw the stone taken from the tomb. [2]And she ran and came to Simon Peter and to the other disciple whom Jesus loved and told them, "They have taken away the Lord from the tomb, and we don't know where they have laid him." [3]Then Peter went out and the other disciple, and they came to the tomb. [4]And the two ran together; and the other disciple outran Peter and came to the tomb first. [5]And he stooped to look in and saw the burying cloths lying, but he did not go in. [6]Then Simon Peter also came following him, and he went into the tomb and he saw the burying cloths lying. [7]And the napkin, which had been on his head, was not lying with the burying cloths, but had been rolled up in a place by itself. [8]And then the other disciple, who had come first to the tomb, also went in and saw and believed. [9]For as yet they did not know the scripture that he must rise from the dead. [10]Then the disciples went home again.

[11]Mary was standing outside the tomb, weeping. As she wept she stooped to look into the tomb, [12]and she saw two angels in white sitting (one at the head and one at the feet) where Jesus' body had lain. [13]And they said to her, "Woman, why are you weeping?" She told them, "They have taken away my Master, and I don't know where they have laid him." [14]When she had said this she turned away, and saw Jesus standing! (And she did not know that it was Jesus.) [15]Jesus said to her, "Woman, why are you weeping? whom are you looking for?" Supposing that he was the gardener, she said to him, "Sir, if you have taken him away, tell me where you have laid him and I'll take him away." [16]Jesus said to her, "Mary!" She turned and said to him in 'Hebrew,' "Rabbouni!" (which means Teacher). [17]Jesus said to her, "Do not cling to me, for I have not yet ascended to the Father; but go to my brothers and tell them, 'I am ascending to my father and your father and my God and your God.' [18]Mary Magdalene went and announced to the disciples, "I have seen the Lord" and that he had said these things to her.

[19]On Sunday when it was evening and the doors were shut where the disciples were for fear of the Jews, Jesus came and stood in their midst and said to them, "Peace to you." [20]And when he had said this he showed them his hands

---

440. The scene in 21:1–14, in its present form a resurrection appearance, very possibly originated in the pre-Johannine source. But there it was not an Easter story, but a sign occurring at an early point in Jesus' ministry. (See pp. 66–67.) Thus it is not to be treated here.

and his side. Therefore when the disciples saw the *Lord* they were overjoyed. [21]**Then Jesus said to them again, "Peace to you. As the Father has sent me, so I also send you."** [22]**Now when he had said this** he breathed on them and said to them, "Receive *the Holy* Spirit." [[23]**Whose sins you forgive are forgiven; whose you retain are retained.**]

[The Thomas episode (vv. 24-29)]

In the *first* story, the scene of the empty tomb, the Evangelist perhaps introduces the symbolism of the night in which Jesus' followers find themselves (**while it was still dark**—see 6:17 in its present form). But beyond this preparation for the epiphanies in the second and third stories, 4E here concentrates all redactional attention on introducing the beloved disciple into the story.

As I have said, we cannot undertake a comprehensive examination of all that this figure represents in the Johannine Gospel. In particular the contrast set up between him and Peter goes beyond the scope of this passage.[441] We can, however, observe how the source has provided some of the raw materials with which 4E has refashioned this scene. The coming of the two disciples to the tomb together imitates and replaces Peter's joining Mary in the source (with the consequence that Mary's presence again at the tomb in v. 11 is not now accounted for). That the beloved disciple stoops to look into the tomb (v. 5) is like Mary in the second episode, and what he sees is the same as for Peter in what is now the next verse.

Only v. 7, the head covering, adds a new element. Peter is the first to see it—presumably it is to be imagined as not visible to one looking in from outside since it was **folded up in a place by itself**—but it is only the beloved disciple who understands; when, following Peter's lead, he too entered (v. 8), **he saw and believed.** The head cloth thus becomes a kind of *sign*,[442] and his faith does not require as basis either an appearance of the risen Jesus or empirical evidence of his identity (in contrast to both Mary and the rest of the assembled body of disciples on the one hand and to Thomas on the other). The sign is a private one, evoking faith in the beloved disciple alone. Peter does not yet believe, as the following verse (9) now serves to explain. That verse thus no longer primarily conveys expectant hope as in the source (Peter wondered, for they did not *yet* know . . .). It becomes instead an accounting for the difference between the beloved disciple and the others (*he* believed, but as yet *they* did not know . . .). His faith, evidently, is to be understood as all the more exemplary since it was not prepared for even by scriptural prophecy.

From a fairly simple appearance to Mary by the risen Jesus, the Evan-

441. This contrast is of still greater importance in the second half of chap. 21.
442. Here I am indebted to Schneiders, "Veil."

gelist has transformed the *second* episode (vv. 11–18) into a more complex *revelatory event*. This is accomplished by various means:

a. If the middle clause of v. 12 has been inserted—it was only a matter-of-fact and somewhat gratuitous detail if it had been found in the source: the angels seated **one at the head and one at the feet** where Jesus' body had lain—its meaning is not at once clear. But it is just possible that here at last we find the fulfillment of the Johannine promise made in 1:50–51.[443] There, at the climax of the conversion of the first disciples, Jesus spoke of "greater things" to be seen, and added, "You will see . . . the angels of God ascending and descending on the Son of Man." In 5:20–21 such "greater works" are apparently related to the divine act of raising the dead. But nowhere in the Gospel does this arresting promise receive even remote fulfillment—unless, rather subtly, in the present detail of the angels at the tomb.[444] They obviously are not ascending and descending; but Jesus himself, having come down from the Father, is about to ascend—that is the final thrust of these three scenes in their present form. Perhaps then the angels "at his head and at his feet" are somehow like the angels in Jacob's dream, going up and down the ladder between heaven and earth, the ladder here which is Jesus, the Son of Man, himself. Thus may this curious detail at the virtual end of the Gospel fulfill that pivotal promise of chapter 1. If so it is all the more notable that the promised vision, though not apparently understood, is given to a woman. And Mary receives it alone, apparently she need share it with no one. Yet for the reader too the promise is now fulfilled.

b. Mary's reply (v. 13b) to the angels' question—a question that was originally rhetorical, it seems—serves now to heighten the suspense. For this answer 4E paraphrases her report to Peter from v. 2, in words more suited to the circumstances: "Because they have taken away *my Lord* and *I* do not know where they have laid him." This repetition of her earlier bewilderment momentarily delays Jesus' appearance. It also repeats the theme of her not knowing, to be found also in 4E's addition at the end of v. 14: **and she did not know that it was Jesus.** Verse 15 stretches out this lack of recognition: Jesus echoes the angels' question, and Mary mistakes him for the gardener. By her words to him ("Sir, . . . tell me . . .") she prolongs the mistake. Thus when Jesus now merely calls Mary by name (v. 16a), it has the effect at last of a divine disclosure, a sudden heavenly breakthrough into the mundane.

443. I owe this striking suggestion to Robert H. Smith of Pacific Lutheran Theological Seminary. See his *Easter Gospels*, 161–62.

444. The promise is addressed to more than one person ("You [pl.] will see . . ."), but is spoken only to Nathanael. If it is fulfilled by Mary's seeing the angels, there is here a similar disregard for strict consistency. And nothing corresponds in an obvious way to the first part of the promise ("You will see heaven opened").

c. That Jesus' directive to Mary has to do not with the Easter good news but with his imminent ascension to the Father is the effect of the two insertions in v. 17 (**I have not yet ascended . . . / I am ascending. . .**). This is evident also from the awkward addition at the end of v. 18; in the source Mary reports simply, "I have seen the Lord," but 4E appends to the direct discourse report the ill-fitting clause **and that [Jesus] had said these things to her.** The resurrection appearance, then, is no longer primarily a demonstration of Jesus' greatest miracle but has become instead only an occasion for Jesus to reveal what still lies ahead. The divine revelation that his entire activity on earth comprised is now at an end. Even more important than Jesus' being raised from the dead is that he now is returning to the Father; the time of the incarnation is over.

Since this is so, the *third* scene, originally Jesus' confirmatory appearance to the disciples (vv. 19–23), becomes instead a *valedictory*. The disciples had hidden themselves, **for fear of the Jews.** Jesus breaks into their despair with the double word of **Peace** (vv. 19d, 21a),[445] and from their disillusionment sends them out into the world to continue his very own heavenly mission, now coming to an end (**Just as the Father has sent me, even so do I send you**—v. 21b). To this, 4E or a later hand adds the bestowal of the traditional authority to forgive sins (vv. 22–23), which, with the gift of the Holy Spirit (as we can now understand it—see, e.g., 14:26 and the absolute use of "the Spirit," *passim*), empowers the followers of Jesus to carry out their newly received mission.

In the second and third scenes, then, what was originally demonstration of the miracle of the resurrection has become instead *christophany*, a manifestation of Jesus and a revelation of his imminent return to the Father from whom he had come. The appearance stories readily lend themselves to such a shift, and—as C. F. Evans notes ("Resurrection," 116)—for 4E the resurrection as such is in a way redundant with her or his presentation of the crucifixion. That was itself already Jesus' exaltation, at the least the first step in his re-ascension into heaven. All that the account of the resurrection need accomplish, then, is to fix the actual ascension as the immediate sequel to Jesus' self-revelation to the disciples for the last time. That the resurrection is itself just such a manifestation is what 4E would emphasize.

But in the first story another Johannine theme is hinted at: the relation between seeing and believing. The beloved disciple believes on seeing a kind of sign, that of the head covering of Jesus (v. 8b). Peter and the other

---

445. The first greeting was found already in SG (v. 19d), but 4E calls attention to its now theophanic significance by inserting "Having said this" (v. 20a) before continuing with the traditional display of hands and side. Then to introduce the addition of solemn words of divine commissioning (v. 21b) the greeting is repeated (v. 21a).

disciples must wait for Jesus to appear to them, and then though their joy is explicit their faith is only implied.[446] The contrast between the beloved disciple, and Mary and the assembled disciples is clear; but chiefly it is with the scene about Thomas's faith that 4E draws the contrast.

The Evangelist evidently creates the chapter's final scene (vv. 24–29) out of materials taken from the source in the preceding stories. The tradition lying behind Luke 24:36–43 (Jesus' appearance to the eleven) is also drawn on. And here as earlier in 11:16 the figure of **Thomas known as the Twin** from the source (now at 21:2) is used. Thomas becomes the type of the one who can, or rather will, only believe if he sees. And this sight is not so much of a sign as of what we would call empirical evidence: **Unless I see in his hands the print of the nails, and place my finger in the mark of the nails and place my hand in his side, I will not believe** (v. 25b).[447] His demand is not rejected; Jesus complies with it so that Thomas will **be not disbelieving but believing** (v. 27), and the confession of faith that ensues is wholly appropriate (**My Lord and my God**—v. 28).

But yet that faith is met with a question: **Because you have seen me, do you believe?** (v. 29a).[448] And the scene, indeed the entire Gospel, ends with a pronouncement of benediction upon the faith of those like the beloved disciple but with even less to rely on: **Blessed are those who have not seen and yet believed.** The whole of Jesus' earthly deed, as encapsuled in this consummating chapter, is Christophany Understood by Faith (see further on this passage in part 2.B). Chapter 21, falling as it does outside the Johannine and pre-Johannine conclusion of the Gospel (20:30–31—see the next section), is very likely post-Johannine. In any case its author has made out of what was evidently a pre-Johannine messianic sign of Jesus a climactic resurrection appearance (see this part, sec. 5, [Post-]Johannine Redaction). This episode (vv. 1–14) is filled by its redactor with what appears to be sacramental or ecclesiastical imagery. That author has then appended to it: an extended dialogue between Jesus and Peter, apparently intended to cancel Peter's three denials of Jesus in chapter 18 by his three professions of love for Jesus here (vv. 15–19); a

446. The source perhaps gave a glimmer of such faith on Peter's part, if it showed him wondering at the empty tomb; and on the other hand it also evidently showed the assembled disciples disbelieving Mary's good news. If so, 4E has removed both these elements implying faith or the lack of it, in order to reserve the issue of faith for the Thomas story.

447. R. H. Smith, in a private communication, points out how emphatically graphical and physical is the test of the risen Jesus' identity as described in this insistence by Thomas. Jesus' invitation simply paraphrases—"Put your finger here, and see my hands; and put out your hand, and place it in my side" (v. 27a). Contrast the more general invitation, preceded by no insistence from the disciples: "See my hands and feet, that it is I myself; handle me, and see" (Luke 24:39).

448. Sometimes v. 29a is taken as a statement rather than a question, but this makes no real difference to the sense.

discussion of the status of the beloved disciple (vv. 20–24); and finally
(v. 25) a second conclusion to the Gospel, mirroring that at the end of
chapter 20. But because none of the material in this chapter, with the
exception of vv. 1–14, is recognizably derived from a source, it does not
lend itself to redaction-critical interpretation, and in any case cannot be
assumed to be Johannine.

Analysis

This passage has had extensive attention, yielding a great variety of views as to
the separation of tradition or source from redaction. But many of these attempts
are flawed—from our standpoint—either by a preoccupation with the question of
historicity or an interest in harmonizing the Johannine account with the Synoptics,
or both.[449] Because of the many difficulties in the chapter, I can claim no certainty
for the following analysis. Nevertheless it may have some reliability simply because
by now it can draw on the source analysis of all the narrative in 4G, and is not—
like most other studies—carried out in isolation from the rest of the Gospel.[450]

• In v. 1 we have a succinct account of the tradition of the women coming to the
open tomb, more fully told in all the Synoptics. The chief difference is that only
Mary Magdalene appears here (as in the Longer Ending of Mark, 16:9, which is
possibly a tradition independent of the Synoptic accounts).[451] There is reason to
ask, then, whether one or more other women, variously named in the Synoptic
versions, have dropped out of this account (see on "we do not know" in. v. 2b
below). Mahoney suggests that this was so and due to 4E's "proclivity to simplify
his *dramatis personae.*"[452] That is possible, since in the Evangelist's hands the
episodes that follow (Peter with the beloved disciple, and Thomas) are narrowed to
focus on single individuals. But it is slightly more likely that the concentration on
one figure, known in her own right in the tradition, has occurred prior to 4E.

The Evangelist's only addition here may be **while it was still dark,** which is
slightly redundant after **early;** the phrase is not found in the otherwise closely
parallel opening of [Mark] 16:9, and it may display Johannine symbolism (see
comment, this section, beginning of Johannine Redaction).

• In v. 2 Mary's shock at finding the tomb empty is not related, only her
response: **she ran and came to Peter** and reported her understanding of what she
had seen and her dismay. Undoubtedly **the other disciple** in v. 2a (as also in vv. 3,
4, and 8), and certainly his description here as the one **whom Jesus loved,** is to be

449. On the other hand, Neirynck's article, "Empty Tomb," has as its agendum support
for the overall view that 4E knew and used the Synoptics, making source theories superfluous.

450. This is the last of the three passages Dauer (*Johannes und Lukas,* 207–89) analyzes to
show dependence of the pre-Johannine source on the present text of Luke; see further, this
part, excursus B.

451. That block, usually known as [Mark] 16:9–20, is found in a number of MSS but is
missing in the oldest and best and is commonly regarded as a post-Markan addition to Mark
16:8, when that verse evidently was seen as an inadequate or a defective ending.

452. Mahoney, *John 20:1–10,* 225. In both Matthew and Luke, but in different ways, the
cast of characters from Mark 16:1 is simplified. But what Mahoney considers a trait of 4E
may as well be true of the predecessor.

195

attributed to 4E, as elsewhere in the account of the passion,[453] and so we may suspect that the source read "to him" (rather than "them") after **said.**

Mary's words ("They have taken the Lord from the tomb . . ."—v. 2b) might seem premature, in view of the fact that we will be told of her looking into the tomb only in vv. 11–12 (and—as we shall see—by Johannine imitation in vv. 5–6); but that episode must originally stem from a separate tradition that the pre-Johannine author has joined to this one. Here Mary, although she has not looked into the tomb, simply expresses what is implied in the women's silent fear in Mark 16:8, namely that the entrance stone's removal[454] must mean that Jesus' body has already been taken away or even stolen. (Mark is analogously expanded by Matthew and Luke each in its own way.) Her absolute use of *ho kyrios* ("the Lord") is not uncommon in resurrection accounts, but since Mary is not yet aware that Jesus is risen it perhaps means only "the Master." The plural **we do not know** probably reflects, as we noted, an earlier version of the story in which Mary Magdalene was not alone. But in any case v. 2b is best attributed to the source.

• For our analysis in v. 3 there may be very strong support in Luke 24:12, a verse often held to be post-Lukan—as so it may be, though it is found in important MSS. In any case, while it has many details in common with this passage in 4G, it appears to be independent of canonical 4G, since it lacks "the other disciple" altogether (nor can it be the source of the pre-Johannine text here [*pace* Dauer, *Johannes und Lukas*]). According to Luke 24:11–12, Peter on hearing the report of the women, including Mary Magdalene (v. 11), goes to the tomb, stoops to look into it, and finding only the burying cloths goes home wondering (v. 12). (On this controversial verse in Luke, see further R. H. Smith, *Easter Gospels*, 111. He observes [p. 241 n. 31] that "a majority of the editorial committee of the United Bible Society project think Luke and John drew [here] from a common tradition.")

Verse 3, then, without **the other disciple,** is similar to Luke 24:12 (whether or not authentic to that Gospel). See this part, n. 453: Peter alone goes to the tomb on hearing that it was open. If, as it appears, Mary returns to the tomb with Peter, the plural reading in the present text of the Gospel **(they came to the tomb)** could be pre-Johannine.

• Verses 4–6a are Johannine: "the other disciple" and his footrace with Peter; his looking into the tomb but not entering; and Peter's coming (redundant with the end of v. 3). Verse 6b smoothly follows v. 3: on hearing Mary's report, Peter comes out, goes with her to the tomb, and enters it, seeing **the burying cloths.**

453. See the singular verb at the beginning of v. 3. It is conceivable that the "other disciple" here and in the places listed above is pre-Johannine, along with Peter and Mary Magdalene. See the unnamed disciple in the pre-Johannine narrative at 18:15–16 (in the high priest's house). But the function of this figure throughout the present episode is entirely Johannine, and because of the grammatical anomalies we have noted it seems better to regard the entire phrase—"the other disciple whom Jesus loved"—as the product of 4E's insertion (see just below, on Luke 24:12). We leave open the possibility that this figure somehow corresponds to a historical (or at least traditional) person and is not simply the product of Johannine invention—a question we do not attempt to resolve.

454. In the present text of chap. 19, there is no mention of the tomb's having been closed with a stone, as is assumed in chap. 20 and is common to all Synoptic accounts. Its absence from chap. 19 would stem simply from the fact that once-separate traditions underlay that chapter and chap. 20, respectively.

• Mention of the handkerchief used as head covering (the whole of v. 7) is a postscript (there was no mention of it with the burying cloths in chap. 19) and its detailed description here (**not lying with the burying cloths but folded up in a place by itself**) is out of proportion with the narrative's flow. The verse is probably redactional, 4E perhaps having borrowed from the Lazarus tradition for the handkerchief (11:44) but describing its function somewhat differently—why, we cannot say ("upon his head" here, Lazarus's "face wrapped" in chap. 11)—and then elaborately calling attention to its disposition in the empty tomb.

• And verse 8 on the one hand takes up the Johannine themes in vv. 4–5 and on the other logically collides with the evidently traditional v. 9: the belief of the "other disciple" is hardly explained by the fact that "as yet they did not know the scripture."[455] Thus, vv. 7–8 extend the Johannine insertion of vv. 4–6a. In the place of v. 8 we may conjecture that, following v. 6b, the source said of Peter that he "wondered" (see Luke 24:12).

• Culpepper (*Anatomy*, 23) suggests that an offstage narrator's comment such as v. 9 is likely to stem from 4E. This could be, but it is more likely that it is 4E's predecessor who is the narrator in question here and who adds the parenthetical explanation ("For as yet they did not know the scripture . . ."). Such interest in the fulfillment of prophecy is typically pre-Johannine, whereas 4E is usually concerned with the fulfillment of *Jesus*' words. The style ("not yet" and "know") would seem Johannine except that the form of the adverb (*oudepō*) is pre-Johannine at 19:41 and found in a Johannine context only once (7:39—a gloss?), whereas 4E uses *oupō* eleven times (Darton, *Concordance*, 407), and this form of "know" is pre-Johannine also in v. 2.

• In v. 10, perhaps an original "And *he* returned home" has been altered by 4E to conform to the addition of the beloved disciple.

• With v. 11 a second episode begins, the appearance of Jesus to Mary Magdalene.[456] Analysis in this story (vv. 11–18) is difficult, as the varying attempts show (see, e.g., B & L, 459). The most striking phenomenon is the presence of several doublets, in the space of only a few verses, with details and phrases used

455. One could treat the logic here as elliptical: the beloved disciple believed *despite* the fact that they did not yet know. But that would require us to attribute v. 9 to the Evangelist, and, as we are about to see, it appears more likely to be a traditional part of the story.

456. Wink ("Sexual Politics") suggests that underlying vv. 1–10 and 11–18 there were not originally separate stories but a single account involving only Mary Magdalene (possibly with other women). This comprised roughly v. 1 followed by vv. 11–18. Then 4E has inserted more or less as a block the story of Peter and the beloved disciple (vv. 2–10; many other critics analyze the story this way, for various reasons), perhaps with the intent that the original witnesses of the empty tomb be men and thus able to vouch for the resurrection legitimately. But vv. 2–10 are not homogeneous, for they contain aporias. And in fact neither Peter nor the beloved disciple acts as a witness; after their visit to the tomb they simply return home and are not singled out again. Very possibly Peter's introduction into a scene which in all versions of the tradition includes only the women was in fact made so as to upstage the women, as invalid witnesses. But if so this was done at a stage *earlier* than 4E's redaction (see this part, n. 436). The Evangelist's sole interest is to introduce the beloved disciple as in some way equal to, and greater than, Peter.

either earlier or later in the chapter.[457] Since one element in each of these pairs is found in vv. 11b–14a, some see that block as a redactional insertion by 4E,[458] but I suggest, contrariwise, that it is largely pre-Johannine and that it is the basis for much of the imitation before and after it. Thus, for example, the beloved disciple stoops to look into the tomb in v. 5 just as Mary does here in v. 11b; the question to Mary in vv. 13a and 15 is the same; on the other hand her reply in v. 13b imitates the source at v. 2.[459]

● The description in v. 12 of the angels' position in the tomb is overfull, the dangling phrase **one at the head and one at the feet** probably a redactional insertion prematurely referring to **Jesus' body**, mentioned only in the next clause. That there are **two angels in white sitting** is simply a variant of the tradition, Mark having only a *young man* in a white robe sitting *on the right side* (16:5), Matthew one angel in *raiment white as snow* but descending from heaven (28:2–5), and Luke two *men* in *dazzling apparel* and *standing* (24:4).

● Mary's reply (v. 13b) to the angels' question, replicated from the source at v. 2b, has been adapted to fit its present context: "*my* Lord," "*I* do not know," omission of "from the tomb."

● Mary originally gave no reply here but instead **turned away,** perhaps in grief (v. 14a). The verse's opening phrase (**saying this**) often concludes a Johannine insertion.

● Schnackenburg may be right that Mary's failure to recognize Jesus (v. 14b) is not the typical Johannine misunderstanding,[460] but it is nevertheless probably Johannine, together with Jesus' initial words to Mary (v. 15a), which reiterate verbatim the angels' question of v. 13a (**Woman, why are you crying?**). But then his next words (**Whom do you seek?**), would be pre-Johannine. Her reply together with the preceding explanation (v. 15b: "Supposing him to be the gardener,[461] she said to him . . .") lacks the spareness typical of the source's narrative and seems designed only to heighten the suspense introduced by v. 14b (**she did not know that it was Jesus**).

● That suspense leads in v. 16a to Jesus' christophanic address to Mary, calling her by name. The awkward repetition of her turning—why would she turn to speak to Jesus when she was already speaking with him?—must be Johannine.

● Mary's astonished address of Jesus (**Rabbouni!**—v. 16b) resumes the pre-Johannine course of v. 15a. Only the parenthetical explanation of the Semitic word (not actually **Hebrew**) is Johannine: **which means teacher;** see 4E's translation of **Rabbi** in 1:38.

● In v. 17a the puzzling **Do not touch me** is probably not Johannine, colliding as

457. Namely, Mary's stooping to look into the tomb (vv. 5, 11b–12); "Woman, why are you weeping?" (vv. 13a, 15); "They have taken away [my] Lord and [I] do not know where they have laid him" (vv. 2, 13b); Mary's turning (vv. 14a, 16).

458. So Schnackenburg, more or less, following Hartman, "Osterberichte."

459. Thus, I now separate the question (v. 13a) from the reply and attribute the former to the source (contrast *TGOS*, 139).

460. As I mistakenly held in *TGOS*, 140.

461. Mention of "the gardener" might stem from the source, which locates the tomb in a garden (19:41—uniquely in all the resurrection traditions, as Schnackenburg observes); but equally it can be part of 4E's redactional elaboration.

it does with Jesus' invitation to Thomas in 4E's scene at the end of the chapter (v. 27). Johannine redaction accounts for only the justification of the prohibition (**for I have not yet ascended to the Father**—v. 17b), which interrupts the continuation of Jesus' instructions to Mary. At the pre-Johannine level the warning to her then evidently means "Do not cling to me but [rather] go. . . ."

• The present content of the report she is to carry to the disciples (v. 17d) is obviously Johannine (**I am ascending to my Father and your Father and my God and your God**). It may have replaced something in the source, such as the promise (found in Mark and Matthew) that the disciples will see Jesus in Galilee.[462] But more likely the message was not specified, being obvious: simply "Tell them [that is, what you have seen]," for that is what she in fact does (v. 18—she **went and announced to the disciples, "I have seen the Lord!"**), and only the ill-fitting phrase appended there (**and that he had said these things to her**—v. 18b) is redactional.[463] That the disciples to whom Mary is sent are called by Jesus his **brothers** is found at Matt. 28:10.

• We hear nothing of the disciples' response, but it can be conjectured that originally they may have refused to believe and that 4E has suppressed the notice, so as to limit such disbelief to Thomas in the episode about to follow (20:24–29).[464]

• In v. 19a—which begins the third and last episode in the source—the pleonastic and perhaps unnecessary reminder of the date (**on that Sunday**) may prepare for the Johannine story of Thomas, which takes place exactly a week later. That the doors were closed **for fear of the Jews** is Johannine.[465]

• That Jesus came and **stood in the midst [of them]** (v. 19b) is found, in slightly different form, in Luke 24:36a, and so possibly pre-Johannine here, as perhaps in 1:26b. Jesus' greeting at the end of the verse (**Peace to you**), to be reiterated by 4E in v. 21, is probably traditional as well, a special case of the general greeting, "Shalom."[466] The greeting of peace is found in the same context also in [Luke] 24:36b, which may reflect an independent but parallel tradition.

• In v. 20 Jesus' showing the disciples **his hands and side** is surely pre-

462. The Evangelist, not unlike the Lukan author, may have had reason to suppress a return to Galilee at the end of the story of Jesus, in view of the geographical schema of the present Gospel (see part 2.F)—a consideration probably weighing against the Johannine authorship of chap. 21.

463. Once again 4E puts the word of Jesus alongside and superior to a traditional element, sometimes a prophecy of scripture, here a deed of Jesus and his greatest one.

464. See further *TGOS*, 142–43.

465. The element of fear as a general reaction to the resurrection is found under various forms in all the Synoptic accounts (esp. Mark 16:8), so the redactional addition here might be only "of the Jews," except that the entire phrase *dia ton phobon tōn Ioudaion* is certainly Johannine at 7:13 and 19:38.

466. Despite the Johannine "and having said this" immediately following; that phrase ordinarily follows a redactional insertion. Here it seems only to call attention on the Johannine level to Jesus' revelatory presence. The greeting's affinity with the Johannine Jesus' words in 14:27 ("Peace I leave with you, my peace I give to you") is no problem for assigning it to the source. In fact, strictly speaking the saying in chap. 14 makes the present scene redundant; 4E has only let it stand from SG.

Johannine.[467] Their joy at recognizing and seeing him risen is most apt as the climax of the source's resurrection account.

• Verse 21 seems entirely Johannine: repetition of the peace from v. 19; Jesus sent by "the Father"; the precise correspondence between the Father's action toward Jesus and that of Jesus toward the disciples (**As the Father has sent me, even so I send you**—see 17:18).[468]

• The bestowal of "holy Spirit" (v. 22) and the authority to forgive sins (v. 23) are undoubtedly based on traditional materials.[469] In an integrated SG the former is clearly the completion of the divine promise implied in the Baptist's testimony to Jesus ("he who baptizes with holy spirit"—1:33) and thus must stem from the source.[470] The authority over sins is more difficult to assign, but seems not to be a pre-Johannine concern. It may have been introduced by 4E, having perhaps some connection to the Johannine tradition of the Lamb of God "who takes away the sins of the world" in 1:29; but the resemblance is loose at best. Possibly it is a post-Johannine addition.

• The entire Thomas episode (vv. 24–29), beginning with the afterthought ("Now Thomas . . . had not been with them when Jesus came"), is 4E's addition and possibly creation. It builds mainly on elements found earlier in the chapter, in particular the third story; yet that passage is altogether oblivious of this episode that now follows it. The general disbelief that we postulated for the source after v. 18 is here dramatized in the person of Thomas, who is known to 4E from SG (21:2) and twice earlier was made to serve a dramatic purpose (11:16; 14:5).[471]

---

467. See the similar but slightly different account in Luke 24:39[–40] where it is "hands and feet" that he shows them. His **side** here is consistent with the spear wound of 19:34, replacing the feet that, like his hands, had been pierced with nails.

468. The resemblance to Luke 24:49 ("I send the promise of my Father upon you") is only superficial.

469. See Brown, 1022–24.

470. The same promise, usually overtranslated as "the Holy Spirit" (on our rendering, see this part, n. 51, on 1:33), finds no completion in Mark; the authors of Matthew and Luke each fill this lack in their own way (Matt. 28:19d [perhaps]; Acts 2:4).

471. See further *TGOS*, 142.

The Closing

SECTION 20 (20:30–31a)
THE AUTHOR'S SUMMARY

Pre-Johannine Source
20 [30]Now Jesus did many other signs in the sight of his[472] disciples, which are not written in this book. [31]Yet these are written that you may come to believe that Jesus is the Christ, the Son of God.

The source thus ends on a sonorous note: "Now while it is true (*men*) . . . nevertheless (*de*). . . ." This rhetorical device expresses both a concession and a double claim. The author acknowledges that only a selection of the miraculous deeds of Jesus is included, but thereby claims (first of all) that such activity was even more extensive and impressive than the book can show.[473] But at the same time (second) what is shown is sufficient.

For the first time we hear the pre-Johannine writer consciously addressing readers; he or she has written a **book**, with a clear purpose relative to them: **That you may . . . believe.** The intent is to give the basis for faith, and the form of the verb (**come to believe**) suggests the onset of faith—conversion.[474]

The portrayal of the signs provides both the necessary and the sufficient basis for faith. It is as if the latter-day readers (those addressed in v. 31a)

472. There is some good MS evidence to suppose that instead of "his disciples" the original text of 4G read "the disciples." But clearly nothing hinges on the matter for our purposes.

473. The later paraphrase of this verse in 21:25 thus correctly interprets, while exaggerating, this implicit claim: "There are also many other things that Jesus did; were every one of them to be written, I suppose that the world itself could not contain the books that would be written."

474. The MSS differ here, some showing the present subjunctive (*pisteuēte*), others and perhaps the better ones the aorist (*pisteusēte*). Heekerens (*Zeichen-Quelle*), cited by Neirynck ("John 4,46–54," 369), at one time held that the present was the authentic reading and should be translated "that you may continue to believe," suggesting that the purpose of SQ was as a *Lehrschrift*, a manual for the instruction of the faithful. He then shifted to favor the aorist and to regard SQ as a missionary writing ("that you may come to believe"). But both readings may in fact mean the same, the former understood as an inceptive present. I too hold that SG was a missionary tract, at least originally—did the variant reading represent a change in use with the passage of time? But I doubt that the issue can hinge on the translation of this one verb, even if its form were certain.

are thought of as having seen the signs, not literally of course but nevertheless really, as they are **written in this book.** Unlike Thomas, in the Evangelist's added scene (vv. 24–29) they are not contrasted with, but rather likened to Jesus' **disciples** who believed on the basis of the signs done **in [their] sight** (v. 30).[475]

The content of the faith thereby engendered is simply a christology but with all that that includes: **that Jesus is the Christ, the Son of God.**[476]

The two titles used here of Jesus are not new to the reader, whether of SQ, which these verses must originally have concluded, or of a fuller SG, with passion and resurrection inserted. The titles appear at the very start of the book. John the Baptist, who bears witness **that all might come to believe** (1:7), testifies that he himself is not **the Christ,** making it clear that the title belongs instead to Jesus (1:20). And he explicitly avows that Jesus is **the Son of God** (1:34). Then, in the opening scene's sequel, the chain of witness on the part of the first converts takes up the messianic title in its Semitic form (*Messias* [1:41]—author and readers were evidently at least partly bilingual), and that chain culminates in both titles used together: Nathanael acclaims Jesus as **Son of God** and adds, in what is clearly a paraphrase of "Christ," **You are the King of Israel** (1:49).

In the sign stories themselves titles rarely occur.[477] But in the passion narrative, to which 20:30–31 was probably the conclusion already at the pre-Johannine stage, messianic titles are common. **King of Israel** is the acclamation of the crowd at Jesus' Entry into Jerusalem (12:13), and thereafter the clearly equivalent **King of the Jews** appears four times (18:33, 39; 19:3, 19). "Messiah"/"Christ" does not occur, nor does "Son of God,"[478] but all the titles in the combined source have only one message: the unique agent of God, so long expected, has appeared and demon-

475. The preposition *enōpion* (only here in 4G, vs. *emprosthen,* frequently) is usually translated "in the presence of," but its more literal meaning (above) is probably not far from the surface here. On the question of how faith comes about, in SG and in 4G, see further, part 2.B.

476. Thyen (*"Literatur"*) holds that these two verses are a post-Johannine insertion made by the anti-docetic author of the beloved-disciple passages (19:35; 20:2–10, 18–29). But he thereby inverts the meaning of these verses, arguing that for their author they have to do not with Jesus' messiahship per se but with his *identity* with the Christ, against those who would deny that the Christ is identical with, limited to, the historical person Jesus. Presumably Thyen would translate: " . . . believe that the Christ, the Son of God, is Jesus." While the use of articles in this clause would permit this construction, it makes no sense of v. 30, for how can the earthly deeds of *Jesus,* however impressive, be used to demonstrate that the otherworldly Christ is to be identified with him? See Addendum.

477. Evidently there is no need to explain that what the signs signify is just that Jesus is the Messiah. It is the witnesses' believing response that is highlighted, and that very faith of course attests to Jesus' messianic status. The notable exception is the acclamation of the crowds immediately after the feeding: **Surely this is the Prophet who is to come into the world** (6:14). This title is synonymous with Christ, and just as it too was disavowed by the Baptist so it is expressly applied to Jesus at the culmination of the Galilean ministry.

478. The distinct origin of the passion tradition is no doubt accountable for this variation in titles used.

strated his messianic authority, his divine sonship. This is the pre-Johannine book's single-minded witness.

Johannine Redaction

The Evangelist's only change is the addition of v. 31b: **and that believing you may have life in his name.**

4E writes for a community that is, of course, further removed in time from its roots than was true when the source was written, and—what is more—drastically separated emotionally and spiritually by the rift between synagogue and church (or rather the expulsion of the church *by* the synagogue). At several points (all redactional) the Gospel shows evidence that such a break has intervened between the writing of the source and the time 4E takes up pen to transmute the source into the Gospel we now read. (Very likely this traumatic experience is also a major motivation for the *writing* of the Gospel, since the source—whose context was entirely the Christian movement within Judaism—has now become obsolete.) The problem (1) of latter-day belief is raised by this temporal difference: how shall second- and third-generation Christians, out of touch with the experience of eyewitnesses, believe? And the problem (2) of theological inadequacy in the earlier Christian proclamation and faith is raised, after the expulsion of Christians from the body of Judaism.

It is the former problem that 4E addresses in the Thomas episode, and now coming immediately after it these verses gain a new meaning. The reader is one who now, unlike Thomas, has not seen (contrast the original purpose of the source and its expression in v. 31a—see Pre-Johannine Source in this section). For that reader, contrary to the expectation of 4E's predecessor, not even reading of the signs constitutes compelling evidence. The failure of SG any longer to convert unbelievers had shown that. But since there is no other basis for faith, **Blessed are those who do not see**—who only trust on the basis of what they can read—and so believe (v. 29b). Such trust is not misplaced. If anything, 4E makes a greater claim for such a basis than did the source.[479]

But mere faith in Jesus' messiahship has been proved inadequate (the second problem). To believe that he was the Christ in the context of Judaism had been soteriologically sufficient, for it then included a theology of salvation. What had been awaited, longed for, had come ("We have found the Messiah"), and all else followed. But once that context was taken away, once Christianity was torn loose from its Jewish moorings—as it had for 4E's time and community—belief in Jesus' status, belief merely **that [he] is the Christ,** is not enough. It must lead—in a way partly comparable to but now also distinct from the whole Jewish mystery of

479. If "these" of v. 31 is, in the Johannine context, intended to mean not just the signs but "these things" (i.e., all that the Gospel contains, and especially Jesus' teaching), the basis is in fact broadened.

salvation—to **life in [Jesus'] name**. The Evangelist affirms the necessity of coming to faith, but unless it persists[480] and results in an enduring relationship, what 4E elsewhere (and some MSS here) can call eternal life, it is of no value.

The Evangelist elsewhere uses the early Christian metaphor of faith in the **name** of Jesus (see 1:12; 2:23; 3:18),[481] as well as praying in his name. It is thus only a small step to summarizing Christian salvation as **life** in his name, "life" being also a frequent Johannine term.

The Gospel of signs, the good news of Jesus' messiahship, has necessarily been augmented by this fuller message of salvation. What there was only implicit, 4E now has made explicit. It is no longer sufficient simply to believe that Jesus is Messiah, even thereby to become in some sense like his first followers. Thus the good news of 4G is clear: Belief and Life in Jesus' Name.

Analysis

• The last two verses of chapter 20 present a well-known difficulty. Although a connection with the preceding scene of doubting Thomas can be made out (see this section, Johannine Redaction), it is not entirely natural. Here there is no contrast between two kinds of faith, as in that scene; no mention of belief without seeing.

• A greater difficulty is that we hear of signs for the first time since chapter 12.[482] It is widely held that these two verses, less any redaction they might contain, originally concluded a Signs Source in the narrow sense, where they would immediately have followed the last of a series of miracles. This was undoubtedly true at one stage in the editorial development of the Johannine narratives. But it is conceivable and (it is our contention) likely that prior to the work of 4E the passion account had been joined to a Signs Source. The latter's original ending was then moved to follow the resurrection stories. This new context would have been quite satisfactory (prior to the Johannine redaction) since for PQ the resurrection is Jesus' greatest sign (2:18–19)—it is not a sign at all for 4E[483]—and the disciples have just been mentioned (20:20).

• The only clear aporia in the two verses is caused by v. 31b, which in form and content reads like an afterthought and differs grammatically from v. 31a.[484] It is clearly Johannine.

480. Hence the present participle and subjunctive in v. 31b, with the durative force of that tense.

481. In the Johannine context it very likely replaces the older biblical symbol of the name of Yahweh.

482. This problem was felt by some early scribes, who added that these signs (of 20:30) were done "after he rose from the dead."

483. As we saw in this part, sec. 19. The detail of the headcloth (20:8) is a kind of minor sign, but not explicitly, and it is perceived only by the beloved disciple.

484. *Present* participle and subjunctive ("continuing to believe . . . continue to have") contrasting with *aorist* subjunctive in v. 31a ("come to believe"). (Some MSS show the latter as a present subjunctive, but very probably by assimilation to the verse's second half.)

Excursuses: Studies in the Pre-Johannine Source

Having reconstructed SG as fully as practicable, and before turning to the synthetic summation of the theological movement from source to present Gospel (part 2), we need to give special attention to two issues concerning the hypothetical source: (A) its literary form or genre and (B) its relation to the Synoptic Gospels. Then we can attempt (C) a brief summary of the source's character.

A. THE SOURCE'S GENRE

1. A Gospel

I have spoken just now of the source, in the singular, and we shall deal with the question of its integrity—whether signs and passion had come together in a common genre at the pre-Johannine stage—in A.2. But first we must ask the question of genre of each component of SG separately. So we consider SQ by itself—that is, the Signs Source in the narrower sense. What was its literary character, its *Gattung*?

a. We can say at once, as before, that it was no mere string of sign stories, such as the several clusters of miracles used by the Markan author. Rather, SQ was a coherent document, organized and integrated within itself. What is more, it was already **a gospel**—a primitive and bare one, by later standards, but a gospel nevertheless. Both its form and its content display this.

As Bultmann already saw *(Gospel of John)*, the Signs Source was an articulated narrative, from its opening introductory narratives onward. Similarly, it had an unusually explicit conclusion (20:30–31a), in which it refers to itself as a book *(biblion)*[485] and comes formally to an end. Further, most of the individual stories, and very likely all, lead each to the next, in a carefully conceived geographic order for Jesus' performing of the signs, a minimal but unusually logical itinerary.

In its relatively brief way, then, SQ by itself is comparable to the flow of the later Gospels, and indeed, compared to Mark at least, moves forward in a more controlled and consistent story line and has a tighter and more evident structure.

But though resembling in smaller scope the continuous accounts of all four canonical Gospels, and thus *a* gospel in form, it is not automatically **Gospel** in substance. For ultimately Gospel is not a genre but a matter of message. *Eu-*

---

485. Uniquely among the Gospels (unless *biblos* in Matt. 1:1 refers to the entire Gospel; more likely it identifies only the genealogy of Jesus [1:2–17] or at most the birth narrative [chaps. 1—2]).

angelion, which means good news, necessarily involves *kēryssein,* proclamation. *A* Gospel is a book, then, that announces the good news of Jesus the Messiah.

But then on this count too SQ is one of the purest versions of Gospel we possess or, as in this case, can reconstruct. It does not use the term "good news," but placed alongside the others, its message is more explicit, its announcement the most distinct: "We have found the Messiah ... the Son of God, the King of Israel!" (1:41, 49). The Markan Gospel calls itself "good news" explicitly (Mark 1:1), and the Matthean and Lukan Gospels repeatedly use either that noun or the verb ("evangelize") in its original proclamatory sense. But in none of them is the fact and the epitome of the good news so lucidly and forthrightly presented as in SQ.

After Jesus is found and named by the first disciples, he elaborately justifies their discovery by performing the deeds, the signs (such as those of Moses and Elijah) for the Coming One so long expected. And for the closing of the pre-Johannine book its author is confident that this single affirmation is both self-evident and sufficient: "Jesus did many other signs in the sight of his disciples [the original recipients of the good news and its traditioners] which are not [necessary to be] written in this book; but these are written that you [the readers] may believe that Jesus is the Christ, the Son of God" (20:30–31a). What was evident already in John the Baptist's testimony ("this is the Son of God"—1:34), it is now at last only necessary to state outwardly as summary.[486]

Thus, on the basis both of its form and content, SQ was one of the first of the Christian Gospels to be written, purer, simpler, and thus almost certainly earlier than Mark.

If we compare SQ to that other, more widely recognized hypothetical pre-canonical writing—Q, the saying source commonly thought to underlie Matthew and Luke—we can still call SQ the earliest of the Gospels, even if later than Q,[487] *since Q is not really a Gospel.* It is, rather, only a collection of the sayings of Jesus, which though they imply a christology (Jesus the revealer of true wisdom, perhaps) do not proclaim that fact outwardly. More important, there is in Q no narrative base (barely any narrative at all, and none connecting the collected units of tradition editorially). But narrative is essential to all explicit statements of good news, from the earliest pre-Pauline thumbnail formulas (such as Rom. 1:3–4; 1 Cor. 15:3b–5), through the so-called Apostles' Creed, even to the highly meta-physical creeds of the fourth and fifth centuries.[488] Instead, Q seems to have been set in a trajectory leading in an eventually unacceptable, semi-Gnostic direction

---

486. The Markan Gospel opens with almost identical words, adding only that this is "Gospel"; perhaps this was necessary at the beginning since the proclamation is not so palpable in that Gospel's more complex representation.

487. In dating these two theoretical documents one cannot be more precise than to say that they both appear to stem from a time stretching anywhere from the late 40s to the mid-60s of the first century.

488. Thus, the objection (as by Lindars, *Behind 4G,* 31) that a book ought to contain the teaching of Jesus to be a Gospel is simply unfounded. Indeed, to make the teaching of Jesus about the kingdom of God serve as a proclamation about Jesus was anomalous at first, as the relatively small role that teaching plays in Mark shows. The writing Paul sent to the Romans would perhaps best be called Gospel if it were not outwardly a letter and now set among his other more occasional letters.

(such as we see more clearly in the so-called *Gospel of Thomas*), alien to the historical, narrative affirmations of what had been the earliest, and eventually became normative, Christianity.[489]

It should be recognized that we are designating SQ alone, without a passion narrative, as Gospel and therefore a Gospel. It is true that a combined source (signs followed by passion), of which as we shall try to show below the final pre-Johannine narrative source consisted, is more self-evidently a Gospel than SQ alone, simply because our later canonical Gospels all have roughly this shape.[490] But we can say that SQ alone was an early, perhaps the earliest, Gospel we know.

b. What about the Passion Source, then, that clearly arose separately from SQ (at least the clusters of tradition making it up stemmed from an altogether different motive)? Is it in a sense Gospel too?

Fundamentally, we must say no to this question. The pre-Johannine passion narrative has the function of apologetic—not of proclaiming but justifying, not good news but argumentation. For how could Jesus, if he was Messiah, have died in the shocking and unacceptable way that he did? That is the question addressed in the assembling of passion traditions, the initiating theological problem. The answer is, of course, simply that scripture required this death, a rationale tying together the whole connected account. The intent is not to announce but to answer, so as to correct and reassure. (And just possibly it was the messianic proclamation of SQ that required the development in the same community, first, of a passion story and, eventually, its attachment to SQ.)

Yet in the end PQ, including the resurrection,[491] does announce good news, the supreme news—better still than that Messiah had come. In spite of Jesus' death and the inexplicability even of the empty tomb, Mary Magdalene makes the astonished announcement, comparable but superior to that earlier made by the disciples at the beginning: "I have seen the Lord!" (20:18). So even PQ, separate from SQ, becomes in the end a kind of Gospel.

It follows, then, that when SQ and PQ were combined, the sum would be still more both Gospel and a Gospel than each of them individually. But we must now address the question when that combination would have taken place, that is, whether on the part of the pre-Johannine author or only later, at the Johannine level by the Evangelist.[492]

489. For this reason, no doubt, Q had to be brought into the evangelic framework by both Matthew and Luke, albeit in quite different ways. While SQ also must be adapted by 4E, it is treated with such respect that it becomes the structural basis for the finished gospel, as was not the least true of Q for Matthew and only minimally for Luke.

490. Hence I entitled my earlier study *The Gospel of Signs*, but I have come to realize that the evangelic character of SQ does not depend on the question of an attached passion narrative; see my article "Christology," 501.

491. While the resurrection story was very likely not originally part of the passion tradition, in the hands of the pre-Johannine author of PQ it is added to the passion story and made one continuous narrative, beginning in a theological problem and concluding in the proclamation of the risen Jesus.

492. Those who have espoused the existence of two such pre-Johannine sources mostly held that the two were distinct until the time when the Evangelist would have combined them, joining them with other (mostly discourse) material, into the present Gospel. This was one of the major objections, widely made, to *TGOS*. But in his article, "Johannine Chris-

2. A Combined Signs and Passion Source

Frequently in this work I have spoken of the narrative source—in the singular—and referred to it as SG (Signs Gospel), denoting by that siglum a combined pre-Johannine Gospel of signs and passion. We must now give justification for this usage, especially since until now we have been careful at virtually every point to treat the two kinds of pre-Johannine material separately and we have repeatedly postponed the question when they were combined.

Each was in some sense already Gospel. But what grounds are there to suppose that together they constituted a continuous narrative at the disposal of 4E, one that began with John the Baptist and concluded with the resurrection and the pre-Johannine author's summary?[493] This would be a Signs Gospel in the full sense, the resurrection then both an overcoming of the problem of Jesus' death and the last and greatest of his christological deeds.

a. One basis for the contention that the two had already been joined together when 4E used them is the handful of instances of **stylistic overlap** between PQ and SQ. These have been termed meager in number, and so they are on an absolute scale. But the very existence of these data gives telltale indications of redactional continuity between the two narrative sources at the pre-Johannine level. That is, the data are evidence that the same editorial hand appears to have reworked, and to that degree stylistically integrated, the two once-separate sources or bodies of tradition—and to have done so prior to the work of 4E.

There are two kinds of such evidence, in both cases mostly inconspicuous stylistic details that would have been used unwittingly by an author or editor.

First, there are elements of style that can be regarded as characteristic of the pre-Johannine material and that are to be found in both SQ and PQ. While not always peculiar to the source within the NT, yet they appear comparatively rarely in the Synoptics and are largely or wholly absent from the rest of 4G:[494] In most cases they represent Semitisms and are reminiscent of biblical language.

    i. The phrase "Now ___ was . . ." (*ēn de*) as the opening of an explanatory parenthesis;[495] similarly, the introductory phrase "Now there was (a certain)

---

tianity," 245–46, D. M. Smith began to consider the hypothesis of a combined Gospel of signs and passion, holding that it "makes a certain sense in view of the *Sitz im Leben*, as well as the functioning of the document" and adding that if a milieu of Jewish-Johannine debate obtained "a passion . . . narrative would have become a necessity [for a Signs Source]." (On the matter of what occasioned the joining of signs and passion, see below, 2.b.) In "Setting," 235–38, he has moved to a clear assertion of the likelihood that signs and passion were combined prior to 4G.

493. I treated this question in a preliminary way in "Christology" (498–500). In first reconstructing the pre-Johannine source material (*TGOS*) I had not set out, as has sometimes been supposed, to find a combined Signs Gospel, but instead I stumbled upon the evidence, at first sight only telltale, that the two sources had been redactionally combined prior to the Johannine stage.

494. Given SG's relatively short length (roughly one-fifth the bulk of 4G, and far smaller in relation to the Synoptic material) these data are all the more striking. In the lists of pre-Johannine occurrences those in SQ are separated from those in the passion material by a double slash (//). Data are based mostly on Darton, *Concordance*.

495. Once only in the Synoptics (Mark 15:25), but by my count thirteen pre-Johannine instances (1:40, 44, 4:6b; 6:10; 11:18; 11:38//18:10, 13, 28, 40; 19:14, 19, 23) and one Johannine (18:14); 11:2 is very likely post-Johannine.

. . ." (*ēn de* [*tis*]).[496]

ii. Various characteristic uses of *ek*: After a noun (= "made of");[497] after a numeral (= "one [etc.] of");[498] and finally, again after a noun but describing origin ("of," "from among").[499]

iii. *hōs* with a numeral (= "approximately . . .").[500]

iv. *oun* ("So") after a command, the compliance usually repeating verbatim the wording of the command.[501]

v. *onoma autōi* ("his name was . . ." [lit., "name for him"]).[502]

vi. Singular verb with double subject, often "he and . . ." (*autos kai*).[503]

More generally, in this first category of the style characteristic of SG is the interest in circumstantial detail of time and place and situation, a gratuitously "factual" preoccupation (whether accurate or not). A partial list would contain: six stone jars holding twenty or thirty gallons (2:6), "yesterday at one o'clock" (4:52), about one hundred yards off (21:8), half a year's wages (6:7), "a city of Samaria called Sychar . . . Jacob's well was there" (4:5–6), and so on / / Malchus (18:10), known to the high priest (18:15), Gabbatha/Lithostratos (19:13), in 'Hebrew,' Latin, and Greek (19:20), about seventy-five pounds (19:39), and so on.

Second and inversely, some very common elements of *Synoptic style* are found rarely in 4G, but there always in the source material, and in both SQ and PQ; by contrast, 4E uses analogous but different locutions:

i. *hekastos* ("each," "every") instead of the Johannine *pas*.[504]

ii. *eutheōs* ("immediately") for the Johannine *euthus*.[505]

iii. Adverbial *prōton* ("first"); the uniquely Johannine equivalent has the article (*to prōton*).[506]

496. Always without a predicate or participle, this appears in the Synoptics only twice (Mark 15:7; Luke 23:38), but in 4G nine times, at least seven of them in the sources: 2:6; 4:6a, 46; 5:5; 11:1; 21:2//19:41. It is clearly Johannine only at 12:20, and perhaps at 3:1, both undoubtedly by imitation. The analogous Synoptic usage, very frequent, is *kai ēn*. A characteristically Johannine usage similar to these two pre-Johannine forms with *ēn* is found in the five explanatory and usually introductory notices of date, always of a Jewish holiday (5:9; 6:4; 7:2; 9:14; 11:55; see also Mark 14:1). All other Johannine explanatory parentheses begin with *touto* or a relative pronoun (e.g., 1:41–42; 6:6).

497. Three times in 4G, always pre-Johannine (2:15; 9:6//19:2, the latter paralleled in Matt. 27:29).

498. Fifteen times or more in the Synoptics, fourteen times in 4G, of which all but two (7:50; 20:24) are pre-Johannine: 1:35, 40; 6:8, 70–71; 21:2//12:2, 4; 13:21; 18:17, 25–26.

499. Eight instances in the Synoptics, six in 4G, of which at least four are pre-Johannine (3:1; 4:7; 6:11, 13//18:3). It is evidently imitated by 4E in 18:3.

500. Ten times in the NT outside of 4G, eight times there, all pre-Johannine (1:39; 4:6; 6:10, 19; 21:8//19:14), and probably also 11:18 and 19:39.

501. Perhaps seven times in 4G, all pre-Johannine (1:39; 6:10, 13; 9:7; 11:41; 21:6//19:29).

502. Five to seven times outside 4G, thrice there (1:6; 3:1//18:10).

503. At least nine times in 4G, seven pre-Johannine (1:35, 45; 2:2; 4:53//2:12; 18:1b, 15) and two Johannine (3:22; 4:12).

504. Ten distinct times in the Synoptics, three in the pre-Johannine sources (6:7//16:32b; 19:23); *pas* is found once in the source, in a proverbial saying (2:10).

505. Seventeen Synoptic occurrences, three pre-Johannine (5:9; 6:21//18:27).

506. Twenty-four times in the Synoptics, three pre-Johannine (1:41; 2:10//18:3).

iv. *syn* ("together with") for the very frequent Johannine use of *meta*.[507]

v. *prōi(a)* ("next morning," "early"); 4E uses *tēi epaurion* instead.[508]

These examples could be extended, but they will suffice to show that a stylistic unity obtains between the two kinds of narrative source material: style on the one hand unique to the source and on the other more Synoptic-like than the Johannine material. (It appears that quite possibly the author of SQ is responsible for this overlap with PQ, since the style characteristics are usually more frequent in the signs than in the passion material, even though the latter is half again as long. That author has, then, adapted the preexisting passion tradition and only lightly retouched it when combining the two sources.)

Further, we see that the source is far from stylistically colorless, in no way a mere collection of verses where distinctive Johannine locution happens to be absent.[509]

b. But if on the level of style the source's author has retouched the preexisting narrative and on the level of structure has joined them together smoothly (as we saw in 12:37–40), the **Johannine composition** does not show this kind of smoothing. Thus, the pre-Johannine join of the two kinds of material is to be found in the present Gospel not at a point of Johannine transition but still in the same pre-Johannine passage. And the major Johannine alteration, the insertion of the massive Farewell Discourse of chapters 14—17, is made not at this joining of signs and passion but later and within the pre-Johannine story of the Last Supper. The Evangelist, in short, appears to be unaware of the pre-Johannine seam at 12:37.

c. Still more telling in favor of the pre-Johannine combining of signs and passion is the evidence at the level of **plot**, of story line. From almost the beginning of the

---

507. More than one hundred times in the NT as a whole, only three in 4G and all of them pre-Johannine (21:3//12:2; 18:1). Apart from the theological use of *meta* so typical of 4E, that author also uses it in the everyday sense like the source's *syn* (see esp. 20:24, 26). PQ also uses *meta* several times (18:2, 18b, 26; 19:18).

508. (1:41); 21:4//18:28; 20:1.

509. Ruckstuhl ("Language," 141) refers to the source's "pale face." He seeks to refute my detailed use (*TGOS*, part 4: 203–18) of his style characteristics (*Einheit*, part 2) to show that SG is relatively free of Johannisms.

I concede that my conclusions were in some ways hasty. Thus, Ruckstuhl diminishes the percentage of Johannine characteristics absent in the source by observing that many of them are used "exclusively in discourse material, most often in elevated speech" or "only exceptionally found in narrative material" ("Language," 131–32). But this only means that they are not to be used in asking the question of the distinctiveness of the source's style; in other words, that Ruckstuhl's original list of fifty characteristics must be reduced to twenty-six. Then the proportion of the characteristics not found in the source remains significant, especially when we consider the likelihood that the Evangelist, perhaps unwittingly, will have imitated pre-Johannine style (e.g., the Semitic "believe in," with preposition instead of dative) or borrowed a usage in the source and elaborated it (e.g., taking the rare form *helkuein* ["draw"] and giving it metaphoric meaning; or the so-called partitive *ek* ["one of . . . ," "a woman of . . . ," "officers of . . ."] and making it into the distinctively Johannine phrase "some [many, none] of"). Similarly, the Evangelist's reuse of pre-Johannine material will have occasioned the insertion, again probably unconsciously, of typically Johannine particles (e.g., historical *oun*). Thus stylistic blurring is to be expected.

Ruckstuhl himself admits that the Gospel contains "source material . . . [which has not] been integrated into the world of Johannine thought and terminology" (ibid., 141). That it also has not "kept the unmistakable signs of an independent pre-Johannine existence" is disproved by the distinctive style we have outlined above.

Gospel in its present shape there is a preparation for the shocking fact that the magisterial Jesus of the signs will be subjected to arrest and execution. This forewarning is made subtly in the portrayal of the interrogation of the Baptist, more expressly in the scattered references to Jesus' coming "hour" (beginning with 2:4), and most explicitly in the continual animosity of "the Jews" and their repeated attempts to put Jesus to death (from 5:18). So the death of Jesus, when it comes, is no surprise whatever, and indeed it is regarded as no theological problem, for it has become the culmination of Jesus' work, his victorious "lifting up" whereby the Son of man who came down from heaven returns there in glory. (In a somewhat different way Mark too prepares the reader from the beginning for the denouement of the cross.)

But nothing of the sort appeared at the pre-Johannine level. Underlying the Johannine unity is an earlier tension, which is not evidence against the eventual combining of signs and passion but on the contrary the circumstance that required it: the discontinuity of signs and passion due only to the separate origin of SQ and passion tradition.

An independent Signs Source, a Gospel of Jesus' messiahship, would have come into existence and been useful for a time by itself, for converting non-Christian Jews within the synagogue (see A.3). It would have had no need to take notice of the way Jesus' life had ended. But before long the contradiction between a self-revealing Messiah and the well-known fact that Jesus had suffered, and in fact had died an ignominious death, would be felt and found intolerable. How can it be that the wonderworking Son of God died on a cross? A Signs Source by itself, without giving a hint of the way Jesus' life had ended, would then either become useless or would have to be expanded to recount the death and explain it in a way consistent with his self-evident messiahship. In short, the passion tradition would have to be incorporated into the miracle-working source to keep it theologically relevant.

And the passion tradition contained already the answer to the contradiction; indeed that need had probably occasioned the composition of the passion story in the first place, at least the beginning of the process. In it the death of Jesus is remembered not simply as and because it occurred but in order to *justify* it; PQ contains its own apologetic. The means to this explanation is of course the motif of prophecy fulfillment. The scriptures, read through the eyes of Christian faith looking for such an explanation, predicted that the Messiah would suffer and die; the very details of that slowly unfolding drama were foreshadowed in Psalms and Prophets and Law. So the pre-Johannine author need only remind the reader of this preparation in salvation history as the answer to the question why Jesus had died as he had.

The passion story, then, recounts Jesus' death in a way that recognizes and answers the very problem that the death had posed for a self-sufficient and wholly affirmative SQ.[510] It provides a rationalization for Jesus' death in terms of divine necessity. Just as Jesus' messiahship was demonstrated in SQ on the basis of

---

510. So apt is PQ for the solution of the theological problem raised by the christology of a wonderworking Messiah that one could imagine the pre-Johannine author of SQ to have penned it for the purpose. But because the pre-Markan passion account demands the same genesis, we must perhaps suppose that the tradition was available already to our author.

underlying OT expectations and prototypes (Moses- and Elijah-typology, as we shall see [A.3]), so in the passion tradition, and far more openly, the death is perceived as acceptable because it was foreordained, it had to occur. (This apologetic element will no longer be of use to 4E, yet typically of that redactor it is allowed to remain.)

Further, the resurrection not only helps to resolve the problem of the cross, in a sense to undo it, but it becomes—consistent with the signs tradition now prefixed to the passion story—Jesus' chief sign, for he raises himself in accord with the promise he had given, the sign he had pointed ahead to, in the Temple Restoration (2:18–19).[511]

And SQ's original ending (20:30–31a) can easily move to the end of the resurrection story. At the level of the present Gospel it is anomalous there, since the signs it summarizes have not been mentioned for some eight chapters, and the promise of the resurrection sign is found roughly ten chapters earlier still. But on the pre-Johannine level of a combined SQ and PQ, the closing is entirely fitting, the resurrection coming just before it.[512]

Before going on to the last and most telling of the reasons for supposing a pre-Johannine merging of signs and passion (d, below) we must digress for a moment to pursue further the genre of the combined sources. We have already said that the result is clearly a Gospel; but in view of this evidence for a structural unity imposed upon signs and passion prior to the Evangelist's reworking of the source material, what kind of Gospel would have resulted?

Certainly not, as for the present 4G, "one continuous [and victorious] passion narrative."[513] And since signs and not the passion still predominate in an SG its genre is hardly, like Mark's, "a passion narrative with introduction."[514]

The only way to characterize the combined source's genre is to call it, as we have loosely done throughout, a *Gospel of signs*. It is a Gospel of *signs*, since an account

511. Originally part of the passion narrative's "prelude," once signs and passion are joined, this passage becomes the transition between the two halves; it now points ahead to the resurrection as the last and greatest of the signs, a meaning that event had not previously had.

512. Mention of the disciples as the audience for the signs (20:30a) also makes sense at the end of the resurrection story, where the disciples figure so clearly; at the end of the signs, in most of which, after 2:11, they do not appear at all, their mention—although tolerable and necessary for the closing's purpose—was not so natural.

513. (See my "Christology," 504.) This phrase hardly does full justice to the genre of 4G, as we shall see presently, but it is used here as a kind of shorthand for contrast with the genre of the source.

514. Mark's framework (ministry of healings followed by passion) has not at all provided the model for the reconstruction of the pre-Johannine source or in any way suggested the hypothesis that it included both signs and passion, as some critics have imagined. As I have said, the possibility only slowly dawned in the course of my original source analysis. Haenchen ("Literatur," 303) speaks of the source of 4G as "a kind of coarsened [*vergröberten*] Gospel of Mark," not suggesting something derived from Mark but simply a work rough by comparison with it, more primitive, rudimentary. And Reim (*Hintergrund*, 212–24) thinks of the pre-Johannine source as a "fourth synoptic Gospel." The analogy of the Hellenistic "aretalogy" about a "divine man" (an account that could include both marvelous deeds and impressive death) is not of very much use (as I once held, "Christology," 501); for the death of Jesus at the pre-Johannine stratum is in itself anything but impressive or noble, even from the standpoint of the final resurrection.

of Jesus' miracles, and especially his resurrection, remains the most obvious and explicit function of the book. In it Jesus shows himself by means of his christological deeds. And that self-presentation continues throughout, to the end of the passion story.

It is also a *Gospel* of signs in that by the signs the good news of Jesus' messiahship and his final overcoming of death is proclaimed; it is thus, in technical language, a thoroughly kerygmatic work.[515] SG's genre, then, is different from, and somewhat more rudimentary than Mark's; it is not yet, as for Mark, a proclamation of the death of Jesus, but of the one who was Messiah despite his death. The reader believes in Jesus even though he died as criminal, because he had performed the signs of the Messiah. But this is not to say that SG grew backward from the passion tradition, as perhaps Mark, or was a function of the longstanding problem of that death. Rather, the development—in the pre-Johannine community, at any rate—seems to have taken place in just the opposite direction. The miracles, once they had become messianic signs,[516] eventually demand that the cross also be accounted for and made subservient to the same christology; the passion, culminating in the resurrection, becomes almost a *sēmeion* in its own right. The combination was forced, evidently, by the pre-Johannine author's intention that the miracle tradition be used for missionary purposes. The very conception of a book of signs requires eventually gathering up into the same work the death of Jesus. In this way the source's genre was born.

Thus it may be this otherwise unknown author who was first to create a Gospel—simply an account of the deeds of Jesus that culminate in his death and resurrection.[517]

d. Finally, we consider the strongest evidence for a pre-Johannine Gospel combining signs and passion, namely the fundamental **theological unity** in the two halves and its sharp difference from the theology of the present Gospel.

It is patent that the central, indeed virtually the only, theological theme in the signs is a simple christology, the fact that Jesus is Messiah. While other issues are not absent, as we shall see in part 2, they are always secondary and implicit. But if this christological focus is true of the signs, of SQ by itself, it is also true, less obviously, of the pre-Johannine passion narrative. For Jesus' death is not recounted for its own sake, and certainly not "soteriologically" (as being redemption or any kind of salvation), but once again christologically, so as to demonstrate who Jesus is, namely, the one who dies according to OT prophecy. His death is apologized for

515. See p. 206, on *kēryssein*.

516. No minor step. A miracle story per se (the literary form of *novelle*) is not the same as a sign episode, which may but does not necessarily involve the same literary form; e.g., 2:1–11, at one point a pronouncement story. A sign involves not only a miracle but an overt christological claim.

517. On Talbert's typology the finished 4G, along with Mark, comes closest to his Type B: "written to defend against a misunderstanding of the savior and to present a true picture of him," by means of a "myth of origins for a . . . Christian community" (*Genre*, 135). But SG is a different form altogether; it falls under Talbert's Type E, exemplified by Matthew and "written so as to present the career of Jesus both as a legitimation of his [messianic status] and as a hermeneutical [= interpretive] clue to its meaning" (ibid., 134); its myth is one of "divine warranty."

simply to reconcile it with the christology of the signs. Even his teaching, which appears in rudimentary fashion and only in the passion, in every case calls attention to himself (see part 2.A). Finally, the resurrection too is obviously christological, and becomes united with SG's first half, by serving as Jesus' greatest act of self-presentation.

By contrast, the unifying theology of 4G as we have it is not at all christology (though an important concern of 4E is to deepen and qualify the source's presentation of Jesus' status). Rather, it is salvation (soteriology)—how Jesus' teaching and death give eternal life; and it is revelation (epistemology)—of the nature of knowing and believing. The signs were only mediate ways of knowing Jesus, and his death not at all; but in the present Gospel the latter is no longer accidental and problematic but a matter of affirmation, for by it the Son of Man, having come down from heaven, reveals his own glory and "draw[s] all men to [him]self" (12:32).

And the resurrection, so critical for SG, is now not quite a postscript to Jesus' death but still only an occasion for Johannine explanations of the role of the beloved disciple (20:2–10, and subsequently by the Evangelist or a later editor in chap. 21) and especially for the all-important and crowning Johannine episode of questioning Thomas (20:24–29), both figures having to do with the themes of knowing and validly believing.

Have we not, then, found good reason to speak of a unified pre-Johannine source, a Gospel of signs?

3. An Early Christian-Jewish Gospel

We use this double phrase[518] in the strictest sense to describe SG. For that document is Christian in the most literal way: it espouses belief in Jesus as the *christos*, the Messiah. It is as simply "Christian" as imaginable, that is, it is nothing more than messianic, its focus is pure and single-mindedly christological. And it is Jewish simply because the idea of Messiah is comprehensible only within Judaism. In distinction from the paths that Christian ideology and sociology would soon follow, it has no interest in Gentiles, there is no evidence of the need to reinterpret or reject Torah, the incorporation of pagan or Hellenistic concepts has not yet been envisaged.[519] We have, then, a document from an early and pure Christian Judaism.

518. Following Martyn, "Glimpses," I use this form of the adjective, rather than the more common Jewish-Christian, to remind that the earliest Christian movement took place fully within Judaism. It involved Jews who—by virtue of their belief in Jesus as the Jewish Messiah—had become confident "Messianists," Christians. To distinguish them from other Jews, we call them Christian Jews. (The reverse term properly refers to a much later period, when some Christians were still Jewish, unlike the Gentile majority that made up the church. As distinct from other Christians, they were Jewish Christians.)

519. Nicol (*Sēmeia*, 66–67) shows in detail how fully Jewish the pre-Johannine source is: its knowledge of Palestinian geography and customs, its use of Aramaic terms, Semitic sentence structure (short sentences, with verb first, and simple connectives), LXX references to Elijah and Elisha, Jewish concepts (eschatological prophet, sign), and so forth. That the Cana story may have had a pagan provenance (see this part, sec. 3, end of Pre-Johannine Source) is no exception.

That it was written in Greek (there is no clear evidence of translation from an earlier Semitic) makes it no less Jewish. In fact, it appears to be addressed to an audience that is minimally bilingual, familiar with a number of Aramaic terms (*Rabbi, Messias, Cephas, Bethesda, Siloam, Thomas*) and also "Hebrew" equivalents for Greek terms used (*Gabbatha, Golgotha*). Whereas the Evangelist will later insert explanations or simple translations from Semitic terms into Greek (*Teacher, Christ, Peter, "sent," Didymos* [or Twin]), the pre-Johannine author goes only from Greek back to Aramaic.[520]

The intended audience of SG—or at least of the Signs Source (SQ), the earlier of the two components of SG—would have been simply Jews in the synogogue in the author's Greek-speaking city. And the purpose of the author (see 20:30–31a) would have been to convince the readers that because of his signs Jesus is the Jewish Messiah come at last.[521] The Signs Source,[522] then, was a missionary tract.

At a somewhat later date, and after the objection had been raised that the expected Messiah could not have ended his life on a Roman cross, the passion tradition would have been added—with 12:37–40 created as transition and acknowledging for the first time the failure of belief in the signs by the Jewish leaders. Very likely the passion tradition had already reached a fixed form; whether written or still oral, it was literary, that is, authored, so that at most it would have needed only some minor redaction on the part of the author/editor of SG. We saw (A.2.a) that at most points the hand of the author of SQ has only lightly retouched the passion story; yet there are some indications of structural parallelism that seem to show accommodation of the two components (SQ and PQ) to each other on the editor's part. For example, the three selfless denials of John the Baptist, really his confession of Jesus (1:20–21), are to be contrasted with the three self-serving denials of Jesus by Peter (18:17–27);[523] and the promise of Jesus' baptizing with holy Spirit (1:33) is to be seen as fulfilled in his bestowal of holy Spirit at the end of the resurrection appearance (20:22).

We have called this document early, and so we must now consider the question of its date. It is certainly older than Mark, for (a) its passion narrative represents a theological stage earlier than Mark's (still an apologia, like Mark's passion source, and without any theological affirmation of Jesus' death per se such as in Mark itself) and (b) it shows no awareness whatever of the destruction of the Temple or

---

520. Using (*ho legetai*) *Hebraïsti* ("which in Hebrew means," or simply "is called"), whereas 4E writes (*met*)*hermeneuein* or *ho legomenos* (meaning "translated [*or* called]," that is, in Greek). See further, this part, n. 173.

521. See further excursus C, on the source's provenance and purpose.

522. I retain this title, despite Robinson's objection (*Trajectories*, 236), following Haenchen's then as yet unpublished MS of his commentary, that only in 4G are the miracles truly signs in the sense of "having symbolic meaning." The present Gospel does use the word, and in this sense in part. But the pre-Johannine Gospel thinks of Jesus' deeds as more than miracles—in short, as signs of his messiahship. It cannot be called merely a miracle source, such as underlies Mark. The distinction between the source's understanding of a sign and 4E's must be expressed in a less overt way than Robinson proposes.

523. Some find a parallel also between the scene that follows the Baptist's affirmations, the conversion of the first disciples (1:35–50), and the scene that precedes Peter's denials, the hearing in the high priest's house (18:13–16).

even the possibility.[524] (It is only in the Johannine redaction of 2:19 that Jesus' saying is related to the physical destruction of the Jerusalem shrine.) The document, as we saw, represents a Christianity entirely comfortable within Judaism and unaware of the possibility of any other home. The conflicts to be experienced later, in the present Gospel's setting, are absent altogether. And if Paul's battles were earlier, which is not certain, they are due to the question of admission of Gentiles into the church, an issue altogether missing from SG (and only barely present, evidently, in the finished Gospel).

We have, then, one of the earliest, and certainly purest, expressions of Christian Judaism, roughly contemporary no doubt with the sources and traditions lying behind the Synoptics, with which material SG is somehow in touch. But at least one of the Markan sources is probably later, that lying behind Mark 13, for our source knows nothing of the problem of delay of Jesus' return (the parousia), or even of the concept itself. (See Addendum.)

We can thus imagine a dating in the 40s or possibly the 50s of the first century—roughly contemporary with Q—and hence SG will be the earliest Gospel known to us (unless a kind of *Urmarkus* appeared at about the same time). Thus, the genre gospel must have emerged independently in SG and Mark. As Robinson (*"Gattung,"* 104) has put it, "the view that one distinctive Gattung Gospel emerged *sui generis* from the uniqueness of Christianity hardly seems tenable."

B. THE SOURCE AND THE SYNOPTIC GOSPELS

The relation of 4G to the Synoptic Gospels is an issue with a varied history.

1. It was by far the earliest critical question to be raised in the history of Christian interpretation of the NT. Awareness of the differences between this Gospel and the other three led to the ancient recognition that—although strictly there was only one Gospel in four versions—that fourth version was unique. So long as it, like the others, was thought to be based on eyewitness accounts, the question of 4G versus the Synoptics was dealt with by treating 4G as different in intent and method from the other three, as "the spiritual [that is, theological] gospel," assuming (incorrectly) that the Synoptics were primarily factual and nontheological. This view prevailed until modern times.

2. But the eyewitness basis for the Gospels was then gradually rejected—for why, if eyewitnesses, would the authors depend one on another for sometimes verbatim accounts of Jesus' deeds and sayings? Our Gospel was the last to lose its eyewitness authority, since the beloved disciple—whoever he may have been—was claimed from ancient times and, uniquely, in the text itself (21:24) to be the author. But even this view was finally abandoned. (The beloved disciple may be the authority behind the traditions of 4G but not the literary author.) Once it was accepted that even 4E was late and anonymous, it was then widely assumed that 4G

---

524. Rensberger ("Politics") identifies a sociological and political element still evident in 4G in tension with Johannine tendency and stemming from the period prior to the catastrophe of A.D. 70. For example, the presence of Romans at Jesus' arrest, Pilate's fairness, etc. See further, this part, n. 301.

must be dependent on the Synoptics, at least in a loose and perhaps untraceable way.

3. This view too was rejected eventually, and there grew up instead a widespread consensus that 4G is quite independent of the Synoptic Gospels.[525] If 4E knew them (and even that was doubted) "he" did not make use of them, but rather was in touch only with the Synoptic tradition, that is, the tradition lying behind the canonical Synoptics and even possibly continuing alongside them. This at last opened the way for a source theory to account for 4G's Synoptic-like material.

4. But now for the last decade or more the question has been reopened.[526] A number of scholars hold that the best explanation for the somewhat intricate relation between 4G and the Synoptics is that 4E has freely and creatively rewritten some of their material, having knowledge of at least one and perhaps all three. The theory of 4E's free *relecture* of the canonical Synoptics rather than more precise redaction of sources is held as a preferable alternative to the theory that hypothetical and now lost documents underlie 4G. And certainly that would be so if the text of 4G can adequately be explained by just such a connection (loose and imaginative, as it is) to the first three Gospels.

But there, precisely, is the problem, as I see it. If only the Synoptics lie behind 4G, only very loosely occasioning it, and not a parallel but distinct set of traditions or sources, we are helped very little to understand 4G better, to follow the method and meaning of 4E, by a comparison with them. One can only imagine how that author may have used them, guess why it was done as it was. The ingenuity is in trying to show how 4E might have used the Synoptic material in this way or that, not in understanding from a careful comparison of source and present Gospel the resultant picture of Johannine theology. It is just the controls that redaction criticism provides that are lacking in the view of dependence on the Synoptics and that we need in coming to terms with the otherwise so subjective and elusive task of understanding the Johannine theology.

There exists, however, a clear-cut test for determining whether the canonical Synoptics underlie 4G, or whether they only exist alongside it: Can elements of the uppermost layer in the Synoptics, that is, the Synoptic authors' redaction be found in 4G, or only the stuff that the Synoptic evangelists themselves redacted? For then we could be sure that 4E knew the Synoptic Gospels, and not merely the tradition they contain. So far as I have been able to determine, only the latter is to be discovered in 4E (see, e.g., my article "Jesus and Peter"). But recently Dauer ("Johannes und Lukas") has boldly proposed that the canonical Gospels underlie—not simply 4G, but SG as well! He attempts to demonstrate this in just the way one should: by isolating, in three stories that 4G has in common with Luke, the Lukan redactional material. And he believes that we find traces of this material in 4G. If that were so, it obviously would prove also Johannine dependence on Luke, at least in these instances. But Dauer's method is torturous and his identifi-

525. This consensus began to form with the appearance in 1938 of Gardner-Smith, *Saint John*.

526. Signaled by Neirynck's paper, "John and the Synoptics," at the 1975 *Journées Bibliques de Louvain*, published in de Jonge, *L'Evangile de Jean*, 73–106. Since then the Leuven school (including esp. Sabbe and now Van Belle and Selong) has led the way in usefully questioning what had become an unconsidered assumption in Johannine studies.

cation of the Lukan redaction questionable, as Neirynck has shown ("John 4, 46–54").

Instead, so far as I can see, the best explanation for the complicated way that Synoptic-like material appears in 4G is that it derives from a roughly common tradition, mediated to 4E by SG. (But see Addendum.) The situation for 4G is closely analogous to that for Matthew and Luke, SG and Mark in this case playing similar roles. That is, both 4G and the two later Synoptics derive from an earlier written source.[527] That source represents the stage at which traditions are for the first time put into writing.

The author of SG, and of SQ and PQ still earlier, then shares with "Mark" the distinction of creating the Gospel genre. (Each clearly did so independent of the other, and in a highly distinctive way.) It also appears that the pre-Johannine author was the earlier of the two.[528]

I do not rule out the possibility that 4E was acquainted with one or more of the Synoptics. This could account, probably more by unconscious imitation than direct borrowing, for the very loose parallels, often only structural, that occasionally appear.[529] But there seems to me no evidence at all that the Synoptic-like material found in 4G was mediated only through such acquaintance. The combination of close, sometimes verbatim, parallels to the Synoptics and often gratuitous differences from them—differences that cannot be accounted for as Johannine redaction but rather are such as the vagaries of oral tradition would produce—is only adequately explained by the Evangelist's use of a written source that was itself dependent on Synoptic tradition. To account for these phenomena by means of loose dependence by 4E on the Synoptics requires stretches of the imagination greater than I can make and gives us no understanding of why the changes that 4E supposedly made would have been made. The Synoptics then become a resource available to 4E but not a source, and that author remains just as mysterious in his or her intent and purpose as before.

C. THE CHARACTER OF THE SOURCE[530]

Was the source written or oral, and did 4E only use it from memory? This question involves distinctions of far less moment in the ancient world than today.

527. More than one, in fact: Matthew and Luke from Mark and the sayings source, Q, and 4G from SG and whatever form the traditional material took that comes to the surface in the Johannine discourses.

528. See the end of excursus A.3. It is one of the problems for Dauer's theory that it postulates a date for SG posterior to the completion of the canonical Synoptics, at the end of the first century or later, while the character of that material, however already somewhat derivative (as in the understanding of Jesus' miracles), is patently primitive and early, as the still-apologetic thrust of PQ attests.

529. Attention is sometimes called, for example, to the similarity between Mark 6 and 8 on the one hand and John 6 on the other: the feeding of the crowd, a miraculous episode on the lake, talk of bread (or leaven), Jesus' self-disclosure, and the defection (or hardening) of some of the disciples. This is held either to demonstrate Johannine dependence on the Synoptics (as if Mark must have been dependent on her or his own chap. 6 as source for chap. 8!) or on a pattern that must have come to the source from a tradition in common with the Synoptic. On a quite different level, Glasswell ("Relationship," 110) hints that in 1:7 the Evangelist shows acquaintance with Mark 1:1–4: *apostellō, egeneto Iōannēs*. But the evidence shows equally that the *pre*-Johannine author is in contact with Synoptic tradition.

530. Here I partly paraphrase and expand my earlier sketch in *TGOS*, part 5: 223–25.

Nevertheless, it is clear from 20:30–31a that it was "written" and referred to itself as a "book." Because 4E's reproduction of it is more faithful and detailed than Matthew's and Luke's use of Mark, we can probably say that 4E had the source at hand as she or he wrote.

If the question of provenance is difficult in the case of an extant Gospel, it is more so for our hypothetical one. Nevertheless it is a safe assertion that the source sprang from *a Christian-Jewish milieu*. This judgment is made, first of all, on the basis of its linguistic character. Its quite unstilted though sometimes Semitized Greek may suggest that it nevertheless is not a translation of a Semitic original, but author and audience are no less Jewish for being Greek-speaking. They seem in fact to have been at least minimally bilingual: the text is interspersed with (1) Aramaic words which the author (unlike 4E) felt it unnecessary to translate (place names, *Messias, Kēphas*, and so on); (2) Greek words to which the *Semitic* origin is added (usually with *Hebraïsti*); and (3) certain words used interchangeably in Greek and Aramaic (*Messias/Christos, rabb[oun]i/kyrios/didaskalos*).

The unself-conscious Jewishness of the source is borne out also by the lack of concern with either the Gentile question or issues of Torah: circumcision, fasting, Sabbath. While this can be argued only from silence, in the lattermost case it is noteworthy that when 4E wishes to take up the Sabbath question, it cannot be found in the source but must be quite artificially introduced (5:9b; 9:14). Similarly (except in PQ, where it is purely apologetic), there is no deliberate use of the OT, such as one finds in the Gentile Gospels of Mark and Luke, in Matthew's elaborate anti-Pharisaic proof-texting, or in the Johannine debates on issues of Jewish exegesis. (For the latter, see Martyn, *History and Theology.*)

The Judaism of the source is unlike the Pharisaism that is found in the canonical Gospels and that presumably reflects the dominance of the Pharisees after A.D. 70, when all those documents were written. There is no preoccupation with the Law, whatever, or with theological issues we normally associate with first-century Judaism. We see, then, a quite different Jewishness reflected in this work. No doubt the picture we get is partial and in many ways unique to this document and the situation that evoked it. Nevertheless, it may help to emphasize how partial is our picture of the religious situation of Jesus' time and shortly afterward and at the same time to add to that picture.

As to the question of the source's place of origin, it can be pointed out that the evidence which suggests to some a Syrian rather than an Asia Minor provenance for the finished Gospel belongs largely to the source. There obviously are close contacts with Palestinian tradition, customs, and geography. But whatever its roots, the Greek-speaking community which used the source as a Gospel could have existed in almost any part of the Hellenistic world.[531] (The same provenance probably obtains also for 4G, after the expulsion of the Christian Jews from the local synagogue with which they are still in polemical debate.)

We are on firmer ground as to the intent of the source, for in 20:30–31a (cf. 1:7c) the author states the purpose explicitly. The Gospel is a missionary tract designed to show (presumably to the potential Jewish convert) that Jesus is the Messiah

---

531. But see now Wengst (*Bedrängte Gemeinde*, 97), who locates the Johannine community with great specificity "between A.D. 80 and 90 . . . in the southern part of the kingdom of Agrippa II . . . [in] the territories of Gaulanitis and Batanea" (northern Transjordan).

since he works the signs, so like those of Moses and Elijah, that the awaited divine agent was expected to display. No doubt the audience was meant to see itself in the persons of the original disciples, for the description of their conversion, by means of a chain of witness (1:36–49), is paradigmatic. And the disciples, who first believed (2:11c), are present in almost all of the sign stories. It is taken for granted that belief, as with the disciples, would be the inevitable response. The suggestion of missionary terminology in 4:53 is consonant with this end, as is the exemplary way the witnesses to many of the signs "believe in him." (It is, among other things, this unifying purpose that differentiates the source from a mere collection of stories.)

Faith on the reader's part is meant to be immediate and automatic. The possibility of the signs' failure in this is not considered. And the intent of producing faith, though not yet specified as to object, is clear from the beginning in the mission of John the Baptist (1:7), and it is altogether explicit in the conclusion: "These are written that you may believe that Jesus is the Messiah, the Son of God" (20:30–31a).

At the same time, the book has in mind among its readers, though not addressed to them directly, also the missioners who are to be spreading the good news and to approach the potential convert. The first disciples' sharing their faith (1:35–49) is exemplary also for them, the disciples' latter-day counterparts in the church; they are to follow the procedure modeled there, and from the very beginning in the figure of John (1:7c).

(On the matter of date, see the end of excursus A.3.)

The theology of the source, both expressed and implied, is too full to be summarized.[532] It is extensively laid out in the Source subsections of each division of part 2.

But an especially important observation must now be added. Whether or not SG represents, as I hold, the very earliest of the Gospels in one way or another accessible to us (earlier, that is, and more basic than Mark) it is nevertheless the only truly Christian-Jewish document we possess. It is thus at an earlier remove from the very first forms of the post-resurrection faith than most other data we possess. This is particularly useful in seeing what a Christianity would be that had not begun (as even Paul did in the course of his correspondence) to see itself *over against Judaism*. This Christian document is thus uniquely devoid of any hint of anti-Jewishness such as we find in every other expression of early Christianity.[533] Perhaps for this reason (besides the fact that evidently 4E totally reproduces it in 4G) it was later lost: its Jewishness would have proved an embarrassment when Christianity found itself confronting Judaism frontally as a separate and rival religion.

---

532. But see *TGOS*, 228–34, for an earlier attempt.

533. Schüssler Fiorenza (*Memory*, 105–7) has lucidly identified this problem. It is, of course, just this matter which so distinguishes SG from the redaction it received at the hands of 4E, when Johannine Christianity has become almost wholly defined in opposition to Judaism.

Part Two

THE THEOLOGICAL DEVELOPMENT FROM SOURCE TO PRESENT GOSPEL

Introduction

In part 1 our chief concern was to trace, section by section, (1) the thought of the pre-Johannine source and (2) the way that the Johannine Gospel redacted it. We now need to bring together in a systematic way the ideological content of each of the two literary stages and to show explicitly how the theology shifts as we move from SG to the present Gospel. Both theological levels are visible still in the Gospel as it stands before us, because of the extraordinary way that 4E has adapted the source, so as to leave reasonably intact (and therefore recoverable) the form and even much of the wording of the source—at the same time putting it to new use. The Johannine respect for the work of the predecessor shows through, alongside the evident resolve to reinterpret and sometimes correct it.

There is only one overt theological thrust in SG—the demonstration of Jesus' messiahship—and it is to be found in virtually every passage. This is presented unmistakably in his miracles—which are no longer simply wonders, as in the tradition, but explicit "signs" of Jesus' status. Less overtly but no less really does Jesus' messiahship unify the account of his death and resurrection.[1] Nevertheless, there are varieties within the thought of the predecessor, sometimes in the form only of hints or undeveloped ideas.[2] Now we take a closer look at that variation, especially since it sometimes provides the germ from which the Evangelist's more developed theology stems.

By contrast to the univocal thrust, at least on the surface, of SG, in 4E's reuse of each of the stories a number of themes emerge. Consequently we now look at those themes in a comprehensive and orderly way, gathering together the major threads that surface in the Johannine redaction, threads

1. Because of this relative uniformity of theology at the pre-Johannine level of material in the narratives, we have not found it either necessary or even possible to characterize a distinctive theological message particular to each of the stories in the source, as we have interpreted them one by one. All convey in one way or another the same proclamation: Jesus is Messiah. See this part, n. 3.

2. For example, the theology latent in the symbolism of the water and wine ("the best wine" saved "until now" at the wedding at Cana) or in the life which Jesus gives (the healings, the feeding story).

223

that sometimes were faintly visible in the source. In this way we can understand more clearly the theological hints in the source, and even more the many ways the Evangelist has both adapted them and added greatly to their meaning. It is a function of the Johannine redactional achievement that these themes are to be found throughout the narratives of the Gospel and are not confined to the more purely Johannine discourses.[3]

At the risk of an overly categorized appraisal of the intellectual achievement of these two first-century writers—the canonical author (4E) and the predecessor—it will be useful nevertheless to look at their thought according to the classic theological issues that head the sections of part 2. In the process we shall discern the emergence of the one from the other, the Johannine from the pre-Johannine, with the continuities and discontinuities that that development entails.

It is almost certainly not the case that this development took place overnight, or without mediating circumstances. We are to think of an evolution, not a sudden shift. Nevertheless, it seems to me that the overwhelming factor in that evolution was the powerful creativity of one mind—the Evangelist's—making dramatic new use of an older work. It is for this reason that we concentrate on the two literary achievements, 4G and the earlier document that held such authority for it, and do not attempt to reconstruct the intervening events that influenced the Evangelist's redaction of the source. I find highly persuasive the detailed reconstruction of Martyn in his *History and Theology,* in particular his proposal that expulsion of 4E's Christian community from the synagogue has occasioned many of the differences between source and extant Gospel. (This has been taken up and usefully extended by Brown in *The Community of the Beloved Disciple.*) Nevertheless, the data for such a reconstruction of events are to be found entirely within 4G and in the earlier source, so far as it can be isolated from the canonical text. For that reason we concentrate on the theological shifts observed empirically in the two texts themselves.

---

3. Within this richness there is usually one dominant theme in a particular story, sometimes comprehensive of others also present but in any case standing out from the others. Thus, without undue artificiality we have been able to identify a central Johannine motif in each story, naming it in a capitalized summarizing phrase at the end of each subsection of Johannine Redaction in part 1.

A. Messiahship

The technical term "christology" functions as shorthand for a powerful cluster of ancient theological issues having to do with the Jewish hope for the Messiah, questions that concern not just human thought but human destiny as well: Who will the Messiah be? Has he already come? What does it mean for human life if he has? More specifically, the term has to do with what Christians—who by their very name show themselves to be essentially concerned with christology—believe about Jesus of Nazareth, why they believe it, and its significance for the history of the world. As we have observed, 4E's source, the work of the predecessor, is almost wholly and single-mindedly preoccupied with christology, with proclaiming that Jesus was, or rather is, the Messiah and that both his miraculous deeds and the events at the end of his life display simply that fact in an unmistakable, undeniable way.

For the source (and so for 4G) the term Messiah, Christ, needs no explanation; the document stems from a theological context—its version of first-century Judaism—in which the figure and the expectation it embodies are both taken as givens.

We have now to pull together the various ways that this highly concentrated christological purpose is accomplished in the source and suggest what its ramifications are. Then we shall be able to see more vividly the extent to which the present Gospel has reaffirmed that earlier purpose, and also how far it has been modified by altering the thrust and even some of the content of the source. Consequently it will appear with a clarity otherwise not available to us—and this is the advantage of redaction criticism—how the Johannine purpose and meaning are to be understood. The Evangelist's proclamation, while frequently christological, is no longer predominantly so, but one can only perceive what that proclamation is against the background of the theological milieu in which it developed. We certainly cannot trace the shift, the theological flow, that lies back of the canonical Gospel without beginning at the center of the source's message.

Source

Whether it had been combined with a passion source or stood alone (but see part 1, excursus A.2), the fundamental pre-Johannine document is a presentation of Jesus' signs—*demonstrations of his messiahship.* In every one of the seven (or eight) miracle stories, it is solely Jesus' identity—his christological status—that the narrative intends to convey. The wondrous deeds of Jesus are not worked to help those in need (though that in fact occurs) or to astound (though astound they sometimes do). They do not display Jesus' compassion or skill. They are done, and we are shown them, solely to make clear who Jesus is.

This central christological impact does not emerge gradually; it appears at once for the reader as he or she takes up the pre-Johannine book.[4] John the Baptist, who by his own strenuous insistence is not the Christ, not Elijah, not the Prophet (1:20–22), came rather to bear witness; his function is purely christological. He testifies to another who, it is understood, is bearer of the titles the Baptist refuses and who, even before he is named, is identified further as the Son of God (1:34). The thrust of this undifferentiated cluster of messianic titles is clear: all are expressions of the same affirmation. And in the ensuing scene of the disciples' conversion (1:35–49) the list is first repeated—"We have found Messiah . . . Elijah . . . the One of whom Moses wrote [namely the Prophet] . . . ," "You are the Son of God," "Lamb of God," "King of Israel."

In the miracles themselves this kind of designation is sometimes explicit ("Surely this is the Prophet who is to come into the world"—6:14). More often, at least as the text of the source is now recoverable, it is left to us to supply the title, presumably any one of the several christological labels.[5] In either case, the response of the original witnesses is the key; the reader is to put him- or herself in the shoes of those who "saw and believed." Belief is the paradigmatic response (2:11c; 4:53b). Even when it is not named we see people responding with implicit faith in Jesus' messiahship: the first disciples attach themselves to Jesus solely on hearing who he is (1:35–49), his mother knows what he is about to do at Cana (2:5), the official trusts what Jesus tells him (4:50), and so forth.

In the case of the first two or three miracle stories, and perhaps originally in more of them, Jesus' deed is summarized simply as a sign, its meaning evidently wholly understood in that term. That is, the miracle is

---

4. Many ancient documents, including some within the NT, were not intended to be read but to be listened to. But that the pre-Johannine author intends a reader (whether aloud or silently to oneself) is the best interpretation of 20:31a, even with its second-person plural.

5. Since the titles, the various namings of Jesus' standing, have already been supplied at the beginning. As the plot of the source advances, it is not that each miracle convinces the reader further that Jesus is Messiah, or adds a new dimension; rather, the advance we see is how more and more people believe in his messiahship.

worked purely in order to demonstrate; what it demonstrates, Jesus' messiahship, is taken for granted by author and reader. Christology is paramount, obvious, sufficient. If at one or two points Jesus "shows" himself to the disciples (as possibly in 2:11b; 21:1, 14), we are to understand that it is just this messianic identity that is conveyed. And many times, by means of supernatural knowledge (e.g., 21:4) and unusual power (the minor miracles within the larger event), the same is underscored.

In the pre-Johannine passion material too a distinguishable but not altogether dissimilar christological concentration obtains. The message of the account overall is apologetic. That is, it is concerned with the defense of the Christian belief: how can it be that Jesus suffered and died as he did? The question is essentially christological: it presupposes as its starting point that Jesus is Messiah; it is just his standing that makes the manner of his death a problem. And the solution is simple: "these things happened in order to fulfill scripture." The Hebrew Bible, by means of its prophecies, is understood to be the biography of the Messiah. Therefore the repeated display of the events of Jesus' death as fulfilling those prophecies[6] is simply one extended christological assertion. Read with the eyes of faith, the scriptures show that, just as in his miracles, so in Jesus' dying and rising from the dead the messianic goal of history was coming to pass.

Besides this element's punctuation of the passion story, there is another kind of christological concentration. The person of Jesus is everywhere focused on, his sayings—the only words of any consequence that he speaks in the narrative tradition—in every case call attention to himself ("in three days I shall raise it up," "the day of my burial," "I'm he," and so forth).

What is missing altogether is attention to the effect of Jesus' death, the possibility that it accomplished anything theologically. The soteriological (i.e., saving) dimension that shapes the passion tradition in its more developed forms (in 4G and to some extent also in the Synoptic Gospels) is simply not present in the pre-Johannine source (see further 2.D). Instead, all has to do with who it was that was dying, how that death could be reconciled with his person.

Consonant with this exclusively christological preoccupation in the passion story is the matter of Jesus' kingship. The title "King of Israel," used loosely at the end of the source's introduction, appears once again, dramatically proclaimed in the Entry into Jerusalem (12:13).[7] Consequently, the question of this kingship is inquired into by Pilate (18:33) and sufficiently

6. Most notably in the account of Jesus' execution (19:24, 28, 36–37) but also in the stories of the Temple Cleansing (2:17) and Triumphal Entry (12:15), and—though there is no quotation—in the resurrection (20:9).

7. We saw in part 1, sec. 13, how narrowly christological this episode appears in the source, compared to the Synoptic accounts.

227

if obliquely answered by Jesus (v. 37a). That the soldiers satirically hail Jesus by the title (19:3) is to be understood as conveying ironic truth. And while its appearance placarded on the cross (19:19) is ostensibly only a statement of the crime for which he is executed, on the deeper level it expresses the theological heart of the crucifixion.

Finally, in the pre-Johannine passion account just as in the signs, Jesus acts like the Messiah. He functions as prophet and judge in the Temple (2:13–22), refers to God as his Father (2:16), undergoes suffering without complaint (the background for this understanding of the event in Isaiah 53 is evident), and consequently even in the midst of his execution is somehow victorious over it.[8] Most dramatic of all, he raises himself from death, the greatest of his miracles.

Throughout the two pre-Johannine narrative traditions (signs and passion), then, there runs a simple, fundamentally christological current. It takes a variety of forms but shares the theological limelight with no other motif. (On the precise nature of Jesus' messiahship, see this part, n. 114.)

Present Gospel

How does the Johannine Gospel handle the concentrated christology of its source material while also reinterpreting it?

1. To begin with, it emphatically reaffirms and, by implication, defends the source's christology. It does not discard or edit away the miracles' portraying Jesus as wonderworking Messiah. On the contrary, it makes them the very basis for its presentation of the public ministry (chaps. 1— 12). Although we here bypass the question how 4E views the validity of faith based on signs (see part 2.B), nevertheless we can note that belief in Jesus as the Christ is repeatedly portrayed in 4G as the appropriate response to the miracles; to that extent the christology remains central.

The messianic faith is especially evident in the case of the official at Capernaum (4:46–54). In the source the man had shown implicit trust in Jesus' ability to heal. With 4E's handling this becomes an initial and explicit act of faith that Jesus has already healed his son (v. 50b) and is subsequently confirmed upon his return home (v. 53). As with the earlier miracle at Cana, the event remains a "sign" that Jesus has done (v. 54). Even when most of the witnesses to a miracle do not believe (most pointedly in 4E's greatly extended telling of the story of the blind man in chap. 9), the one healed remains a paradigm for faith in Jesus' unique status.

What is that status? We have seen that in SQ a number of titles—Christ, Elijah, the Prophet, Son of God, Lamb of God, King of Israel—cluster

---

8. This perspective is only implicit in the source, to be greatly extended by 4E. What is absent altogether is any theme of degradation or tragedy, such as in Mark or Luke.

together to convey an essentially single theological affirmation: that Jesus is the Messiah of Jewish expectation. With one exception ("Elijah"), the Gospel takes up all these titles. (One of them, "Lamb of God," is emphasized by making the Baptist both reiterate and expand it [1:29].) In this respect, as in others, the source has seemed to some so "Johannine" as to be irrecoverable (or even imaginary), for the simple reason that 4G has appropriated the central message of the predecessor as much as possible. A good deal of what appears, from a first glance at 4G, to be distinctive of its christology has in fact been adopted from the source. The source is of course loosely "Johannine," not in the sense that it originated with 4E but rather just the reverse.[9]

2. If 4G takes over the predecessor's theology, it nevertheless does not leave it unchanged. Whatever messiahship meant in the source (it is usually undefined), 4G takes pains to make it clearer: it is not to be understood in a political or earthly sense. Thus, in the adaptation at 6:14–15, what in the source had been a natural and proper acclamation of Jesus as "the Prophet" now becomes a misguided attempt to "take him by force and make him king," and rightly leads to one of the Johannine Jesus' many withdrawals in the face of improper acceptance. The Evangelist does not reject Jesus' kingship, of course, so immovably is the title "King of the Jews" implanted in the passion tradition. But unlike the predecessor— who, as in the synoptics, shows only Jesus' ambiguous response to the question of his kingship put by Pilate (18:37)—4E expressly makes Jesus assert that his kingship is "not of this world" (18:36). The twofold context of this qualification is important: Jesus here encounters simultaneously the secular power of the "world," in the person of Pilate, and the more immediate world of 4E's Christian experience, the power of "the Jews." In the face of both expressions of earthly rule it is made clear that Jesus' authority is different altogether.

In this way 4G qualifies the inherited christology, and also more than once corrects it, in each case in a passage having to do with the Baptist:

a. If for the source the Baptist is "sent from God" (1:6), this designation

___

9. To illustrate the extent to which pre-Johannine christology has interpenetrated 4G's theology, we could look briefly at a somewhat esoteric debate among scholars about the christologies of the Gospels. It has been asked whether any of them are akin to a contemporary category, both "pagan" and Hellenistic Jewish—that of the "divine man" (*theios anēr*). This figure was a sort of magician, known as a "thaumaturge" (a worker of wonders) and thought to have divine powers, who wandered about the ancient world, gathering a following and inspiring accounts ("aretalogies") of his impressive exploits. It can be asked, then, which of our two authors, that of SG or 4G, was more influenced by, or at least closer to, the divine-man figure. In the end, however, the comparison is self-contradictory, for in both the pre-Johannine and Johannine christologies there is some correspondence with the divine-man figure but also divergence from it. See further my article "Christology," 490–94; also D. M. Smith, "Milieu," 168–72. The Dionysian cultic background that may explain the origin of the one sign at Cana (see end of part 1, sec. 3) is apparently unique to it.

is now eclipsed by the repeated Johannine affirmation that Jesus is the one "sent by the Father" (first at 3:17, and in many other places, most notably six times in chap. 17).

b. John's witness to Jesus as Messiah is of course taken up by 4G and singled out as the sole function of the forerunner (1:7, 32). But that testimony turns out to be insufficient: only God can bear witness to Jesus, and that God does so is the bold claim of the Johannine Gospel, vis-à-vis Jewish controversy over the matter of christology. This is especially clear in chapter 5, where the issue of Jesus' status comes to a head. Jesus bears witness to himself, but the reader—particularly the skeptical one—is not expected to believe this testimony. Even that of the Baptist, valid as it is, is inadequate. Rather, it is only the Father who bears witness to the Son, and that Jesus does the Father's "works" (the Evangelist's paraphrase of the pre-Johannine term "signs") demonstrates this (5:31–37).

c. Finally, and most pointedly, 4E rejects for Jesus one of the pre-Johannine titles used to express his messiahship: "Elijah." We saw that in the source this title is implied as appropriate to Jesus by the Baptist's rejection of it, along with "Prophet" and "Christ," for himself. Following the lead of Martyn we held that a probable announcement by Andrew of Jesus' status—"We have found Elijah"—has evidently been excised by 4E at 1:43.[10] Why?

The answer seems to lie in chapter 3, where the Johannine Jesus—in polemic with first-century Jewish speculation about ancient worthies who had ascended to heaven, returning to earth with the secret mysteries—asserts that "no one has gone up into heaven except he who [first] came down from heaven, [namely] the Son of man" (3:13).[11] The Evangelist both asserts (in passing) Jesus' preexistence and rejects the possibility of any revelation except by Jesus. If that is the author's intent, as it appears to be, the figure of Elijah—especially as a "type," an ancient model, for the role of Jesus—must fall away, since Elijah is the one biblical figure who is reported to have already gone up into heaven and whose return from there is expected.

Thus Jesus can no longer properly be understood as he is in SG—rather loosely and perhaps even carelessly—to be only an Elijah-returned, for Jesus' origin goes back not to the time of early Israel but to the very "beginning" (1:1–2).[12] On the other hand, the title "Prophet" is still acceptable; it denotes not a Moses-*redivivus* but a new Moses, "like" him (Deut. 18:15) but undeniably greater (see further just below).

10. See part 1, sec. 2, on 1:43 and the reference there to Martyn's article, "Elijah."

11. Here I am indebted to Dunn ("Let John Be John," 321–25) for identifying this controversy between the Johannine church and its Jewish opponents.

12. See again Martyn, "Elijah."

3. Above all, 4E greatly enhances and deepens the christology taken over from SG. The wonderworking Messiah of the source becomes the speaker of revelatory words—the discloser of divine truth—and this role overshadows the thaumaturgic and even the self-revelatory function of the signs. (Indeed in 4E's hands the miracles are not simply signs but the very "works" of God [e.g., 9:3].) Often the germ of this revelatory element is to be found in the pre-Johannine story; words spoken by Jesus, more or less matter-of-factly, in the course of the working of a sign or in simple discourse in the passion story become the basis for Johannine theological disclosure. Those very words are first of all taken as sacred: reiterated by 4E for emphasis (4:50–53; 5:11–12), shown to have stunning effect in themselves (18:6–8), sometimes placed on a par with scripture as fulfilled prophecy (2:22). Further, most of the original stories are now only the starting point for extended discourses by Jesus, speaking as if from heaven. In them the heightening of christology is obvious, especially since the content of much of this teaching is itself the lofty Johannine christology.

A notable example is the discourse between Jesus and Martha inserted into the raising of Lazarus (11:21–27). The miracle, in its pre-Johannine form, is of course the most suggestive christologically, or so at least in 4E's eyes, for it has been made the climax of Jesus' public ministry, whereas it may have had a less prominent place in the source, viewed there as simply one among a number of equally telling signs. At any rate, for the Evangelist the fact that Jesus can raise Lazarus from death uniquely signals his divine status, and this is elicited in his conversation with Martha. Ostensibly it is a discussion about resurrection, the question whether anyone can be raised before "the last day." If Jesus had come in time, Martha believes, her brother would not have died, but once dead he is beyond the reach of even Jesus' miraculous powers. At most God might give a resurrection in answer to Jesus' request. To this limited faith in Jesus' capability he reveals his true nature, correcting the subordinationism it implies:[13] he himself is "resurrection and life." Not his wonderworking facility, not even his special influence with God, but he himself is both subject and object of the revelation. His very revealing of himself with the theophanic "I AM" discloses this. So when in response Martha makes the christological confession, using the traditional terminology ("the Christ, the Son of God"), it has wonderfully new and exhaustive meaning.

A way that early Christians commonly expressed christology was by means of typology, the statement or more often the suggestion that Jesus

---

13. Later in the story (11:41c–42) 4E portrays Jesus in fact praying to God, but here too in such a way that Jesus is not subordinate to God. On the contrary, God always hears his prayer and the point is solely to show that Jesus is God's co-equal agent. It is this way of speaking that earlier evoked "the Jews' " charge of ditheism in chap. 5.

was to be seen as a new and greater version of a significant figure from the Jewish past. In the source there is no real typology. There are hidden allusions to both Moses and Elijah as earlier miracle-workers, but otherwise Jesus is only the one "of whom Moses wrote," and strictly speaking he is identified as Elijah-come-again, rather than Elijah's antitype. In 4E's hands, things are rather different. We have seen just now how the Elijah identification is suppressed. On the other hand, the typology of Moses becomes all-important, probably because of church/synagogue argument in 4E's own time, reflected in the discourses (e.g., 5:45–46; 6:32; 9:28–29). From the very beginning of the Gospel the comparison and contrast between Jesus and Moses is made in a passage (1:17) that has a double meaning: Just as the law was given through Moses, so also grace and truth came through Jesus Christ (the first meaning). But also: Whereas only the law was given through Moses, by contrast grace and truth actually came through Jesus Christ.

Moses typology is a common theme in the Gospel, and in every case Jesus the antitype overshadows Moses the foreshadowing type. Moses has borne witness to Jesus, not vice versa. He prophesied that God would raise up a prophet like him (Deut. 18:15); Jesus of course is that prophet, but he is more. Moses gave bread from heaven; so also does Jesus, but the bread he gives bestows eternal life. And if in the end human beings ("the Jews") prefer to hear Moses, they thereby deafen themselves to the greater one, Jesus.

Besides this typological deepening and transcending of the Moses image, 4G introduces into the narrative material a new title altogether: "Son of Man." (It is not a Johannine creation, of course, for it appears, in rather different form, throughout the Synoptic Gospels, and in 4E's use it shows evidence of a long prehistory in the tradition, evidently independent of the narrative sources used.) For 4E the Son of Man is always an exalted title[14] and one which from the beginning of Jesus' public ministry expressly transcends even the christophanies of the pre-Johannine Jesus through the miracles. Its introduction, by Jesus himself, brings to a climax the conversion of the first disciples and their confession of Jesus and becomes for the Evangelist the supreme title: Jesus asks Nathanael, Do you believe because I had foreknowledge of you? You will see far more than this. "You will see heaven opened and the angels of God ascending and descending on the Son of Man" (1:50–51).[15]

Consonant with this enhancement of Jesus' titles and their content is the

14. The Son of Man has descended from heaven and re-ascends (3:13; 6:62), has authority to execute judgment (5:27), has God's seal and gives the bread of life (6:27), is lifted up (8:28; 12:34) and glorified (12:33; 13:31).

15. The allusion to the theophanic episode of Jacob's ladder, connecting heaven and earth, is clear.

way 4E intensifies the lordliness of Jesus as it is found already in SG. The performer of signs had already given indications of his foreknowledge; and the Messiah who must die to fulfill scripture and to occasion his greatest sign had appeared as in a way sovereign over even his executioners.[16] It will be self-evident by now how greatly 4E heightens this supremacy of Jesus. Throughout his ministry he speaks as one from heaven, answering his critics with a sonority altogether foreign to the Synoptic Jesus and only faintly hinted at in the few words about himself in PQ. But particularly there, in the Johannine reshaping of the passion, Jesus appears as victor, even when at the mercy of his enemies. He freely goes out to those who seek to arrest him and, "knowing all that will befall him," gives himself up with a word (the divine I AM) that lays low his hearers with its theophanic impact. His earlier prediction, that none of those given to him would be lost, is—necessarily—fulfilled.

This sovereignty is especially evident in the trial before Annas, where he challenges and in turn interrogates the high priest. With Pilate his calm is in direct contrast to the governor's baffled and frenetic questioning, now of Jesus, now of "the Jews." It is most of all at his death that he displays his true messiahship: he goes out to Golgotha freely, carrying his own cross; his true kingship is publicly and officially proclaimed; and he dies "knowing that all was completed" and uttering as his last and triumphant word, "It is accomplished."

But the fullest expression of Jesus' divine status and function is surely to be found in the Johannine use of the term "glory" *(doxa)*. Throughout Jesus' public activity his role was to reveal the fullness of his nature, and this is already signaled in 4E's redaction of the conclusion to the first sign (2:11). There he does not simply show himself to his disciples, as perhaps in the source (see part 1, sec. 3, on this verse). To be sure that is still the case, but what he finally displays is his divinity: "he manifests his glory." By itself, this alteration in the pre-Johannine reading might be barely noticeable. But of course it takes up the term, and the meaning, that climaxes the Johannine prologue (1:1–18). Whatever we are to make of that stunning and problematic passage and of its pre-Johannine history, and however much weight we are to give to the first two clauses of v. 14, it can hardly be disputed that for 4E an important, and perhaps the central, meaning of the fact that "the Logos became flesh and dwelt among us" is precisely that as a consequence "we have beheld his glory, such glory as that of God's only-begotten."[17] By prefacing the Logos hymn to the opening of SG, 4G has transformed a purely Jewish-messianic view of

16. Richter notes that this sovereignty is apparent also in the pre-Johannine accounts of the Temple Restoration, the Triumphal Entry, and the Arrest (*Studien*, 286).

17. Against Richter (*Studien*, 285–86) I see the theology of *doxa* as altogether a Johannine development.

Jesus into a cosmic christology. For this only-begotten Son of God, who shows God's glory, is the preexistent Word, God's partner at creation and very self-expression (1:1–3).[18]

We can sum up the christological affirmations of source and present Gospel, and the development that takes place between the two, in this way: For SG it is sufficient to demonstrate, in every way possible, *that* Jesus was the Messiah. The Johannine Gospel, on the other hand, has provided a wealth of meaning to *what it meant to be* Messiah.

---

18. A question often put to the Johannine christology, and by extension, to the pre-Johannine as well, is whether and how far they are *docetic*, that is, whether the divinity of Jesus, so clearly portrayed by 4E and in various ways implied by the predecessor, is to be understood as in some way excluding true humanity from his nature; whether, in short, he only "seemed" to be human (as the Greek word underlying the term docetism suggests) and so was not really human at all but divine instead. (As the reader knows, this kind of question—and particularly the meaning of the terms divinity and humanity as they apply to Jesus, and whether they are mutually exclusive in the way the question suggests—preoccupied the Christian church for several centuries before it was in some fashion resolved in the famous christological formulas of the fifth century.)

Certainly the Gospel is moving in a direction that will end up as docetism, for it came to be espoused as their special scripture by that school in the second century. But was it intending to advocate a docetic position? It has been said that in 4G, Jesus is like "a god striding over the face of the earth," and that implicit in this likeness is a kind of "naive, unreflecting docetism." (On these phrases, from Käsemann [*Testament*], and the issue they raise, see again my article "Christology," 494–98.) Some of the elements that give rise to these characterizations of 4G's christology stem in fact from the source—a Jesus who only demonstrates, if not his divinity, his supernatural power. His aloofness in the present Gospel has its origin in the single-mindedly signs-working Messiah of the source, evidently unconcerned with human need or response. But the Evangelist gives a more nuanced portrayal of Jesus, certainly one less naive and unreflecting. On the one hand it intensely heightens the divinity of Jesus in such a way that it is this Gospel, far more than the other three, that gives rise to the christological problem facing the church. On the other hand, however, this Jesus is undeniably and expressly human (more so than in SG—see O'Grady, "Human Jesus"), contradictory as the details that support this may seem.

So the question of docetism is not a very productive one; it oversimplifies and labels, ignoring the form of these issues with which 4E had to deal, namely, ditheism. For the Gospel so emphasizes the divinity of Jesus that its Jewish antagonists could only understand it as the ultimate blasphemy, making him "equal with God" (5:18; see also 19:7). Jesus is fully divine, one with the Father, yet not separate from the Father, not "a god [in his own right] striding. . . ."

B. Signs and Faith[19]

We began to synthesize the theologies of the Johannine Gospel and its predecessor, as they can be seen in comparison with each other, by centering on the heart of the pre-Johannine author's message, its christology. The present Gospel maintains much of this meaning, adapts it, even heightens it, but we sensed also that it would not be at the very center of its message: if Jesus as the Word of God has manifested his glory, the aim was nevertheless not solely to display his identity.

We have now to look at a matter that is almost equally important to any Signs Source or Gospel, and in a way more basic: namely, at the signs themselves, the miracles displaying Jesus' messiahship. They are of course the vehicle for faith in that messiahship—both for those who witnessed them and equally, in the design of the pre-Johannine author, for later readers. But this is simply assumed by the source. It is 4G that takes special interest in this matter, particularly in correcting in part what the predecessor implies, and in greatly extending the question of the genesis and character of faith.

So as we take up this topic, in the case of SG we go behind the christological heart of its message, and then, with the present Gospel, move out beyond it.

Source

The very term "sign" (*sēmeion*) is fundamental to the pre-Johannine document. The first two or three of the miracles that form its heart are still in 4G expressly called signs, and we may wonder if all of the seven were not once so designated, their original endings ("This was the [fourth] sign Jesus did . . .") having been lost in 4E's reordering.

The term's usage in the source is distinctive. The same word is found in the Synoptic Gospels, but most characteristically in the narrator's third-person description of a demand made to Jesus for a sign—a demand which he refuses categorically ("No sign shall be given to this evil generation"). Implied in this Synoptic usage is skepticism, even suspicion, about Jesus'

19. For an earlier treatment of this topic see my article "Jesus' Signs."

credentials; a sign is demanded as legitimation, and sometimes we learn that those seeking the sign were "testing" Jesus, perhaps even tempting him.

On one occasion, the Restoring of the Temple (2:18–19), SG shows awareness of this legitimizing function of a sign, but the situation is different. Those driven out of the Temple by Jesus (or the officials, possibly) ask him to justify his deed ("What sign do you show us for doing these things?"—diction not unlike that found in several of the Synoptic passages), but as is not the case in the other Gospels he responds directly and at once—and with the promise of his resurrection. The element of menace is missing and the request for a sign is patently regarded as valid.[20]

In the more common use of the word, in connection with the miracles, there is no questioning whatever of Jesus' power and authority. On the contrary, far from refusing to work signs he proffers them; his public work is purely and simply the performing of the miracles. They do in fact provide legitimation for his activity, or rather for his status—that is precisely what the signs signify—but never in the face of doubt. If they create faith, as they invariably do, it is as the people's spontaneous response to the initiative of Jesus, never as an overcoming of skepticism at their insistence. (The example of Nathanael, 1:46, is no exception.)

The signs in SG, then, are positive and authentic, and they constitute the whole of Jesus' activity. In view of this fact it is interesting that nowhere in SG is Jesus himself understood as a sign, as two or three times in the Synoptics (Luke 2:34; 11:30; see Matt. 24:30). Presumably this is so because Jesus and his activity do not point to something else (God's kingdom). Rather, he is himself the subject of the signs; they point to him. His activity in SG entirely takes the place of the coming of the kingdom in the Synoptic tradition.

But what precisely is a sign for the pre-Johannine author? It has sometimes been suggested that for him a sign is a miracle in the literal sense— an astounding deed, a "wonder" (the Latin derivation of the English word "miracle"). It is then an event comparable to the "mighty acts" (*dunameis*) of Jesus in the Synoptic Gospels. But the pre-Johannine signs, as Richter succinctly puts it ("Semeia-Quelle," 284), are not wonders at all but pure demonstrations of Jesus' messiahship. In contrast to the effect Jesus' miracles have in the Synoptics, for SG they never produce wonder or fear but always belief. They are not prodigies that in themselves astound; rather they point beyond themselves, they demonstrate. Thus they are not finally miracles but purely signs.

---

20. Theissen (*Miracle Stories*, 296–97) is perhaps right that in the Synoptics Jesus' refusal is no rejection of signs as such but a punishment to "this evil generation." Nevertheless, our point is that this refusal is simply missing in SG. See further, just below, on the sign demand in the present Gospel.

Their automatic and unvarying effect is faith; SG does not conceive the possibility that those who see them will fail to believe. In the words of Robinson ("Kerygma and History," 55), their effect is "direct, unambiguous, nonparadoxical, causal." They show to all who see them that Jesus is Messiah; he is both their author and their subject. The pre-Johannine writer's sole reason for portraying them, indeed for writing a book, is just to produce such faith (20:31a).

Present Gospel

In thoroughgoing contrast to SG, the Johannine redactional treatment of Jesus' signs and their relation to faith is complex. As usual, the source's understanding is reaffirmed, adopted as valid in itself. But it is also corrected in a number of ways and extensively deepened; in particular, issues wholly absent from SG are raised, about both the genesis and validity of belief.

For the present Gospel the deeds of Jesus remain signs. It takes up SG's term and repeatedly uses it, perhaps more often than did the source[21] and usually in favorable light. Whereas in SG the term was (with two significant exceptions) always used in the singular, for 4G it usually appears as a plural, in a generalizing way that emphasizes the great number of the signs.[22] So there is on 4E's part fundamental acceptance of the source's central statement, namely, its portrayal of Jesus' work as the doing of signs.

But 4G does not limit itself to the predecessor's understanding of the signs; on the contrary, at this very point it considerably expands and extends the source.

First, it clarifies what is only implicit in SG, namely, that the sign is not to be taken either too seriously, as something in itself, or too casually, as merely a means to an end. As we shall see further, in two seminal verses (4:48; 6:26) the Evangelist rules out the possibility of such improper or inadequate attitude to the signs: the stance that, on the one hand, concentrates on the miraculous per se (6:26) or that, on the other, wants a miracle only in order to believe (4:48; see 20:25).[23]

21. Twelve times by 4E (2:23; 3:2; 4:48; 6:2, 26, 30; 7:31; 9:16; 10:41; 11:47; 12:18, 37) as against five surviving pre-Johannine instances (2:11, 18; 4:54; 6:14; 20:30).

22. See esp. 7:3; 11:47; 12:37. The source's numbering of the individual signs served a different purpose, not amassing them but calling attention to each one in turn. Even when it speaks of "many other signs [that] Jesus did" (20:30) it does not emphasize the magnitude of Jesus' activity so much as insist that even a brief selection of the signs suffices to demonstrate his messiahship (v. 31a). (Here I differ with Robinson, "Kerygma and History," 55.) And 12:37 stresses the great number of the signs only to assert ironically the mistaken attitude of the Jerusalem authorities.

23. As the Gospel now stands and in contrast to what we find in SG, wonder is sometimes a response that is allowed, even encouraged (as in 5:20), but sometimes also it is met with Jesus' gentle directive, "Do not marvel . . ." (3:7; 5:28; see also 7:21).

In the second place, for 4G a sign is not merely a demonstration of Jesus' messiahship. This basic assertion of the predecessor is not denied, but 4E seeks to break out of its limitations. The signs are not simply indices of Jesus' authority,[24] so that to believe them would be merely to believe *that* he is the Messiah, to believe *in* him only as Messiah. (Such was a sufficient understanding of the signs at the level of the source.) For the present Gospel they convey all that, but also a deeper understanding—namely, of what it means that Jesus is Messiah—an understanding, in short, of his divine sonship. This christology is clear early in the redaction of the source, from 4E's assertion, in the midst of the conclusion to the first sign, that in that deed Jesus "manifested his glory" (2:11b), so that when the disciples then believe in him (v. 11c) it is now in this fullest sense; they truly understand who he is.[25]

Third, 4E raises the question of the true author of the signs. For the source it was simply Jesus who performed them, and they were done solely to call attention to himself as Messiah. Even the resurrection is regarded as his own deed (2:19). The present Gospel does not wholly eliminate the initiative of Jesus; far from it. It adopts the usage characteristically associated with "sign" in SG (the verb "to do" [*poiein*] with Jesus as subject) and uses it still more frequently,[26] usually with the generalizing plural ("did signs"). But it is not content to depict the signs as acts merely of Jesus. Whereas in SG it was entirely natural that he should perform signs, in 4G there is need to explain how it is that he is able to do them. It is his divine origin that accounts for the signs, as Nicodemus recognizes (3:2). Without that "he could do nothing" (9:33). Evidently it is the importance of this point that leads 4E to introduce a second term *(erga)* for the signs and to assert that Jesus does only the "work(s)" of his Father (4:34; 5:17).[27] They are not deeds in themselves but part of the total activity of God in Jesus; together with Jesus' words they stem from God (14:10).

Without displacing the older understanding of the signs, then, 4G expands it. They both demonstrate Jesus' divine sonship and comprise the deeds of God, and these two ways of understanding Jesus' activity are not in tension with each other. As worker of signs he is at once the agent of God's acts and the revealer of God's nature. The signs of the Messiah, inherited from the source, have become expressions of the incarnation.

24. They are, in fact, finally not signs of Jesus' authority at all, but of God's (5:19).

25. The pivotal change here is the addition of the term "glory"; if the source had already stated that Jesus "manifested himself" (as we considered possible) it was only in the sense of displaying the fact of his messiahship to the disciples.

26. Ten times; see also 10:41.

27. For this reason, surely, when the Johannine Jesus (as distinct from 4E or others) speaks positively of his own deeds he uses *erga*. On the two occasions, also Johannine, when Jesus uses *sēmeia* it is in criticism of the crowd: 4:48; 6:26. (In other instances, that is, when either the narrator or other figures speak, it is not so clear-cut.)

We must now consider that aspect of the signs most important for 4G, as for the predecessor, namely, their relation to *faith*.

The source presupposed a direct and uncomplicated connection between sign and faith. Each of the original sign stories very likely ended with some evidence of belief in Jesus on the part of the witnesses, as the immediate and inevitable response to the sign.[28] This belief was portrayed as both automatic and yet also spontaneous, and that it is meant to be understood as the goal of all Jesus' miracle-working activity is clear from the closing words of SG: "these [signs] are written that you may believe that Jesus is the Christ, the Son of God" (20:31a).

The Johannine Gospel does nothing to deny this relationship between sign and faith. Repeatedly and in various ways we see that 4G takes it for granted.[29] Jesus is depicted calling for such belief, at least as a concession to human weakness (14:11), and thanking God for a miracle that will evoke it (11:40–42). The three discourses that now are attached to a sign (those in chaps. 5, 6, and 9) are all intrinsically concerned, and each in a number of ways, with faith.[30]

It is striking, therefore, that the Johannine Jesus goes out of his way to criticize those who "seek" a sign in order to believe. This is first evident, subtly, in the Johannine handling of the Temple Cleansing (2:13–22).

Prior to the redaction the episode was part of the passion story. The request for a sign that is integral to the story (2:18) roughly corresponds to the Synoptic question, following shortly after the Cleansing, on the part of the Jerusalem authorities. In SG the question is no more surprising than in the other Gospels, but it lacks all suggestion of impropriety on Jesus' part or trickery on the part of his questioners, such as in Mark 11:27–33 pars. Furthermore, Jesus proceeds without hesitation to meet the request—not, to be sure, with a sign, but with the promise of a sign, and his greatest one, namely, the resurrection (v. 19).

In the Evangelist's hands the thrust of the passage is quite different. Now separated from the passion material and placed after the first Galilean sign, the act in the Temple becomes itself a kind of sign, as 2:23 and 3:2 show. So when the subsequent request for a sign is made it has become inappropriate; Jesus has just performed a messianic sign, in his Restoration of the Temple (see also 6:30). The material for this understanding of the deed was already present in the source, but there, in the context of the

---

28. Only three examples have survived the Johannine redaction (2:11c; 4:53b; 6:14) and it is perhaps no accident that this element remains only in stories set in Galilee; see F, in this part.

29. See esp. 11:47–48: "This man performs many signs. If we let him go on like this everyone will believe in him." See also 2:23; 7:31; 11:15; among others, all Johannine passages.

30. See 5:24, 38, 44, 46–47; 6:29–30, 35–36, 40, 47, 64, 69; 9:18, 35–36, 38.

passion, its role as sign was not brought out. That the request, now a demand, displays misunderstanding is first implied by putting it into the mouth of "the Jews" and then made explicit in their literal misappropriation of his saying (vv. 20–21). And the connection between the sign done in the Temple and that promised after Jesus' death is pointed up by the element of the disciples' remembering in vv. 17 and 22 (both Johannine insertions).

Early in the Gospel, then, an improper request for a sign is portrayed. At various other points such a request is criticized, whatever the circumstances. Jesus' mother is rebuffed by him when she only implied the need of a miracle for the sake of the wedding guests (2:4). He reproves the official seeking to save his son's life, implying that he insists on signs only for the sake of faith (4:48). And Jesus' brothers urge him to show himself in Judea by means of his "works," only proving their lack of faith (7:3–8).

Yet in each of these cases Jesus proceeds to grant the request. He changes water into wine, promises the sign of his resurrection, heals the boy, goes up to Jerusalem. Signs as the basis for faith are thus treated ambiguously. Why? The key is the question how a sign is requested or will be understood, an issue quite foreign to SG. Two striking verses are relevant here, both of them inserted into a pre-Johannine context.

The first passage is 4:48. In response to the official's request that Jesus come and heal his son, Jesus says to him, "Unless you people see signs and wonders [note the double phrase] you just will not believe." There is disagreement about the intent of the verse, which interrupts its context so awkwardly. With its use of the second-person plural, is it addressed to the Galileans specifically, into whose region Jesus has just come (4:43–45), or to humankind in general? In either case it is probably (this also is disputed) to be understood as a rebuke. Yet if it is not to jar intolerably with what follows, we must hold that 4E does not intend to rule out all faith based on signs. Rather, in addition to any broader reference it may have, it is designed in the immediate context to test the man's request for a healing, and to criticize only faith that demands the miraculous—signs, that is, understood merely as wonders. So understood, the signs would cease to be truly signs; in focusing on the wondrous their signifying role would be ignored.

In the second instance, at 6:26, there has been no request as yet. (That follows in v. 30, where it has become altogether inappropriate.) Jesus comments on the crowd's response to the miracle of the loaves: "You seek me not because you saw signs, but because you ate your fill of the loaves." The tone is not altogether clear; is it meant as pure rebuke or somehow also a word of encouragement? But in either case it can hardly be disputed that here Jesus holds "seeing signs" as preferable to "eating one's fill of the loaves."[31] That is, to witness a miracle, even to benefit from it and seek out its author (as the crowds do in vv. 23–24), and yet not to perceive it as a sign is to miss its point. A sign, while valid as the basis for faith, must be understood as a true sign. And to be understood, "seen," it must be recognized as full of meaning beyond the miraculous.

In this connection, it is noteworthy that the Gospel adds to the significatory effect of the various miracles by giving them *symbolic* meaning in every case, a meaning almost wholly absent from the pre-Johannine form of the stories. This symbolism is sometimes introduced with no more than a phrase or verse inserted, sometimes by the addition of an entire discourse. The following list is not exhaustive: Judaism contrasted with Christianity (2:6b), salvation as life (4:53a), Jesus' "working" (5:9b and following), the Christian passover (6:4), Jesus as dispelling darkness (6:17b), "the bread of life" (6:27–51), "day" and "night" and the light of the world (9:4–5; see 11:9–10), Jesus' mission (9:7), sight and blindness (9:8 and following; see also 8:12), "I am resurrection" (11:21).[32]

The proper attitude toward signs is made clear in another way, by the verb "to know," that is, to perceive—found in the signs material at 2:9b; 4:53a; 11:22, 24; 21:4, 12. The signs are intended to convey the knowledge of who Jesus really is. Thus, when he prays at the tomb of Lazarus, it is "so that they may believe that thou has sent me" (11:42). Anything short of this ultimate theological perception is inadequate. It is the same requirement, apparently, that accounts for the flaw in the Jerusalemites' faith at 2:23–25; they have seen the signs and as a consequence believed. This would be entirely sufficient in the context of SG, but as typical of "the Jews"—Jesus' "own" *(hoi idioi)* and representatives of "the world" (1:10–11)—they do not "know" him; it is rather Jesus who knows them (2:25). (See further in F, in this part, on Jerusalem and "the Jews" as theological symbols.)

The signs, then, are a crux by which people's faith is determined. "Properly understood as signs, they evoke genuine faith; understood as arbitrary miracles, they create hardening."[33]

We need now to look still more closely at the role of signs in the genesis of faith, for 4G gives great attention to this. In particular we must consider the relation of seeing signs and believing. It is 4E who introduces the

---

31. The verb *(chortazesthai)* is clearly pejorative; the phrase is roughly paralleled in the next verse by "laboring for the food that perishes."

32. From whosever hand, the symbolism in 21:1–14 (see part 1, sec. 5, Johannine Redaction) also belongs in a list such as this.

33. Hartman, "Osterberichte," 203 n. 17. See also 12:40.

element of sight into the context of the signs,[34] and thereby raises the question of the various ways the two verbs, seeing and believing, can be connected. At the pre-Johannine level there is only one such relationship: sight (most often implicit) leads unfailingly to belief (cf. 3, below). In 4G, on the other hand, the situation is complex:

1. We may consider first of all the combination *seeing and yet not believing*. The failure of the signs is a possibility simply not countenanced in the original SQ. They are "written so that [the reader] may believe" (20:31a), and no doubt in the case of every sign depicted the witnesses are to be understood as simply believing in this straightforward way. Whether the impression given is a deliberately ideal one or in fact corresponded to the experience of the community in which SQ arose, there is an inevitability in the effect of Jesus' miraculous activity.

(Eventually, of course, the problem of Jesus' death would have raised question about the signs' indubitable basis for faith. But it would have been met before long by the addition, or production, of a passion narrative in which that death is given theological justification, which is just the agendum of the pre-Johannine PQ. At most, the problem would have been addressed directly in the brief notice underlying 12:37–40; but even there the question is only why the officials plotting Jesus' death did not believe in the signs, not the general issue of signs as valid basis of belief for all.)

The situation is quite different in 4G. The Johannine church found a changed reception to the proofs of the source; its new situation with respect to the synagogue very likely presented these Christians for the first time with the fact of unbelief.[35] In any case, 4G is concerned to explore the nature of faith in a way the predecessor had not done, making the failure of the signs an important theme.

The concern appears, in general terms, already in the prologue (1:10–11), and it is loosely expressed throughout the Gospel in the use of "the Jews"/"Judeans" as symbols of the misunderstanding and rejection of Jesus. The Evangelist addresses this broad theological problem—why do some, indeed most, fail to believe in the face of the signs?—in the conclusion to the first half of the Gospel (12:37–41).

---

34. As at 2:23; 4:48; 6:26; 7:3; see also 4:45; 6:2, 30; 12:40. By contrast, SG speaks of seeing a sign only once (6:14, possibly the germ of 4E's enlargement) and otherwise uses only the formula "Come and see" (1:39, 46; 4:29; 11:34); in all cases the automatic and uncomplicated result of seeing is believing. A Mosaic background to the Johannine elaboration seems likely: Deut. 29:2–3 (Moses summarizes all the signs the Israelites have "seen" the Lord do); also Deut. 6:22; 7:19. Further, the usage obviously bears relation to the more purely Johannine theme of seeing the divine glory (1:14; 11:40; 12:41).

35. Here as elsewhere the reader is referred to Martyn, *History and Theology*, who convincingly proposes that the expulsion of the Johannine Christians from the Jewish community provided the sociological context in which belief on the part of potential converts has become costly, and lack of belief is even officially encouraged.

Originally, the kernel of this pivotal passage would have served as bridge between SQ and PQ (preceded only by the Temple Cleansing and Official Conspiracy) and would have explained the officials' decision to put Jesus to death in spite of the public success of his miracles. But in the Johannine structure, this important passage comes at a later point, after the Anointing and Triumphal Entry, and thus at the end of the Johannine Jesus' ministry "to the world," before turning in the Last Supper to his disciples as audience for his last discourse (chaps. 14—17). The notice serves, thus, to summarize the whole of Jesus' activity and the general response to it (now characterized as negative).

This bridge both parallels and contrasts with the original ending of SG, which 4E retains as the conclusion to the passion narrative and the Gospel as a whole (note especially the verbal similarities and contrasts between 12:37 and 20:30–31). In it the whole of Jesus' ministry is expressed as paradox: "Though he had done so many signs before them, yet they did not believe in him, so that the word spoken by the prophet Isaiah might be fulfilled. . . ." Despite the repeated instances of belief in the face of Jesus' signs, 4G can characterize his public ministry as failure: a failure attributable not to Jesus, of course, but to those who would not believe or whose belief was not valid. It is a failure finally that is to be understood—by means of the much-used passage from Isaiah—as part of the divine economy. Not just a few wrongheaded priests with hardened hearts, but the human context of Jesus' entire ministry has failed to believe.

The same paradox was expressed already in 1:10–11 and in the proverb Jesus cites at 4:44: just as Jesus' "own" could be expected to receive him, so ought the signs to produce faith, but they do not. Many of the Jews, "many even of the authorities" (12:42), believe, but in most cases (Nicodemus being the notable exception) this faith comes to nothing, and Jesus' ministry closes on a somber note. Seeing the signs cannot be counted on to lead to belief.[36]

2. So far we have looked at one way that sight and faith can be related, or in this case found not to be related: seeing and yet not believing. A second—*not seeing and therefore not believing*—raises the special question of the second- and third-generation Christian's faith, which we shall postpone for the moment. But the circumstance in general has already been discussed in different form: the inability, even the refusal, to believe without a sign, as 4E so negatively characterizes the official's request for a miracle in 4:48. It is implied also in 6:30: "What sign do you do," the crowds ask following the miracle of the loaves, "that we may see and

---

36. It is interesting that in 12:37 the failure of the signs is not stated in terms of seeing; we do not read, as we might have expected, "Though they had seen so many signs, yet they did not believe." The explanation no doubt lies in the fact that here 4E is employing material from 4G, where Jesus' performing of the signs, not their audiences' response, is paramount.

believe you?" The outrageousness of this demand is self-evident: Jesus had just given a sign greater than Moses' manna in the wilderness! The importance of this matter for 4E is evident from the Gospel's climactic episode, that of unbelieving Thomas (20:24–29) who avowed, "Unless I see . . . I will not believe" (v. 25).[37] To be unable, still more to be unwilling, to believe without seeing is inexcusable.

3. Each of these negative combinations of seeing and believing is matched by its positive counterpart. Just as 4G disapproves of the one, it commends the other. The failure of the signs has for its opposite the condition of *seeing and therefore believing*. In discussing the valid relation between sign and faith we have already noted that for 4G sight that leads to faith will be appropriate so long as the faith is genuine and treats the signs truly as signs.

In that very discourse (chap. 6) in which Jesus criticizes the demand for a sign (the insistence on seeing in order to believe), 4E shows at the same time that seeing and believing are naturally and appropriately associated: ". . . everyone who sees the Son and [consequently] believes in him" will have eternal life (v. 40).[38] The same teaching is made more extensively in 9:35–38.

At the very inauguration of Jesus' ministry, before the signs begin, the Johannine Gospel affirms the positive value of seeing. In SG Nathanael was moved to a profound confession of Jesus by his passing display of supernatural knowledge (1:48–49). The Evangelist gives important amplification to this little scene in several ways (vv. 50–51). The validity of Nathanael's confession is not questioned; on the contrary, it is explicitly named belief, as was not so in the source, and Nathanael is promised greater faith, based on seeing: "Do you believe [merely] because I said to you, 'I saw you under the fig tree'? You shall see greater things than these [and consequently believe still more]. . . . Amen Amen I say to you, You shall see . . . the Son of man." (The programmatic function of this episode is evident from the shift to second-person plurals in its culminating pronouncement.)

The only instance where belief based on seeing signs is treated as invalid is in 2:23–25, but of course it is not the paschal pilgrims' having seen the signs that nullifies their faith, which follows naturally enough from that sight. Rather, it is something "in humanity" that calls this faith in question; the passage has to do not with the proper genesis and nature of faith but with the Judeans as symbols of Jesus' rejection (see F, in this part).

---

37. On this passage, see further just below. Thomas does not speak of seeing a sign, but the verbal parallel to 4:48 is clear.

38. That it is Jesus, not merely a sign, that is seen makes no difference here, in the light of the seeing of signs in vv. 2 and 14. Indeed, Jesus criticizes the Galileans for not seeing signs, that is, perceiving their true nature (v. 26), and, when they have seen, for not believing (v. 36).

And elsewhere (6:26) 4E implies a distinction between seeing and seeing, sight that is purely physical and that which perceives theological significance. The former can produce positive response to Jesus ("seeking him"), can even lead to belief (just as in 2:23), but it is not truly to "see signs." And a similar point is implied in that other pivotal verse, 4:48: to see signs-and-wonders is not to see signs in the full and proper sense.

In SG no attention was drawn to the seeing of signs; consequently the question precisely who it is that witnesses them was not raised. The participants in the story, of course, are the witnesses, and if the source's author were asked if anyone besides them also sees the signs she or he would surely have answered, "Yes, you who read my book" (see 20:31a). But with the Johannine emphasis on the validity of sight-leading-to-faith the question of the subjects of such seeing becomes an issue, and it is necessary to distinguish between the actual witness and the vicarious one. That is, while 4G knows of a profounder kind of seeing, it can treat the seeing of signs quite literally, in the sense of eyewitnessing, and so distinguish it from the belief on the part of the reader that subsequently is based upon it. Thus 4E introduces into the crucifixion scene the one who "saw [the blood and water from the side of Jesus and] has borne witness . . . that you also may believe" (19:35, patterned in the latter part on the source's 20:31a). But at the same time a kind of faith that does not depend on sight must be provided for.

4. This is accomplished in the combination of the two verbs that is certainly the most important for 4G, *not seeing and yet believing*—the positive counterpart, of course, of the second combination, not seeing and therefore not believing.

Those in the Gospel who do see signs are undoubtedly intended by 4G, as by its predecessor, to be models for the reader, so that merely to read of the signs is in some sense to "see" them. But in a more real sense the situation of the second-generation, or later, Christian, as 4E realizes, is that he or she cannot see, but is dependent on the witness of others, and this circumstance may become a barrier to faith.[39] It is just this consequence that is ruled out. Belief on the basis of others' reports is satisfactory; but belief without any such reliance is superior. It is even superior to believing on the basis of immediate concrete evidence.

Thus in 4:48 Jesus challenges the official who asks him to heal his son (and through the official all the Galileans, who had just seen Jesus' deeds and consequently welcomed him) by questioning whether the man must see proof in order to believe. In this way Jesus sets a test for the official, a

---

39. At the end of the Samaritan episode (4:42) the woman's fellow townspeople declare with evident relief, "It is no longer because of your words [reporting what you saw] that we believe, for we have [seen Jesus and] heard for ourselves, and we know that this is indeed the Savior of the world."

test that he then clearly passes. In the Johannine redaction he is portrayed in his obedience to Jesus' command ("Go . . .") as believing simply Jesus' word, that his son is already healed (v. 50b); that faith-without-seeing is subsequently ratified, when the man hears (and presumably then sees) the evidence of the healing (vv. 51–53).[40]

This paradoxical superiority of faith-without-seeing is the point of the story of Thomas, which 4E evidently creates and with which the Gospel comes to its dramatic close (20:24–29).[41] The passage serves to complete the schematic structure of the Gospel. Thus Thomas's climactic confession of Jesus (v. 28) parallels and supersedes that of Nathanael at the very beginning of Jesus' ministry (1:49), and the form of Jesus' reply there (question followed by pronouncement, 1:50) is replicated in his final word to Thomas (20:29). The episode itself, the entire chapter, indeed the whole Gospel—all culminate in this saying from Jesus. "Have you believed because you have seen me?[42] Blessed are those who have not seen and yet believe." This is one of two beatitudes in the Gospel, and the other is spoken only to Jesus' immediate disciples (13:17). Here, insofar as it validly believes, the whole church—past, present, and future—is blessed.

The implication is clear: belief without seeing signs is a superior form of faith, and we will consider below the last issue by which 4G develops the concept of faith, namely, the portrayal of deepening degrees of faith. But before leaving the question of the relation of belief to sight, we must observe that 4E portrays two more ways of combining the verbs, namely, by reversing their order.

5. In its negative form—*not believing and therefore not seeing*—this phenomenon is vividly dramatized in chapter 9 by the Pharisees' metaphoric blindness stemming from their refusal to believe. They claim to see, denouncing the former blind man for his lack of insight, but by their refusal to believe they show themselves at the end of the chapter to be blind. They stand in contrast to the man, who exemplifies just the opposite condition.

---

40. It is apparent here as elsewhere (see, e.g., the preceding note) that seeing and hearing are in this context interchangeable for 4G; Jesus' role is to show the works of the Father for believers to see and to speak the truth for them to hear. Both are grounds for valid faith.

41. If chap. 21 is Johannine, it nevertheless functions only as a postscript to the Gospel proper. Although the Thomas episode contains traditional material I nevertheless find it impossible to isolate any pre-Johannine version of the story. It has also been worked up by 4E largely from elements in the preceding passage—compare v. 25a with v. 18, v. 26 with v. 19, and v. 25b with v. 20.

42. Jesus does not say "because you have seen signs." The problem for the latter-day Christian is not only that such a one has not seen the signs and must, like those who heard of Jesus during his lifetime, depend on the reports of others, but that he or she has not seen—cannot now see—Jesus. In a sense, of course, Thomas has seen a sign, the sign in Jesus' hands and side of his identity with the crucified One and so of his resurrection, but that too is no longer available, and so the ensuing beatitude is necessary and sufficient.

246

6. The positive combination of the two verbs—*believing and therefore seeing*—does not refer to restoring the blind man's sight, as it might in the Synoptics. Neither in SG nor in 4G is faith ever the component of a miracle. The seeing in question here is of another order. The man has of course already seen Jesus with his new-gotten eyesight, as Jesus tells him (v. 37). His subsequent act of faith gives him a different kind of sight, so that he can at last "worship" Jesus (v. 38). It is on this spiritual level that he exemplifies in his belief the end for which Jesus "came into this world," namely, "so that those who do not see may see" (v. 39). In just this way Jesus says to Martha, at the tomb of Lazarus, "Did I not tell you that if you would believe you would see the glory of God?" (11:40).

The seeing that results from faith is a central affirmation in 4G. It has to do with true understanding, which is so often portrayed, in contrast to the baffling lack of understanding even on the part of those who see. Thus Nicodemus, in chapter 3, has clearly seen the signs Jesus has done (2:23; 3:2) and initially believes somehow in Jesus ("You are a teacher come from God"). But when Jesus begins to lead him to an understanding of the salvation he brings, by being "born from above," Nicodemus quickly shows that he does not understand in the least (3:10), evidently because as "a ruler of the Jews" he here exemplifies the same kind of opacity as the authorities in chapter 9. (Later Nicodemus will vindicate himself— 7:50–51; 19:39.) The Evangelist had already displayed this contrast, between those who understand (usually "know") and those who do not, in 2:9 (the servants at the wedding feast vs. the steward), and it recurs in many other places. Equally the beloved disciple is the exemplar of Christian understanding. At the tomb he sees the head-cloth of Jesus (a kind of sign, though it demonstrates nothing more than the absence of Jesus' body) and believes, that is, understands (20:8). In chapter 21, when the other disciples do not recognize ("know") Jesus the beloved disciple does (v. 7).

To enable humanity to understand, to know, to see in this way is the chief work of Jesus: "No one has ever seen God; the only Son . . . has made him known" (1:18).

We turn finally to 4E's depiction of degrees or, better, *levels of faith*—a major enhancement of the source. There faith was understood in a single way: belief in Jesus as Messiah on the basis of his signs. The inevitable consequence of a miracle was its witnesses' confession of Jesus' messiahship. Even the variety of titles applied to Jesus was presented on a single plane, each interchangeable with any other.

The Evangelist, by contrast, sees in faith a complex phenomenon. We have already seen that faith not dependent on signs is regarded as superior (14:11; 20:29). The various expressions faith can take, and the relative value to be assigned them, are dramatized by 4E in several passages that depict progressive stages of conversion. Thus in chapter 4 the Samaritan woman, the crowd of her fellow townspeople, and the Capernaum official, and in chapter 9 the blind man—all are led by Jesus, in different ways and sometimes by several steps, from a less to a more adequate faith.

The second and third of the three passages in chapter 4 introduce the element of belief in Jesus' word as the vehicle for the progression of faith. In 4:39–42 4E expresses the response of the crowd at Sychar: "many Samaritans from that city believed in [Jesus]" and at first this was only "on account of the woman's word" (v. 39). After they find Jesus and he stays with them, "many more believed on account of his word" (v. 41), and they tell the woman that now they believe not on account of what she has told them but what they have heard for themselves (v. 42a). Her word had led them to Jesus as a first step so that it could have its effect on them—they come to "know" that he "is indeed the Savior of the world" (v. 42b).

Similarly, and more demonstrably, in 4:46–54 4E has explicitly used the device of Jesus' word to portray the official coming by stages to full faith in him. In SG the man, on hearing Jesus' assurance, "Go, your son will live," had simply complied with it (v. 50ac). This obedience no doubt implied a kind of trust in what Jesus had said. But not till the man had heard confirmation of Jesus' promise did the pre-Johannine reader learn that he believed (vv. 53–54). The Evangelist deftly transforms this. By the insertion of v. 48 there is raised the question of the valid basis of faith; the man's trust is put to the test, a test that he survives: he immediately repeats his request that Jesus heal his son, receives the assurance, believes Jesus' word (Johannine insertion, v. 50b), and goes. This faith in Jesus, without seeing, is clearly exemplary, and so on the one hand it is only ratified when the man meets his servants, but on the other it is thereby quite naturally extended to "his whole household" (v. 53b).[43]

The progressive deepening of faith is shown most fully in the case of the man born blind, as 4G elaborates the simple miracle by a dramatized series of dialogues (chap. 9). Here it is not only a matter of a changed basis of belief (Jesus' word) but also of a deepening awareness on the man's part, consequent to his healing, of who Jesus is. At first he knows only that "a man called Jesus," of unknown whereabouts, healed him (vv. 11–12). Then, challenged by the authorities, he is moved to confess that Jesus is a

---

43. We were in doubt in part 1, sec. 4, whether to take v. 53a—"The man knew that [the time of the boy's recovery reported by the servants] was the hour Jesus had said to him . . ."— as pre-Johannine or Johannine. But, in either case, its meaning in the context of 4E's story is evidently that the official came to "know" (in the Johannine sense) on the basis of his prior faith: a case of believing and therefore seeing. Liebert ("Fourth Gospel") interestingly shows, by means of a structural analysis of 4G, that the stages in human developmental theory are roughly paralleled in 4G. It is not surprising, perhaps, to find that all of the data she mounts is part of the Johannine layer in the episodes she adduces.

prophet (v. 17). The officials declare that Jesus is a sinner (v. 24), on which question the man initially pleads ignorance but, pressed to explain his simple acceptance of Jesus' power, he affirms that he must be "from God" (v. 33). Then Jesus meets him, confronting him regarding his faith: "Do you believe in the Son of man?" The man at first fails to understand whom Jesus means by the title, but once he is told the man believes and—validating his faith and the full understanding it includes—worships Jesus (vv. 35–38). Against the background of the authorities' faithless rejection of Jesus, the man serves as a model of Christian conversion.

A roughly similar exchange takes place in the first part of chapter 4, between Jesus and the Samaritan woman (vv. 7–29). We cannot tell what earlier material, if any, 4E makes use of here, but the force of the passage in its present form is clear enough. At first Jesus is to the woman simply "a Jew" (v. 9). On hearing his suggestion that far from depending on her for a drink he can give her "living water" she ironically wonders if he is greater than the patriarch Jacob (v. 12). Soon, from Jesus' supernatural knowledge of her former life, she "perceives" that he is "a prophet" (v. 19). Led further by Jesus' puzzling words she proclaims her faith in Messiah, a prophet par excellence (v. 25). He announces to her that he is just that one, and although she does not fully understand or believe it she finally comes to wonder in the hearing of her fellow townspeople whether Jesus could be "the Christ" (v. 29). She evidently is not to be understood as a type of the true believer, like the blind man of chapter 9; for in the end she provides only the "words" on which others' faith is initially based (see just above, on vv. 39–42). But her moving from initial ignorance of Jesus' identity to very nearly full realization is nevertheless meant, once again, to show how faith can grow and understanding mature.

A deeper example is found in Martha, who in chapter 11 is led by Jesus to the full realization that he is the source of Life itself, a believing that conveys the deepest seeing. At first (v. 21) she addresses him as "Lord" (*kyrie*), meaning perhaps simply "Sir" or—since she goes on to express her faith in his healing power (v. 21b) and in his influence with God (v. 22)—more likely "Master." Jesus then promises that her dead brother Lazarus will "rise again," for the reader an obvious announcement of what he is about to do. Martha, however, understands it as only a reassurance of the resurrection that awaits everyone "at the last day" (vv. 23–24). Thereupon Jesus proclaims, "I am [the source of] resurrection and life," available to anyone through faith (vv. 25–26). When asked if she has such faith Martha at once displays that now, led by Jesus, she does; she both understands and confesses him as "the Christ, the Son of God who is come[44] into the world"

---

44. *Erchomenos* here can hardly be taken as having only future, or even merely continuous reference in the present.

(v. 27). Martha's example is paramount as the last instance, in the public ministry of Jesus, of one coming to full faith in him.[45]

This then is the meaning of signs faith in the Johannine Gospel: the perception of Jesus as the ultimate sign, the one sent from heaven to make God known. Yet faith, even understood in this fullest way, is not the end point of the Gospel. This is evident from the all-important addition 4E makes to the source's ending. The signs are written not only that the reader may believe in Jesus but also that "believing you may have life in his name" (20:31b). In the final analysis, the Evangelist's work is not, like the predecessor's, a "gospel of signs," but a message of salvation. For the source the chief sign was Jesus' resurrection—chief in that it showed Jesus' messiahship more decisively than any of the other miracles. For 4G the chief sign is rather Jesus' death, by which he gives life.

We must, therefore, proceed to explore first how at the Evangelist's hands christology gives place to salvation, to soteriology (see C in this part), and then the meaning given to the death of Jesus (see D in this part).

---

45. Yet even she fails, at the moment of Jesus' command that the tomb be opened (11:39b), to believe in the miracle's possibility (a less important failure than not seeing Jesus' identity in his works). It is just conceivable that this detail is pre-Johannine, though no natural place for it is to be found in the reconstructed source.

C. Salvation[46]

Soteriology, the idea of salvation, as a distinct topic in 4G has seldom been treated in detail,[47] perhaps because the concept seems to include the whole of Johannine theology. One might expect, of course, to find it especially in the discourses, and to that extent not susceptible to redaction-critical investigation of the narratives. That may be, but soteriology is not limited to the sayings of Jesus in 4G. By looking at the pre-Johannine narrative source with the concept of salvation in mind one finds the germ of the later Johannine theology and at the same time sees the latter's distinctiveness all the more clearly.

Source

I have summarized the theology of SG as follows (*TGOS*, 228):

> In contrast to almost every other early Christian document we possess, its message is not that a new age has dawned, not that salvation is made available in Jesus, not that suffering and sin and death are now destroyed, not that the Spirit is bestowed. . . . It affirms simply that "Jesus is the Christ, the Son of God." . . . His miracles are recounted simply as legitimating signs of his messianic status. Even the healings are christological, not soteriological. . . .

It is necessary now both to amplify and to qualify this statement.

In its explicit theology, 4E's narrative source is exclusively christological, and in the most literal sense. It seeks to demonstrate solely that Jesus is the Messiah: In his ministry he repeatedly performs the signs of the expected Christ and in his death he fulfills OT prophecy. What is expected in response is simply belief in that messiahship (1:7c; 20:31a). SG

46. For an earlier treatment of this subject see my article "Soteriology."
47. But see Lattke, "Erlöser," and more recently Turner, "Soteriology." As his title implies, Lattke deals with salvation as redemption, an approach that slightly distorts the resulting picture of Johannine soteriology, for despite its later Gnostic use in that regard there is nothing of the concept of rescue in the Gospel, and the sense of redemption as a ritual transaction, underlying the very occasional use of *apolytrōsis* by Paul and the Synoptics, is missing in 4G. Turner looks at the question largely from a Pauline perspective. Further, he misunderstands my redaction-critical approach, supposing that SQ is identical with chaps. 2—12 of the present Gospel (Dodd's "Book of Signs" in the outline of 4G he gave in *Interpretation*, 289–90) and thus failing to see the theological movement from a christological source underlying those chapters to the soteriology now dominant in them.

251

does not consider, as the Johannine Gospel later does, what messiahship means, but simply the fact that Jesus is Messiah. This single-minded aim of the work is probably a reflection of its apparent purpose: to serve within the synagogue as a tract for potential Jewish converts to belief in Jesus.

Besides christology, the theological issues that we find in other early Christian literature apparently do not arise for the source as worthy of explicit attention; they are irrelevant to its purpose. The question of salvation is such an issue. There is of course no such thing as a christology that is not also soteriological. The very idea of the Messiah carries with it a message of salvation—at the least political salvation, more often eschato-logical and spiritual salvation as well or instead. Lying behind SG's christology, then, there must have been the whole weight of Jewish soteriology. But it is never expressed. We find none of the usual words having to do with saving (*sōzein*, etc.);[48] nor any of the Johannine terms— life, grace, truth, light—synonymous with salvation; and certainly no hint of Pauline or Synoptic language (redemption, justification, forgiveness).

Nevertheless, within this densely christological work there are elements that are potentially—already implicitly—soteriological, some of which in fact 4G will take up to express its concept of salvation.

The source begins with two introductory episodes implying salvation: John the Baptist's testimony to Jesus (1:19-34) and the subsequent con-version of the first disciples (1:35-49). And even before these episodes begin we learn, in two brief sentences, of a sort of plan of salvation underlying them: the Baptist has been "sent from God" to bear testimony so that human beings, "all," in fact, "might believe" (1:6-7). Though never spelled out, for the source the act of coming to belief—belief solely in Jesus' messiahship—is surely understood to some extent soterio-logically, and the Baptist as the inaugurating witness to Jesus' messianic ministry sets in motion God's saving plan for the world. Even if the "all" excludes any but the Jewish world (and the author gives no clue that we are to understand it more inclusively), the salvation implied, indeed the salvation-history, is all-pervasive.

The depicted activity of the Baptist (1:19-34) is entirely christological, namely, to bear testimony to the coming Messiah. In contrast to the Synoptic portraits, the Baptist here appears neither baptizing nor preach-ing repentance, only testifying. But a scheme of salvation—inherent in the advent of the savior—is implied.

Implicit salvation history finds further expression in the conversion of the disciples (1:35-49). The pre-Johannine author attaches great impor-

48. An exception may be the title "Savior of the world," which possibly already in SG was the confession of the Samaritans in response to their encounter with Jesus (4:42). But even here the phrase is entirely christological in intent. See this part, n. 66, on the possibility that the assertion in 4:22 ("Salvation is of the Jews") is also pre-Johannine.

tance to the disciples, and the story of the first conversions is intended to be both an emblem (the Christian community of the saved begins to form) and a model (the Christian is the one who, like the first disciples, follows Jesus and stays with him).[49] Salvation is inaugurated.

In its pre-Johannine portrayal, the whole of Jesus' public ministry—his repeated performing of signs—results in faith in him on the part of the witnesses. It is surely no exaggeration to say that, for this author, to believe in Jesus is to be saved. Thus the constant theme of belief is not only christologically demonstrative but by implication also a portrayal of people coming to salvation. This is true, evidently, already in chapter 1. Verse 7 suggests it (the Baptist bears witness "that all might believe"), and although nothing is said subsequently in this chapter of faith on the part of the new disciples, that is because the author has chosen to let their conversion, with its repeated confession of Jesus' identity, come to its climax of belief only after the first sign (2:11c). Nevertheless, alongside the author's intent to identify Jesus as Messiah is the concomitant soteriological affirmation of what it means for the believer that the Messiah has come.

The seven miracles of Jesus that make up the heart of the source have been selected from a much greater number, as the author tells us (20:30). We can safely guess that this selection was not made at random but was intended to be representative, comprehensive, sufficient. This is evident from the lack of duplication among the seven and from the balance the selection shows. And it is just possible that the signs have been chosen specifically to display various aspects of the salvation that the coming of the Messiah entails.

Three of the miracles (those now found in chaps. 2, 6, and 21) demonstrate in various ways the bounty that the Messiah provides. In each of them the overabundance of Christ's sustaining work is clear: more than one hundred gallons of wine, five thousand men fed (not counting women and children) with baskets left over, fish nets too heavy to haul. No doubt tradition is partly responsible for this prodigality, but the source can hardly have failed to see all this as a representation of the abundance of the messianic age. It uses no eschatological language, yet there are hints that in these stories we are to see the metaphor of the messianic banquet. Each of the three miracles results in a kind of feast; in each the final abundance is contrasted with an earlier dearth; and in the first, an actual wedding banquet, the story culminates in the steward's declaration: "You have kept the good wine until now" (2:10). It is not clear how far this traditional

---

49. "Follow" is used pointedly three times (1:37, 40, 43) and evidently in a technical Christian sense. Similarly "stay" (or "remain") is emphasized (three times in 1:38–39) and implies a sense of community.

253

logion, once no doubt the climax of the story, is emphasized, but that it stands with the prominence it has suggests that its soteriological implication is meant to sound. If so, the turn of the ages, the "now," otherwise nowhere alluded to, proclaims itself.

Two of the signs show Jesus healing longstanding afflictions: a thirty-eight-year lameness (5:2–9) and congenital blindness (9:1–7). In each the dramatic change in the sufferer's condition is boldly conveyed—"he took up his bed and walked," "he came back seeing." The possibility of soteriological interpretation is left open.

The most dramatic miracles show Jesus restoring to life a boy at the point of death and Lazarus four days dead. Rescue from the finality, the oblivion, of death is both the clearest metaphor for salvation and itself dramatic expression of it; no matter how hopeless the human condition, how finite and vulnerable, the wonderworking Messiah—in the very act of displaying his stature—gives life by a word alone. In the case of the official's son that word is the simple directive, "Go, your son lives" (4:50): at once reassurance to the boy's father and itself the healing, life-giving command that banishes the threat of death. This word is without parallel in the Synoptic versions of the story. That the later Evangelist has emphasized it by the repetition in v. 53—though we left open the possibility that this duplication was found already in the source—does not obscure the fact that already for the source the saving assertion is given prominence by its paraphrase in v. 51. Jesus is of course not called the giver of life—it will remain for 4E to make the christological (still more, the soteriological) fact explicit (see 11:25)—but in the pre-Johannine story he is nevertheless just that.

The point is clearer by far in the source's account of Lazarus. I have said (TGOS, 229) that there is no assertion there that the power of death is destroyed in Jesus' act, and that is strictly true; the attention is entirely on Jesus' messianic power. Yet details in the story hint at a soteriological struggle. Jesus' indignation in 11:33, while probably solely thaumaturgic at an earlier stage of the tradition, is for SG very possibly a suggestion of cosmic conflict in process of being overcome. The depiction of Lazarus' coming forth from the tomb at Jesus' command and his unbinding (vv. 43–44) can perhaps be taken as further evidence of an implicit symbolic soteriology.

A further episode, the miraculous crossing of the sea, while perhaps not strictly a sign in itself, shows the disciples in difficulty and presumably anxiety. Into this situation Jesus comes, bringing rescue. At the same time his appearance strikes fear in them and this he quiets (6:18–21). One may ask whether in this story 4E later found the seed of the Johannine portrait of Jesus as both judge of men by his very presence (3:19) and the bringer of comfort (16:33). In any case, the soteriological potential is already in place.

Nowhere does SG treat salvation explicitly. Yet it would have been apt if the source had made some such citation of messianic prophecy as in Luke 4:18 ("He has anointed me . . . he has sent me to proclaim . . . recovering of sight to the blind . . .") or summary of Jesus' deeds as in his answer to John the Baptist ("The blind receive their sight and the lame walk . . . and the dead are raised up," Matt. 11:4–5 = Luke 7:22–23).[50]

We have concerned ourselves until now with the nature of salvation, the question what it meant to be saved, according to SG. While the answer is nowhere on the surface, it is nevertheless certainly there. Two other questions demand consideration to complete our investigation of the pre-Johannine soteriology. The first has to do with the questions who is saved and how that salvation is appropriated.

That the believer reading or hearing SG is meant to see her- or himself as somehow the beneficiary of the various miracles seems clear from the otherwise unnecessary presence of the disciples at most of the signs. The disciples were simply the first believers, and in all but one of the miracles they somehow figure. For example, they appear at the beginning and end of the Cana wedding story (2:2, 11) and are mentioned in the introduction to the second miracle (2:12a). Their presence in some cases is contrived and a product of the pre-Johannine author's redaction.[51] This suggests that salvation was meant to be seen as coming not only to the person originally healed or raised or fed but to all disciples, all believers, as well.

A further expression of the same idea can be found in the episode of the official's son, where the miracle results in the conversion of a whole household (4:53). The account of the conversion of the disciples is also paradigmatic. There we find individuals coming to salvation, and what is especially striking is the way that salvation spreads, by a kind of chain reaction: from Andrew to Peter, then to Philip and Nathanael. The power of the message of Jesus' messiahship is obvious; once it is at work on earth it does not falter, as the subsequent seemingly automatic belief of the miracles' witnesses shows. (See B, in this part, on the fact that the failure of the signs, a Johannine theme, is lacking in SG.)

50. Despite the prominence of exorcisms in the Synoptic tradition, it is noteworthy that these summaries contain no reference to exorcism (unless "release to the captives" is such a metaphoric allusion), and that SG similarly lacks that kind of healing. Of the miracles cited by Jesus to the Baptist, SG lacks the cleansing of leprosy and the healing of deafness.

51. Especially in the stories of the blind man (9:2) and Lazarus (11:7). In the feeding of the multitude the disciples figure somewhat more prominently than in the Synoptic parallels (6:3, 5, 7, 8, 10, 12). In the miraculous catch of fish (21:2–14) they are of course principals, but only there. Solely in the healing of the lame man (5:2–9) are they not mentioned.

For the predecessor then, salvation comes to anyone who believes, at least within the context of Israel. Faith defines both the recipient and the means of claiming the salvation. In contrast to the Synoptic summary of the Christian good news (e.g., Mark 1:15), there is no place here for repentance as a condition of salvation alongside faith, except perhaps as Israel had long since repented (cf. how that element is entirely missing in the pre-Johannine account of the Baptist's message). The long-awaited Messiah has come; simply to believe in him is to appropriate the salvation implicit in his expectation.

The other question to be put to the pre-Johannine author's soteriology has to do with the objective *means* of salvation. Later Western theology has taught us to think always of the death of Jesus in seeking an answer to this question. But various NT writings—the early letters of Paul and the Synoptic Gospels—remind us how little early Christians were concerned to develop a soteriology in this way. It is especially true of the pre-Johannine source. The death of Jesus is given prominence if, as I believe, a combined pre-Johannine source contained both signs and passion; it comprised about one-half of the work's bulk. Thus on the basis of weight at least we can call it, if not with Mark a "passion narrative with introduction,"[52] nevertheless a presentation of the death of Jesus. Yet nowhere, so far as we can now tell, did the pre-Johannine author consider Jesus' death as itself effective in accomplishing human salvation.[53]

For this author, the death of Jesus had not yet been taken up into the good news as even an implicit concept of salvation. Its handling is entirely apologetic, something to be accounted for and excused, since it seems to contradict the christology of Jesus' signs. Through the author's ingenuity it is made instead to buttress Jesus' messiahship by the device of prophecy fulfillment. In PQ, then, just as in the signs, the emphasis is preponderantly christological. But at the same time, as we shall see in D in this part, SG lays the groundwork for the Johannine doctrine of the death of Jesus by providing its raw materials.

To summarize, in inverse order, what we have seen so far: SG apparently

---

52. See part 1, excursus A.2, on the source's genre. The signs of Jesus are not simply a prologue to his death; on the contrary, they are fundamental, and his passion is something to be explained in their light.

53. See further D, in this part. The phrase "Lamb of God" was evidently ascribed to Jesus in SG (1:29), and very possibly in origin it would have had soteriological meaning, whether in a Jewish or an early Christian context. But in the pre-Johannine material it has come to be solely christological, simply another in the list of synonymous messianic designations piled upon Jesus in the opening episodes. The soteriology of the explanatory phrase "who bears the sin of the world" (1:29) appears to be Johannine. In the source's account of the Sanhedrin Conspiracy against Jesus there is what appears to be the germ of a theology of atonement: "that one man die for [*hyper*] the people" (11:50). But if a soteriological potential exists here, there is no reason to suppose that it was realized by the author, since at the pre-Johannine level the preposition was undoubtedly to be understood only in the sense "instead of."

never considered the question (1) how salvation is accomplished but simply holds the unexamined assumption that it comes with the arrival of the Messiah. A more nearly explicit soteriological issue is rather (2) how humans receive the salvation that the Messiah brings, and to that there is a straightforward answer: they do so by believing in Jesus as the Christ. Finally, although the source does not openly ask (3) what salvation consists of, yet by implication it takes an important step toward supplying the answer, namely, by portraying people finding health and sustenance and life itself at Jesus' hands.

Present Gospel

The first thing to be said about the Johannine handling of the source is that it takes what is fundamentally a christological document—one containing at most soteriological implication, but always explicitly focusing on Jesus' messianic stature—and makes it instead overtly and centrally soteriological. A comprehensive way of characterizing 4E's redaction of the source is simply this movement away from an exclusive attention to christology and toward soteriology.

In correcting the source's all but single-minded preoccupation with christology 4E does not suppress that christology. (See, e.g., part 1, sec. 3, on the redaction of 2:11.) Christ is central for 4E, just as for SG.[54] But christology is no longer central; it is now secondary to soteriology. That is, it is not sufficient in the Evangelist's eyes simply to believe in Jesus' messiahship; christology by itself—such was the theological burden of the source—is inadequate. For 4E one must not only believe, yes, "that Jesus is the Christ, the Son of God," but also understand that so to believe is to "have life in his name" (20:31c).

If we consider in detail the Johannine redaction of SG with respect to soteriology, we can put the same three questions used in summarizing the source and thereby quickly narrow the issues. The first question, namely, of 4E's interpretation of the death of Jesus, is a problem in its own right, to be taken up in D, in this part. Here we are concerned not with what might be called objective soteriology (what God has done to save the world) but with a subjective one: what salvation amounts to from the human standpoint (the third question).

To the second question, how do human beings come to salvation? 4G gives a rather different answer from the predecessor's: There is no necessary equation between belief and salvation, between seeing signs—even

---

54. On this passage, see further just below. I want to be clear about both the continuity and the discontinuity between source and canonical Gospel on this score, since Woll (*Johannine Christianity*, 157) somewhat misunderstands what I have said in the article that preceded the present discussion ("Christology"). He characterizes the relation I see between pre-Johannine and Johannine authors as "polemical," a term I would not use.

believing in them—and perceiving Jesus' glory, having "life in his name." Yet at the same time, faith for 4G, just as in a simpler way for the source, somehow *is* salvation if it is legitimate. All this we have already seen (see B, in this part).

We are left, therefore, with the third question and the one for which the source provides so much unrealized potential: What does salvation amount to?

A look at the incidence of the Greek terms underlying the idea of salvation does not lead us very far. True, unlike the source 4G occasionally uses *sōzein* (six times), and also *sōtēria* and *sōtēr* (once each),[55] but—in the words of Foerster (*"sōzō, k.t.l.,"* 997)—"the theological distinctiveness of John's Gospel does not come to expression" in the use of such terms. Instead of them, 4E prefers a number of poetic metaphors, the most important of which is "life," and particularly "eternal" life. Various writers have sketched the importance and meaning of this term in the Johannine vocabulary.[56] Here we want to show what insight redaction criticism can shed on the matter. We begin with the striking clause added by 4G to the concluding lines of the source. The present Gospel was written, it tells its readers, not only so that they may believe in Jesus' messiahship, but also and supremely "that believing you may have life in his name" (20:31b). 4E can thus summarize the purpose of the entire Gospel.

We are not surprised by this declaration; already in a number of places it is prepared for.[57] In fact, a close look at the prologue and the way 4G integrates the opening lines of the source with the traditional christological hymn shows in part how this idea arose. In 1:7 the Evangelist takes up the source's understanding of the Baptist's role of witness and further defines it by the insertion of v. 7b: John came "to bear witness to the light." But this passage now interrupts the hymn; and the light, as the immediately preceding lines of the hymn tell us, is none other than "life" (1:4–5). Both of these terms, *phōs* and *zōē*, in their pre-Johannine use in the hymn, probably had a meaning that was more cosmological than soteriological. But in being combined by 4E with the salvation-historical account of the Baptist, with which SG began, they become necessarily soteriological. Life, eternally coexisting with the Father, is intended for human beings as their light and is only accessible to them, in the Johannine scheme of things, because at a particular point in time God sent the Son, prepared for by the Baptist. Salvation as life is available because of this historical fact.

In the two passages we have just examined, from the end and the

55. These latter uses may possibly be pre-Johannine.
56. Most usefully Brown 1:505–8, and Schnackenburg 2:352–61.
57. For example, 3:15—"that whoever believes in him may have eternal life." See also 3:36; 5:21; 6:33, 47.

beginning of the Gospel, respectively, the concept of salvation as life is simply thrown out in summary fashion by means of the Johannine insertions. But in some of the narratives the idea of life was occasioned or even suggested already in the source, so that it can then readily be expanded by 4E. The first and simplest of these is the story of the official's son, where SG twice affirms that the boy "lives" as a result of Jesus' healing word (4:50–51). As we have seen, it is probably 4E who underscores this by declaring it a third time with a literal quotation of Jesus' word (v. 53a). Evidently for the present Gospel it is the salvation Jesus bestows that matters, not simply the physical healing of a dying boy. His life in the profounder sense is focused on, and its universal application (as the second-person plurals in v. 48 show).

In the same chapter, using a traditional story of the woman at the well,[58] 4G introduces a discourse on the subject of "living water" which alone can quench thirst and comes from "a spring welling up to eternal life" (4:10–15; see 7:37–38).

A similar elaboration is found in the Johannine development of the miracle of the loaves (6:26–65). There 4E: (1) distinguishes between perishable food and that which "endures to eternal life" (v. 27), (2) identifies Jesus as himself the "bread of life" that comes down from heaven and permanently satisfies human hunger (vv. 33–35), and finally (3) claims that while the manna in the wilderness brought death, by contrast Jesus gives immortality (vv. 48–51).[59]

Further, in the raising of Lazarus, by inserting the dialogue with Martha, 4E makes Jesus not so much a worker of signs as the bestower of resurrection and life (11:20–27).

Thus simple miracle stories containing a hint of soteriology are taken and from them a comprehensive theological doctrine is made.

For the Evangelist life is set in ontological opposition to death. The origin of this and the other dualities in 4G is a much-disputed question.[60] Without attempting here to answer it fully we can yet observe that a rudimentary form of some of the dualism, in this case the life/death contrast, lay before the Johannine writer already in SG in more than one instance. The boy at Capernaum is "at the point of death" but "lives"; Lazarus is already dead and buried when he is raised. There is no way of

58. At the end of part 1, sec. 7, we considered the possibility that this episode derives from SG. Whether that is true or it is an independent tradition that 4G has used is unimportant for present purposes.

59. And whether the disputed passage 6:51b–58 is to be regarded as Johannine or post-Johannine, for present purposes it can be seen as a further expression of these various ideas, in eucharistic terms.

60. See the intriguing suggestion of Martyn ("Glimpses") that one source of this dualistic way of viewing reality was the sociological and psychological alienation the Johannine community experienced in its expulsion from the synagogue.

knowing whether life or death were thought of by the pre-Johannine author in any but their literal meaning, but it is not a huge step to a spiritual understanding of them.[61]

The most characteristic Johannine word for salvation, then, is life, and ultimately it is not a quality or state to which Jesus brings humans but it is Jesus himself. "I am resurrection and life," he declares (11:25; see 14:6). He does not accomplish, rather, he is salvation. By his coming, as "the Son" sent from "the Father," he both shares in the act of saving and gives to the world the life that he himself is. (Thus, whereas the heightened christology of 4E finds expression in all five words of this I AM-saying, the christology-become-soteriology does so only in the last three words of it.)

This much is quite new in the redaction of SG; yet no one who had grown up with the source as the church's Gospel could, on reading 4E's striking advance beyond it, find offense in what has been added, for it has both drawn out the theological potential hidden in the source and extended it in a way that makes its original meaning clearer and deeper. (Even the christology of the source, for example, is only underscored by the redaction.)

What we have just said does not minimize the differences between the two Gospels, for the Johannine transformation is a radical one. The source is a Gospel of signs, demonstrating Jesus' messiahship; its soteriology is entirely subjected to christology. While this emphasis is not diminished in 4G—on the contrary—it is a Gospel not only of signs, that is, of Jesus and his identity, but much more of salvation itself, of life. Or rather, it finally asserts that the two are one, that to know who Jesus is and to believe in him is to live (20:31). Presumably 4E's experience, and that of the church, showed that christology alone is insufficient; belief in Jesus, unless understood soteriologically, is finally of no account.

So far we have dealt with life as the most important Johannine metaphor for salvation. There are others, as is well known, and some of them are just as clearly rooted in the source. We can look at them more briefly.

However problematic a redaction-critical analysis of the prologue must be, given the uncertainty of the source question there, we cannot fail to pay attention to the phrase "grace and truth," which occurs twice in a handful of verses (1:14, 17) and seems to me most likely to stem from 4E's own hand. Both its origin and precise meaning are debated, but that it is meant to express the very essence of salvation in all its plenitude is beyond dispute.[62] "Grace" does not occur again in 4G; "truth," with its cognates, on the other hand, figures prominently.

---

61. The passages promising physical resurrection "at the last day," whether original or not, are peripheral to this chief Johannine affirmation.

62. Notice v. 16 in particular, and *plērēs* in v. 14.

The term appears most often in contexts having nothing to do with source material, but its background must include the traditional story of the Samaritan woman to whom Jesus reveals the truth about herself. From this hint 4E develops the portrait of Jesus as bringing people to salvation by means of his teaching the truth, as the redactional ending of the same story shows: "And many more believed because of his word" (4:41). Later, Jesus' words are said to be not merely a means of salvation but salvation itself; they are "spirit and life" (6:63).[63] Finally Jesus simply identifies truth with himself (14:6; see 18:37).

For the present Gospel, then, Jesus' primary mission is no longer that of wonderworker but teacher and revealer. If the source already suggested this by showing him revealing his identity in the signs, 4G has made the role paramount and given it explicitly salvific impact. Jesus is the Son of Man whom the willing believer will see (1:51); in his signs it is his glory that is manifested (2:11b; see also 1:14c); when he appears to his disciples, both before and after his death, it is not only reassurance that is proffered but his saving presence (6:17b; 21:7).

"Light" is a Johannine metaphor of salvation closely related to truth. Jesus is himself "the light of the world" (8:12; 9:5; 12:46; and see 1:4–5, 9), and when he comes to the disciples in their isolation and darkness he brings safety (6:17–21). The light metaphor may have suggested itself in the first instance because of the source's story of the blind man. That episode has become in 4E's hands not so much a healing as a conversion; the sight the man receives is primarily spiritual. The idea of salvation as seeing, with its many related themes, now permeates the Gospel, running from Nathanael (1:50–51) to Thomas (20:29). (See B.3, in this part, on "seeing and therefore believing.") But perhaps the most intensely soteriological instance of all is to be found at the end of the prologue: "No one has ever seen God; the only Son . . . has made [him] known" (1:18).

We could go on to look at other metaphors for salvation—for example, knowledge, with its opposites ignorance and misunderstanding; these too have been occasioned by episodes in SG (e.g., 2:9, 20–21). But it will be more profitable at this point to look in greater detail at 4G's relation to the implicit soteriology that we saw to be already present in the source's miracle stories. In general 4E fails to take up and draw out many of these elements. They are allowed to stand but, clearly, other concerns predominate.

This is true in the first instance of the miracles of abundance. At Cana what is important now is not the astounding miracle but the splendor of Jesus' self-revelation (2:11b). Again, in the miracle of the loaves it matters

---

63. This is repeated in v. 68 in slightly different form. Peter says to Jesus, "You have the words of eternal life," which is Johannine paraphrase for the probably traditional confession in the next verse ("You are the Holy One of God").

not that a great crowd is fed so much as "that nothing be lost" of the bread left over (6:12c).[64] In both stories, then, the physical preoccupation of the older tradition, itself concerned in some way with salvation, yields to more symbolic soteriology.[65]

The two stories of healing in Johannine handling come in for considerable change of meaning. Not that they are altered internally—their pre-Johannine form stands more nearly intact than in some of the other miracles—but rather they are transformed into mere occasions for extended controversy between Jesus and "the Jews" (the discourses in chaps. 5 and 9). The point is no longer primarily that salvation, in the form of healing, comes to individuals, but that in the face of these happenings many do not believe and so stand in contrast to salvation (see further, just below, on the phrase "the Jews").

Finally and similarly, in the stories of resurrection, what is now at stake is not the rescue of two people from death—note how in both cases Jesus seems to resist the appeal of need (4:48; 11:6; see also 2:4)—but the revelation which the miracles convey and the faith thereby engendered. In this way the salvific character of the two stories is all but forgotten on the individual level, but at the same time radically broadened and deepened. In the healing of the official's son, the source affirmed already that not only was the boy healed but that the father and "his whole household" (4:53) came to belief as well. 4G further extends the circle of people affected by the miracle; in v. 48 through the official he challenges perhaps the whole of Galilee ("You people won't believe . . .") so that when he and his household do believe the test has obviously been met. Similarly, in the raising of Lazarus the context has been widened; Martha, even more than Lazarus himself, now stands for all to whom Jesus brings resurrection and life.

We come back in these stories, then, to the metaphor of life with which we began. In it is comprehended the nature of Johannine salvation and the end point of all Jesus' miracles.

There remain two soteriological questions that are peculiarly Johannine. The first is the question of the realm of salvation: Who is saved? and, especially, where? in what context?

Though the question evidently did not occur to the author of SG, we have already asked it and it was obvious what the answer would be. Salvation comes to those, presumably Jews in the synagogue, who believe

---

64. The meaning of the clause is disputed, but it certainly looks forward both to the ensuing discussion about food that perishes (6:27—the same verb) and to the promise that Jesus not lose any of his own (6:39; 18:9).

65. The same is true, even more clearly, of the way that what was probably the source's third miracle, of bounty, in chap. 21 becomes an epiphany: the catch of fish is unimportant compared to the risen Jesus' self-revelation. Whether the redactor here is 4E or a later editor the motif is the same as the Johannine one just explored.

in Jesus as Messiah. The issue of Gentile faith is evidently not relevant, so that the "all" of 1:7c, just as the second-person plural of 20:31—thus at both the very opening and the closing of the work—must refer only to Israel.[66] Unlike 4G, the source was not forced to question this traditional context of salvation.

The present Gospel is no more concerned with the Jewish/Gentile question as such than the predecessor. The term "nation," in its plural form the Jewish designation for Gentiles, always refers to Israel in 4G. *Hoi Ioudaioi* has for 4E not an ethnic but a purely religious meaning; its opposite is not the Gentiles, but Jesus' "own," that is, Christians. (This is true whatever is meant by "the Greeks" of 12:20.) That 4E poses this new contrast between Jews and Christians, presumably because of the rift between church and synagogue experienced by the Johannine community since the source was written, forces the question of the realm of salvation. And the issue is just that, a contrast between two realms.[67] "The Jews" stand somehow outside salvation for the Johannine author. That "salvation is from the Jews" (4:22) means only that it had its historical origin in Judaism. Though the possibility that individual Jews, even leaders among them, will become believers is always kept in mind, "the Jews" as a whole represent "the world," which most often in 4G has a negative meaning. (See F, in this part.)

Yet the two realms are not set in an ontological opposition, like that between light and darkness, truth and falsehood. "The world" is both the realm in which Jesus is rejected and at the same time that to which he comes as savior.[68] Similarly it is among *hoi Ioudaioi* that Jesus properly works and in whose place *(Ioudaia)* he finds his home (4:44). Whatever reinterpretation is required, 4G can comfortably include both 4:22 (Salvation is from the Jews) and the probably traditional confession of 4:42 (Jesus as savior of the world). Thus the Gospel is not, in any ordinary sense, either anti-Jewish (but see F, in this part) or otherworldly. Yet it was the failure of "the Jews," of "the world," to believe in Jesus that caused 4E to deal with salvation as a problem.[69] They are consequently made to

---

66. Prof. David Flusser has suggested to me that the much-debated phrase "Salvation is from the Jews" (4:22), together with the intra-Palestinian rivalry between Mount Zion and Mount Gerizim reflected in the accompanying conversation, is pre-Johannine and more appropriate to the milieu of SG than of 4G. This is quite plausible. For the Johannine understanding of the phrase, see below.

67. So rightly Lattke, "Erlöser," 18.

68. Lattke ("Erlöser," 23) seems to me mistaken in attempting to maintain such a radical dichotomy by excluding the crucial text 3:16–17 (in particular, "God sent the Son into the world . . . that the world might be saved through him"; see also 12:47) as a mere piece of tradition not representing 4E's own mind.

69. It is mainly in connection with these phrases that 4G uses the term "sin": 8:21–24; 9:41; 15:22–24; 16:8–9; see 2:23–25. See also B, in this part, on the failure of the signs.

represent the other side of salvation, the refusal to be saved. Strictly speaking they stand in the Gospel as foils, serving to show by contrast what salvation is. (See further F, in this part, on the meaning of *hoi Ioudaioi.*)

Who are saved? All who believe, showing themselves thereby not to belong to "the world." (There, in a nutshell, is the ambiguity of the Johannine doctrine of election.) 4G thus retains the soteriological criterion of SG, but the locus of salvation is not the synagogue, not the world, though the revelation has taken place there. Where it is is harder to say, for 4G never uses the concept church as a realm over against the world. (See E, in this part.) Its view of salvation is in a way sectarian, but it is not sufficient to say, with Lattke, that salvation for 4E finally means "redemption [note the shift] from the world." The Johannine Savior does not come to separate human beings from within the world; rather, the world is both the object of his mission (12:47) and that which he has "overcome" (16:33). But since the world finally separates itself from the believers in the face of this revelation, the real locus of salvation is Jesus present with "his own."[70] If there are more ecumenical thrusts in the Gospel[71] they are finally overpowered by the preoccupation with the Christian's isolation in a generally hostile world.

The other issue in which 4G goes beyond its source is the question of the *time* of salvation. We defer consideration of it to a separate section (see E, in this part).

In conclusion, we remind ourselves that it is especially salvation that informs the Johannine redaction of SG. It has transformed a single-mindedly christological document, all the while maintaining that original thrust, into still more a Gospel of salvation.

---

70. We remember the important promise that Jesus will not lose any of his followers (18:9).

71. Notably in 1:29 (the Lamb of God "who takes away the sin of the world") or 11:51–52 (the prophecy that Jesus would die "for the nation, and not the nation only").

D. The Death of Jesus

The stance of 4E's predecessor toward the death of Jesus is simple but ambiguous. In this respect it is like other instances of early Christian thought so far as we can identify them (e.g., Paul's early letters [2 and 1 Thessalonians] or the passion source underlying Mark). For all these thinkers the crucifixion is not at all the center of theological concentration. At best it is to be accounted for and somehow accepted but hardly embraced; at worst it is an event that is to be ignored or explained away. It is always the shameful deed of humans directed against God's Messiah. For these early interpretations, in contrast, for example, to the mature Paul (Galatians, Romans) or the Markan evangelist, the death plays no overarching role, and this is certainly the case in the pre-Johannine source, and obviously in the case of a Signs Source in the narrow sense (SQ). In the miracle stories there is no indication, or even hint, of the death that awaits the wonderworking Messiah, and equally in their preface (the witness of the Baptist and the conversion of the first disciples) we find no suggestion, like that in the Synoptic Gospels, that he who preceded Jesus or those who follow him will suffer the same fate as he.[72] If we have to do with a Signs Gospel, with passion account appended to signs (SG), there was in it no preparation for Jesus' death even at the end of the public ministry, such as the predictions of the crucifixion and resurrection in the Synoptics. Certainly none of the allusions to Jesus' hour, his time of glorification, that now punctuate 4G were to be found in the source.

In the pre-Johannine passion narrative itself (PQ) what binds the episodes into one is no sense of the completion of a purpose (apart from the highly schematic motif of prophecy fulfillment) but only the inevitable succession of one event upon another, leading to the awful end. When that end arrives it is not commented on, as in Mark with the rent Temple veil and the centurion's confession, in Matthew with the cataclysmic signs, or

---

72. One might think to find a hint of Jesus' death in the phrase "Lamb of God," used by John the Baptist in directing his own followers to the discipleship of Jesus. But, as we have observed more than once, the cryptic designation has only a christological thrust for the pre-Johannine author; any allusion to Jesus as victim is simply ignored.

in Luke with the pathos of the departing crowds. Rather, the whole story is told with matter-of-fact directness. The death is reached as swiftly as possible, leading then immediately to the resurrection story.

At the pre-Johannine level it is preeminently the events of Easter that make the death of Jesus tolerable: the resurrection reverses the crucifixion, it explains away Jesus' incomprehensible execution. Dealing with the death in this way is central already in Jesus' prediction in the Temple, in what was perhaps the opening episode of the pre-Johannine passion account: "Destroy this sanctuary and in three days I shall raise it up" (2:19). The saying points forward to the possibility of Jesus' death at the hands of others ("If you destroy . . ."), and by Jesus' prediction in a way permits it; but at the same time it points chiefly beyond that death, to Jesus' greatest sign, and only thereby makes that death acceptable. The author has taken an old saying, possibly of the destruction of Herod's Temple, and by a play on words made it an announcement, yes, of Jesus' problematic death but, more prominently, of the resolution of that theological problem in his resurrection.

In the story of the Anointing at Bethany, too, the nearing death is adumbrated. Jesus declares that the act is "for the day of [his] burial" (12:7) and possibly goes on to observe that "you do not always have me" (v. 8). But the story is carefully introduced with the reminder (v. 1a) of the death of Lazarus which has already resulted in resurrection. If Lazarus's dying points forward to the death of Jesus, his restored life even more reassures of Easter.

Thus, even at the outset of the pre-Johannine passion narrative there is no theology of the approaching end but rather an attempt to come to terms with it by denying its finality. This perhaps reflects the earliest Christian responses to the events of that problematic Friday, once it had to be addressed theologically.

Nevertheless, the source does subject the event of Jesus' death itself—the unavoidable fact of it—to theological reflection in the process of redacting the passion story that comes to it from tradition. If God, or rather Jesus himself, reversed the crucifixion on Easter day, nevertheless the Friday, though not Good, is in some way not altogether incomprehensible in God's dealings with humanity. However painful and baffling, it is yet seen as prepared for in God's economy: *it fulfills prophecy.* In this way it not only is, after all, acceptable, appropriable by the Christian; it also comes to have a limited theological significance in itself. This is not to say that the death of Jesus accomplishes anything soteriologically (it is surprising how little such a perception is explicit even in the Synoptic Gospels), but in fulfilling what had earlier been prophesied the cross comes to make sense as part of the plan, the drama, that God was accomplishing in the appearance of his Messiah. It remains a terrible human crime, but one that can be understood as accepted by God and thus taken up into the Gospel message. God foreknew, and thus through the prophets (and the psalmist) foreordained, the otherwise shameful death of the Messiah.

The source has no overt salvation history. At most it takes for granted that what happened in Jesus' lifetime was part of God's intent in human history; such was implied already in the Jewish concept of messiahship, which SG presupposes. But there is little pre-Johannine reference to earlier events in a divine plan, and what there is is entirely proleptic, pointing ahead always to the events of Jesus' life. The Baptist appears, "sent from God," as the beginning of the Christian story of salvation. The preparatory role of past figures in Israel's history—Moses, Elijah, the prophets—is touched on but never examined. But in connection with Jesus' death a sort of minimal salvation-historical perspective surfaces.[73] Insofar as that death, with the events surrounding it, is understood as the fulfillment of scripture, it comes to consummate God's preparation for it earlier in Israel's experience. Specific prophecies are assembled and cited to explain what takes place at the end of Jesus' life. This device of prophecy fulfillment is used in the source at least five times,[74] and brief as it is in each case it carries substantial theological weight. We therefore now examine each of the instances in some detail.

1. At the beginning of the events that end in Jesus' burial—we cannot say "Jesus' cross" since the form of his execution is not emphasized—in the Restoration of the Temple, we are told by means of scripture that Jesus' end is both inevitable and acceptable: **It is written, Zeal for your house will consume me** (2:17, from Ps. 69:10). Just possibly it is Jesus himself who announces this, as continuation of his authoritative assertion in v. 16 ("You shall not make my Father's house a house of business"); more likely the author speaks in this way directly to the reader. In either case, the predecessor is surely responsible for adding the comment (see part 1, sec. 10, on 2:17), and it explains that Jesus' prophetic deed in the Temple had been revealed beforehand in scripture itself; it took place, we

---

73. Grech ("Testimonia," 323) rightly observes that the device of prophecy fulfillment, which we are about to examine in the case of 4G's predecessor, unmistakably involves "a salvation-historical pre-understanding" on the part of any writer who uses it.

74. In 2:17; 12:14–15; 19:24, 28, 36–37; probably also 12:38a; and see 1:23 and 20:9. Note that citation by the narrator, the implied author, is distinctive of PQ. This is the case in the five passages listed (with the possible exception of 2:17); further, certainly at 12:38a, perhaps in 1:23, and also somehow in 20:9 (without actual quotation). In all other cases in 4G it is either Jesus who cites the prophecy (6:45; 7:38; [8:17]; 10:34; 13:18 [possibly a traditional citation, once a part of SG, but 4G has rewritten it, putting it on Jesus' lips]; 15:25; 17:12; in some of these cases Jesus speaks in a most Johannine fashion of "your law" or "their law"), or his interlocutors (6:31; 7:42) quote the scripture; and on one occasion the disciples "remember" it (2:17 [in its present form]; see also 2:22 and 12:16).

267

are to understand, **because** [*hoti*][75] **it is written.** . . . But not only is Jesus' provocation in the Temple explained, so also is his death that here is set in motion. By a play on the word **consume** and an alteration to future tense[76] both Jesus' "zeal for [God's] house" and his resulting death are accounted for. In the working out of divine history he is filled with a passion that motivates his messianic act of purification—and at the same time he will be destroyed by it. Thereby his death is interpreted beforehand as inevitable and hence tolerable. Such is the theological freight carried by this single notice.

2. The next such citation of scripture appears, in the original arrangement of the source, almost immediately after the first: in the theological comment (12:37–40) that must have followed the Officials' Plot (which itself stemmed from the Temple Cleansing). Isaiah 53:1 is quoted, and also the famous Isa. 6:10. As we saw in part 1, sec. 11, the citation formula here is the most radical of the various versions used: these things happened "so that the word of Isaiah might be fulfilled" (v. 38a). The passage has a major role in the redactional arrangement of tradition by the pre-Johannine author; it forms the bridge between signs and passion and accounts for the sharp discrepancy between the two portraits of Jesus' life they convey. Just as the original ending of SQ now completes the combined Signs Gospel—and, incidentally, overcomes the paradox expressed here—so this passage brings to an end the unclouded messianic success of Jesus' signs and both introduces and allows for the dark events that now begin to unfold.

3. A scripture citation is found in almost the next episode, the Triumphal Entry into Jerusalem (12:15). Once again this notice appears to be the work of the source's author.[77] The Synoptic tradition lacked explicit quotation of the Zechariah passage that clearly underlies this episode; only Matthew, consistent with its interest in such proof texts, adds it.[78] In SG

75. Or, conjecturally, "as" (*kathōs*).

76. The Masoretic Text of Ps. 69:10 has the perfect. While LXXB shows a future, it is usually held to be an assimilation to this passage in 4G; the parallel phrase in Ps. 119:139 has the aorist. See further, Freed, *Quotations*, 8–10.

77. The implicit use of Ps. 118:25–26 ("Blessed is he who comes in the name of the Lord") in the crowd's acclamation in v. 13b is no doubt traditional. To this the source has added as its own comment the explicit fulfillment of Zech. 9:9 in vv. 14–15 that we here examine.

78. This has occasionally been understood as suggesting a dependence here on Matthew, but I attribute it instead to a coincident interest in the scriptural basis for the event. The explicit use of the prophecy is all but called for by the story itself, and Matt. 21:4–5 cites it in rather different form, at a different point in the story, and with a different citation formula. So, as elsewhere, there is no reason here to posit literary dependence between any of the Synoptics and 4G.

the event is first told and then, as an appended theologoumenon, we hear: **As it is written, Fear not, daughter of Zion; behold your king comes, sitting on the colt of an ass** (Zech. 9:9).[79] Once again an event is explained by its prophetic preparation—Jesus fulfills scripture in his entry into the city as Messiah—and at the same time his end is accounted for. The latter is less evident here, and we might understand the relevance to Jesus' death to be only the very general one provided by the passion context of the story. But two allusions within the quotation subtly suggest a passion reference. Though not explicit, as it is in Matthew, the lowliness of this Messiah is evident from his foreordained posture, seated on a young donkey, and is perhaps thus consistent with his coming subjection to an ignominious death. The substitution of the phrase "Fear not" (where Zechariah reads "Rejoice") both sounds an ominous note and at once seeks to dissipate it. The fact that these events fulfill scripture reassures the reader and makes more tolerable the catastrophe that is about to take place.

The remaining citations, three of them, are found in brief compass in the crucifixion scene: 19:24b, 28b, 36–37. Thus at the point of Jesus' death itself the theological concentration intensifies. Correspondingly the assertion of divine necessity, implied only in the first two citations, now becomes explicit. Each time we learn that the prophesied events take place **in order** that the scripture be fulfilled. In each case the very literalness of the fulfillment underscores this necessity.

4. In the first instance of the three (19:24), the narration ignores the redundancy of Hebrew poetic parallelism ("They divided my garments among them / For my clothing they cast lots"—Ps. 22:19). Instead it meticulously shows the soldiers on the one hand singling out the garments (*himatia*) among the four of them and on the other deciding to throw dice for Jesus' seamless tunic (*chitōn*)[80] rather than tear it. The little episode has evidently been written backward from the citation with which it now ends. The syntax joining description of the soldiers' acts with the psalm quotation is not altogether smooth[81] but the meaning is clear; all of these things happened—happened solely, we might say—"so that the scripture might be fulfilled." The soldiers' heartless and careful greed is remembered in detail, but only its theological significance matters.

5. That Jesus' cry of thirst from the cross (19:28) fulfills prophecy—the second instance—is stated only parenthetically and the prophecy fulfilled

---

79. Syntactically, the clause is a continuation of v. 14, but as comment it has a kind of independence comparable to 2:17.

80. Corresponding rather artificially to the singular noun "clothing" (*himatismos*) of the quotation.

81. The half-verse is a dangling dependent clause: "In order that the scripture. . . ."

is only alluded to,[82] but it is no less explicit that Jesus' ordeal, and the cruel offering of vinegar or sour wine, takes place simply **so as to complete the scripture.**[83]

6. The third and climactic, and the most horrifying, portrayal of prophecy fulfillment in the death scene surrounds the violence contemplated and done to Jesus' dead body. Once again the account has apparently been composed with the scripture, this time a pair of passages, in mind. On finding that Jesus had already died, the soldiers do not in fact break his legs (a practice apparently designed brutally to hasten death). Instead one of them pierces his side with the spear, causing a wound which though posthumous is no less shocking (19:32–34).

But the scriptural justification for these offensive acts is dominant, and the by-now-familiar theological affirmation finds its fullest and most sonorous expression here, at the end of the account of Jesus' arrest, trial, and execution, with only his burial remaining: **These things took place—** all of them, the whole event of Jesus' death, apparently, as well as the details just recounted—**so that the scripture might be fulfilled** (v. 36a).[84]

Then the two passages themselves are quoted. The source for the first ("His bone shall not be broken") is not certain, for the reading here has apparently been adapted. Either a psalm of suffering (34:20) or one of the directives for preparation of the Paschal Lamb (Exod. 12:46; Num. 9:12) is referred to, but the precise OT context is irrelevant. It is the divine necessity operating in Jesus' death that matters, and that has already been displayed in the minute fulfillment of the quoted scripture. One might see the preservation of Jesus' body from assault as evidence of God's intervention, protecting the Messiah, if it were not for the spear wound that follows. Evidently the author's sole intent is simply to justify what happens—to explain the event as a whole by means of the divine necessity of a few particular details.

So also with the second half of the double citation ("They shall look on the one they have pierced"—Zech. 12:10). There seems to be no interest here in irony, pathos, or even blame, certainly no suggestion of beholding God's revelation in the cross (the latter will perhaps be the Johannine

---

82. Unless the one Greek word translated "I thirst" is simultaneously both cry and quotation, but then no OT passage quite fits. (The general description of thirst described in Ps. 22:15 is sometimes suggested.) More likely the passage in mind is not quoted, and then Ps. 69:21 ("For my thirst they gave me vinegar to drink") fits both the cry itself and in particular the soldiers' response to the cry in the following verse.

83. The variation in verb here—"completed" (*teleiōthēi*) in place of "fulfilled" (*plērōthēi*)— may be Johannine, in line with 4E's use of the verb in vv. 28 and 30. On the other hand, it may be a pre-Johannine synonym for "fulfilled," on the basis of which 4E added the double use of it.

84. The finality is emphasized by the introductory conjunction "For" (softened in a few MSS to "And" [*de*], probably because of 4E's insertion of v. 35).

understanding). Rather, once again, the function of the quotation is only to explain and make acceptable, and the means to that end is the recognition that all, even the smallest detail, had been foreordained and that therefore all was allowable, comprehensible.

What shall we make of this device, the repeated use of OT "testimonies," as they are technically called? We said that it is the chief way the source comes to terms with the fact of Jesus' death, not simply viewing it as having been reversed, and so undone, by the resurrection, but asking how it could be understood in itself. The way that question is answered is essentially apologetic, attempting to resolve the theological, and indeed psychological, problem presented by the crucifixion. Jesus had died the death of a common criminal, and nothing in messianic expectation had prepared the first Christians for such an end's coming to the one they believed, despite the crucifixion, to be Messiah. The contradiction had to be faced and overcome. The very telling of the story of his death, perhaps the earliest connected account assembled by Christians, is itself a recognition of the problem, and the telling had somehow to resolve the problem.

It is apparent that the OT, the Christians' only scripture, was influential at many points in the reconstruction of the story. Once it was read in the light of Jesus' fate, any detail, especially in the psalms of innocent suffering but not only there, might be understood as a puzzle piece making up part of the biography of the Messiah, the plan of what had to be. This implied connection between prophecy and the events of Jesus' death would thus have been present already in the tradition available to our author as she or he either assembles or, more likely, adapts that tradition. So in this explicit citing of the biblical passages the logic of the underlying hermeneutic principle is made central and forthright.

At the beginning and end of the story this basic fact of divine causation, of preparations laid down long ago coming at last to pass, comes boldly to the surface: At the outset Jesus purged the Temple and so initiated his official persecution "because it is written" that this would occur, and his Entry into Jerusalem, unmistakably conveying his messiahship, took place "as it is written." But especially at the end the outrages visited on him—the callous plundering of his only remaining possessions, vinegar given for his agonizing thirst, the mistreatment of his dead body—were in accord with prophecy and so took place fittingly. "These things occurred in order to fulfill scripture."

Therefore all was somehow allowable; the problem of Jesus' death is somehow overcome. Further, since it had to be, since it was part of the divine plan for human history, it was in some sense even to be welcomed. Jesus' crucifixion is not seen as good; it accomplishes nothing positive. It remains a necessary evil. But because necessary it is at least satisfactory

271

that it took place, that the drama was seen through to the end, to be capped—and reversed—by the resurrection.

There are two other pre-Johannine occurrences of the motif of OT fulfillment. One is also in the passion account, or rather its sequel; on Easter morning Peter left the empty tomb "for as yet he did not know the scripture that [Jesus] must rise from the dead" (20:9). The lack of an actual citation of scripture suggests that the author here is wanting only to show that if Jesus' horrifying death was necessitated in stark detail by the divine plan, so much more was the resurrection that reversed it.[85]

At the very beginning of SQ we are told that the Baptist is the voice crying in the wilderness "as the prophet Isaiah said" (1:23).[86] Thus the combined SG—like, in narrower scope and greater detail, the passion account itself—is framed by prophecy fulfillment.

The same motif of divine necessity and a calm sense of acceptance is conveyed by Jesus himself as PQ portrays him. Taking altogether different form from Jesus' predictions of the passion in the Synoptics, nevertheless a similar perspective appears in this account as well. At the Temple Cleansing Jesus announces, obliquely but clearly, that he will both die and be raised: "Destroy this temple[87] and in three days I will raise it up" (2:19). Similarly in the Anointing at Bethany Jesus quietly prepares his disciples for what is to come. What Mary does is "for the day of my burial" (12:7). And possibly he adds that "you do not always have me" (v. 8).[88] Very likely also—in the original account of the Last Supper though it is now not recoverable—Jesus is portrayed as having predicted that Judas would betray him, Peter deny him, and the disciples forsake him (see part 1, sec. 14).

At the arrest Jesus willingly gives himself up (18:4–5) and openly announces his acceptance of "the cup" awaiting him (v. 11). In the Synoptic accounts the latter appears instead in the intensely private scene in Gethsemane, and the struggle there depicted is at most only faintly reflected in SG (12:27). The impression is one of unquestioning acquiescence, indeed cooperation, in his coming death and is unique to this

---

85. The resurrection tradition was originally distinct from the story of Jesus' suffering, but the same theological motif has been added, probably prior to SG.

86. This instance is possibly traditional (see, e.g., Mark 1:2) and then not the product of redaction as in the other cases. This might account for the fact that it does not share the wording "as it is written . . . ," found both in Mark and later in the source itself.

87. The force of the imperative here is at least conditional (If you destroy . . .) and more likely either predictive (Since you will destroy . . .) or even permissive (Go ahead and destroy . . .). Jesus' awareness of what is to befall him seems to be implied.

88. The imminence of Jesus' death in this otherwise warm occasion of affection and loyalty for him is perhaps also hinted at by the double reminder at the outset that Lazarus, one of the hosts of the meal, was "the dead man" whom Jesus had raised "from the dead" (v. 1).

account. Perhaps it provided the germ for 4G's subsequent portrayal of Jesus magisterially presiding over his own end.

But thereafter, having willingly allowed his arrest, Jesus submits to the mercy of the forces that would destroy him. He is mistreated in the house of the high priest and mocked and scourged before Pilate, during which he mostly keeps silent. At the execution his anguish is not emphasized, nor (quite possibly) does he utter significant words from the cross. All that occurs had to take place and so, evidently, its recounting is appropriately factual, unemotional, accepting.

Does the death as such have no significance then? Certainly it is not salvific. If Jesus' condemnation is "in place of the people," as Caiaphas perhaps declared (11:50), that is only in explanation for the reader of the authorities' unwarranted rationalization. Very little is made, in fact, of their responsibility for his death; it is assumed but hardly emphasized.[89] At most Jesus' death is faintly paradoxical. The charge placarded on his cross declares to the believer that despite (hardly because of) his degrading death he is Messiah, **King of the Jews.** This christological affirmation,[90] though not the only thrust of the passion account, would have afforded the otherwise anomalous combining of the signs tradition or a Signs Source in the strict sense, with the passion tradition, to produce what we call SG, a combination that I believe to have occurred at the hands of the pre-Johannine author. The good news that this Gospel proclaims is first and last Jesus' messiahship, self-evident in his signs and even discernible at his execution (though not yet with the forthright emphasis on that paradox that we find in Mark).

As we said to start with, the death of Jesus for the predecessor is ambiguous. It is wholly ignored in his public ministry, finally explained away by the resurrection, and only with difficulty accepted as inevitable—in OT prophecy and Jesus' own predictions. It is not yet his "passion,"[91] the cross is no metaphor of humankind's redemption or joyous reminder of the Messiah's love, the Friday is in no sense Good. Yet that execution is understandable, appropriable. The story can be told in detail, and if the motive is what is technically called apologetic the telling nevertheless is done without embarrassment. It has become a part of the Gospel.

---

89. They are acting in fulfillment of Scripture. It will be 4E who assigns the blame and in a way that surpasses all the other Evangelists.

90. As we have observed, a christological motif is implicit in the words of Jesus throughout the passion story, all of which in one way or another call attention to his person.

91. We have used this term only as a conventional designation for the composite tradition of the events surrounding Jesus' death, not with any of the later theological connotations of the redemptive, vicarious suffering of Jesus. Even the divine necessity accruing to the death does not yet make it, as in the Synoptic Gospels, Jesus' appointed destiny, a path he must deliberately follow.

273

Present Gospel

Käsemann has maintained that the death of Jesus in 4G—that is, for 4E—is relatively unimportant, present only as a concession to tradition; the passion account is "a mere postscript which had to be included" but which 4E could not "fit . . . organically into his work" (*Testament*, 7). This assertion, perhaps intentionally, has provoked renewed attention to the place of Jesus' death in Johannine theology. Mostly it has met with disagreement.[92] Martyn helpfully observes that such truth as it contains applies not to 4G but to the pre-Johannine source.[93]

If when 4E began to write there were available two still-separate traditions—signs and passion—and that author combined them into the Gospel format recognizable in all its four canonical versions, then clearly 4E took pains to include the death of Jesus in the account of the glorified Son of God. Its role, far from problematic, must then be somehow central. But even if, as I hold to be more likely, 4E found signs and passion already combined, the death was not simply included by default but was itself chosen to display in full preeminence the very glory of Jesus, to crown the whole story of his self-disclosure. As is well known, 4G is unique in this among the Gospels. The resurrection, which elsewhere in Christian thought so universally has the role of revealing Jesus in glory, becomes now only a kind of postscript to the death, ratifying what in the Johannine presentation had already been manifested on the cross.

It is true, as Käsemann says, that there is in 4G no passion journey up to Jerusalem depicted "as a process which leads from lowliness to glory" (*Testament*, 7). (Jesus goes up to Jerusalem a number of times in 4E's portrayal, for reasons that we have still to examine; see F, in this part.) But in fact Jesus is never in this Gospel shown in lowliness at all; from the beginning he is the incarnate Son of God, and his divine glory is always in view. So it is all the more striking that in the very first of the signs—that is, from the start of his ministry, which throughout is really nothing other than his public self-revelation—we hear of his "hour" and that it "has not yet come" (2:4). Into the Cana miracle's traditional timetable of eschatological consummation (the "now" in v. 10) 4E has introduced reference to a still-future time, and it will soon be evident that it is no other than Jesus' glorifying death. In the Gospel there is no progress toward that moment, by natural stages, any more than the disclosure of the messianic secret in Mark is gradual or logical. The glory is both present throughout and

92. For example, Meeks's review of Käsemann, 419.

93. "Source Criticism," 262: "To paraphrase Käsemann's statement . . . and apply it to [SG], the passion comes into view only at the very end, is provided with virtually no preparation, and is overshadowed by Jesus' signs which find their proper climax in his resurrection." I would add only that since it comprises roughly half of the hypothetical SG the passion narrative is somewhat more than appended postscript.

uniquely revealed at the crucifixion. The notice in 2:4, then, and others like it cannot be viewed—in Käsemann's phrase—as only "a few remarks that point ahead to [the crucifixion]"; they have instead signal importance.

In the Temple Restoration, the episode after the wedding at Cana, as 4E has rearranged the source, Jesus' death is focused on—now together with his resurrection. Far from dissipating a traditional concentration on the passion, as Käsemann suggests, 4G here brings it forward into the inauguration of Jesus' earthly activity. This event for the first time forces the attention of "the Jews" on his public deeds, every one of which will again and again provoke their opposition to him, so that the last of the deeds finally ensues in his destruction. But there is no progression, no building up of causation, only a repeated pattern which, once all of Jesus' "works" have been "manifested," will then take its course.

In still the next episode—Jesus' conversation with Nicodemus in chapter 3—the central place of the crucifixion comes more clearly into focus, for the reader if not for this "ruler of the Jews." At the climax of his mystifying words to Nicodemus Jesus introduces the theme of the ascent and descent of the Son of Man (v. 13). The latter is developed at some length in vv. 16–21, probably the most famous passage in the Gospel: the love of God that motivates the sending of his Son into the world. But before attending to that assertion—the initial and fundamental expression of the divine glory—the Johannine Jesus pregnantly points forward to the still-future expression of the same glory, namely, his lifting up (3:14–15). This brief passage is worthy of close inspection.

The Evangelist evidently had available much the same raw materials (in 20:19–23) that Luke used for his account of Jesus' ascent into heaven after the resurrection. In view of the explicit Johannine dogma of Jesus' descent from heaven, such an ascent, a re-ascension, would seem indispensable. It is striking, therefore, that here in chapter 3 the Evangelist chooses not that Easter episode but instead the cross as the consummating moment of Jesus' ascent. The reference to his death is perhaps not at once obvious, but the striking use of the passive voice—**the Son of Man must be lifted up**—gives a strong clue.

This understanding of the saying will be confirmed in the passion account, and in a typically Johannnine way—by showing ahead of time that what will take place is a fulfillment of Jesus' prophecy. Pilate suggests to those who bring Jesus before him that they pass judgment on him themselves, and they ("the Jews") refuse, citing their incapacity to carry out a sentence of death (18:31). But the significance of this claim is not primarily the inevitability of Jesus' fate. Rather, it is that he himself controls what is occurring; the exchange between governor and accusers takes place, we learn, **in order to fulfill the word Jesus had spoken signifying by what kind of death he would die** (v. 32). A Jewish execution, presumably by stoning, would not have shown Jesus' glorification in death; the Roman crucifixion, thus, is taken not as abasement but on the contrary as being "lifted up."

We note here that the pre-Johannine formula—"in order that the scripture might be fulfilled"—is adopted by 4G but applied now to Jesus' own word which here, as in other passages, has an authority equal, in fact probably superior, to the Hebrew Bible's. But returning to Jesus' initial announcement in 3:14 we see that 4E also makes use of scripture, not strictly as prophecy but instead for purposes of typology. The strange story of Num. 21:8–9 becomes a foreshadowing of Jesus' exaltation on the cross: **Just as Moses lifted up the serpent in the wilderness, so must the Son of Man be lifted up.** The salvific effect of Moses' act[94] is paralleled and surpassed; both purpose and consequence of the crucifixion is **eternal life** for anyone who believes.

This soteriological statement is reaffirmed and extended in one of the two later reiterations of the present passage; in 12:32 Jesus solemnly declares, **I, if I am lifted up from the earth, will draw all to me.** A christological resonance is also evident, which the other reiteration makes explicit: **When you have lifted up the Son of Man, then you will know that I AM** (8:28).

We have, then, in this theme of Jesus' "lifting up," which briefly resurfaces three more times in the Gospel, a dense cluster of meaning central to 4G's understanding of Jesus' death.

So far we have examined the first three episodes in the Johannine portrayal of Jesus' ministry—the wedding at Cana, the Temple Cleansing, and the dialogue with Nicodemus—and found that in each of them the death of Jesus is in some way singled out and pointed toward. And in each case motifs are set down that will reemerge at various points in the Johannine presentation of the pre-passion ministry. We saw how the third such motif, the image given to Nicodemus of Jesus' exaltation, is used, and it is well known how the second, that of the Jewish opposition to Jesus, punctuates the Gospel.[95] We need to return to the first motif, that of Jesus' "hour."

In at first declining his mother's request for a miracle Jesus distances himself from her ("Woman, what have I to do with you?") and declares, **My hour has not yet come** (2:4). It is not at once apparent what this means, but it strongly implies that the goal of Jesus' public manifestation is not the working of the miracles that nevertheless provide the structure of

94. In the time of the exodus, anyone who looked at the fiery serpent Moses held up on a pole would avoid God's punishment and live.

95. This appears first even before Jesus is on the scene. The pre-Johannine account of the Baptist's witness has become in 4G a menacing interrogation by those sent "by the Jews" (1:19) and "from the Pharisees" (1:24).

the ministry; it will be something more than them and coming after their completion. And perhaps the reader can sense that Jesus' "hour" connotes both the suffering he must undergo (his hour of testing) and at the same time his greatest moment (his finest hour). Certainly these implications will emerge.

In the next statement of the motif, now as 4E's comment in 7:30, the threat to Jesus from the authorities has become explicit ("They sought to arrest him"), but it cannot be carried out "because his hour had not yet come." Not only does the full expression of his earthly work wait until the proper moment; the human events that precipitate it similarly can have no effect until the right time. All is within a divine timetable, a scenario that will come to its climax precisely at Jesus' death.

Earlier in chapter 7 an exchange between Jesus and his brothers closely related to the foregoing takes place. They urge him to "go to Judea" for the Feast of Succoth to "show the works you are doing" so as "to be known openly" there, to "show yourself to the world" (vv. 3–4). The parallel with their mother's request in chapter 2 is evident but several elements are new: the importance of Judea and, as will appear, specifically Jerusalem, the explicit call for Jesus' self-manifestation, and in v. 5 the evaluation of the brothers' request as reflecting their lack of belief in Jesus (an extension of the distance between him and his mother suggested earlier). All of these elements will contribute to the conception of Jesus' death: it will take place, of course, in Jerusalem, it will be the full manifestation of his purpose to the world, and only some will be able to appropriate it. That the death as unique event is in view here is clear from Jesus' response: **My time[96] has not yet come, but your time is always at hand. The world cannot hate you, but it hates me** (vv. 6–7a). Then, just as Jesus for the moment refused the miracle his mother had proposed, so here for the time being he chooses not to go up to Jerusalem as his brothers had insisted. But in each case once *attention has been drawn to his death*—that is, when the theology has been made clear—the requests can be acceded to; the refusal of the request is only for the purpose of pointing up the central act of his dying. (As so often, plot is totally subservient to message.)

Finally, at the conclusion of the public ministry and the inception of the Last Supper, 4G plangently signals to us that the passion narrative is formally beginning:[97] **Now before the feast of Passover, when Jesus**

---

96. The term used, *kairos*, is even more apt than *hōra* of 2:4 and 7:30 and surely synonymous with it, according to 4E's wont. Similarly the verbs used here and in the reiteration in v. 8 for the time's delay—"not yet at hand" (v. 6), "not yet fulfilled." (v. 8)—paraphrase the assertion—made already twice—that Jesus' hour had "not yet come."

97. Thus 4G incorporates the so-called prelude to the passion, with which the pre-Johannine account of Jesus' death began, backward into the first half of the present Gospel: The Temple Restoration, of course, has been put very early, and the Official Conspiracy, Anointing, and Triumphal Entry now also become part of the culmination of the public ministry; the passion itself, then, is in no way a postscript. It has its own time, its own place in Jesus' story, most carefully prepared for, defined.

277

knew that his hour had come to depart out of this world . . . (13:1). In this solemn introduction several important assertions are made: the death of Jesus is associated with Passover (see below, on 11:51), Jesus himself knows and thus presides over what is to follow, and his "hour," until now postponed, has at last come and is explicitly synonymous with the end of his life.

In all these ways, then, 4E reminds us periodically during the first half of the Gospel that the crowning and unifying event in Jesus' manifestation to the world will be none other than his death. But how is the death itself presented? We have been prepared to understand it both as divinely ordained, in line with SG,[98] and as a glorification, a Johannine contribution. We have now to look at the Johannine portrayal of the event itself, that is, at the redaction within the passion material. We turn back to the episodes of the so-called Prelude to the Passion; though now the climax of the public ministry, they still look forward to the passion soon to begin.

Passing over the Temple Cleansing story, which we have already considered, we come to the Official Conspiracy against Jesus (11:46–53). This once evidently followed immediately on the Temple Cleansing, representing the authorities' response to Jesus' provocative act at the very center of the Jewish cultus. Whether part of an independent PQ (as once it must have been in any case) or already joined to an SQ, at the pre-Johannine level it was the first indication of the conflict that would soon eventuate in Jesus' death. But not so in 4G, and we need to look at that conflict in the first half of the Gospel.

There has been no slow progression of opposition to Jesus; rather, it stands out almost from the first—implicitly in the official treatment of the Baptist and overtly in the response to Jesus in the (now early) Temple Cleansing. Then we see it, in very nearly its full naked force in chapter 5. When Jesus has healed the lame man and it has been reported to "the Jews," the fact that the healing occurred on the Sabbath leads them to "persecute" Jesus (v. 16), and when he identifies his working of the healing with the activity of God ("my Father") they seek "all the more to kill him" (vv. 17–18). Nothing prepares us for the sudden sharpening of theological conflict (the mere healing is all at once taken as an expression of ditheism, Jesus "making himself equal with God"—v. 18b) or for the suggestion that the resolve to do away with Jesus is not new ("all the more"). But it accounts for the vehemence of this opposition, and from it there is no building, only the periodic reminder of its continued presence (7:1, 19,

98. The present Gospel has simply included, like virtually everything in the source so far as we can tell, the pre-Johannine apologetic that all takes place "in order to fulfill the scripture."

25; 8:59; 10:31; 11:8).[99] We have here not historical causality but a portrayal of a cosmic struggle between good and evil necessarily taking place in the events of Jesus' life.

Thus the outcome of the Sanhedrin's meeting, taken up directly from the source, sounds anticlimactic and redundant if read as simply a narration of events: **So from that day they formally decided to put him to death** (11:53).[100] Nor can it be understood, as it is in the other Gospels, as a decision at last actually to arrest Jesus. We have already heard on two occasions of their attempt to seize him (7:30; 10:39)[101] and each time they were prevented: "his hour had not yet come," "he escaped from their hands." They are but players on a stage, and the play is not to be understood on the level of cause and effect, leading slowly and steadily to the denouement. Rather, the conflict between Jesus and "the Jews" is stylized and two-dimensional.

But in what was said at the Sanhedrin's meeting, as 4G has shaped it, we glimpse something new of the Johannine understanding of Jesus' death. On the one hand the authorities[102] are filled with fear and despair, faced as they are with Jesus' inexorable effect on the people: **What are we to do? . . . All will believe in him and the Romans will come . . .** (11:47–48). This vestige of political concern is no longer apposite in 4E's day, after the catastrophe of A.D. 70; only the religious fear is real. The Evangelist depicts it as craven and ignorant. Caiaphas himself tells them, **You know nothing at all, you do not understand** (vv. 49–50). Even the counsel that he goes on to express—**It is expedient that one man die for the people lest the whole nation perish** (v. 50)[103]—is said **not on his own accord but being high priest that year he prophesied** (v. 51). So Caiaphas too is simply an unwitting player in the predestined drama.

On the other hand 4G adds considerably to the significance of Jesus' death. Caiaphas's "prophecy" in 11:51 means to convey to the reader a soteriological understanding; Jesus would die "for the nation," where the

99. This opposition will eventually broaden out to include the intent to put Lazarus to death as well (12:10).

100. The Sanhedrin here enacts as if for the first time (the abruptness in the source still comes through) what on the Johannine level had been policy all along.

101. And the attempt will be repeated still again, immediately after this scene, at 11:57.

102. Their description here—"chief priests and Pharisees"—reflects the two levels of the Johannine drama, the time of the historical Jesus, when only the priests would have had authority to convoke the Sanhedrin, and 4E's own time, when only the Pharisees remained as Jewish leaders.

103. His words are probably traditional, reflecting a situation prior to the Jewish war, when "the Romans" could still "come and destroy our Holy Place." And in that context, as we saw (part 1, sec.11), Jesus' death "for the people" would have meant only "instead of them."

preposition now surely means "on behalf of." It would be not merely a substitutionary death but now a fully redemptive one. We cannot know very precisely what is in view here, for 4E does not spell it out but instead further builds on it in the next verse (v. 52). Very likely the background here is the sacrificial theology surrounding Passover. The present Gospel has earlier extended the source's bare christological title **Lamb of God,** which would have connoted at most a substitutionary sacrifice, by adding the qualifying clause **who takes away the sin of the world** (1:29), and we can surmise that something of that meaning is intended here in the notion of Jesus' dying "for the nation." Though Judaism has become the Johannine Jesus' opponent, and indeed because of that, his death must and will deal with that sin, one unknown to SG (see C, Source, in this part, on repentance).

But 4G does not leave the matter there. In v. 52 it adds the comment: **And not for the nation only, but to gather into one the children of God who are scattered abroad.** Does this all-important verse seek only to assure that "the children of God" includes Diaspora as well as Palestinian Jews? Or does it go beyond Jewish categories—all the while affirming the original soteriological context that "the nation" possessed—to think of a new people of God which would include and give unity to isolated and fragmented humanity? (See further, just below and p. 293, on 12:20–23.) Does it only comfort Israel, or also challenge her limited assumptions? In any case the brief but important affirmation of the salvation conveyed in Jesus' death is unmistakable.

We can now move a little faster. In 4G's handling of the Anointing at Bethany (12:1–8) the death of Jesus is taken for granted, but Mary's act toward Jesus is seen as almost premature ("Let her keep it for the day [sic] of my burial") since, evidently, Jesus' hour had still not yet come. But at the same time the imminence of that death is now heightened; all emphasis is on the hostile authorities' response to Jesus, and even to Lazarus (12:10).

The next episode—the Entry into Jerusalem (12:12–15)—Jesus' approaching death, his eventual glorification (possibly including the resurrection), will allow the disciples at least eventually to understand this entry into the city (v. 16). But for the moment the authorities once again react with dismay at what is taking place (v. 19).

Here 4G adds a brief but structurally vital scene (12:20–23), one evidently not based on anything in the source. Included among those who were flocking to Jesus were some **Greeks** (Gentiles, evidently), and when Jesus is told *this* he makes at last the exalted declaration: **The hour has come for the Son of man to be glorified** (v. 23). Here then is the turning point in the Gospel; the moment which repeatedly was **not yet** is now reached. The public ministry of Jesus is on the one hand complete, evidently because "the children of God scattered abroad" (11:52) have now begun to find inclusion in Jesus' following. But on the other hand the ministry of signs has ended in failure, a failure elaborately explained in both SG and 4G (12:36b–43).

Jesus' agony therefore begins (12:27—"Now my soul is troubled"), and while for the moment it takes place in the presence of a crowd (v. 29), just as much of the passion will occur in public, it is 4E's intent to portray Jesus here turning at last from "the world" to the privacy of his own community of followers. In the tradition, of course, the Last Supper demands such a setting, and here 4G makes use of it (chap. 13). But we can say little redaction-critically of the Johannine handling of that tradition since it has been so drastically reshaped.

We can however discern several clearly Johannine notices, brief but telling: (1) Jesus *knows* that "his hour" is at hand, and it is defined here as the time "for him to pass [*metabē*] out of this world to the Father" (13:1), since "he had come out from God and was departing [again] [*hypagei*] to God" (v. 3). (2) Further, it expresses Jesus' *love* for "his own who are in the world," a love which he held "to the end" (v. 2). (3) Finally, in his death "the Son of God is glorified, and in him God is glorified" (v. 31). His death, then, is no longer only a necessary evil but the culmination of Jesus' mission, with clear christological and soteriological import.

The Last Supper has become the occasion for 4G to introduce in a direct way its understanding of the approaching crucifixion and the attendant meaning for Christian life. Thus the four chapters (14—17) of Farewell Discourse that follow flow out of the themes already introduced in the account of the meal itself. We cannot expect here to do justice to the complex construct that 4E has created, and although strictly speaking Jesus' words are all spoken in the context of his approaching death they in fact stand apart as a major Johannine statement about the church's life later on in the world. Since they at last inaugurate the time of the passion as 4E constructs the drama, we thus turn to consider the Johannine redaction of the passion account proper (chaps. 18—19).

Three themes prevail in the Johannine portrayal of Jesus' passion: his sovereignty in the face of death, his self-manifestation by means of it, and the responsibility of "the Jews" for it.

1. Still more than in the Synoptics (where Jesus appears sometimes in charge, sometimes at the mercy of the events taking place) and certainly in clear contrast with the pre-Johannine PQ (where only divine necessity countervails) 4G shows Jesus presiding magisterially over his passion. At the arrest he knew "all that was to befall him" (18:4) and in fulfillment of his own foreordination protects the disciples from his fate (vv. 8–9). Before the high priest he calmly questions his mistreatment (v. 23). Pilate

throughout is baffled and helpless (e.g., v. 38), whereas Jesus has predicted even the method of his own execution (v. 32) and has at his disposal forces superior to Rome's (18:36; 19:11). He goes out freely to his execution (19:17) and at the very end knows that all is over (v. 28a). The term used in this last instance (a form of *teleioun*) is important; it is repeated twice again in the space of three verses. It means, of course, not termination but completion; all of Jesus' mission here comes to its climax. His very thirst consummates "the scripture" (*teleiōthē*, v. 28b), and his final word is the majestic, "It is accomplished" (*tetelestai*, v. 30a). Both Jesus' person and work are fulfilled, at last and precisely here in his dying. The death of Jesus is for 4E his greatest sign. (Contrast SG, in which that role goes of course to the resurrection.)

2. The second theme is related. Just as Jesus' purpose on earth has been—from one perspective—only to reveal the truth, as he tells Pilate (18:37), and to speak "openly to the world" (v. 20, before the high priest), so his death is characterized as none other than revealing his glory. At the moment of his arrest his divinity is disclosed; in giving himself up he utters the theophanic I AM, laying low his pursuers (18:5–6). And where, in the Synoptic Gospels, prodigies of nature attend his death, all that is needed in this Gospel is his word of completion, of fulfilled revelation.

3. So the death of Jesus focuses the Johannine message. In it his victory over evil is accomplished. At the same time, however, 4G is at pains to assign blame for the death, the third theme, and in fact in the same people to identify the locus of the evil. It centers in "the Jews." We shall give extended attention to this phrase (see F, in this part), in particular its origin, taking note of the disastrous effect it has had on subsequent treatment of Jews by Christians. For the moment we can observe simply that the religious authorities (and the whole Jewish nation)—ostensibly of Jesus' day, in fact of 4E's—are seen as entirely responsible for his death. From the beginning and throughout "they" both oppose and fear him. They formally plot the death, they "hand over" Jesus to Pilate, and after the condemnation Pilate hands him back to them as if it is they who carry out the crucifixion. They stand, it is clear, for the world that sets itself over against God. They do not so much bring about Jesus' death as share in the polarity that it reveals. There is no circumstantial, causal flow of events; rather, there is a kind of constant understanding that "the Jews" will destroy Jesus.[104]

Nevertheless, although 4G is determined to portray "the Jews" in this way and thereby—more than any other Gospel, and certainly in a way uncountenanced by the predecessor—to affix responsibility for Jesus'

---

104. For this reason, evidently, some of the details of the source's Jewish trial may have been dispersed throughout the story of Jesus' day-to-day interactions with "the Jews." See part 1, sec. 16, Johannine Redaction.

death, at the same time the theological achievement that the death has become is even more pervasively stressed. The Gospel, in other words, can be seen as *one extended passion narrative*.[105] Both protagonist and antagonists (Jesus and "the Jews") convey from the beginning the meaning of that Friday. The portrayal of the death of Jesus is not at all 4G's concession to tradition but stands at the heart of its message. That death shows, christologically and soteriologically, what the good news is. For the first time—and here one must think of both Paul and the three other canonical Gospels, to say nothing of the pre-Johannine Gospel—4E shows that Friday to be Good.

---

105. Contrast with what was said above (part 1, excursus A.2) on the question of the source's genre.

E. Eschatology and Community

Eschatology—a concept and even a term mostly foreign to the modern mind—was altogether central in the early Christian consciousness. The followers of Jesus would have shared in the widespread Jewish expectation that the age's end (in Greek, its *eschaton*) was drawing near, even that the end of the world as it was known was at hand. From the very first, then, they were preoccupied with the question how the movement Jesus led might fit into this apocalyptic hope. If there is scholarly disagreement about Jesus' own teaching on the matter during his lifetime,[106] it is agreed that after his death, with the rise of belief in his resurrection, his disciples began to integrate what had now been seen to take place into the eschatological world view. When would the old age end now? they asked. Had the new one come nearer, was it not now clearer to the imagination? Was not Jesus the One who would soon appear to bring in the new age unmistakably for all to see? Were not his followers those who already had in some way a membership in that coming age and who only awaited his return?

There was, in short, a sense of something having changed, of a new reality in the old hope. But it remained essentially a hope, something looked forward to in the future. It was Jesus' return that still needed to take place and for which the Christian must wait. For only then would Jesus be the Messiah; at most he was now only the Messiah-designate (Rom. 1:4; cf. Acts 3:20). The Christian was one who simply knew now beforehand who the Messiah would be and could share in the expectant hope of his appearance as Messiah.[107]

As the first Christian century wore on, the eschatological issue became still more pressing, for the old age seemed to continue and the looked-for return of Jesus did not occur. The delay of his appearance, of his Parousia,

106. See most recently Borg, "Non-Eschatological Jesus."

107. The hoped-for Parousia, then, was not to be solely his return, his "coming again," but his appearing, his "presence" for the first time as Lord. Only 4G will present Jesus during his lifetime as having "come" already, and it is a confusion of that belief with the still-future hope that creates the hybrid idea of a "second coming."

became a theological problem. Even Paul, by midcentury, had had to come to terms with it. And each of the Gospels addresses it one way or another. Among the canonical Gospels, only 4G lacks as a fundamental affirmation the expectation that Jesus will return, that the end is still to come.[108] Instead there is the dominant impression that the end is already present, and the explicit claim that Jesus, before his ministry, had "come down from heaven." (There is no attempt to connect the incarnation with the birth of Jesus.) Except for a few vestiges of the older eschatology (they are not later additions—see this part, n. 108) it is implied that after his death Jesus went away not to return again but that in the Paraclete, the Holy Spirit, he is eternally present. This so-called realized eschatology, as distinct from the older and far more widespread futurist eschatology, is not altogether unique to 4G.[109]

In 4G there is almost nothing of the future expectation, as we have seen, and the forthright assurance that the end time has been realized is at the heart of the Gospel's theology. But how has 4E arrived at this major theological advance? Has that author made the step, simply ignoring— more or less eradicating—the belief in Jesus' return, if it was contained in the tradition? If so, what would have led to such a shift, without a trace of the process by which it came about?[110]

108. There are a few places where what seem to be vestiges of a future eschatology appear (e.g., 12:48), not integrated into the otherwise thoroughly "realized" (that is, already fulfilled) eschatology running through 4G. (But see Carroll, "Eschatology," for a convincing attempt at such an integration. He does not contradict what is said here about the dominance of realized ["present"] eschatology.) In chap. 6, for example, Jesus four times speaks of those he will "raise up at the last day" (vv. 39–40, 44, 54). It has been suggested that these instances are all the result of post-Johannine addition, attempting inadequately to harmonize 4G with the Synoptics. But if they were part of the Johannine message, they are minor and in the end are all but contradicted by the more dominant view. In his dialogue with Martha Jesus implicitly corrects her expectation of "the resurrection at the last day" (11:24).

109. In his later letters Paul comes to the position that the death of Jesus is the central event of salvation and that, since it has already occurred, in that sense the end time has arrived. (See particularly 2 Cor. 6:2; Gal. 6:14–15; Rom. 3:21.) But Paul does not relinquish his belief that Jesus would return to consummate the new age; instead he combines and extends the older future eschatology with the newly perceived realized one. The Synoptic Gospels, in various ways, do the same.

110. Aune's lengthy treatment of 4G in his *Cultic Setting* develops a complex theory of how the Johannine community's experience of the presence of Jesus and of the fact that he had already accomplished human salvation must have originated; namely—to summarize Aune's argument far too simply—it would have arisen in the context of worship, especially the eucharistic cultus, and under the influence of various religion-historical trends that must, he holds, have been available to the Johannine community. I question whether Aune's explanation is necessary. I am thinking here not of the intricate ways the eschatological stance of 4E finds expression in the discourses, which Aune so extensively analyzes, but rather of the question of the origin of that stance. He deals exclusively with the discourse material in 4G, and thereby, I would maintain, overlooks the key to the germ that the narratives contain, as is so often the case in the study of Johannine thought.

I hold that the Evangelist has not created the realized eschatology but, rather, has sharpened a pre-Johannine affirmation, namely, that the Christian does not look to the future for the completion of salvation. (The tradition underlying 4G, then, never knew the belief in a future appearance of Jesus.) The Gospel explicitly presents the work of Jesus as the already consummated end; but the Johannine writer has simply inherited this realized eschatology. The narrative source used by 4E already displayed an eschatology implicitly but entirely realized. The fact of Jesus' messiahship fully visible in his lifetime is taken for granted in SQ, and it is to be seen simply in the miracles Jesus had done.

Paul had understood Jesus' death as messianic (1 Cor. 1:23—"a crucified Messiah") and perhaps also his birth (Phil. 2:7), but he nowhere points to Jesus' earthly career as itself an expression of that messiahship. And the Gospels, all of whose authors know of course that Jesus is the Messiah, at the same time show some reserve in portraying Jesus fully present as Messiah. Mark's messianic secret expresses this reserve most fully, and the tradition of Jesus' sayings about the "Son of Man" still convey similar ambiguity.

So to focus, as SQ does, on the deeds Jesus performed as evidence, indeed proof, of his messiahship, and therefore evidence that the messianic age had in fact arrived—to display Jesus simply being the Messiah—is the unique contribution of SQ; it thereby stands alone among the very early Christian literature known to us.[111]

My thesis, then, is that the eschatology in SQ is sufficient explanation for the rise of the so predominantly realized eschatology of 4G and of the discourses in particular.

We now turn to the pre-Johannine narrative tradition for evidence of the claim I make.[112]

Source

There is no explicit assertion in SQ that the end has arrived or even that a new age has dawned. On the surface, the only indication that such eschatological event is nevertheless occurring is a negative one, the lack of any future expectation. This lack in itself is noteworthy, given the prominence of that hope in almost every other version of early Christian tradition, but in a hypothetical document such as SQ an argument from silence is not decisive. Beneath the surface, however, there is clear enough evi-

111. The collected miracle stories underlying the Markan Gospel probably intended to show something not altogether unlike this, namely, that Jesus is the Son of God, or at least a kind of Divine Man. But they were not explicitly messianic, and certainly not seen as overt demonstrations (signs) of that eschatological status; nor have they become such in Mark.

112. D. M. Smith ("Milieu," 173), on rather different grounds from mine, agrees that the "lack of apocalyptic perspective . . . was already a feature of the miracle tradition in the form in which it was adopted by 4E."

dence that in fact this pre-Johannine document is based on the premise of a realized eschatology. Jesus is the Christ, the One whose earthly appearance had so long been awaited. That he can be shown working the signs of the Messiah means, obviously if still unexplicitly, that the new age has now at last appeared.

Of course we do not know what varieties of christology and eschatology were beginning to appear in the many Christian communities known to have existed but which left us no record. But among the extant early literature the pre-Johannine source alone represents a clear-cut change from what were surely the earliest futurist expectations. Jesus is now portrayed, during his lifetime, expressly and unequivocally as the Messiah. His deeds are recounted solely to convey this christological fact. He is not the one who causes wonder or curiosity, one about whom a question arises, as still in the Synoptics; he is, simply, the Messiah. That is asserted from the beginning (1:26b: he "is standing among you," v. 41: "We have found the Messiah!"), and all of his deeds convey it. The traditions of his earthly life have been carefully sorted; not his words but his acts, and not all of them but only his miracles—and merely a selection of them (20:30–31)—suffice. Further, they are presented not for their own sake but with an accompanying interpretation, a consistent hermeneutic: all of them are *signs*, that is, demonstrations of his messianic status.[113]

In PQ, his death too is recounted so as not to cast any doubt on the fact. The cross does not, as it will in Mark, itself express his messiahship, but all the same is carefully portrayed so as to show that there is no conflict with the fact of that messiahship (see this part, D).

SG, then, has a curiously single-minded, even narrow focus. Whatever else its implied readers might have known, this work is altogether unconcerned with the question how Jesus' messiahship affects history, and so far as we can tell the future is simply not in view. Quite obviously the joyous fact that he is present (1:26b) as the Christ is sufficient. Just as it implies a soteriology—the ills of humankind are healed and their hunger fed (C, in this part)—so equally it conveys an eschatology. The time has at last come: "This is the Son of God" (1:34); "We have found the Messiah . . . Elijah . . . [the Prophet]" (1:41, 43, 45); "This is truly the Savior of the world" (4:42); ". . . the Prophet who is to come into the world" (6:14). It matters not that he is unlike the political savior so widely awaited, that the world is not radically changed.[114] He has come, and that is eschaton enough.

113. Not all of the miracles are now accompanied by the overt designation of sign. But the effect of each miracle on the witnesses is evident; either the witnesses acknowledge Jesus' messiahship (6:14) or now in the Johannine redaction object to it.

114. Clearly, the messianic expectations held by both author and audience of SQ were neither Davidic nor apocalyptic. The role that Jesus fills was to be seen not in the political conquests of a king or the supernatural display of a cosmic savior but in the miracles of Elijah, in the signs of the prophet like Moses.

At most the pre-Johannine author only hints at the eschatological implications of Jesus' messiahship. In the first of the signs, Jesus appears at a wedding feast, which is perhaps to be understood as symbolic of the messianic age. What he provides is "the good wine . . . saved until now." His raising of Lazarus surely implies that the old age of death is at least no longer fully present. In PQ, the fact that Jesus purges the Temple, enters Jerusalem as King of Israel, and finally raises himself from the dead is also full of meaning about the turn of the ages. But everything is directed to the question who Jesus is. What that implies eschatologically has to be taken for granted.

An intimate correlative of eschatology is community. The new age would necessarily involve, or create, a people. The individualistic eschatology that moderns usually understand as Christian (particularly, immediate life after death) is virtually missing from the ancient mentality.[115]

But, again, all attention to the nature and constitution of the eschatological community is missing in SG. The Baptist announces Jesus "so that all [that is, all Jews] might believe," and the disciples are simply those who are first to do so and to remain with Jesus. Potentially the "church" of the new age is the membership of the synagogue, of all of Jewry, to at least local representatives of which the document is addressed. In calling that membership to belief in Jesus, to become Christian Jews, it anticipates no change in sociological condition. Even when the Baptist's promise that Jesus would bestow the Holy Spirit is in the end accomplished—uniquely among the Gospels, and full of both eschatological and ecclesiological implication—nothing is said to draw out that theological potential.

It remained for 4E to educe the eschatological and still more the ecclesiological potential of the source(s).

Present Gospel

The Evangelist's radical extension of the source's christology (which we have already treated) has far-reaching eschatological results. If Jesus is now not simply the long-expected Christ but the eternal Son of God come down from the Father, all of history is fundamentally affected. Jesus is not just the Messiah who at last appears from within history, as evidently both in

---

115. Paul imagines a wait, a "sleep," for those who die before the end, and then a rejoining with the eschatological community (1 Thess. 4:16–17; 1 Cor. 15:51). Only when confronted with the prospect of his own untimely death, like that of Jesus, does he imagine that he singly might "leave and be with Christ" (Phil. 1:23; note also Luke 23:43, Jesus' promise to the criminal crucified with him, but hardly to be generalized to all Christians), and soon the collective realized eschatology of 2 Corinthians overshadows any such individual view of resurrection (see esp. 5:14b, 17).

Mark and in the pre-Johannine source.[116] He represents the inbreaking of cosmic time into the merely earthly. His very appearance brings the old age to completion (to use non-Johannine language) and brings the glorious new age which had only been imagined in the futuristic eschatologies. In the Johannine perspective the fulfillment that early Christians still looked for, associated with Jesus' *re*appearance, has taken place. In his life on earth Jesus has already, and once for all, appeared. In 4G the Incarnation replaces the Parousia; the fact of Jesus' exalted status on earth obviates the hope in a heavenly vindication and glorified earthly manifestation still to come. Jesus' final re-ascent is not a prelude to his eventual return but only a postlude to the descent that has already occurred. Thus the locus of the christological event has radically moved from future to present, and the by-now-traditional order of ascent and descent is reversed.[117]

But this eschatological shift is not the deliberate transformation that a comparison with the other Gospels suggests, for 4E begins with an early Christian document that, so far as we can tell, knew only of the arrival at last of the messianic age and had no expectation of a still-future fulfillment.

Consequently, there is no role to be played by a Messiah returning to earth in glory.[118] What was only an unimagined lack in SQ is now in 4G unnecessary and unimaginable. Jesus' time on earth, his incarnation, is already the consummation of all time. For that reason it is expressed in both his words and deeds in a supernatural, unearthly way, with the qualities that Jesus' glorified reappearance would have in the future eschatologies transferred to his portrayal during his lifetime. Thus, in effect, the end has already occurred, the consummation of history has taken place. A kind of timelessness pervades the Johannine Jesus' ministry and teaching. Even the last judgment, which the older eschatology inevitably included in its almanac of the future, is now bound up with Jesus' presence on earth (3:17–21).[119]

Still more, Jesus' death signals the transition from old to new. If his life is shown as in a way timeless, it nevertheless moves toward an end, his

116. See Mark 1:9: "In those days Jesus [also] came and was baptized . . .," and John 1:29, 37, 41: "[John] saw Jesus coming . . . and they followed Jesus . . . and [Andrew] said to [Simon], 'We have found the Messiah'."

117. This is graphically shown in a comparison of Acts 1:11 ("Jesus . . . will come in the same way as you saw him go into heaven") with John 3:13 ("No one has gone up to heaven except the one who [first] came down from heaven") or with 16:28 ("I came from the Father and have come into the world; again, I am leaving the world and going to the Father").

118. The situation is quite different in the Johannine epistles, which with Brown, *The Community of the Beloved Disciple*, I take to belong to a later time and to stem from an author writing under changed circumstances and using to some extent different early traditions.

119. See ibid., 50–51.

"hour," his "time." And that moment is simply his passion, death, and burial (as in a similar way in the Synoptics). But even the death is transformed by the Johannine perspective of a realized eschatology. In the pre-Johannine passion source it had been a necessary evil, something to be explained away. In Mark it is paradoxically an evil human deed and at the very same time the way God reveals Jesus' divine sonship. In 4G, where that sonship is displayed from the beginning, what in Mark is the astonishing paradox of the cross is here a knowing irony. While it may appear to represent the world triumphing over God's Christ, in fact it is not only his triumph but the consummation of all that he came to reveal. When at the moment of his death he says "It is finished," he indicates both that his life is ending and also that the world's end has been achieved. Or rather the two are one; his life is the disclosure of ultimate reality, so that its termination is the fulfillment of that mission. That Friday can now at last be called Good, as we have seen.

For 4E, then, it is no longer the resurrection (as in PQ, or a combined SG) but the cross that is Jesus' chief sign. He more than once "signifies" how he will die. The ostensibly horrifying deed of raising him up on the cross for all to see and despise is in reality his moment of glorification, his exaltation, and the act by which he "will draw all human beings" to himself (12:32).

I have said that there is little in 4G suggesting Jesus' return; it has become unnecessary and irrelevant. To be sure, in chapter 14 Jesus twice says to the disciples that he will come again to them (vv. 3, 18). This could be the vestige of an older eschatology. But if one reads closely, the event described as Jesus' return is now meant (I hold) to be his still-future resurrection, his return from death (for of course this is said at the Last Supper, before his crucifixion). "The world" will not perceive this coming again, but only the disciples. His going away, then, is the temporary fact of his death, for which the chapter prepares the disciples.[120]

In the succeeding chapters Jesus' going away is permanent (16:10) and has to do not with his death but presumably his subsequent ascension to the Father (20:17). Once the culmination of his incarnate life had been reached, including Good Friday and Easter, he would no longer appear on earth. The language from chapter 14 is now explicitly reinterpreted (16:16–17), and the consolation now is the sending of the Paraclete in his stead. In both cases, however, the reference to the future is not to a still-

120. There is reason to think that chap. 14 is an early form of the Farewell Discourse. That it ends with the traditional phrase inaugurating the arrest ("Rise, let us go hence"—see Mark 14:42) suggests that it is concerned primarily with Jesus' approaching death and the disciples' proper understanding of it. The chapter has now been supplemented by chaps. 15—17, which considerably alter and extend its reference. For a recent arguing of this view of chap. 14 in the development of the Farewell Discourse, see Woll, *Johannine Christianity*, 9–12. See also Beutler, *Habt keine Angst*.

uncompleted eschatological moment but only to the working out of what has already been accomplished.

The foregoing paragraphs suggest how the vibrant germs of implicit realized eschatology in the source available to 4E get their working out in the greatly expanded Gospel that writer produces. We have not done full justice to that working out, but have identified the resources provided by the sources themselves. It is obvious that the problem of the origins of the realized eschatology has only been pushed a stage further into the past (that is, to the level of the sources), but there it is simpler to account for. It was a relatively short step from a mere remembering of Jesus' miracles to their evaluation as signs of the messianic end time.

The Synoptics, clearly, have not taken that step (nor had the pre-Markan collection of miracles). Instead they show a refusal to understand and hence portray Jesus' *dynameis* as messianic proofs (signs in the technical sense used in SQ). This reluctance may stem from Jesus himself or it may represent a later polemic developed against the sort of christology characterized by the demand for a sign,[121] or both. In any case, it is a reluctance not felt by the community that produced from the miracle tradition a carefully constructed document displaying Jesus as the wonder-working Messiah, a document that, even before it was combined with a passion narrative, must be thought of as Gospel: it univocally proclaimed the good news that the Messiah had come and shown himself, able to heal and feed and raise from the dead.

The pre-Johannine passion narrative, originating from a quite different motive, shows nevertheless the same christological concern, though negatively expressed: Jesus was no less the Messiah because of his shocking death. The logic to sustain this claim is highly eschatological in its implication. The scripture had foretold that, and even in detail how, the Messiah would suffer (for example, the parting of his garments, his thirst, the treatment of his dead body). Since all this is displayed as having taken place, then the coming of the Messiah, that is, the realization of all eschatological hope, has itself patently taken place. A common eschatology, then, joins the two narrative sources, signs and passion, and so do compatible, even reciprocal christologies.

The source's hope was "that all might believe" (1:7)—all Jews, that is—and that they would accept their long-awaited Messiah. This, then—an Israel restored and consoled at last—would be the new community of faith.

121. One often described—with limited usefulness, I would hold—as a *theios anēr* christology. See this part, A.

But by the time 4G was written that clearly has not occurred, and would not. Whereas the pre-Johannine author and readers had found their home wholly within Judaism, now Christians have been expelled from their spiritual home, exiled from Jewish faith and people. The problem of community arises for the first time, and with great urgency. The first disciples who had represented—as they hoped—merely the beginning of what would be a national conversion instead now constitute the entirety of the believing community, together with any who subsequently joined themselves to their number. In SG they were emblematic of a long and continuing chain of people coming to faith. For 4E they represent, rather, the relatively small church, decidedly limited in numbers. Jesus can speak of them as his flock threatened by the dangers of the world, his little children who fear to be left as orphans. The body of Christians is but a sect over against the dominant Jewish religion—and it is disoriented, dispirited, afraid. They are surrounded by a foreign and hostile "world,"[122] and it is the role of the departing Jesus to console and strengthen them. In the Johannine portrayal he speaks to them in terms that convey bonds of community: "friends," "brothers," "children."

But along with this concession to the sociological reality of the Christian life there is both a great limitation and an enormous theological claim. The cost is that as a sect the community sacrifices the universal ethic of Jesus (love of neighbor, of enemy), whether known to them in the early pre-Johannine tradition or not. It is now an ethic of love that applies only within the small church: love of one another, of brother (there is no mention of sister), of Jesus, just as he has loved them (13:34–35). The new theological claim is one that must have given great confidence to the small body of believers: Judaism is defunct, it is only the "world," having nothing to do with Jesus' kingdom. Christianity is the new and true religion,[123] the completion of Jewish imperfection. The "true Israelite" Nathanael is the exemplar of Christians and their vision of "greater things"; they see Jesus replacing Jacob's ladder, the ancient and ambiguous connection between God and the chosen people (1:47–51). This new Christian community is the good wine saved until now, the true manna from heaven. Its members are sheep who know the true shepherd, followers of the true and living way. Moses gave only the law, but grace and

---

122. But from the standpoint of the Jewish leaders, at least as the Gospel portrays them more than once, "the world" has gone after Jesus and is lost to Judaism. Is this simply Christian hyperbole, a wishful dramatization of panic in the Jewish camp? Or does it reflect the alienation and disaffection that any schism brings, the sense of loss felt also on the other side of the Jewish-Christian rift?

123. There is, of course, no term for it as a separate religion, nor any awareness that that is what it is becoming; it is known simply as "the truth," "life," perhaps—as in Acts—"the way."

truth came through Jesus Christ.[124] He died for the sake of "the whole nation" of Israel, and "to gather into one" all Jews dispersed throughout the world—as the high priest Caiaphas unwittingly prophesied (11:50–52). Indeed, there is the hint that Gentiles, too (if that is the referent of "the Greeks" of 12:20–23), may be part of the new community of faith.[125] A hint only, yet hardly negligible—they appear on the scene at this one point, at the very end of the public ministry of Jesus, and immediately he declares that his "hour" has come.

So we have found that the Christian community countenanced by 4E is on one hand small and beleaguered, and on the other hand simultaneously full of hope on a global scale. But what is the essence of the new belonging, with meaning not only for the fledgling church but promise as well for a world awaiting salvation? It is now more than faith in the messianic accomplishments of Jesus, filled though they are with soteriological implication. It is finally a spirituality, a mysticism unique to 4G.[126] Jesus is one with his followers, just as he and the Father are one. They "abide" in him and he in them. If absent, he is yet always with them, they are not alone.

In the foregoing we raised the issue of Christianity's relation to Judaism, since by 4E's time it was becoming a separate religion. Because the view of Judaism, the image of "the Jews," is so important in the Gospel, and so controversial, we devote the final section to that question.

---

124. Here (1:17), just as at many other points, the dominant meaning is not the only one. If Judaism is replaced by Christianity, it also provides the new faith's essential matrix, its preparation, the soul out of which it springs. That verse from the prologue, pointedly lacking a conjunction between its two clauses, means also *"Just as* the law [with all its grace and truth] was given by Moses, *so also* in Jesus Christ."

125. In 4G there is only this slight evidence, and nothing whatever in the source, of the question concerning the admission of Gentiles to Christian belief which so preoccupies most other first-century Christian literature.

126. But not altogether unlike a Christ-mysticism found also in the letters of Paul. It is beyond the scope of our study to give an extensive interpretation of this Johannine spirituality, which has no redactional basis in SG. Only the discovery of a key to unlock the composition history of the discourses will make such a redaction-critical investigation possible.

F. Theological Locale:
Jesus' Itinerary and "the Jews"[127]

Until now in this part we have been concerned mostly with the classical categories of NT theology—christology, soteriology, the theology of Jesus' death, and eschatology and ecclesiology. Only the section on "Signs and Faith" was demanded by the distinctiveness of Johannine thought. Now, finally, we turn to a topic notoriously peculiar to 4G: the use of the phrase "the Jews." It is my thesis that this can be understood only as a function of the Johannine employment of geography in a symbolic and schematic way, an itinerary of Jesus that is patently complex by comparison with the other Gospels. Topography—Jesus' whereabouts as in itself significant—conveys a theological meaning that will be seen to center around the Johannine view of "the Jews."[128]

A comparison of 2:23–25 with 4:43–45 quickly and strikingly illustrates this Johannine device. In the former passage those—presumably the Jews (or Judeans—see below) of Jerusalem and others who have come to the feast—who see Jesus' signs and consequently believe in him are nevertheless not to be trusted; they typify humankind,[129] and their faith is suspect. By contrast, in chapter 4 the Galileans who had been in Jerusalem for that very Passover believe in Jesus on the basis of the same deeds, and quite

127. Some of the material in this section can be found, in earlier form, in my article "Theological Use of Locale."

128. This interpretation finds its origin in Lightfoot's highly intuitive study (*Locality*, 89–105, 145–58) where he recognized many of the points I try here to document redaction-critically. Simultaneously with my own earlier work ("Theological Use of Locale"), Davies (*Gospel and Land*, 319) has also asserted that in 4G "Topography subserves Theology."

129. See vv. 24–25: "all," "humanity" (*anthrōpos*—the latter used twice). Brown (*The Community of the Beloved Disciple*, 72 n) identifies those mentioned in 2:23–25 with a particular group in 4E's sociological situation. I accept that such a group perhaps inspired the portrait in these verses. But they function in the Gospel as not simply one group among others in the Johannine ecclesiological context but as representatives of all "Jews" (and as such of humanity as a whole) who stand in dialectic contrast to the attitude of those symbolized, as we are about to see, by the "Galileans." (See this part, n. 131, on Ashton's distinction between reference and sense.) Von Wahlde, in several articles (notably "Terms" and "Critical Survey"), insists quite rightly that the complexity of the use of "Jews" and of the many other "terms for religious authorities" does not permit a simple treatment of the phenomena, and he would probably fault the present study on this account. I allow for variety within the use of the term *Ioudaioi* but think nonetheless that its most common and certainly its fundamental meaning is the one we now pursue.

clearly their belief is valid. To be sure, it is put to the test by Jesus in the story which this brief passage now introduces (4:46–54). The official who comes to Jesus seeking healing for his son is challenged as typical of those who will believe only if they see "signs and wonders" (v. 48); but in the person of this representative individual, and in the context of 4:43–45, Galilean faith passes the test (vv. 50b, 53b).

Why? What is it about the locale of those who see signs and believe that determines the validity of their belief? This is the puzzle we seek to understand in this section. That it is a deliberate literary fiction is clear from the fact that 4E repeatedly and pointedly calls our attention to that region of Palestine where, at any particular point in his public ministry, Jesus is to be found. Galilee is often singled out, and Jesus' travels to and from that region are emphatically noted in redactional comments. But still more are we made to think of Judea as the place of Jesus' activity. Three times in the course of a few chapters Jesus makes his way to Galilee in the north (1:43; 4:3; 6:1), and three times he still more pointedly reenters Judea (2:13; 5:1; 7:10). This format stands in contrast to the far leaner geographical framework of Jesus' ministry found both in the Synoptic Gospels and in the source.[130]

An essential clue to what the device means is to be found in the fact that, in Greek, Judea is etymologically simply the place of the Jews. Thus *Ioudaia* could as well be translated "Jewry" as "Judea"; and *Ioudaios*, which is of course usually translated "Jew," equally means "Judean."[131]

---

130. That Jesus' itinerary in any of the Gospels is a construct of the author in question was long ago demonstrated by Schmidt, *Rahmen*. In *Tradition* (233–47) Dodd attempted to attribute the geographical framework in 4G to tradition, but this was carefully refuted by Meeks, "Galilee and Judea." Schein's work, *Way*, takes a simpler view of the entire Johannine geography. He treats it as historical (and a basis therefore for a modern pilgrim's devotional approach to the holy land). This is an imaginative way of introducing the reader to literary pilgrimage, not to say the actual believer-pilgrim to Israel/Palestine, but it necessarily involves filling in Jesus' itinerary with intelligent guesses about the route he took in moving from place to place. Many of the data in the Johannine tradition are historical in some sense, but it will be obvious that I do not take the present arrangement of these data to be factual, in 4G any more than in the Synoptics.

131. In a recent unpublished paper ("Judeans"), Meeks now proposes that the best translation of *Ioudaios*—not simply in 4G but in general usage of the first century—may in fact be "Judean," since "neither of our categories 'religion' and 'race' had been invented in antiquity." Just as today anyone whose origin is Greece, however many generations back, may be thought of as Greek, so "Judean" in the Roman world "may refer either to people residing in Judea or to the community of resident aliens in a diaspora city whose origin was Judea and who preserve their identity" thereby. Lowe (*"Ioudaioi"*) earlier argued, too simply, that the term, usually translated "Jew(s)," always in 4G has the basically territorial meaning of Judean(s); but he allows that among "Diaspora Jews the word had already a secondary religious meaning" (p. 107). This would then apply also to the Christian Jews who appear (according to Martyn, *History and Theology*) to constitute the Johannine community. More recently Ashton (*"Ioudaioi"*) has considerably qualified and deepened Lowe's point and observed the difficulty finally of expressing adequately in English what the term means. He raises the distinction between reference (*Ioudaioi* obviously refers to the Jews who are the Christians'

That the people take their name from their place is hardly surprising; but 4E's insistence on both "the Jews" and the region of Judea suggests that something more than what is merely factual is intended.

This matter is important to an understanding of the Johannine good news. Still more, it is of considerable significance for the history of Jewish-Christian relations throughout the centuries.

Source

In contrast to what we have just been saying about the present Gospel, the source is not concerned with region at all. It uniformly supplies the particular place where Jesus' deeds occur, but it seldom identifies those places by region. The reader is either expected to know the part of Palestine in which Cana,[132] Capernaum, and the Sea of Tiberias[133] are to be found, and that Jerusalem (with its environs) is in Judea, or more likely is not expected to be concerned with the matter of region at all.

Like the Synoptic Gospels[134] the source shows Jesus working initially in Galilean sites. This ministry is brief yet carefully articulated. Only at its completion (again as in the Synoptics) does Jesus go to the south, and there (unlike Mark and Matthew) he has another brief ministry of signs, separate from the events associated with his death.[135] This dual ministry, then, is distinctive of 4E's source; and—uniquely in Gospel tradition—it may have contained even the occasion for Jesus' change of locale, namely, the death of Lazarus. Yet there is no hint even in that story of interest in region as such.

In our outline of the source in part 1 we distinguished the signs in Galilee from those in Judea. But this way of speaking of the format of the source is in a way misleading, for SG nowhere makes such a regional distinction. We found (part 1, sec. 6, Pre-Johannine Source) that the feeding of the multitude, with its sequel on the sea, forms a kind of fitting climax to the first half of the signs sequence, and the acclamation of Jesus in response to the feeding itself ("Truly this is the prophet who is to come

---

opponents in the Johannine community's experience) and sense: symbolically, the term *means* "humanity" (just the interpretation I had earlier espoused—in "Theological Use of Locale," an article Ashton seems not to know).

132. Depending on the source's reconstruction at 2:1 and 4:46. It may very well be only 4E who there has introduced a second time the datum that Cana is in Galilee.

133. Possibly it is only 4E who has identified this as the Sea of Galilee—see part 1, sec. 6, on 6:1.

134. Though clearly not because of any dependence on them in this respect; more likely in accordance with the very rough shape of Jesus' ministry in historical fact.

135. It is difficult to say that this latter has any basis in Synoptic tradition. In Mark the journey to Jerusalem and all activity there are integrated with the passion narrative. Only the author of Luke, in a quite different way from our source, makes activity in Judea a significant and distinct part of Jesus' ministry.

into the world"—6:14) serves as culmination of the conversions that Jesus' signs evoke. Yet the source takes no notice of this as a Galilean period; it identifes these events neither with Galilee nor its inhabitants, as 4E will do.

When we speak of a dual ministry, then—one part in Galilee and the second in Judea—we do so solely from the perspective of later Johannine redaction, or from our awareness of the geography of Palestine. (Were the source's readers equally conversant?) In the source there is simply a ministry of seven signs which happen to fall into two regional parts.

This is not to say that the author of the source has no concern for itinerary. On the contrary, the articulation of Jesus' signs is more coherent and logical in SG than in the Synoptics. This, of course, is partly a function of the selectivity used in constructing Jesus' ministry of signs in SG, but at the same time the flow of Jesus' ministry seems carefully constructed: from Cana in the hill country down to Capernaum by the sea; after the catch of fish on the sea (if included in SG), the feeding on the far shore and the miraculous crossing (and stilling of the storm), bringing Jesus back to Capernaum. Then we are in Bethany on the outskirts of Jerusalem, at the pool of Siloam nearby the city, and finally at the pool of Bethesda in its center.

This is all preceded by the Baptist's testimony and the conversion of the first disciples. Where did these occur, according to the source? No notice of locale, if one was given, has survived.[136] Bethany-beyond-Jordan has been supplied by 4E (1:28). But evidently a northern locale is implied, continuous with the ministry that is about to begin.[137] The Baptist's followers, who become Jesus' disciples, are from a Galilean town, just as those who then are immediately converted (1:44). Jesus' origin is also Galilean, as in all the traditions (vv. 45–46). So a northern venue for the Baptist is evidently supposed, but the region of Galilee is never named; presumably he baptizes in the Jordan either north or south of the Sea of Galilee, but even the river is not mentioned (except in the Johannine v. 28).

In the combined SQ and passion narrative, the events of Jesus' last days in their own way show a similarly straightforward spatial logic: In the Temple (the Sanhedrin's meeting), out to Bethany, formal entry into the city, the Last Supper, a garden across the Kidron, the high priest's house, the Pretorium and Lithostrotos, Golgotha, a nearby garden tomb, the disciples' meeting place.[138]

---

136. Unless Aenon-near-Salim (3:23) was once part of SG and has been displaced by Johannine redaction, as I held in *TGOS*, 179. But if so it gives us little help, since its location is now unidentifiable.

137. Despite the Synoptic tradition's association of the Baptist with the Judean wilderness, more than once it has been suggested that either in fact or according to another tradition he worked in the north. See Flusser (*Jesus*, 31) and Brownlee ("Whence?" 170–74).

138. Only the Last Supper and Jesus' appearance to the gathered disciples now lack ex-

So the source can be seen to follow a carefully conceived geographical plan. It is thus all the more striking that the reader is in no way asked to be aware of either Galilee or Judea as such, and never of their inhabitants in a symbolic way. Indeed, for SG all the participants are simply taken for granted as Jewish, and so is the Christian movement itself.

Present Gospel

In the canonical Gospel, by contrast, the matter of geography is of central importance and its role is intricate. The source's closely knit geographical articulation and its roughly equal interest in both Galilean and Jerusalem settings for the ministry of signs may have inspired the Johannine interest in itinerary, but in any case the present Gospel shows a radical reworking. Beginning from the source's very first scene, 4E has introduced a preoccupation with region as such.

• At 1:28, interrupting the Baptist's profession of Jesus, there is a prominent notice of locale. This is not at all the kind of matter-of-fact but casual datum found so often in the source, and there always within the introduction to a scene. Instead it constitutes a self-contained and pointed declaration: "These things took place in **Bethany beyond the Jordan**, where John was baptizing." We note first of all the region specified: The Baptist announces the appearance of Jesus outside of Judea.[139] Prior to declaring this, 4E has introduced the detail that the Baptist is under interrogation by those who come "from Jerusalem" (1:19; see also v. 24). Already a kind of polarity, and one tinged with hostility and danger, has been established between Judean and non-Judean territory.

This is the first of four notices of locale that have been introduced into the pre-Johannine narrative of Jesus' ministry. They seem not to be entirely Johannine redactional creations but evidently come to 4E by independent tradition, two of them at least associated with the Baptist. What is notable is that each of them, as they now appear, contains not only a highly particular place-name but also an explicit naming of region:

---

plicit locales. But just possibly the latter is to be understood as Peter's house, to which he returned after visiting the empty tomb (20:10); and quite likely the former has been lost in 4E's drastic redaction (chap. 13).

139. Transjordan is not named merely to distinguish this Bethany from the village of the same name near Jerusalem, which of course will not figure in the Gospel for many chapters, but also and perhaps chiefly to identify the place's region. It is likely that during the first century part of Transjordan was under Judean rule. But clearly the Evangelist is either ignorant of this or more likely unconcerned with political fact, as appears at the end of chap. 10: Jesus "again went away across the Jordan" to Bethany (10:40), and from there said, "Let us go into Judea again" (11:7). For attempts (misguided, I believe, so far as the Johannine understanding is concerned) to place this Bethany either in Judea (and identical to the Bethany of Mary and Martha) or in Galilee, see respectively my article "Theological Use," 67, and Brownlee, "Whence?" 167–74.

Bethany-beyond-Jordan

Aenon-near-Salim—associated with Jesus' transfer to "the Judean countryside" (3:22–23—but see further below)

Sychar—"a city of Samaria" (4:5)

Ephraim—"away from [Judea] . . . near the wilderness" (11:54—see below)

Two of these notices (Sycar and Ephraim), together with the return to Bethany-beyond-Jordan at 10:40, now also provide a place of withdrawal from Judea on Jesus' part. (At 1:28 Jesus has not yet entered Judea.) Aenon, on the other hand, occasions a continuation of Jesus' Judean sojourn, marked by controversy (3:25). Already, then, we begin to see that Judea alternates and contrasts with non-Judean territory in the Johannine Jesus' ministry.

• But in considering the notices akin to 1:28 we have gotten ahead of ourselves and must return to chapter 1. A regional emphasis now obtrudes also within the second scene of SG, the account of the first disciples' conversion. At 1:43, interrupting the chain of witness and thereby dividing the scene in half (much as the insertion of 1:28 broke apart the first scene), the Evangelist tells us that "Jesus decided [lit., willed] to **depart for Galilee.**" Evidently the placing of the subsequent scene in the region of Galilee—presumably away from Judea and its emissaries—is vital to the Johannine purpose. It is declared ahead of time, and it overrides even the disciples' recognition (and also, naturally, the reader's) of who Jesus is.

We have seen that in the source the next scene, the first of the signs, was at last carefully located, in Cana, but that very possibly no regional identification was given, 4E being responsible for introducing **of Galilee** even in 2:1. At the very least she or he has emphasized the Galilean locale by reiterating it in 2:11, and again at 4:46.[140]

If Capernaum, the site of the succeeding episode in SG, is not explicitly located by 4E in Galilee, nevertheless the introduction to that episode (4:43–45) accomplishes the same function. The Galilean setting is all the more evident since in the meantime the source has been broken open and the great block of material, 2:13—4:42, has been introduced and set in Judea, patently contrasting with the Galilean locale of the two miracles now separated by this insertion.

• Not one but several redactional notices make this unmistakable. The first of these is at 2:13, interrupting the original transition from first to

---

140. See also 4:3, 43, 54. Inserting "of Galilee" in 2:11a and 4:54b considerably changes the source's meaning. Originally these notices were simply enumerations of the first two signs; now they locate the signs. "This [was] the beginning of the signs Jesus did (at Cana)" has become "It was in *Cana of Galilee* that Jesus did this beginning of the signs." At 4:54b the pre-Johannine reading "This was the second sign Jesus did" is now altered to "Jesus did this second sign after he had come *from Judea to Galilee.*"

second sign. At the pre-Johannine level this took Jesus from Cana to Capernaum (v. 12a). That journey remains but now becomes almost pointless; v. 12b has been introduced as an attempt to give it independent standing ("with his mother and brothers, and they stayed there not many days") but only barely succeeds in this. The Evangelist is preoccupied with the need to take Jesus suddenly to Jerusalem. The occasion introduced here, as twice again later (5:1; 7:2), to provide alternation between northern and southern regions is an event in the Jewish festal calendar.[141]

An episode found much later in SG, and indeed not from among the signs at all but from the prelude to the passion story—the Restoration of the Temple—is now the event that provides substance for Jesus' sudden visit to Jerusalem (2:14–22). It is clear from the Johannine handling of that episode (see part 1, sec. 10) that it has come to have altogether new meaning in its present setting, a meaning integral with the geographical alternation between south and north. What had, prior to the Johannine redaction, been a story of prophetic and christological self-expression has now become far more controversial. In its original setting it had occasioned the Conspiracy against Jesus, to be sure. It no longer has that role, which is taken over by the Lazarus sign. Instead it introduces at the very beginning of Jesus' ministry an element of antagonism from "the Jews," and also the theme of misunderstanding and belief. For it is now a *sign*, paralleling the first sign just worked in Galilee; but Jesus' antagonists fail altogether to perceive it. Seeing Jesus' deed in the Temple, "the Jews" can only ask, "What sign do you show us for doing these things?" (v. 18); and they wholly misunderstand his explanation (vv. 20–21).[142] Even those who appear to respond positively to the sign in faith are characterized as untrustworthy (vv. 23–25).

There follows the discussion, largely of Johannine invention, between Jesus and Nicodemus (3:1–10). This representative of "the Jews" (or should we say "of the Judeans"?) correctly perceives who it is that Jesus'

141. What is the significance of this calendar, especially the repeated mention of the feast of Passover (see 6:4 and 11:55, both Johannine as well)? (The Passover in 13:1 is very likely pre-Johannine; see part 1, sec. 14.) Is a paschal theology, and in particular one interpretive of Jesus' death, intended? But then why is nothing made of this overtly and why does 4E also use the unnamed feast in 5:1, and the feasts of Succoth at 7:2 and of Hanukkah at 10:22? Does the Jewish liturgical year, and especially its lectionary, shape and interpret the events by which Jesus' ministry is structured? I see no way of answering these questions with any confidence. Redaction criticism does not authenticate the various theories of paschal or lectionary schemas underlying the Gospel. For this reason I think it valid to treat the festal notices as chiefly, and perhaps only, a device used by the Evangelist in the service of the theology of locale.

142. Verse 18 is largely pre-Johannine, but the request for a legitimating sign was valid in the story's original context. Now, however, it is "the Jews" who ask, and their question becomes inapropos since Jesus' act is unmistakably a sign, as v. 23 shows. Verses 20–25 are wholly Johannine.

signs show him to be, and yet he fails to understand in any but a literal sense what Jesus teaches.

● Next Jesus goes with his disciples **into the Judean countryside** (3:22).[143] This move is not a withdrawal but simply a continuation of the southern sojourn, paralleling the Galilean transfer to Capernaum in the present form of 2:12. Its function is primarily to introduce the account of the Baptist's simultaneous activity at Aenon-near-Salim (3:23–24). The latter's spatial relation to Jesus in v. 22 is not stated, but presumably it is to be understood as nearby and therefore in Judea.[144] John's baptizing and making disciples is now secondary to Jesus' (v. 22b), for a dispute immediately arises with "a Jew [or some Jews]" (v. 25) and leads to the question why Jesus is more successful than the Baptist (vv. 26–36).[145] For our present purpose it is only noteworthy that the motif of Judean antipathy has been reasserted and that Jesus' very popularity will now force him to withdraw from Judea.

● The opening verses of the following chapter (4:1–3) constitute a most important redactional notice, negatively evaluating this last episode and the Judean sojourn in general: **Now when the Pharisees heard that Jesus was making and baptizing more disciples than John, he left Judea and departed again to Galilee.**[146] Because of the official Jewish opposition Jesus withdraws a second time to Galilee. Activity, especially successful activity, on his part cannot be allowed to continue in Judea. But Jesus, while responding to this threat, is not at its mercy; he himself takes the initiative to leave Judea again, as he did in 1:43.

This time the journey is not simply named but filled with an episode in Samaria. This section, vv. 4–42, is undoubtedly based on a traditional kernel which may once have been found in the source (see the end of part 1, sec. 7, Analysis). The Evangelist has made of this tradition, namely, the story of Jesus and the woman at the well, an account of the progressive

143. Literally, the Greek reads "into the Judean [or Jewish] land," and sometimes this is taken to mean the region of Judea as a whole and hence to clash with what precedes, in which Jesus is clearly already in Judea. But with the noun "land" (gēn) here only the rural part of Judea is meant, since 4E consistently uses simply *Ioudaia* to mean the region as a whole.

144. In v. 26 the Bethany of 1:28 is referred to from the standpoint of Aenon as also "beyond the Jordan." Schein (*Way*, 203) tentatively places Aenon in Samaria. If this was the case historically, 4E nevertheless gives no indication of a Samaritan locale but on the contrary implies a Judean one. Schein correctly observes that in Greek the name is literally Aenon-near-the-Salim (or Salem), but unless we can be sure, as we cannot, of the reference of the term Salim it is unclear whether the article should be translated or not; in Greek "Jerusalem," for example, sometimes appears with an article.

145. The datum that Jesus himself baptized (here and 4:1, and contradicted by the gloss of 4:2—see the following note) is unique to 4G and presumably serves the purpose of Johannine anti-Baptist critique, as the assertion of Jesus' greater success shows.

146. These verses have clearly suffered some post-Johannine additions. Part of the opening clause of v. 1 ("the Lord knew") and the whole parenthesis of v. 2 are evidently late additions. When these are removed we have the purely Johannine notice just quoted.

recognition by the woman of who Jesus is. This implies faith on her part but even more it results in enthusiastic acceptance of Jesus by **the Samaritans** (vv. 39–42). Further, within this section 4E has introduced the theme of widespread missionary potential (fields white for harvest—vv. 31–38). The implication is that, in contrast to Judea, Samaria is a place of positive and authentic acceptance of Jesus.

As he arrives at last in Galilee (4:43–45) this kind of acceptance is shown all the more. The Galileans' reception of Jesus is wholehearted and, when subjected to the test of sincerity and proper basis, proves to be altogether sound. (See the discussion of this passage, in comparison to 2:23–25, at the beginning of this section.) Evidently, then, in every region but Judea, Jesus is validly responded to.

But Galilee is the chief pole in the contrast with Judea. The Samaritan episode was only an interlude, for at its conclusion the theme of 4:3 is resumed: **After the two days** [of his stay in Samaria] **he departed to Galilee** (v. 43). The rest of the chapter is punctuated with reminders that it was to Galilee that Jesus withdrew (vv. 45, 46) and especially that **he came from Judea to Galilee** (vv. 47, 54). For this reason, the startling Johannine comment in vv. 44–45 is all the more significant: Jesus left Judea for Galilee because "a prophet has no honor in his own country," and when he came to Galilee he was vigorously welcomed. But we shall leave till later the interpretation of this pivotal notice (see 3, Judea, below).

• The sudden transfer of Jesus' activity **to Jerusalem** once again, which so artificially and jarringly is accomplished by 5:1, further exemplifies and indeed underscores the regional polarity. In sharp contrast to the Galilean official of 4:46–54, the lame man healed on this occasion in Jerusalem (vv. 2–9a—a story moved forward from a probable later point in SG) proves to be anything but a loyal disciple, and before long Jesus finds himself engaged by "the Jews" in provocative and antipathetic controversy, such that soon they seek his life itself (v. 18).[147]

• The famous anomaly at 6:1, which has led to such hypothetical explanations as that chapters 5 and 6 have been rearranged (whether accidentally or by deliberate post-Johannine redaction; see part 1; sec. 6), is most simply to be explained as a product of 4E's imposed geographical schema. What in the source had been simply a journey across the Sea of Tiberias, following the healing of the official's son in Capernaum (possibly with the miraculous catch of fish intervening), has now—after the insertion of the sudden transfer to Jerusalem in chapter 5—become a journey from Jerusalem back to Galilee, indeed to **the far side of the Sea of Galilee** (as 4E here evidently renames it).

147. It is irrelevant to 4E that Jesus is even more provocative than his antagonists, with his christology that threatens the very monotheistic basis of Judaism: "As the Father raises the dead and gives them life, so also the Son gives life to whom he will" (v. 21).

Jesus is back again in the familiar and friendly territory of Galilee, but perhaps the situation is not altogether as before. In fact, in this, the last of the Galilean episodes, the response to Jesus, while positive and valid in its reception—"Truly this is the Prophet who is to come into the world"—proves to be overenthusiastic (**they were about to seize him and make him king** . . . so Jesus "perceives") and thus necessary for him to elude (vv. 14b–15). Similarly the amazed response of the crowds to the subsequent miraculous crossing of the lake is now both understandable and yet misdirected (vv. 25–26).

Immediately there ensues a debate between Jesus and these crowds which is reminiscent more and more of the suspicious, hostile questioning Jesus has met in Judea prior to this point. Indeed these crowds are before long identified twice as "the Jews" (vv. 41, 52). There is, of course, nothing in itself anomalous about Jews in Galilee, until we remember that in 4G "the Jews" and Judea are in some sense inseparable (see below on 7:1).

We are told also, in a parenthetical notice, that these events took place **in the synagogue at Capernaum** (v. 59). Once again there is nothing factually striking about a Jewish synagogue in Galilee, but in the ears of the Gospel's first readers, who would themselves have just experienced expulsion from the synagogue (9:22; 12:42; 16:2),[148] this detail signals Jewish antipathy to Jesus. We remember further that this episode, again according to a Johannine notice, takes place when **the Passover, the feast of the Jews was at hand** (6:4). No doubt that detail is in part preparatory of the substance of the debate between the Jewish crowds and Jesus—namely manna/bread-from-heaven and the question whether it is Moses or Jesus who best provides it. But the Passover notice, especially coming in the opening of the chapter and prior to the two miracles that give rise to the debate, must be intended to place these events, while taking place in Galilee, in a context that is analogous to the conflicts during earlier feasts of "the Jews" in chapters 2 and 5.

Thus in chapter 6 Galilee is becoming a place of some ambiguity. This is all too painfully shown at the end of the chapter (vv. 60–66): **many even of Jesus' disciples fell away and no longer went about with him**. The immediate occasion of their defection is Jesus' difficult teaching about himself as the giver of the true manna, in fact, as himself that very bread from heaven. But at the same time we can connect this falling away with the antipathy to Jesus on the part of "the Jews" who have appeared in—shall we say penetrated into?—Galilee. That Galilee is still a place of Jesus' following, the origin and home of his disciples, is clear from the affirmative note on which the chapter ends, the Johannine equivalent of Peter's

148. See Martyn, *History and Theology*.

professing Jesus' messiahship (vv. 67–71). But the final reminder that even one of the chosen disciples will betray him means that the period of Galilee, of predictable and mostly authentic acceptance of Jesus, is ending.

● So it is somehow surprising that chapter 7 begins by telling us that Jesus chose to remain in *Galilee*. That he "would not"[149] go about in Judea, since "the Jews" sought to kill him (7:1) is more understandable. But in this sentence 4E summarizes and evaluates the events of chapters 5 and 6 as a whole, and in particular the schematic significance of Galilee and Judea respectively. If there has been any doubt up until now about the Johannine use of locale to represent both a people and an attitude, it is dispelled by 7:1b: **he would not go about in Judea, because the Jews sought to kill him**. Judea is the place of "the Jews" and of danger and rejection. Once they are also to be found in Galilee and there act antagonistically toward him, Galilee is no longer the place of safety and acceptance, except momentarily.

The artificiality of this presentation of geography—or rather its highly constructed nature—is evident enough in what immediately follows in chapter 7. Jesus is urged by his brothers, who thereby (we are told) show their lack of faith in him, to go to Judea so as to present himself to "the world" (vv. 3–6). Jesus refuses to follow his brothers' bidding, much as he had demurred from his mother's request for a miracle at the wedding party in Cana and the official's plea for his son in Capernaum. Yet here, just as earlier, he then proceeds to accede to the urging. We are told that he went up to Jerusalem—it was the "Jewish" Feast of Sukkoth (v. 2)—only in secret (v. 10b), because his **time has not yet come** (we are reminded of his word to his mother) to manifest himself publicly to "the world." Yet very shortly he is preaching publicly in the Temple.

The Evangelist's purpose, obviously, is not to present a factually and psychologically consistent sequence of events, but rather to convey in this dramatic way the symbolic meaning that is to be attributed to locale and to the timing of Jesus' ministry.

Hereafter Jesus returns no more to Galilee—evidently we have exhausted the Galilean episodes available from the source[150] and Galilee has become no longer the safe place it was. Yet the alternation continues between Judea with its attendant threat, on the one hand, and places or regions clearly to be distinguished from Judea or Jerusalem, on the other.

Jesus' withdrawal at the end of chapter 8 from a renewed attempt on the part of "the Jews" to put him to death (v. 59: "So they picked up stones to

---

149. The same verb (lit., "willed") as that used in 1:43 on the occasion of the first withdrawal to Galilee.

150. With the exception of the catch of fish, which 4E either chooses to save until after the resurrection or, more likely, has simply omitted (to be restored by an early post-Johannine redactor). See further this part, n. 154.

throw at him; but Jesus hid himself and left the Temple")—bringing to an end the long controversy in the Temple that began in chapter 7—does not this time take him out of Judea, but it suggests nevertheless that it is Judea's inhabitants who create the regional polarity.

• At the end of chapter 10, when "the Jews" again take up stones to kill him in response to his Hanukkah discourse in the Temple, Jesus overtly leaves Judea again for the relative safety of Transjordan and the place where the Baptist had born witness to him in the beginning (10:40–42). This site, clearly Bethany-beyond-Jordan,[151] is a Baptist place, yet—just as earlier—here Jesus is alone the one who reveals himself as Messiah by the signs that he does.

With chapter 11 and the raising of Lazarus, which 4E has saved until this point to serve as the climax of the public ministry, Jesus is summoned to return to Judea, to Bethany on the outskirts of Jerusalem (v. 3). Whereas in chapter 7 his brothers had tried to persuade him to go to the capital and perform just the kind of sign that is now about to take place, here his disciples, rightly fearing for his safety, try to dissuade him from going. But Jesus' time, his "hour" (which at 2:4 and 7:6 [see also 9:4] had not yet come), is now at last approaching. If the disciples in the person of Thomas do not fully understand, nevertheless they courageously agree to accompany Jesus (vv. 7–17). But of course Jesus' presumptuous raising of Lazarus from death, which for Jews God alone can accomplish, results in intensified official opposition to him. Although this is accompanied by curiosity and even eagerness to believe on the part of the people, once again Jesus does not "walk openly among the Jews" but must withdraw (11:54). This time it is to a place which we can no longer locate on a map, but by its very name—Ephraim, one of the eponymous names of the ancient northern kingdom of Israel—and its association with the wilderness it is obviously to be distinguished from Judea.

We have reached the preliminary episodes of the pre-Johannine passion narrative—only one of them having been already used in chapter 2—and so the locale from this point on remains Jerusalem. But the Anointing at Bethany (12:1–8) and the Entry into the city (vv. 12–16) have now been incorporated into the final stages of Jesus' public ministry, and the tension that his entering and withdrawing from Judea earlier reflected continues. If these episodes express acceptance of Jesus on the part of a considerable

151. Why is it not named here? Evidently so as to avoid collision with the other Bethany which, in the present artificial Johannine arrangement, is about to be mentioned and to which Jesus is about to go (11:1, 17). This notice (10:40–42) is of obvious theological significance but is oddly contrived, sketching a curiously empty episode; it reflects only the general fact of Jesus' acceptance outside of Judea. Whether or not based on some tradition—see Bammel, "No Miracle"—it appears to have been designed by 4E expressly for the purpose of taking Jesus away from Jerusalem, so that he can be recalled to Lazarus's bedside.

number of people, they nevertheless finally result in official rejection of Jesus' ministry (vv. 9–11, 17–19).

• Therefore the whole of Jesus' public life can be summarized, with only a certain exaggeration, as one of disbelief, from which he once again withdraws in hiding: **Though he had done so many signs before them, yet they did not believe in him** (12:36b–37).[152] The considerable evidence of acceptance and belief, especially in Galilee but also in the other non-Judean regions—and even, exceptionally, in Judea—is thus finally negligible. In the end all that matters is that "the Jews" have rejected Jesus.

Consequently we now find Jesus turning decisively from public life to the inner world of his "own" (13:1b). Jesus' time has now come (12:23, 27), the playing out of his death must begin. It remains to instruct his disciples—for the space of five chapters—in the meaning of what is now to unfold, and of its aftermath. The private events of the Last Supper provide the occasion for this. Evidently the public events of his arrest, trial, and execution, which comprise the Johannine Jesus' chief sign,[153] his self-exaltation on the cross, can be understood only by the inner world of his church.

If Jesus is in one sense wholly at the mercy of his executioners in chapters 18—20, so that the freedom to enter into the world of Jewry and to leave it again is now lost, yet he is still in control of all that takes place. We shall see him presiding over the events culminating in his crucifixion. And the polarization that characterizes the first half of the Gospel is still at work, particularly in the scene of his arrest, but above all in the trial before Pilate (see part 1, secs. 15 and 17). Jesus against "the Jews," Jewry against Jesus: the geographical schema of chapters 1—12 matches the drama of the passion, making a unity of the present Gospel.[154]

But what does all of this mean? What does the pattern of Jesus' entries into Judea and withdrawals from "the Jews" seek to convey?

152. Originally it was only the Sanhedrin whose disbelief was recognized in this way. With the Johannine rearrangements, the summary now brings to an end the whole of Jesus' ministry to the world, and his chief audience ("the Jews") are thus characterized by the lack of belief in the face of his signs.

153. Contrast SG, for which the death was still problematic but the resurrection was the last and greatest sign.

154. The climax of Jesus' victorious death and resurrection in Jerusalem of Judea (chaps. 18—20) is now supplemented by the appendix of chap. 21, where the disciples are without warning depicted again in Galilee and there see the risen Jesus once more. This chapter is most often attributed to a later redactor, who has employed with considerable redaction what seems to be the one pre-Johannine sign story not used by 4E in chaps. 1—12. In that case its geographical setting can hardly be taken to bear on the schema of chaps. 1—20. If, on the other hand, it is 4E who has supplied chap. 21 (surely as afterthought), there is just the possibility that as Galilee represented the *terra christiana* earlier in the Gospel (see 2, Galilee, below), so here. The Evangelist, if the author, then shows Jesus turning once again from "the Jews" to the region where faith was first to be found. But this is not made explicit, as it usually is in the Gospel proper, and does not seem to be entirely fitting.

It should be obvious that 4E uses topography in a way that is neither incidental nor merely factual. Repeatedly, and usually in purely redactional passages, the author calls attention to Jesus' itinerary as a schema; it must therefore have theological import.

The clearest feature of this schema is the polarity of Judea on the one hand and Galilee, Samaria, or Transjordan on the other. To grasp its purpose, then, we must consider each of these poles, that is, the meaning of the various regions where Jesus appears. What does it mean, for example, that the same signs produce one result in Judea and quite another in Galilee? Why are the inhabitants of a region portrayed as its representatives, personifications of the theological value given to it?

In contrast to the Synoptic Gospels, 4G shows a knowledge of only the four regions we have named.[155] The result is a considerable heightening of interest in each of the regions. Their very paucity emphasizes their ideological importance.[156]

1. *Samaria and Transjordan*

We can begin with the least prominent regions. By contrast to Judea and Galilee they are quite secondary, yet Judea is set in polar contrast with each of them.

● It is only in the episode of the woman at the well (4:4–42) that the Johannine Jesus appears in Samaria, but its symbolic character is clear from the one reference to Samaria outside of chapter 4, namely, in 8:48. There Jesus is accused by the Jews of being "a Samaritan." Coupled with this charge, and demonstrating its gravity, is a repetition of the slander that he "has a demon."[157] It had been leveled earlier in 7:20, is reiterated in 8:52, and will reappear at 10:20, but it is answered only here (8:49), where Jesus explicitly denies it. But he does not refuse the Samaritan identification. Presumably, then, he can be thought of as coming in some sense from Samaria, just as (see below) from Galilee, even though he is a *Ioudaios* (4:9) whose homeland will prove to be Judea.[158]

The Samaritans in chapter 4 stand in obvious contrast with Nicodemus and "the Jews" generally in 2:13—3:36. They come to believe in Jesus first

155. All together the Synoptic tradition knows of fourteen regions of Palestine and its environs, and each of those Gospels shows a number of them: Mark six, Matthew and Luke nine each. On the other hand, 4G names about as many towns and cities as each of the Synoptics. Its focus is clearly on regions, which, though few, are mentioned many times.

156. The pre-Johannine narrative source knows of only two or three regions, so 4E has evidently not narrowed the tradition in this respect. Nevertheless, as regions they come to have import only in 4G.

157. Both understandable and surprisingly mild, following as it does on the heinous charge by Jesus that "the Jews" are children of the devil (8:44); see below, at the end of F.

158. Of course both Judea and Samaria, represented by their respective shrines—in Jerusalem and on Mount Gerizim—are transitory and ultimately of no religious consequence, as Jesus declares to the Samaritan woman (4:20–23).

of all at second hand, through the woman's testimony, but then directly, "because of his word" (4:41), and in the end they make an open profession of faith in him (v. 42): "Truly this is the savior of the world." (See also the Galilean crowd's acclamation at 6:14: "Truly this is the prophet who is to come into the world.")

The Samaritans, then, point up a contrast with "the Jews," their longstanding enemies, and the lack of faith in Judea. The opposite of Jew in 4G is then not Gentile[159] but—on one level at least—Samaritan, and (as we shall see) Galilean.

Transjordan (ancient Perea)—though not named—figures in the Gospel but in an even more deliberate and schematic way than Samaria. Three times we find the Johannine phrase "across the Jordan" (1:28; 3:26; 10:40), and always in connection with the Baptist, whose disciples function as the region's representatives. (a) In chapter 1 they are the first to believe in Jesus, in contrast to the suspicious *Ioudaioi* from Jerusalem. (b) At 3:25 they are engaged in an argument with one or more Jews, resulting in their testimony to Jesus' astonishing success and the Baptist's extended affirmation of Jesus' superiority (vv. 26–36).[160] (c) Finally, in 10:40–42, Jesus withdraws from the *Ioudaioi* to the place of 1:28, where a crowd (presumably the Baptist's followers) observe his superiority to the Baptist, "and many believed in him there."

Baptist Transjordan, then, is a place of faith, and like Samaria stands in contrast to Judea.

2. Galilee

If Galilee seems less prominent in 4G than in the Synoptics, as sometimes maintained, it is only because 4E has so emphasized Judea that it overshadows the northern region, which is if anything more significant in this Gospel than in the other three.

The sharpest indication of Galilee's importance is the succession of Jesus' pointed withdrawals "from Judea to Galilee," and the emphasis repeatedly put on the Galilean destination: 1:43; 2:1, 11; 4:43, 45, 46, 54; 6:1. By contrast, very little is ever made of Jesus' going *to* Judea (as distinct from Jerusalem); rather his departures *from* Judea, or staying away from it, are characteristically emphasized.

159. *Ethnos,* the chief Greek term comparable to our "Gentile," always refers in 4G to the Jews (11:48, 50–52; 18:35). "The Greeks" in 7:35 are the Gentiles. If the same is true in 12:20, which is debated, their momentary appearance on the stage of the narrative only signals its conclusion and further demonstrates that everyone but "the Jews" is faithful.

160. The locale of this episode (Aenon-near-Salim—3:23) is not specified as to region. We surmised that it must be somewhere in the Judean countryside to which Jesus had gone (3:22). But there the Baptist's disciples remind him that it was "across the Jordan" that Jesus' ministry began. Thus, while not taking place in Transjordan, this episode points solely to that region.

Galilee is shown almost always in favorable light. Even when Jesus is about to leave it for the last time, and the response to him there has finally become ambiguous, it is a place of refuge for him (as in 4:1, 44), a place of hiddenness (7:1–13). Primarily, Galilee is to be seen as a center of belief, and Galileans are depicted as a people of faith: the first disciples and the witnesses to each of the signs.[161]

A flaw in Galilean faith appears first at 6:14–15, when Jesus withdraws in the face of the crowd's response to the miracle of the loaves. But here it is only overenthusiastic, hardly invalid; Jesus does not condemn it and his withdrawal is only temporary. By contrast, at 6:26, whatever the precise intent of his word to the crowd ("You seek me not because you saw signs but because you ate your fill of the loaves"), it suggests a more serious defect, which becomes clearer as the discussion continues.

But it is striking that the people here are never named Galileans; rather they soon are identified as *Ioudaioi* (vv. 41, 52), and the scene's setting is reported to be the synagogue in Capernaum (v. 59). (We have already recognized that factually there is nothing odd about the presence of Jews and a synagogue in Galilee, but in the light of the Johannine polarity between Judea and Galilee I suggest it is significant that those who object to Jesus in this final Galilean scene are named "Judeans.") Finally there is a crisis among Jesus' followers, and a falling away of many (vv. 60–66). But once again, even in this worsening situation, the Galilean locale is no longer named. Galilee then, symbolically set in polar contrast to Judea, gives way in this chapter to the presence—shall we say the intrusive penetration?—of Judeans.[162] When Galilee is mentioned again (7:1), it is still in sharp and favorable contrast to Judea.

At the end of chapter 7 Nicodemus reappears, who had earlier represented Jewish failure to understand Jesus (3:1–10). He is still described as "one of them" (7:50), but now he objects procedurally to the officials' determination to get rid of Jesus (v. 51), and this is met with the scornful retort, "Are you also from Galilee?" (v. 52a). The region is obviously used here in a wholly symbolic sense; Galilee is the place of discipleship, and one who wavers from official Jewish opposition to Jesus is thereby suspect of being no longer *Ioudaios* but *Galilaios*.

This brief episode is part of a larger debate among the Jews as to Jesus' place of origin in relation to the messianic prophecies (7:40–52). Some imply that Jesus himself "comes from Galilee" (v. 41), and when on this

161. I allow that there may be historical basis for this view (as Lohmeyer, *Galiläa*, long ago suggested), but the possible origin of the idea in fact ought not to be confused with the theological use of Galilee as symbol, which alone we here attend to.

162. Something similar was true in the interrogation of the Baptist in 1:19–23, ostensibly taking place outside of Judea, in Transjordan.

basis they finally deny that he can be the Messiah (v. 52b) they show that for 4E it is in some sense true that Jesus is a Galilean.[163]

This is not meant factually, of course, for the Gospel's ultimate teaching on this question is that Jesus' true origin is not earthly at all (not even Jewish/Judean). But insofar as Galilee stands for the place of the church and Galileans for believers, Jesus can be said to disprove the scornful Judean belief that "no prophet is to rise from Galilee" (7:52).

Thus, over against the Jews' midrashic insistence that the Messiah must come from Judea, 4E has two answers, which together form a paradox and demonstrate the Jews' lack of understanding: (a) Jesus is indeed from Judea (see below, on Jesus' *patris*), and thus is the true Jewish Messiah; (b) but when the Jews reject him and he is accepted by Galileans, their region becomes the *terra christiana*.

Galilee, then, plays an essential part in the topographic scheme of the Gospel.[164] But the adjective *Galilaios* occurs only once (4:45)—contrast the use of *Ioudaios* over and over again—and Galilean belief is not depicted as normative. It is always simply contrasted with Judean unbelief. We are to look favorably on Galilee, then, but no matter how faithful the Galileans they are finally only a foil to the Judeans.

3. Judea

The world of the Fourth Gospel... is a Jewish world.[165] Apart from Pilate, gentiles hardly make an appearance. The boundaries of John's story are the boundaries of Israel. The imagery and structure of the Johannine argument are... profoundly [Judean].[166]

The most prominent region in the Gospel by far, Judea is explicitly named seven times; even more often it is to be understood, particularly at Jesus' journeys to Jerusalem. But Judea is important primarily because of the great prominence attached by the Evangelist to its inhabitants, *hoi Ioudaioi*. The usual translation of this phrase is, of course, "the Jews."

163. See further, below, on 7:41. I leave aside here the vexed question of the author's at best ambiguous attitude to the Bethlehem tradition of Jesus' origin; see 7:42. We are concerned, as is the author, not with traditional biography (however christological) but with the schematic use of region.

164. Meeks recognized this in "Galilee and Judea." Davies (*Gospel and Land*, 324) insists that not Galilee but Judea is essential to the Johannine schema. Both, of course, are right, as has been seen more recently by Bassler, "Galileans."

165. This is clear at several places in the Gospel where "the Jews" and "the world" are used synonymously, e.g., 18:20: "I have spoken openly to the world; I have always taught in synagogue and in the Temple, where all the Jews come together." See also 7:3–4; 12:19; 18:36. Even though this world has now expelled the Johannine Christians, they still can think of their universe only in Jewish terms.

166. Meeks, "Judeans." For present purposes I have altered the last word of the quotation from "Jewish" to "Judean," in line with Meeks's subsequent argument in that paper that the latter translation for *Ioudaios* is preferable.

But, as we have been keeping in mind, there is no verbal distinction in Greek between Jew and Judean. From several passages, most notably 7:1, it is obvious that 4E identifies all *Ioudaioi* with Judea. Whether they are to be thought of primarily as Judeans or, more probably, Judea conceived as simply the Jewish place ("Jewry"), region and people are inseparable in the Johannine schematic use of topography.[167]

Altogether "the Jews" are named about fifty times in the Gospel, and the phrase is almost always a Johannine insertion.[168] The Jews usually function as real actors in the narrative (in contrast to the relatively infrequent Synoptic use, which is primarily editorial or explanatory). But at the same time the Johannine phrase has a stylized, monolithic effect, virtually obliterating all actual distinctions within first-century Jewish society. Gone are the rich and poor of the other Gospels, sinners and righteous, Sadducees, Herodians, Zealots, scribes, elders, tax collectors, prostitutes.[169]

Why this narrowing, this simplifying, and at the same time the proliferation of the phrase? Who are "the Jews" in our Gospel? What does their place, "Judea," stand for?

● To begin to understand, we must turn at last to that puzzling passage, 4:43–45. There we hear that Jesus completes the withdrawal from Judea which had begun at the beginning of chapter 4. Now at last we have the explanation for this withdrawal. He had departed for Galilee because "a prophet has no honor in his own country *(patris)*" (v. 44). The plain sense of this "testimony," as 4E calls it, is that Jesus leaves Judea because it is his *patris*, his homeland, where he is not accepted.[170]

But in the Synoptics there is another version of this saying, whereby Jesus' "own country" is clearly to be understood as Galilee or some part of

167. We have no reliable knowledge of the Gospel's place of origin. Nor do we know how familiar Evangelist and readers were with the actual geography of Palestine, but very likely far less than we are, so the symbolic use of "Judea" to mean simply "the place of the Jews" may have seemed a good deal less contrived in their time than it does to us.

168. The major exception is the traditional "King of the Jews." The Johannine phrase appears in all parts of the Gospel except for the Farewell Discourse of chaps. 14—17 and the appendix of chap. 21. Some of these instances appear in what are frequently understood as "explanations for Gentile readers"; e.g., in 2:6, the setting out of the water pots is said to be "in accordance with the [rite of] purification of the Jews." More often a feast is described as "the Passover [e.g.] of the Jews." I contend that these are not simply factual parentheses but, like the other uses of the phrase *hoi Ioudaioi*, clues to the theology of locale that the Evangelist develops. For example, see part 1, sec. 6, Johannine Redaction, on 6:4.

169. The only groups mentioned within Israel are the Pharisees and the chief priests, often in association with each other and presumably reflecting simply the Jewish power structure in the author's own time and his or her view of it in Jesus' time. While the chief priests, including the high priest, were known to PQ as Jesus' opponents (11:47; 18:3, 10–14, 19–24; 19:6), I am inclined to think that the Pharisees are almost always the Evangelist's insertion.

170. This is the only intelligible interpretation of the conjunctions in these verses: "(43) . . . he left there for Galilee; (44) for Jesus himself testified that a prophet has no honor in his own *patris;* (45) therefore, when he came to Galilee, the Galileans received him. . . ."

it (Mark 6:4 = Matt. 13:57).[171] A good deal of effort has been expended to reconcile the Johannine version of the saying to the Synoptic.[172] We could, of course, understand Jesus' leaving hostile Judea for a more welcoming Galilean homeland. In fact, in 4E's portrayal Galilee is just such a haven (here, e.g., in v. 45); in the end it is in Galilee, as later elsewhere, that Jesus "remains" (7:9), never in Judea. But because of 4:44 Galilee cannot be Jesus' *patris*. Everything in the Johannine context of the verse demands that Jesus' place of nonacceptance is to be understood as Judea. The whole of the Judean sojourn in 2:13—3:36, summarized in the Johannine notice of 4:1, 3, shows this. It is the paradox of v. 44 that Judea is nevertheless (or should we say thereby?) seen to be Jesus' homeland.

In the immediately preceding passage—the conversation between Jesus and the Samaritan woman—the fact that Jesus is a Jew, and hence in the Johannine scheme of things a Judean, is explicitly stated (4:9, uniquely in the Gospels; see also Pilate in 18:35). It is Judaism that Jesus represents, "the Jews," from whom salvation derives (v. 22). Jesus' *patris* is Judea. Galilee, and to a lesser extent both Samaria and Transjordan, have been places of acceptance for Jesus, but acceptance that is evidently to be taken as unexpected, exceptional. Judea, the place of the Jews, is the homeland of the Jewish Messiah.[173]

The prologue (1:1–18)—which we can take to be Johannine, while based no doubt on an earlier hymn—provides the key to understanding the Johannine paradox. From the Gospel's very beginning we learn that Jesus "came to his own [home] and his own [people] did not receive him" (v. 11—the same term for "own" here as in 4:44). This passage, fundamental to the Gospel as a whole and to the interpretation of Jesus' relation to the Jews, is of course speaking universally, of the eternal Logos's coming

171. In Luke 4:24 the saying appears in still a different form, and there it is applied specifically to Nazareth.

172. See Brown (*The Community of the Beloved Disciple*, 39–40); he notes that Judea was last referred to only at the beginning of chap. 4 and that Galilee is far more prominent here. This ignores the clear reference back to v. 3 in v. 43. Brown posits the sociological importance of Galileans in the Johannine church, citing Matsunaga, "Galileans." This interpretation of the Galileans in chap. 4 makes the same mistake as for the Jerusalemites in 2:23–25 (see this part, n. 129). Carson ("Source Criticism," 424) classifies the various attempts to solve the question of Jesus' *patris*. He criticizes me with inconsistency in not attributing the aporia of v. 44 to Johannine redaction of a source; but it is only an aporia if one assumes the Synoptic understanding of the logion.

173. We are speaking theologically, not biographically. A kind of exception is perhaps 7:41: Some who do not believe in Jesus seem to know that he "comes from Galilee" and on that basis conclude that he cannot be the Christ. In painting this scene 4E may simply be using the historical datum, found in the source, that Jesus is "from Nazareth" (1:45–46; 18:5; 19:19). And, as we saw, Jesus can in some theological sense also be seen to be a Galilean (see above, 2, Galilee). But the important issue is not the truth of this point of view but the invalid logic of some who fail to believe in Jesus.

into the world. But the world is a Jewish world. The savior of the world is the Jewish Messiah; he comes to a world that is innately his.

The world, a Jewish world, has ambiguous meaning in 4G, as the following instances show: "God so loved the world that he gave his only begotten Son . . ." (3:16); ". . . so that the world may know that I love the Father" (14:31); "If the world hates you, know that it has hated me before it hated you" (15:18); "In the world you have tribulation; but be of good cheer, I have overcome the world" (16:33); "My kingship is not of this world" (18:36). It is Jesus' world, to which he came and belongs, yet it has rejected him, so that he and his followers are no longer of the world.

The representatives of this world, with its paradoxical relation to God's Son, are the Jews.[174] It is they whom the divine Logos created and to whom he came. The glory of the Jews is just this fact, that they stand for the whole of humanity. They are as of old the chosen people. Salvation is of the Jews.

The tragedy is that, despite many exceptions, taken as a people "the Jews" reject their Messiah and expel his followers. Indeed, this has been prophesied "in their law" (15:25—see further n. 175).

Thus the story of the Gospel's first twelve chapters is one of failure, from first to last: "He came to his own, and his own received him not" (1:11); "though he had done so many signs before them, yet they did not believe in him" (12:37). In the second half of the Gospel Jesus first prepares his true followers for the world's rejection both of him and them.[175] Then, in the passion narrative, we see how, despite this tragedy—indeed because of it—the Son of God is glorified in the Jews' very act of crucifying him.

On the surface 4G, like Matthew to a lesser extent, is flatly anti-Jewish. The Jews are presented from an external perspective and in a stereotyped way. They are simplistically shown as failing to understand Jesus, as opposing him and seeking to kill him. In fact at the end they are his actual executioners. The consequences of this portrayal for later Christian perception of God's chosen people are notoriously disastrous. The classical anti-Semitism of Christianity is grounded in this Gospel more than anywhere. Anti-Judaism is potential anti-Semitism (as Janis Liebig, cited by Culpepper, "The Jews," has shown).

174. Bultmann recognized this long ago (*Gospel of John*, 86–87).

175. In the Farewell Discourse Jesus never speaks of "the Jews" (with the exception of 13:33, which technically occurs before the discourse begins). Rather he instructs his disciples about "the world." But that "they" are in large part to be understood simply as the Jews is clear from 15:18–25, where the world's rejection is said to be "written in their law." The prophecy quoted here, "They have hated me without cause," is a slight adaptation of a phrase found in both Pss. 35:19 and 69:5 (LXX, 34:19; 68:5).

The sociological milieu in which it arose, however, accounts for this way of understanding the portrait.[176] It reflects the intense feelings of resentment, humiliation, and alienation of a group of Christian Jews who have been made to think of themselves as cast adrift from their spiritual home, from their people, so that they can no longer think of themselves as Jews. They have been expelled from their very world. The Jews instead are now the world outside. The Gospel's original readers are those who have reason to look simplistically and negatively on the Jewish nation, for they have been persecuted, expelled, and perhaps even put to death by it for their faith. That nation, with the power of a majority, has become in their eyes the enemy of the Christian truth.

This situation, if it in fact lies behind 4G, in general both occasions the radical rewriting of SG and specifically calls forth the negative polarity in which "the Jews" are portrayed.

In the context of the Gospel text itself the matter is far more subtle and complex than simply anti-Jewish. However real the Jews' role in the experience of author and readers, they are ultimately symbols of humanity, with a potentially positive role. But empirically they stand for the world that has in fact rejected its Savior and his followers. Like Judea and the rest of the geographical framework, they are theological constructs, belonging to the schema 4E creates to display the paradox of incarnation and salvation.

Thus in intent the Gospel is not anti-Semitic in any racial sense, but theologically anti-Jewish. So complex and subtle a theology of locale and peoplehood as it contains could not long survive the changing circumstances in which 4G soon found itself in the world. By then Christians were not a people persecuted and rebuffed by a dominant Judaism. Rather they had become a majority, with power to persecute the Jews, themselves now in the minority. And in large part because of the language of 4G, the Jews come to be seen as a race different from Christians, a people simply opposed to God and the Messiah. They no longer stand also for the world but on the contrary are viewed at times as scarcely belonging in the world of humanity. They are simply "of [their] father the devil" (8:44),[177] Christ-killers, monsters.

This later distortion of the Johannine meaning—simplistically exaggerating it and treating it literally—is tragically ironic, a misuse which 4E occasioned (carelessly, we may think) but perhaps could not have foreseen. And so in the end the Johannine theological subtlety is "understandable—but not justified."[178]

176. I depend here on Martyn, *History and Theology.* See also Brown, *The Community of the Beloved Disciple.*

177. This passage, difficult enough to fit into the portrait of the Jews in 4G, becomes simply demonic when singled out of that context.

178. Broer, "Die Juden," 338–39.

Bibliography

Aland, K., et al., eds. *The Greek New Testament*. 3d ed. New York: American Bible Society, 1975.

Ashton, John. "The Identity and Function of the *Ioudaioi* in the Fourth Gospel." *NovT* 27 (1985): 40–75.

Attridge, H. W. "Thematic Development and Source Elaboration in John 7:1–36." *CBQ* 42 (1980): 160–70.

Aune, David. *The Cultic Setting of Realized Eschatology in Early Christianity*. Leiden: E. J. Brill, 1972.

Bailey, J. A. *The Traditions Common to the Gospels of Luke and John*. NovTSup 7. Leiden: E. J. Brill, 1963.

Bammel, E. "John Did No Miracle." In *Miracles: Cambridge Studies in Their Philosophy and History*, edited by C. F. D. Moule, 179–202. London: A. R. Mowbray, 1965.

Bassler, J. M. "The Galileans: A Neglected Factor in Johannine Community Research." *CBQ* 43 (1981): 243–57.

Bauer, W., W. F. Arndt, F. W. Gingrich, and F. W. Danker. *A Greek-English Lexicon of the New Testament and Other Early Christian Literature*. 2d rev. and aug. ed. Chicago: University of Chicago Press, 1979.

Becker, J. "Wunder und Christologie: Zum literarkritischen und christologischen Problem der Wunder im Johannesevangelium." *NTS* 16 (1970): 130–48.

———. *Das Evangelium nach Johannes*. 2 Hefte. Gütersloh: Gerd Mohn, 1985.

Beutler, J. *Habt keine Angst: Die erste johanneische Abschiedsrede (Joh 14)*. Stuttgarter Bibel-Studien, 116. Stuttgart: Katholisches Bibelwerk, 1984.

Boismard, M.-E. *Du baptême à Cana (Jean 1:19—2:11)*. Paris: Editions du Cerf, 1956.

Boismard, M.-E., and A. Lamouille. *L'Evangile de Jean*. Synopse des Quatres Evangiles III. Paris: Editions du Cerf, 1977.

Borg, M. "A Temperate Case for a Non-Eschatological Jesus." *Foundations and Facets Forum* 2 (1986): 81–102.

Broer, I. *Die Urgemeinde und das Grab Jesu: Eine Analyse der Grablegungsgeschichte im Neuen Testament*. SANT 31. Munich: Kösel, 1972.

———. "Noch einmal: Zur religionsgeschichtlichen 'Abteilung' von Jo 2,1–11." *Studien zum NT und seiner Umwelt* 8 (1983): 103–23.

———. "Die Juden im Johannesevangelium: Ein beispielhafter und folgenreicher Konflikt." *Diakonia: Internationale Zeitschrift für die Praxis der Kirche* 14 (1983): 332–41.

315

Brown, R. E. *The Gospel According to John.* AB 29 and 29a. Garden City, N.Y.: Doubleday & Co., 1966, 1970.

———. "The Passion According to John: Chapters 18 and 19." *Worship* 49 (1975): 126–34.

———. *The Community of the Beloved Disciple.* New York: Paulist Press, 1979.

Brownlee, W. H. "Whence the Gospel According to John?" In *John and Qumran,* edited by J. H. Charlesworth, 166–94. London: Geoffrey Chapman, 1972.

Bultmann, R. *The Gospel of John: A Commentary.* Translated from 1966 German ed. Philadelphia: Westminster Press, 1971.

Busse, U., and A. May. "Das Weinwunder von Kana (Joh 2,1–11): Erneute Analyse eines 'erratischen Blocks'." *Biblische Notizen* 12 (1980): 35–61.

Buttrick, D. G., ed. *Jesus and Man's Hope.* Pittsburgh: Pickwick Press, 1970.

Buttrick, G. A., et al., eds. *Interpreter's Dictionary of the Bible: An Illustrated Encyclopedia.* 4 vols. and Supp. Nashville and New York: Abingdon Press, 1962, 1976.

Carroll, J. T. "Present and Future in the 'Eschatology' of the Fourth Gospel." Paper read at SBL Annual Meeting, Boston, December 1987. Abstracted in *AAR/SBL Abstracts 1987,* edited by K. H. Richards and J. B. Wiggins, 319. Atlanta: Scholars Press, 1987.

Carson, D. A. "Current Source Criticism of the Fourth Gospel: Some Methodological Questions." *JBL* 97 (1978): 411–29.

Childs, B. S. *The New Testament as Canon: An Introduction.* Philadelphia: Fortress Press, 1984; London: SCM Press, 1983.

Corsani, Bruno. *I miracoli di Gesù nel quarto vangelo: L'ipotesi della fonte dei segni.* Studi Biblici 65. Brescia: Paideia Editrice, 1983.

Culpepper, R. A. *Anatomy of the Fourth Gospel: A Study in Literary Design.* Philadelphia: Fortress Press, 1983.

———. "The Gospel of John and the Jews." *Review and Expositor* 84 (1987): 273–88.

Darton, M., ed. *Modern Concordance to the New Testament Based on the French Concordance de la Bible, Nouveau Testament.* New York: Doubleday & Co., 1976.

Dauer, A. *Die Passionsgeschichte im Johannesevangelium: Eine traditionsgeschichtliche und theologische Untersuchung zu Joh 18,1–19,30.* SANT 30. Munich: Kösel, 1972.

———. *Johannes und Lukas: Untersuchungen zu den johanneisch-lukanischen Parallelperikopen Joh 4,46–54/Lk 7,1–10—Joh 12,1–8/Lk 7,36–50; 10,38–42—Joh 20,19–29/Lk 24,36–49.* Würzburg: Echter, 1984.

Davies, W. D. *The Gospel and the Land: Early Christianity and Jewish Territorial Doctrine.* Berkeley and Los Angeles: University of California Press, 1974.

Dodd, C. H. *Interpretation of the Fourth Gospel.* New York: Cambridge University Press, 1953.

———. *Historical Tradition in the Fourth Gospel.* Cambridge: Cambridge University Press, 1963.

Donahue, J. R. *Are You the Christ? The Trial Narrative in the Gospel of Mark.* SBLDS 10. Missoula, Mont.: Scholars Press, 1973.

Dunn, J. D. G. "Let John Be John: A Gospel for Its Time." In *Das Evangelium und die Evangelien*, edited by P. Stuhlmacher, 309–39. Tübingen: J. C. B. Mohr [Paul Siebeck], 1983.

Duprez, A. *Jésus et les dieux guérisseurs: A propos de Jean*, V. Paris: J. Gabalda, 1970.

Ehrman, B. D. "Jesus' Trial before Pilate: John 18:28—19:16." *BTB* 13 (1983): 124–31.

Evans, C. A. " 'Peter Warming Himself' : The Problem of an Editorial 'Seam.' " *JBL* 101 (1982): 245–49.

Evans, C. F. *Resurrection and the New Testament*. Studies in Biblical Theology 2d series 12. London: SCM Press, 1970.

Faure, A. "Die alttestamentlichen Zitate im vierten Evangelium und die Quellenscheidungshypothese." *ZNW* 21 (1922): 99–121.

Flusser, D. *Jesus*. New York: Herder & Herder, 1969.

Foerster, W. "*sōzō, k.t.l.*" *TDNT* 7:965–1024.

Fortna, R. T. *The Gospel of Signs: A Reconstruction of the Narrative Source Underlying the Fourth Gospel*. SNTSMS 11. Cambridge: Cambridge University Press, 1970.

_____. "Source and Redaction in the Fourth Gospel's Portrayal of Jesus' Signs." *JBL* 89 (1970): 151–66.

_____. "Wilhelm Wilkens's Further Contribution to Johannine Studies: A Review Article" [on *Zeichen und Werke*]. *JBL* 89 (1970): 457–62.

_____. "From Christology to Soteriology: A Redaction-Critical Study of Salvation in the Fourth Gospel." *Interpretation* 27 (1973): 31–47.

_____. "Theological Use of Locale in the Fourth Gospel." *Anglican Theological Review*, supp. ser. 3: *Gospel Studies in Honor of Sherman Elbridge Johnson* (March 1974): 58–95.

_____. "Christology in the Fourth Gospel: Redaction-Critical Perspectives." *NTS* 21 (1974/75): 489–504.

_____. "Jesus and Peter at the High Priest's House: A Test Case for the Question of the Relation between Mark's and John's Gospels." *NTS* 24 (1977/78): 371–83.

Foster, Donald. "John Come Lately: The Belated Evangelist." In *The Bible and the Narrative Tradition*, edited by Frank McConnell, 113–31. New York and London: Oxford University Press, 1985.

Freed, E. D. *Old Testament Quotations in the Gospel of John*. Supplements to *Vetus Testamentum* 11. Leiden: E. J. Brill, 1965.

Freed, E. D., and R. B. Hunt. "Fortna's Signs-Source in John." *JBL* 94 (1975): 563–79.

Fuller, R. H. *The Formation of the Resurrection Narratives*. New York: Macmillan Co., 1972.

Gardner-Smith, P. *Saint John and the Synoptic Gospels*. Cambridge: Cambridge University Press, 1938.

Giblin, C. H. "The Miraculous Crossing of the Sea (John 6. 16–21)." *NTS* 29 (1983): 96–103.

Glasswell, M. E. "The Relationship Between John and Mark." *Journal for the Study of the NT* 23 (1985): 99–115.

Grech, P. "The 'Testimonia' and Modern Hermeneutics." *NTS* 19 (1972/73): 318–24.

Gundry, R. H. "Recent Investigations into the Literary Genre 'Gospel.'" In *New Dimensions*, edited by Longenecker and Tenney, 97–114.

Haenchen, E. "Aus dem Literatur des vierten Evangeliums." *TR* n.f. 23 (1955): 295–335.

———. "History and Interpretation in the Johannine Passion Narrative." *Interpretation* 24 (1970): 198–219.

———. *John: A Commentary on the Gospel of John.* Vol. 1: Chapters 1—6; vol. 2: Chapters 7—21. Hermeneia. Philadelphia: Fortress Press, 1984.

Hahn, F. "Der Prozess Jesu nach dem Johannesevangelium." In *Evangelisch-Katholischer Kommentar zum Neuen Testament*, 23–96. Vorarbeiten Heft 2. Zurich: Bensiger, 1970.

Hamerton-Kelly, R., and R. Scroggs, eds. *Jews, Greeks and Christians: Religious Cultures in Late Antiquity.* W. D. Davies Festschrift. Leiden: E. J. Brill, 1976.

Hartman, G. "Die Vorlage der Osterberichte in Joh 20." *ZNW* 55 (1964): 197–220.

Heekerens, H.-P. *Die Zeichen-Quelle der johanneischen Redaktion: Ein Beitrag zur Entstehungsgeschichte des vierten Evangeliums.* Stuttgarter Bibelstudien 113. Heidelberg: Katholisches Bibelwerk, 1984.

Heil, J. P. *Jesus Walking on the Sea: Meaning and Gospel Functions of Matt 14:22–33, Mark 6:45–52 and John 6:15b–21.* Analecta Biblica 87. Rome: Pontifical Biblical Institute, 1981.

Heise, J. *Bleiben: Menein in den johanneische Schriften.* Tübingen: J. C. B. Mohr (Paul Siebeck), 1967.

Hofbeck, S. *Semeion: Der Begriff des "Zeichens" im Johannesevangelium unter Berücksichtigung seiner Vorgeschichte.* Münsterschwarzach: Vier-Türme, 1970.

Hofrichter, P. " 'Egeneto anthropos': Text und Zusätze im Johannesprolog." *ZNW* 70 (1979): 214–37.

Holst, R. "The One Anointing of Jesus: Another Application of the Form-Critical Method." *JBL* 95 (1976): 435–46.

Jaubert, A. "La comparution devant Pilate selon Jean: Jn 18,28—19,16." *Foi et Vie* 73 (1974): 3–12.

de Jonge, M., ed. *L'Evangile de Jean: Sources, rédaction, théologie.* BETL 44. Leuven: Leuven University Press, 1977.

Käsemann, E. *The Testament of Jesus: A Study of the Gospel of John in the Light of Chapter 17.* Philadelphia: Fortress Press, 1968.

Kiefer, R. "Two Types of Exegesis with a Linguistic Basis." In *Conflicting Ways of Interpreting the Bible*, edited by H. Küng & J. Moltmann, 9–16. New York: Seabury Press, 1980.

Kittel, G., ed. *Theological Dictionary of the New Testament.* 10 vols. Grand Rapids: Wm. B. Eerdmans, 1964–76.

Kysar, R. *John, the Maverick Gospel.* Atlanta: John Knox Press, 1976.

Lattke, M. "Erlöser und Erlösung im Johannesevangelium." In *"Salvation today" in exegetischer Sicht: Ein deutscher Beitrag*, 17–27. Oekumenischer Rat der Kirchen Kommission für Weltmission und Evangelisation. Biblische Konsultation. Bossey, 1972.

Liebert, E. "That You May Believe: The Fourth Gospel and Structural Developmental Theory." *BTB* 14 (1984): 67–73.

Lightfoot, R. H. *Locality and Doctrine in the Gospels.* New York: Harper & Brothers, 1937.

Lindars, B. *Behind the Fourth Gospel.* London: SPCK, 1971.

————. *The Gospel of John.* New Century Bible. Grand Rapids: Wm. B. Eerdmans; London: Oliphants, 1972.

————. "Traditions behind the Fourth Gospel." In *L'Evangile de Jean,* edited by de Jonge, 107–24.

Lohmeyer, E. *Galiläa und Jerusalem.* Göttingen: Vandenhoeck & Ruprecht, 1936.

Longenecker, R. N., and M. C. Tenney, eds. *New Dimensions in New Testament Study.* Grand Rapids: Zondervan, 1974.

Lowe, M. "Who were the *Ioudaioi?*" *NovT* 18 (1976): 101–30.

Mahoney, R. *Two Disciples at the Tomb: The Background and Message of John 20:1–10.* Theologie und Wirklichkeit 6. Bern and Frankfurt a. M.: Lang, 1974.

Marrow, S. B. "*Parrhēsia* and the New Testament." *CBQ* 44 (1982): 431–46.

Martyn, J. L. *The Gospel of John in Christian History: Essays for Interpreters.* New York: Harper & Row, 1978.

————. "Glimpses into the History of the Johannine Community." In *L'Evangile de Jean,* edited by de Jonge, 149–75. Reprinted in Martyn, *The Gospel of John in Christian History,* 90–121.

————. *History and Theology in the Fourth Gospel.* Rev. and enl. Nashville: Abingdon Press, 1979 (first ed., 1968).

————. "Source Criticism and *Religionsgeschichte* in the Fourth Gospel." In *Jesus and Man's Hope,* ed. D. G. Buttrick, 1:247–73.

————. "We Have Found Elijah." In *Jews, Greeks and Christians,* edited by Hamerton-Kelly and Scroggs, 181–219. Reprinted (in slightly revised form) in Martyn, *The Gospel of John in Christian History,* 9–54.

Marxsen, W. *Der Evangelist Markus: Studien zur Redactionsgeschichte des Evangeliums.* Göttingen: Vandenhoeck & Ruprecht, 1956; 2d ed. 1959. (English translation: *Mark the Evangelist: Studies on the Redaction History of the Gospel.* Nashville: Abingdon Press, 1969.)

Matsunaga, K. "The Galileans in the Fourth Gospel." *Annual of the Japanese Biblical Institute* 2 (1976): 135–58.

Meeks, W. A. "Galilee and Judea in the Fourth Gospel." *JBL* 85 (1966): 159–69.

————. Review of Käsemann's *The Testament of Jesus.* *Union Seminary Quarterly Review* 24 (1969): 414–20.

————. "Judeans, Galileans, Samaritans, and the Johannine Christians." Unpublished paper presented to the Seminar on the Social Background of Early Christianity at the General Meeting of the Society of New Testament Studies, Basel, 1984.

Meyer, Ben F. *The Aims of Jesus.* London: SCM Press, 1979.

Michaels, J. R. "The Temple Discourse in John." In *New Dimensions,* edited by Longenecker and Tenney, 200–213.

Miranda, J. P. *Being and the Messiah: The Message of St. John.* Maryknoll, N.Y.: Orbis Books, 1977.

Moloney, F. J. *The Johannine Son of Man.* 2d ed. Rome: Salesian Library, 1978.

Neirynck, F. "The 'Other Disciple' in Jn 18, 15–16." *ETL* 51 (1975): 113–41.

———. "John and the Synoptics." In *L'Evangile de Jean*, edited by de Jonge, 73–106.

———. "De Semeia-Bron in het Vierde Evangelie: Kritiek van een Hypothese." *Academiae Analecta*, Klasse der Lettern 45 (1983): 1–28.

———. "John and the Synoptics: The Empty Tomb Stories." *NTS* 30 (1984): 161–87.

———. "John 4,46–54: Signs Source and/or Synoptic Gospels." *ETL* 60 (1984): 367–75.

Neirynck, F., et al. *Jean et les Synoptiques: Examen critique de l'exégèse de M.-E. Boismard*. BETL 49. Leuven: Leuven University Press, 1979.

Nestle, E., E. Nestle, and K. Aland et al., eds. *Novum Testamentum Graece*. 26th ed. Stuttgart: Deutsche Bibelstiftung, 1979.

Nicholson, G. C. *Death as Departure: The Johannine Descent-Ascent Schema*. SBLMS 63. Chico, Calif.: Scholars Press, 1983.

Nicol, W. *The Sēmeia in the Fourth Gospel: Tradition and Redaction*. NovTSup 32. Leiden: E. J. Brill, 1972.

O'Day, G. R. *Revelation in the Fourth Gospel: Narrative Mode and Theological Claim*. Philadelphia: Fortress Press, 1986.

O'Grady, J. F. "The Human Jesus in the Fourth Gospel." *BTB* 14 (1984): 63–66.

Olsson, B. *Structure and Meaning in the Fourth Gospel: A Textual-Linguistic Analysis of Jn 2:1–11 and 4:1–42*. Lund: C. W. K. Gleerup, 1974.

Pancaro, S. *The Law in the Fourth Gospel*. NovTSup 42. Leiden: E. J. Brill, 1975.

Pesch, R. *Der reiche Fischfang: Lk 5,1–11/Joh 21,1–14: Wundergeschichte, Berufungserzählung, Erscheinungsbericht*. Düsseldorf: Patmos, 1969.

Reim, G. *Studien zum alttestamentlichen Hintergrund des Johannesevangeliums*. SNTSMS 22. Cambridge: Cambridge University Press, 1974.

———. "Johannes 21—Ein Anhang?" In *Studies in New Testament Language and Text*, edited by J. K. Elliott, 330–37. Leiden: E. J. Brill, 1978.

Rensberger, David. "The Politics of John: The Trial of Jesus in the Fourth Gospel." *JBL* 103 (1984): 395–411.

Richter, G. *Studien zum Johannesevangelium*. Regensburg: Pustet, 1977.

———. "Die Gefangenahme Jesus nach dem Johannesevangelium (18,1–12)." In *Studien*, 74–87.

———. "Zur Frage von Tradition und Redaktion in Joh 1,19–34." In *Studien*, 288–314.

———. "Zur sogenannten Semeia-Quelle des Johannesevangeliums." In *Studien*, 281–87.

Rissi, M. "Der Aufbau des vierten Evangeliums." *NTS* 29 (1983): 48–54.

Roberge, M. "Jean VI, 22–24. Un problème de critique littéraire." *Laval Théologique et Philosophique* 35 (1979): 139–51.

Robinson, J. M. "On the *Gattung* of Mark (and John)." In *Jesus and Man's Hope*, edited by D. G. Buttrick, 99–129.

———. "Kerygma and History in the NT." In Robinson and Koester, *Trajectories*, 20–70.

———. "The Miracles Source of John: An Essay-Review of Robert Tomson

Fortna, *The Gospel of Signs." JAAR* 39 (1971): 339–48. (An adaptation of part of "The Johannine Trajectory," in Robinson and Koester, *Trajectories*, 232–68.)

Robinson, J. M., and H. Koester. *Trajectories through Early Christianity*. Philadelphia: Fortress Press, 1971.

Ruckstuhl, E. *Die literarische Einheit des Johannesevangeliums: Der gegenwärtige Stand der einschlägigen Forschungen*. Freiburg in der Schweiz: Paulus, 1951.

———. "Johannine Language and Style: The Question of Their Unity." In *L'Evangile de Jean*, edited by de Jonge, 125–47.

Sabbe, M. "The Arrest of Jesus in Jn 18,1–11 and its Relation to the Synoptic Gospels: A Critical Evaluation of A. Dauer's Hypothesis." In *L'Evangile de Jean*, edited by de Jonge, 203–34.

Schein, B. E. *Following the Way: The Setting of John's Gospel*. Minneapolis: Augsburg, 1980.

Schmidt, K. L. *Der Rahmen der Geschichte Jesu: Literarkritische Untersuchungen zur ältesten Jesusüberlieferung*. Berlin: Trowitzsch u. Sohn, 1919.

Schnackenburg, R. *The Gospel according to St. John*. Vol. 1: Introduction and Commentary on chapters 1—4 (1968); vol. 2: Commentary on chapters 5—12 (1980); vol. 3: Commentary on chapters 13—21 (1982). New York: Crossroad.

Schneiders, S. M. "The Face Veil: A Johannine Sign (John 20:1–10)." *BTB* 13 (1983): 94–97.

Schnider, F., and W. Stenger. *Johannes und die Synoptiker: Vergleich ihrer Parallelen*. Munich: Kösel, 1971.

Schüssler Fiorenza, E. *In Memory of Her: A Feminist Theological Reconstruction of Christian Origins*. New York: Crossroad, 1983.

Segovia, F. F. "John 13 1–20, The Footwashing in the Johannine Tradition." *ZNW* 73 (1982): 31–51.

———. "The Love and Hatred of Jesus and Johannine Sectarianism." *CBQ* 43 (1982): 258–72.

———. "The Structure, *Tendenz*, and *Sitz im Leben* of John 13:31—14:31." *JBL* 104 (1985): 471–93.

Selong, G. "The Cleansing of the Temple in Jn 2,13–22, with a Reconsideration of the Dependence of the Fourth Gospel upon the Synoptics." Ph.D. dissertation. Leuven, 1971. Abstracted in *ETL* 48 (1972): 212–13.

Smalley, S. S. "The Sign in John xxi." *NTS* 20 (1975): 275–88.

Smend, F. "Die Behandlung alttestamentlicher Zitate als Ausgangspunkt der Quellenscheidung im 4. Evangelium." *ZNW* 24 (1925): 147–50.

Smith, D. M. *The Composition and Order of the Fourth Gospel: Bultmann's Literary Theory*. New Haven: Yale University Press, 1965.

———. "Johannine Christianity: Some Reflections on Its Character and Delineation." *NTS* 21 (1976): 222–48. (Now also found in his book by the same title, *Johannine Christianity*, 1–36.)

———. "The Milieu of the Johannine Miracle Source: A Proposal." In Hamerton-Kelly and Scroggs, *Jews, Greeks and Christians*, 164–80. (Now also found in *Johannine Christianity*, 62–79.)

_____. "The Setting and Shape of a Johannine Narrative Source." *JBL* 95 (1976): 231–41. (Now also found in *Johannine Christianity*, 80–93.)

_____. *Johannine Christianity: Essays on Its Setting, Sources, and Theology.* Columbia: University of South Carolina Press, 1984.

Smith, M. *Clement of Alexandria and a Secret Gospel of Mark.* Cambridge: Harvard University Press, 1973.

Smith, R. H. *Easter Gospels: The Resurrection of Jesus According to the Four Evangelists.* Minneapolis: Augsburg, 1983.

Talbert, C. H. *What Is a Gospel? The Genre of the Canonical Gospels.* Philadelphia: Fortress Press, 1977.

Theissen, G. *The Miracle Stories of the Early Christian Tradition.* Edited by J. Riches. Philadelphia: Fortress Press, 1983.

Thyen, H. "Aus der Literatur zum Johannesevangelium." *TR* 42 (1977): 268–70.

Tsuchido, K. "Tradition and Redaction in John 12:1–43." *NTS* 30 (1984): 609–19.

Turner, G. A. "Soteriology in the Gospel of John." *Journal of the Evangelical Theological Society* 19 (1976): 271–77.

Van Belle, G. *De Semeia-Bron in het Vierde Evangelie: Ontstaan en groei van een hypothese.* Leuven: Leuven University Press, 1975.

_____. *Les Parenthèses dans L'Evangile de Jean: Aperçu historique et classification texte grec de Jean.* Leuven: Leuven University Press, 1985.

_____. "Jn 4,48 et la foi du Centurion." *ETL* 61 (1985): 167–69.

von Wahlde, U. C. "The Terms for Religious Authorities in the Fourth Gospel: A Key to Literary Strata?" *JBL* 98 (1979): 231–53.

_____. "The Johannine 'Jews': A Critical Survey." *NTS* 28 (1982): 33–60.

_____. *The Signs in John: Recovering the First Edition of the Johannine Gospel.* Wilmington, Del.: Michael Glazier, forthcoming.

Wengst, K. *Bedrängte Gemeinde und verherrlichter Christus: Der historische Ort des Johannesevangeliums als Schlüssel zu seiner Interpretation.* Biblische-Theologische Studien 5. Neukirchen-Vluyn: Neukirchener, 1981.

Wilkens, W. *Die Enstehungsgeschichte des vierten Evangeliums.* Zollikon: Evangelischer, 1958.

_____. *Zeichen und Werke: Ein Beitrag zur Theologie des 4. Evangeliums in Erzählungs- und Redestoff.* Zurich: Zwingli, 1969.

Wink, W. *John the Baptist in the Gospel Tradition.* SNTSMS 7. Cambridge: Cambridge University Press, 1968.

_____. " 'And the Lord Appeared First to Mary': Sexual Politics in the Resurrection Witness." In *Social Themes of the Christian Year*, edited by D. Hessel, 177–82. Philadelphia: Westminster Press, 1983.

Winter, P. *On the Trial of Jesus.* 2d ed. rev. and ed. by T. A. Burkill and G. Vermes. Berlin and New York: Walter de Gruyter, 1974.

Woll, D. B. *Johannine Christianity in Conflict: Authority, Rank, and Succession in the First Farewell Discourse.* SBLDS 60. Chico, Calif.: Scholars Press, 1981.

Addenda

To p. 149:

For a plausible attempt at reconstruction of a pre-Johannine source for the Last Supper (namely, "Passover" + vv. 4–6, 8–9, 12, 17ab), see now Wojciechowski, "Source," improving on B & L's analysis.

To p. 202 n. 476:

Carson, "John 20:31," holds that the intent of the closing verse of chapter 20, and of the Gospel as a whole, is not christological but "evangelical"—to show not what Jesus' status is but, rather, who the Messiah is. He argues forcibly that the central part of the verse should be translated: ". . . that you may believe that the Christ, the Son of God, is Jesus. . . ." (Carson seems unaware of Thyen's espousal, albeit to a different end, of such a reading of the verse.) I agree with this understanding in large part, but I would apply it wholly to the pre-Johannine source (see p. 201 and its n. 474; 204 n. 484; 213, 215; the purpose of the present Gospel is too complex to be stated in this way or based so heavily on a single verse). But I would continue to hold that a christological purpose is also included, that the two meanings ought not finally be separated. The verse asserts both that *Jesus* is the Christ and that Jesus is the *Christ*.

To p. 216:

Cope, "Earliest Gospel," lends new support to this conclusion.

To p. 218:

Cope, "Earliest Gospel," now proposes that SG is not simply parallel to the Synoptics but, because clearly earlier, possibly known and used by them in some way, and esp. by Luke. This suggestion is more radical than I had dared to be and deserves further investigation. For example, if Luke is dependent on SG, then at the points at which the Lukan and pre-Johannine traditions overlap (see, e.g., pp. 26 n. 28, 96, 102, 106, 108, 144, 175 n. 398, 180 n. 415) more rather than less of the similarity between the two Gospels would be attributable to SG, and my suggestion that not only SG but 4G too was influenced by pre-Lukan tradition would be unnecessary. Further, any evidence that Dauer (*Johannes und Lukas*) found suggesting to him that SG was dependent on canonical Luke would in fact be explained by dependence in the opposite direction.

To Bibliography:

Carson, D. A. "The Purpose of the Fourth Gospel: John 20:31 Reconsidered." *JBL* 106 (1987): 639–51.
Cope, Lamar. "The Earliest Gospel Was the 'Signs Gospel.'" In *Jesus, the Gospels, and the Church: Essays in Honor of William R. Farmer*, edited by E. P. Sanders, 17–24. Macon: Mercer University Press, 1987.
Wojciechowski, M. "La Source de Jean 13. 1–20." *NTS* 34 (1988): 135–41.

(An article that Carson cites was not available to me in time for this study: E. P. Groenewald, "The Christological Meaning of John 20:31," *Neotestamentica* 2 [1968]: 131–40. Similarly, I could make no use of J. C. Meagher, *Clumsy Construction in Mark's Gospel: A Critique of Form- and Redactionsgeschichte* [Toronto Studies in Theology, 3; New York and Toronto: Edwin Mellen Press, 1979].)

Index of Selected Passages
in the Fourth Gospel

Index of Modern Authors

329